Airport
Planning &
Management

Airport
Planning &
Management
4th Edition

Alexander T. Wells, Ed.D.

McGraw-Hill
New York   Chicago   San Francisco   Lisbon   London
Madrid   Mexico City   Milan   New Delhi   San Juan
Seoul   Singapore   Sydney   Toronto

Library of Congress Cataloging-in-Publication Data

Wells, Alexander T.
   Airport planning & management / Alexander T. Wells.—4th ed.
      p.   cm.
   Includes index.
   ISBN 0-07-136009-3 (alk. paper)
   1. Airports—Planning. 2. Airports—Management. I. Title: Airport planning and
management. II. Title.
TL725.3.P5 W452   2000
387.7'36—dc21

00-023082
CIP

McGraw-Hill

A Division of The McGraw-Hill Companies

   4 5 6 7 8 9 0   DOC/DOC   0 6 5 4 3 2

ISBN 0-07-136009-3

*The sponsoring editor for this book was Shelley Ingram Carr, the editing
supervisor was Frank Kotowski, Jr., and the production supervisor was
Pamela A. Pelton. It was set in Garamond per the Gen1AV1 design by
Deirdre Sheean of McGraw-Hill's desktop publishing department,
Hightstown, N.J.*

Printed and bound by R. R. Donnelley & Sons, Inc.

McGraw-Hill books are available at special quantity discounts to use
as premiums and sales promotions, or for use in corporate training
programs. For more information, please write to the Director of Special
Sales, Professional Publishing, McGraw-Hill, Two Penn Plaza, New York,
NY 10121-2298. Or contact your local bookstore.

This book is printed on recycled, acid-free paper containing
a minimum of 50% recycled, de-inked fiber.

Dedication

To the University Aviation Association and its dedicated professional membership, past and present, who have shaped aviation education for the past 50 years.

Contents

Acknowledgments

I am sincerely appreciative of the many public and private institutions that have provided resource material from which I was able to shape this text. In this regard, I am particularly indebted to the Federal Aviation Administration for their numerous publications. Portions of this text were drawn from a special report entitled Airport System Development prepared by the Office of Technology Assessment in August in 1984.

Faculty and students at University Aviation Association institutions who have reacted to material in the previous three editions have significantly shaped this book. To them I owe a special thanks because they represent the true constituency of any textbook author.

I am also indebted to many practicing airport planners and managers for their ideas and to the American Association of Airport Executives (AAAE) who adopted this book in their certification program for a number of years before developing their own material.

Special thanks to Jan Elton for her fast and accurate typing with numerous revisions and deadline dates. Finally, I must thank my wife, Mary, for considerable patience and encouragement throughout the process.

Preface

Fourteen years ago, the first edition of *Airport Planning & Management* pioneered an innovative structure for a basic airport principles course designed for several similar, yet distinct markets: the college student enrolled in an aviation program and someone in the field of airport management or operations who is seeking further education.

The response of both professors and students has been gratifying. *Airport Planning & Management* and its accompanying test bank have been more widely used than any other teaching material for an airport course. In fact, the text was used for a number of years by the American Association of Airport Executives' accreditation program until they developed their own materials.

I have tried to make the fourth edition of *Airport Planning & Management* the highest quality teaching resource available for the airport course. I have worked hard to enhance the best and proven elements of the earlier editions while blending new perspectives from my teaching, research, and aviation experiences.

The whole text has been critically revised, updated, and portions rewritten. Clear and interesting communication has been a priority, as in past editions. Careful explanations, coupled with a focus on the important "basics," motivate learning.

Recognizing that a course in airport planning and management is normally a student's first exposure to the field, the book is introductory, not exhaustive. The focus is on building a foundation in the subject. In this regard, I have been influenced considerably by my experience of 30 years in teaching aviation management courses. The text has been designed to introduce the student to the subject, including the major elements in the planning process and managerial and operations functions carried on at an airport. An appropriate balance of depth and breadth of subject matter was considered based upon my judgment of the needs of the average college student taking this course.

It is recognized that professors will supplement the basic material covered with current applications drawn from their own experiences and timely articles and reports. Students are encouraged to explore and keep abreast of current periodicals such as *Airline Executive, Airport, Airport Business, Air Transport World, Aviation International News, Aviation Week & Space Technology, Business and Commercial Aviation, FAA Aviation News*, and the *Journal of Air Traffic Control.* It is hoped that the ability to reason accurately and objectively about problems facing airports and the development of a lasting interest in airport planning and management will be two valuable byproducts of the text's basic objectives.

Major Changes in the Fourth Edition

The theory and practice of airport planning and management are dynamic, and as new developments occur, they should be incorporated into a textbook such as this one. Also, the reviewers and I are constantly on the lookout for ways to improve the book in terms of clarity and understanding. As a result, we have made several important changes in this edition, including the following:

1 All tables, figures, statistics, key terms, review questions, pictures, and glossary terms have been updated.

2 Chapter 1 includes an historical perspective that has been thoroughly reviewed and updated through the 1990s, including the latest legislation affecting AIP funding, PFC revenues, and the Military Airport Program.

3 The current topics of airport privatization and marketing covered in Chapter 2 have been greatly expanded in this edition. The section on noise and environmental issues has been rewritten.

4 Financial Planning, covered in Chapter 7, has been largely rewritten with more extensive coverage of the Airport Improvement Program, Federal Letters of Intent, and PFCs. Factors involved in airport bond ratings are covered in greater depth.

5 Chapter 9 covering airside technological improvements has been completely rewritten, including the latest airspace developments, operational procedures designed to improve traffic flow, and capacity-enhancing technologies.

6 A new section has been added to Chapter 11, Financial Management, discussing the important topic of rising airport costs. Changes in the residual cost approach to financing and maximization of revenues have been included in this chapter.

7 Chapter 11 has been expanded with revised sections covering the latest pavement maintenance techniques. The topics on bird hazards and airport security have been updated, including the latest research.

The aim of all this revising, refining, editing, and illustrating was to make sure that each student really does get a good feel for the airport planning and management process. Airport planning and management is an important and fascinating career field. Hopefully, every student who reads *Airport Planning & Management* will share my enthusiasm for the field.

Learning Tools

The purpose of this book is to help students learn the basic ingredients in the process of planning and managing an airport. Toward that end, I have used various learning tools that recur throughout the book.

- *Chapter outlines.* Each chapter opens with an outline of the major topics to be covered.
- *Chapter objectives.* After the outline, each chapter includes the broad objectives that the student should be able to accomplish upon completing the chapter.
- *Relevance.* Most of the examples, applications, and extensions of the basic material are drawn from and apply to the environment of airport planning and management of the 1980s and 1990s.
- *Staying power.* The text is designed to have staying power over the years. It emphasizes the basic functions and practices that will not change appreciably over time.
- *Figures, tables, and exhibits.* Important points in each chapter are illustrated with strong visual materials.
- *Logical organization and frequent headings.* The material covered here has been put in a systematic framework so that students know where they have been, where they are, and where they are going in the text. Part I of the text introduces the student to the airport-airway system, including its

structure and historical perspective. Part II includes the major elements in the master planning process. Part III provides alternatives to expanding existing and building new airports through better utilization. Part IV focuses in on the organization and management of airports. Frequent headings and subheadings aid organization and readability.

- *Key terms.* Each chapter concludes with a list of key terms used in the text. The terms can also be found in a glossary at the end of the book.

- *Review questions.* Review questions at the end of each chapter cover all of the important points. Many of the questions are suitable for class discussion.

- *Suggested readings.* A list of suggested readings is included after all chapters for students who wish to pursue the material covered in greater depth.

- *Glossary.* All key terms appearing at the end of each chapter, as well as many other terms used in the text and others of significance in airport planning and management, are included in the glossary.

- *Complete index.* The book includes a complete index to help the student find needed information.

Test Bank

A test bank with over 1200 questions is available for professors who have adopted the book. It is available on disk for use with IBM (and compatible) computers with 3.5-in disk drives. The questions are multiple-choice, true-false, and fill-in-the-blank. Answers immediately follow each chapter's questions.

Organization of the text

The following is an outline of *Airport Planning & Management*, including changes in the fourth edition.

Part I Introduction

1 *The airport–airway system: a historical perspective* provides a historical sketch of the airport–airway system, including the federal legislation that has affected its growth, development,

and funding. The chapter concludes with an assessment of federal airport policy.

2 *The airport system* provides a review of the structure of the system, including the type and number of airports in the United States. The economic importance of airports is covered along with a discussion of current issues and factors affecting the airport system.

3 *Airport system planning* concludes the introductory part with a review of the planning process from the national, regional, state, and local levels. The objectives of the local airport master plan are covered, and coordination at all levels of planning is stressed.

Part II Planning and funding the airport

4 *Airport requirements and site selection* covers the first two phases of the airport master planning process. The first phase includes an inventory of existing facilities, socioeconomic factors, and community values. This is followed by a discussion of forecasts needed and methods of forecasting. Demand/capacity analysis and the environmental impact study round out the first phase. The second phase concentrates on the factors affecting site selection.

5 *Airport layout and land use plans* includes the third phase of the airport master plan. The airport layout plan is thoroughly explored, followed by a complete discussion of all airside facilities. The remainder of the chapter covers the approach layout plan, including FAR Part 77 and land use planning on and around the airport.

6 *Terminal area and airport access plans* is a continuation of the third phase, with a focus on landside facilities. Terminal area plans are analyzed in depth, including design concepts and passenger handling systems. Facility requirements for the air carriers, concessionaires, and others are examined, along with the planning steps involved in determining space requirements. The critical subject of airport access plans rounds out the discussion under this chapter.

7 *Financial planning* is the last chapter under Part II and completes the fourth and final phase of the airport master plan. The financial plan includes an economic evaluation of the entire plan of development. A comprehensive review of financing methods is covered, including federal funding sources, passenger facility charges, airport bonds, private financing, and state funding.

Part III Managing growth

8 *Airport capacity and delay* is the first of three chapters dealing with the problem of how to cope with growth in air travel by utilizing the existing system more efficiently. Part III presents an alternative to expanding and/or building new airports. This chapter defines the growing problem of capacity and delay and discusses the causal factors. Various approaches to reducing delay are completely examined, including new airport development, the use of closed military airfields, intermodalism, diversion of traffic, restriction of access by aircraft type, quotas, differential pricing, and slot allocations.

9 *Airside technological improvements* introduces the student to a number of approaches designed to improve airside efficiency. This is covered under three headings: airspace development; operational procedures; and capacity enhancing technologies. All of the new technological advances either planned or presently being installed are thoroughly covered.

10 *Landside technological improvements* concludes the discussion on managing growth by focusing in on the landside technological improvements designed to improve capacity and reduce delay.

Part IV The management process

11 *Financial management* is unquestionably one of the most important functions of management. This chapter examines the revenue and expense areas in a typical airport. The residual-cost approach and the compensatory approach to financial management are covered in depth. Other areas covered include pricing of airport facilities and services, rise in airport costs, and trends in financial management since deregulation.

12 *Organization and administration* introduces the student to the various types of airport ownership and operation, including governmental, multipurpose port authority, and airport authority. This is followed by a comprehensive review of the organizational structure of a typical commercial airport, including a description of the job responsibilities for key management personnel. The chapter concludes with a discussion of career opportunities in airport management and the important role that the airport manager plays in public relations.

13 *Airport operations* consists of the day-to-day operational concerns of management. Major areas of discussion in this chapter include pavement rehabilitation and maintenance, snow removal, safety inspection, bird hazards, aircraft rescue fire fighting (ARFF), security, and ground support equipment. Many excellent articles appearing in the trade magazines can be used to supplement and complement the subjects in this chapter.

14 *Airport relations with tenants and the public.* One of the important functions of airport management is that of serving as a landlord. The primary responsibilities of management in its relations with the air carriers, concessionaires, and members of the general aviation community are covered in this chapter. The airports' liability exposure is reviewed, including coverages afforded under the basic airport premises liability policy. Chapter 14 concludes with a thorough discussion of one of the major problem areas facing management, that of noise. This discussion includes federal responsibilities, measurement of noise, noise and land use, and local noise abatement programs.

Finally, feedback—from both students and instructors—is encouraged. It is my intention to prepare the best teaching materials I can. Learning should not only be enjoyable, but should accomplish specific objectives. Any suggestions for improving the learning process in the airport planning and management area will be greatly appreciated.

Alex Wells

Part I

Introduction

1

The airport–airway system: a historical perspective

Outline

- The formative period
- The National Airport Plan
- Postwar federal aid to airports
- Airport and Airway Development Act of 1970
- Airport development in the 1980s and 1990s
- Concluding remarks

Objectives

When you have completed this chapter you should be able to:

- Discuss the significance of the Kelly Act of 1925; Air Commerce Act of 1926.
- Describe the purpose of the Civil Aeronautics Act of 1938.
- Summarize the role of the federal government in providing airport aid during World War II.
- Highlight several of the important recommendations made by a select committee in 1944 that led to the Federal Airport Act of 1946.
- Discuss the purpose and major features of the Federal Airport Act of 1946.
- Describe the events leading up to passage of the Federal Aviation Act of 1958.
- Distinguish between the Airport and Airway Development Act of 1970 and the Airport and Airway Revenue Act of 1970.

- Discuss some of the important amendments under the Airport and Airway Development Act of 1976.
- Describe the impact of the Airline Deregulation Act of 1978 on the airport system.
- Summarize the significance of the Airport and Airway Improvement Act of 1982 and the subsequent Aviation and Airway Safety and Capacity Expansion Acts.
- List some of the important provisions under the 1990 act pertaining to PFCs.
- Describe the State Grant Pilot Program and the Military Airport Program.

The formative period

When the Wright brothers succeeded at Kitty Hawk on December 17, 1903, in man's first flight, the place from which they took off could hardly be called an airport. It was, however, ideally suited for the requirements of the Wright Flyer. With the invention of the airplane, it naturally followed that such a machine had to have a place to take off, land, be repaired, and eventually be fueled: an airport.

Historically, the development of civil airports has been an intricate meshing of military, commercial, and private activity. Construction and maintenance of airports was, in general, considered a local responsibility, in contrast to the development of the airway system, which the federal government regulated from the start. Although records indicate operational airports existed as far back as 1909, they were generally indistinguishable from local athletic fields, parks, and golf courses.

By 1912, there were 20 recognized airports in the country, all of which were privately owned and operated. With the outbreak of World War I, civil airport development ceased and all new airports were military. Sixty-seven additional airports were built during the war, but only 25 remained operational following the war.

Early airmail service

The first regular airmail route in the United States was established on May 15, 1918, between New York City and Washington, D.C. The service was conducted jointly by the United States War Department

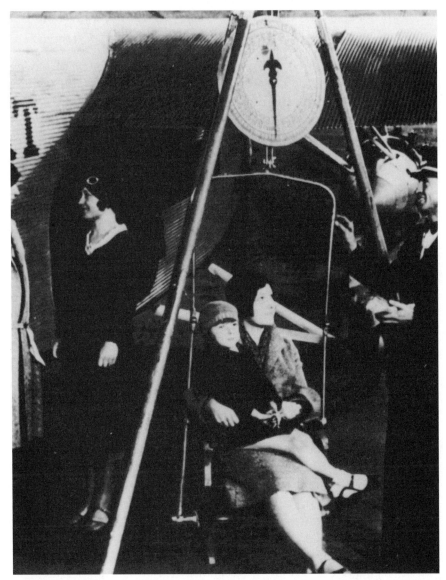

1-1 *Passengers weigh in prior to departure from Chicago Midway Airport in 1927.* Landrum & Brown

and the Post Office Department. The War Department furnished the planes and pilots and performed the operation and maintenance, and the Post Office Department attended to the sorting of the mail and its transportation to and from the airport and the loading and discharge of the planes at the airports. This joint arrangement of the War and Post Office Departments was continued until August 12, 1918, when the Post Office Department took exclusive responsibility for the development of the mail service on a larger scale.

Communities suddenly became aware of the importance of having an aerial connection to the rest of the country. By 1920, there were 145 municipally owned airports and the nationwide airport system was beginning to form. Domestic airmail service grew considerably during the period between 1918 and 1925. Facilities for air transportation had been established, and the desirability of continued direct government operation or private operation under contract with the government was widely discussed. The policy of the United States government in the intercity transportation of mail had traditionally been to arrange with railroads, steamship lines, and other means for its long-distance transportation.

The next stage in the development of the service was ushered in by the Contract Air Mail Act of 1925, the so-called *Kelly Act*, which authorized the postmaster general to enter into contracts with private persons or companies for the transportation of the mail by air. Contracts were let for a number of feeder and auxiliary main lines during 1925 and 1926, and for the portions of the transcontinental airmail route during 1927.

Development of the airway system

On May 20, 1926, President Coolidge signed the *Air Commerce Act of 1926* into law. The object of the Air Commerce Act was to promote the development and stability of commercial aviation in order to attract adequate capital into the business and to provide the fledgling industry with the assistance and legal basis necessary for its growth. The act made it the duty of the secretary of commerce to encourage air commerce by establishing civil airways and other navigational facilities to aid aerial navigation and air commerce.

The regulation of aviation provided for in the act included the licensing, inspection, and operation of aircraft; the marking of licensed and unlicensed aircraft; the licensing of pilots and of mechanics engaged in aircraft work; and the regulation of the use of airways.

In July 1927, a director of aeronautics was appointed who, under the general direction of the assistant secretary of commerce for aeronautics, was in charge of the work of the Department of Commerce in the administration of the Air Commerce Act. By November 1929,

1-2 *Pilots for National Air Transport, one of the companies that would later become United Airlines, preparing for departure from Chicago Midway Airport in 1927.* Landrum & Brown

because of the increasing volume of work incident to the rapid development of aviation, it was necessary to decentralize the organization. Three assistants and the staffs of employees of the divisions under their respective jurisdictions were assigned to the assistant secretary of commerce for aeronautics. These included a director of air regulation, a chief engineer of the airways division, and a director of aeronautics development to assist in aeronautical regulation and promotion. The organization was known as the Aeronautics Branch of the Department of Commerce.

The work was further reassigned by executive order of the president in 1933 to place the promotion and regulation of aeronautics in a separately constituted bureau of the Department of Commerce. An administrative order of the secretary of commerce provided for the establishment of the *Bureau of Air Commerce* in 1934. The bureau consisted of two divisions, the division of air navigation and the division of air regulation.

A revised plan of organization for the Bureau of Air Commerce, adopted in April 1937, placed all the activities of the bureau under a director, aided by an assistant director, with supervision over seven principal divisions: airway engineering, airway operation, safety and planning, administration and statistics, certification and inspection, and regulation.

From 1926 until 1938, the federal government was prohibited by the Air Commerce Act of 1926 from participating directly in the establishment, operation, and maintenance of airports; however, in response to the Great Depression, the Civil Works Administration—from the fall of 1933 up until it was superseded by the Federal Emergency Relief Administration (FERA) in April of 1934—spent about $11.5 million establishing 585 new airports, mostly in smaller communities. The FERA spent its appropriation on 943 airport projects, mostly in smaller cities, with 55 new airports receiving aid.

In July 1935, the Works Progress Administration (WPA) took over the federal airport development work. Under the WPA, there was an emphasis on spending for the larger airports and projects were of a more permanent nature. Under the WPA, about half of the expenses for material and equipment was borne by the sponsors; the remainder, including labor, was supplied by the federal government.

The National Airport Plan

On June 23, 1938, the *Civil Aeronautics Act of 1938* was approved by President Roosevelt. This act substituted a single federal statute for the several general and airmail statutes that had up to this time provided for the regulation of the aviation industry. It placed all the functions of air and regulation of aviation and air transportation in one authority. The new act created an administrative agency consisting of three partly autonomous bodies. The five-man Civil Aeronautics Authority was principally concerned with economic regulation of air carriers; the Air Safety Board was an independent body for the investigation of accidents; and the administrator concerned himself with construction, operation, and maintenance of the airway system.

The personnel, property, and unexpended balances of appropriations of the Bureau of Air Commerce of the Department of Commerce was transferred to the new Civil Aeronautics Authority. The transfer of the responsibilities of the Bureau of Air Commerce to the CAA, effected in August 1938, under the provisions of the act, brought to a close a 12-year period during which the development and regulation of civil aeronautics were under the jurisdiction of the Department of Commerce.

Reorganization of the CAA in 1940

During the first year and a half of its existence, a number of organizational difficulties arose within the Civil Aeronautics Authority. As a result, President Roosevelt, acting within the authority granted to him in the Reorganization Act of 1939, reorganized the Civil Aeronautics Authority and created two separate entities, the *Civil Aeronautics Board (CAB)* and the *Civil Aeronautics Administration (CAA)*. The five-man authority remained as an independent operation and became known as the Civil Aeronautics Board; the Air Safety Board was abolished and its functions given to the Civil Aeronautics Board; and the administrator became the head of an office within the Department of Commerce known as the Civil Aeronautics Administration. The duties of the original five-man authority were unchanged, except that certain responsibilities, such as accident investigation, were added because of the abolishment of the Air Safety Board. The administrator, in addition to retaining his functions of supervising construction, maintenance, and operation of the airways, was required to undertake the administration and enforcement of safety regulations, and the administration of the laws with regard to aircraft operation. Subsequently, the administrator became directly responsible to the secretary of commerce. The term *CAA*, which originally meant Civil Aeronautics Authority, became the Civil Aeronautics Administration.

Early federal aid to airports—the war years

Section 303 of the Civil Aeronautics Act of 1938 authorized the expenditure of federal funds for construction of landing areas provided the administrator certified "that such landing area was reasonably necessary for use in air commerce or in the interests of national defense." War broke out in Europe in September 1939, which prompted Congress in 1940 to appropriate $40 million for *Development of Landing Areas for National Defense (DLAND)*.

Under DLAND, the monies were spent by the Civil Aeronautics Administration, with the approval of the secretaries of war, commerce, and the Navy, for not more than 250 airports necessary for the national defense. Actually, in 1941, work was started on some 200 airports, and an additional 149 were added to the program later in the year. Under this program, government subdivisions furnished the land and agreed to operate and maintain the improved field, and the essential landing facilities were developed by federal funds. This program was coordinated with the work and funds of the other federal programs engaged in airport construction and improvement.

In 1940, the Army Air Corps started expansion, with the result that the previously mentioned program for the improvement of 399 civil airports soon became inadequate to provide the proper dispersion of fields and interceptor bases. The program expanded to comprise 504, then 668, and then a total of 986 airports that received aid under the war emergency.

During the war years the federal government, through the CAA, spent $353 million for the repair and construction of military landing areas in the continental United States. This does not include funds spent by the military agencies. During the same period, the CAA spent $9.5 million for the development of landing areas in the United States solely for civil purposes.

Many of the new airports constructed were planned so as to be useful to civil aviation in the postwar period. As a result, more than 500 airports constructed for the military by the CAA were declared surplus and were turned over to cities, counties, and states for civil aviation purposes. An understanding was reached between the federal government and the sponsor that the facilities would be available to the public without discrimination and to the government in the event of a national emergency.

Section 302(c) of the Civil Aeronautics Act of 1938 directed the civil aeronautics administrator to make a field survey of the existing system of airports and to report to congress with recommendations as to future federal participation in airport construction, improvement, development, operation, or maintenance.

An advisory committee was appointed, composed of representatives of interested federal agencies, both military and civil, state aviation officials, airport managers, airline representatives, and others. The first survey and report, made in 1939, did not result in congressional action, but a revised plan and recommendations submitted in November 1944 were influential in calling attention to the private airport deficiencies of inadequate distribution and inadequate facilities. This 1944 revision of the National Airport Plan was the basis, in part, upon which the Federal Airport Act of 1946 was enacted, so it will be helpful to review its principal recommendations:

　1 That Congress authorize an appropriation to the office of the administrator of civil aeronautics not to exceed $100 million annually to be used in a program of federal aid to public agencies for the development of a nationwide system of public airports adequate to meet the present and immediate future needs of civil aeronautics.

The administrator should be authorized to allocate such funds for any construction work involved in constructing, improving, or repairing (as distinguished from day-to-day maintenance of) an airport, including the construction, alteration, and repair of airport buildings other than hangars, and the removal, lowering, marking, and lighting of airport obstructions; for the acquisition of any lands or property interest necessary either for any such construction or to protect airport approaches; for making field surveys, preparing plans and specifications; supervising and inspecting construction work, and for any necessary federal expenses in the administration of the program.

2 That such a program be conducted in cooperation with the state and other nonfederal public agencies on a basis to be determined by the Congress. That the federal contribution be determined by the Congress in passing the necessary enabling legislation. A good precedent for the proportionate sharing of costs exists in the public roads program, which has operated satisfactorily for many years on a 50/50 basis.

3 That any project for which federal aid is requested must meet with approval of the administrator of civil aeronautics as to scope of development and cost, conform to Civil Aeronautics Administration standards for location, layout, grading, drainage, paving, and lighting, and all work thereon be subject to the inspection and approval of the Civil Aeronautics Administration.

4 In order to participate in the federal aid program, a state shall:

a Establish and empower an official body equipped to conduct its share of the program.

b Have legislation adequate for the clearing and protection of airport approaches, and such other legislation as may be necessary to vest in its political subdivisions all powers necessary to enable them to participate through the state as sponsors of airport projects.

c Have no special tax on aviation facilities, fuel, operations, or businesses, the proceeds of which are not used entirely for aviation.

d Ensure the operation of all public airports within its jurisdiction in the public interest, without unjust discrimination or unreasonable charges.

e Ensure the proper operation and maintenance of all public airports within its jurisdiction.

f Make airports developed with federal aid available for unrestricted use by United States government aircraft without charge other than an amount sufficient to cover the cost of repairing damage done by such aircraft.

g Require the installation at all airports for which federal funds have been provided, a standard accounting and fiscal reporting system satisfactory to the administrator.

5 That sponsors of projects be required to enter into contracts with the Civil Aeronautics Administration ensuring the proper maintenance and protection of airports developed with federal aid and their operation in the public interest.

Postwar federal aid to airports

After the war, Congress turned its attention back to civil aviation with the passage of the *Federal Airport Act of 1946*, which was signed by President Truman on May 13, 1946. It was the purpose of the Federal Airport Act to give the United States a comprehensive system of airports, administered by the Civil Aeronautics Administration. Small communities that needed airports to help develop their social and economic structure were theoretically supposed to benefit from this program.

Congress appropriated $500 million for airport aid over a seven-year period beginning July 1, 1946. The maximum yearly expenditure was set at $100 million. Of the total amount, 25 percent was placed in a discretionary fund to be used as the civil aeronautics administrator saw fit for airport construction. Half of the remaining 75 percent was apportioned to the states, based on population, and the other half, based on land areas. The discretionary fund allowed the administrator to choose the projects regardless of their location. The money had to be spent on operational facilities such as runways and taxiways.

This federal aid program provided that the federal government would pay as much as 50 percent of the cost and that the airport sponsor would pay the balance, or at least 50 percent of the cost. As far as the large cities were concerned, this was excellent because they could issue and sell bonds to pay for their share of the cost; however, for the small cities, even 50 percent of the cost of development was too much of a burden.

For an airport or governmental unit to be available for such aid, it was necessary that the airport be in the National Airport Plan. Under the Federal Airport Act, the administrator was directed to prepare such a plan. In formulating the plan, the administrator had to take into account the needs of both air commerce and private flying, technological development, probable growth, and any other considerations found appropriate.

As a condition to his approval of a project, the administrator had to receive in writing a guarantee that the following provisions would be adhered to:

1 The airport would be available for public use without unjust discrimination.
2 The airport would be suitably operated and maintained.
3 The aerial approaches would be cleared and protected and future hazards would be prevented.
4 Proper zoning would be provided to restrict the use of land adjacent to the airport.
5 All facilities developed from federal aid would be made available to the military.
6 All project accounts would be kept in accordance with a standard system.
7 All airport records would be available for inspection by an agent of the administrator upon reasonable request.

The Federal Airport Program progressed from the paper to the construction stage during 1947, and by February of the following year the Civil Aeronautics Administration had made 133 grant offers to local sponsors totaling $13.3 million. This marked the beginning of the federal government's present participation in construction of airport facilities.

On August 3, 1955, President Eisenhower signed Public Law 211, making major changes in the federal-aid-to-airports program and removed the 1958 time limit prescribed by the original act, as amended in 1950. In the main, these changes established a four-year program with authorizations amounting to $63 million for each fiscal year 1957–1959, made all types and sizes of airports eligible for aid, included airport buildings as eligible items of development, and provided that funds apportioned yearly to states continue on the area-population formula.

Federal Aviation Act of 1958

Recognizing that the demands on the federal government in the years ahead would be substantial, the director of the Bureau of the Budget requested a review of aviation facilities problems in 1955. William B. Harding was appointed as a consultant to the director. Harding, in turn, solicited the help of a number of prominent individuals in aviation to form his committee. In later December 1955, Harding submitted his report. Reporting that the need to improve air traffic management had already reached critical proportions, the group recommended that an individual of national reputation, responsible directly to the president, be appointed to provide full-time, high-level leadership in developing a program for solving the complex technical and organizational problems facing the government and the aviation industry.

Following approval of the Harding Committee recommendations, President Eisenhower appointed Edward P. Curtis his special assistant for aviation facilities planning. His assignment was to direct and coordinate "a long-range study of the nation's requirements," to develop "a comprehensive plan for meeting in the most effective and economical manner the needs disclosed by the study," and "to formulate legislative, organizational, administrative, and budgetary recommendations to implement the comprehensive plan."

In 1956, an event occurred that defied all odds: A TWA Super Constellation and a United DC-7 collided over the Grand Canyon, killing 128 people. Suddenly it was a crowded sky, and the outcry for reform became louder and clearer. If a pair of conceptually obsolete piston airliners could have a midair collision, what would happen with jets?

On May 10, 1957, Curtis submitted his report, "Aviation Facilities Planning," to the president. The report warned of "a crisis in the making" as a result of the inability of our airspace management system to cope with the complex patterns of civil and military traffic that filled the sky. The growing congestion of airspace was inhibiting defense and retarding the progress of air commerce. Concluding that many excellent plans for improving the nation's aviation facilities had failed in the past to mature because of the inability of our governmental organization to keep pace with aviation's dynamic growth, Curtis recommended the establishment of an independent Federal Aviation Agency "into which are consolidated all the essential management functions necessary to support the common needs of the military and civil aviation of the United States." Until such a permanent organization could be created, Curtis recommended the creation of an Airways Modernization Board as an independent office responsible for developing and consolidating the requirements for future systems of communications, navigation, and traffic control needed to accommodate United States air traffic.

Congress was receptive to this recommendation and passed the *Airways Modernization Act of 1957* on August 14, 1957. The purpose of the act was "to provide for the development and modernization of the national system of navigation and traffic control facilities to serve present and future needs of civil and military aviation." The act further provided for its own expiration on June 30, 1960. Appointment of Elwood R. Quesada as chairman was confirmed by the Senate on August 16, 1957.

On May 20, 1958, a military jet trainer and a civilian transport plane collided over Brunswick, Maryland, killing 12 and becoming the third major air disaster within a period of three and a half months. This tragedy spurred governmental action already underway to establish a comprehensive Federal Aviation Agency. Instead of taking two or three years to create a single aviation agency as was predicted, there was a virtual stampede in Congress to enact legislation. The *Federal Aviation Act of 1958* was signed by the president on August 23, 1958. Treating comprehensively the federal government's role in fostering and regulating civil aeronautics and air commerce, the new statute repealed the Air Commerce Act of 1926, the Civil Aeronautics Act of 1938, the Airways Modernization Act of 1957, and those portions of the various presidential reorganization plans dealing with civil aviation.

The law provided for the retention of the Civil Aeronautics Board as an independent office including all its functions except the safety-rule-making powers, which were transferred to the *Federal Aviation Agency*. The Federal Aviation Agency was created with an administrator responsible to the president. The agency incorporated the functions of the Civil Aeronautics Administration and the Airways Modernization Board.

Section 103 of the act concisely stated the administrator's major powers and responsibilities:

1 The regulation of air commerce in such manner as to best promote its development and safety and fulfill the requirements of national defense.

2 The promotion, encouragement, and development of civil aeronautics.

3 The control of the use of the navigable airspace of the United States and the regulation of both civil and military operations in such airspace in the interest of the safety and efficiency of both.

4 The consolidation of research and development with respect to air navigation facilities, as well as the installation and operation thereof.

5 The development and operation of a common system of air traffic control and navigation for both military and civil aircraft.

On November 1, 1958, Elwood R. Quesada, special assistant to the president for aviation matters and chairman of the airways modernization board, became the first administrator of the Federal Aviation Agency.

The Department of Transportation

For many years it was argued that there had been unrestrained growth and considerable duplication of federal activities regarding transportation. In 1966, President Johnson chose to deliver a special transportation message to Congress. He focused in on the need for coordination of the national transportation system, reorganization of transportation planning activities, and active promotion of safety. In his address President Johnson contended that the U.S. transportation system lacked true coordination and that this resulted in inefficiency. He advocated creation of a federal Department of Transportation (DOT) to promote coordination of existing federal programs and to act as a focal point for future research and development efforts in transportation.

Congressional hearings were held on several bills involving most of President Johnson's recommendations. Although some opposition was expressed to specific proposals, there was general support for creation of the *Department of Transportation*. The legislation creating the DOT was approved on October 15, 1966. DOT commenced operations on April 1, 1967, and Alan S. Boyd was appointed the first secretary of transportation.

The agencies and functions transferred to the DOT related to air transportation included the Federal Aviation Agency in its entirety and the safety functions of the Civil Aeronautics Board, including the responsibility for investigating and determining the probable cause of aircraft accidents and safety functions involving review on appeal of the suspension, modification, or denial of certificates or licenses. The Federal Aviation Agency was downgraded to the *Federal Aviation Administration (FAA)*. The administrator of the FAA was still appointed by the president but from then on reported directly to the secretary of transportation.

The act also created within the new department a five-member *National Transportation Safety Board (NTSB)*. The act charged the NTSB with (1) determining the cause or probable cause of transportation accidents and reporting the facts, conditions, and circumstances relating to such accidents; and (2) reviewing on appeal the suspension, amendment, modification, revocation, or denial of any certificate or license issued by the secretary or by an administrator.

Conclusion

During its 24-year lifetime (1946–1969), the Federal Aid for Airports Program generated $1.2 billion in federal aid to airports, all of it drawn from the general treasury. Most of the money—close to $1 billion—was used to build runways and roadways, while the rest was spent on land, terminal buildings, and lighting systems. For all of its success, however, FAAP failed to anticipate the travel boom of the 1960s, which overloaded the country's commercial air routes and prompted carriers to expand their fleets.

Airport and Airway Development Act of 1970

The tremendous growth in all segments of aviation during the late 1960s put a strain on the existing airway system. Air delays getting into and out of major airports began to develop rapidly. Along with the delays in the air, congestion was taking place in parking areas and terminal buildings. Public indignation at the failure of the system to keep pace with the demand for air transportation reached a peak in 1969. It was undoubtedly hastened by the widely publicized touchdown of the first of the new family of wide-bodied jets, the

Boeing 747. President Nixon told Congress in 1969 that stacks of airplanes over the nation's airports were ample evidence that something needed to be done.

It was evident that to reduce congestion, substantial amounts of money would have to be invested in airway and airport improvements. For airports alone it was estimated that $11 billion in new capital improvements would be required for public airports in the 10-year period 1970–1980. The amount of money authorized by the Federal Airport Act of 1946 was insufficient to assist in financing such a vast program. The normal and anticipated sources of revenue available to public airports were also not sufficient to acquire the required funds for capital expenditures.

Congress responded with an idea it borrowed from the interstate highway program: a trust fund supported by taxes on people who used the national aviation system. Such a mechanism, according to its proponents, would shift the cost of increasing the system's capacity from taxpayers to those groups who benefited most directly: passengers, shippers, and aircraft owners.

On May 21, 1970, President Nixon signed a two-title law that was to run for 10 years. Title I was the *Airport and Airway Development Act of 1970*, and Title II was the *Airport and Airway Revenue Act of 1970*. The new legislation assured a fund estimated at the time to generate more than $11 billion in funds for airport and airway modernization during the decade. By establishing an Airport and Airway Trust Fund modeled on the Highway Trust Fund, it freed airport and airway development from having to compete for General Treasury funds, the basic reason for the funding uncertainties and inadequacies of the past. Into the trust would go new revenues from aviation user taxes levied by the Airport and Airway Revenue Act, and other funds that Congress might choose to appropriate to meet authorized expenditures.

Revenues would be raised by levies on aviation users:

1 An 8-percent tax on domestic passenger fares.

2 A $3 surcharge on passenger tickets for international flights originating in the United States.

3 A tax of 7 cents a gallon on both gasoline and jet fuel used by aircraft in noncommercial aviation.

4 A 5-percent tax on airfreight waybills.

5 An annual registration fee of $25 on all civil aircraft, plus (1) in the case of piston-powered aircraft weighing more than 2,500 pounds, 2 cents a pound for each pound of maximum certificated takeoff weight; or (2) in the case of turbine-powered aircraft, 3.5 cents a pound for each pound of maximum certificated takeoff weight.

Advantages of the user-charge/trust-fund approach

The principal advantages of the user-charge/trust-fund approach to revenue raising and funding were that it (1) provided a predictable and increasing source of income, more commensurate with need; (2) permitted more effective and longer range planning; and (3) assured that the tax revenues generated by aviation would not be diverted to nonaviation uses.

First five years under the Act

Two grant-in-aid programs were provided for under the 10-year 1970 Airport and Airway Development Act: *The Planning Grant Program (PGP)* and the *Airport Development Aid Program (ADAP)*. The grant programs were fund-matching assistance programs in which the federal government paid a predetermined share of approved airport planning and development project costs, and the airport owners at the various state and local levels, who were eligible to participate in the program, paid the rest. The 1970 act also provided that the funding authority of the grant-in-aid programs would expire on June 30, 1975, at the end of the act's first five years of operation. The object was to see what, if any, changes needed to be made before further funds were authorized for the act's remaining five years.

The major weaknesses of the Federal Airport Act, which was repealed by the new legislation, were the inadequacy of the resources provided under it and the nature of the formula for distributing those resources. The annual authorization under the old act totaled only $75 million and of this total, the distribution of $66.5 million was fixed by a formula apportioning 75 percent of it by population and area among the states: half in the ratio of each state's population to the total population of all the states, and half in the ratio of each state's area to the total area of all the states. Though the remaining 25 percent of $66.5 million, plus any state's apportionment under the population-area formula if unclaimed for two fiscal years, went into a discretionary fund with certain other funds, this discretionary fund was too small to make a significant impact on critical, high-priority areas.

By contrast, the new airport and airway act increased the total annual authorization by nearly four times for each of the first five years—to $280 million—and it provided a distribution formula improved in the light of the experience under the Federal Airport Act. Of the $280 million, $250 million would be available each year for modernization and improvement programs at air carrier and reliever airports and $30 million annually for general aviation airports.

In its provisions concerning planning, the new legislation reflected not only certain lessons of experience but also the emergence of certain new planning factors. For example, experience under the Federal Airport Act with the National Airport Plan, which covered a period of five years and was revised annually, led to the requirement in the new law for a National Airport System Plan (NASP) covering at least 10 years and revised only as necessary. Notable among factors explicitly mentioned for the secretary's consideration in preparing the NASP, but not mentioned in relation to the NASP, were, among others, (1) the relationship of each airport to the local transportation system, to forecasted technological developments in aeronautics, and to developments forecasted in other modes of intercity transport; and (2) factors affecting the quality of the natural environment.

The provision for planning grants also marked a significant difference between the new legislation and the old. The new law authorized the secretary to make grants of funds to planning agencies for airports' system planning, and to public agencies for airport master planning. At the same time, it authorized a total of $75 million for such grants. Planning grants, however, could not exceed $15 million in any one fiscal year, nor could any such grant exceed two-thirds of an airport project's cost.

Airway modernization also benefited from the increased funding authorized by the Airport and Airway Development Act. Throughout the decade of the 1960s, appropriations for airway facilities and equipment averaged $93 million a year. The new legislation authorized "not less than" $250 million a year for the first five fiscal years for acquiring, establishing, and improving air navigation facilities. A principal beneficiary of this more generous authorization would be the FAA's efforts to automate the air traffic control system of the National Airspace System.

ADAP funding under the act, for which the federal share for large and medium air carrier hubs had been 50 percent, and for the smaller air carrier, general aviation, and reliever airports, 75 percent had initially been $280 million per year. In 1973, under the amendments to the act of that year, the funding level was set at $310 million (Table 1-1).

Total ADAP funds obligated under the act over the five-year period totaled close to $1.3 billion, a figure that exceeded by $100 million the $1.2 billion airport development aid funds disbursed by the federal government in the entire 24-year history of the earlier Federal Aid Airport Program. The $1.3 billion had made it possible for the FAA to provide and fund a total of 2,434 ADAP projects during the five-year period. Of this number, 1,528 had been completed at air carrier locations, 757 at general aviation airport locations, and 149 at reliever airport locations. The beneficiaries included 520 air carrier airports, 624 general aviation airports, and 81 reliever airports. For the air carrier airports, the federal funds expended came to $1.09 billion; for general aviation airports, to $212.8 million; and for reliever airports, to $61.6 million.

With this infusion of additional federal money, 85 new airports were built and more than 1,000 others significantly improved. The improvements included 178 new runways, 520 new taxiways, 201 runway extensions, hundreds of miles of security fencing, and fleets of aircraft rescue, fire fighting (ARFF) equipment. They also comprised some of the most advanced approach-aid equipment available, including 28 instrument landing systems (ILS), 141 runway end identifying lighting systems (REILS) and 471 visual approach slope indicators (VASI).

Table 1-1 ADAP spending (millions), 1971–1975

FY	Amount permitted under 1970 act (authorizations)	Amount approved by Congress each year (appropriations)	Amount actually spent by FAA (obligations)
1971	$280	$170	$170
1972	280	280	280
1973	280	280	207
1974	310	300	300
1975	310	335	335
Total	$1,460	$1,365	$1,292

Source: FAA

The act had served its purpose well during the first five years. Nevertheless, as its obligational authority began drawing to a close, it was clear that the required review was fortunate in its timing. With a sharp increase in air carrier and general aviation operations, mounting environmental and terminal access problems, along with increasing inflation, there was no time to be lost in getting it underway.

Airport and Airway Development Act Amendments of 1976

On July 12, 1976, President Ford signed into law the *Airport and Airway Development Act Amendments of 1976.* ADAP funding levels for the remaining five years under the 1970 act were sharply increased as shown in Table 1-2.

Some of the important amendments included under the 1976 Act were as follows:

1 Expanded the types of airport development projects eligible for ADAP funding. These now included (1) snow removal equipment; (2) noise suppressing equipment; (3) physical barriers and landscaping to diminish the effects of aircraft noise; and (4) the acquisition of land to ensure environmental compatibility. Nonrevenue-producing public use terminal area facilities for the movement of passengers and baggage at airports serving CAB certificated air carriers also became eligible for ADAP funding, except that in such cases the federal share would be 50 percent.

2 Established the "Commuter Service Airport," a new air carrier airport category comprising about 130 airports that served noncertificated air carriers, and enplaned at least

Table 1-2 ADAP funding (millions), 1976–1980

FY	Air carrier airports	General aviation airports	Total
1976	$435	$65	$500
1977	440	70	510
1978	465	75	540
1979	495	80	575
1980	525	85	610
Total	$2,360	$375	$2,735

Source: FAA

2,500 passengers annually. This new airport category was created in recognition of the substantial growth of commercial commuter services during the previous five-year period, their potential for future growth, and the resulting need to assure airports serving them proper development funding.

3 Directed that the reliever airports in the National Airport System, previously grouped for funding purposes with the air carrier airports, be included instead with the general aviation airport category because, aside from their usefulness as relievers, they were basically general aviation airports.

4 Increased the federal share for ADAP grants. For small air carrier hubs, general aviation airports, reliever airports, and commuter service airports, the federal share would be 90 percent for fiscal years 1976 through 1978, and 80 percent for fiscal years 1979 through 1980. For the 67 large and medium hubs in the National Airport System, it went from the previous 50 percent to 75 percent and remained there throughout the entire five-year period.

5 Increased the federal share for PGP grants from 66.7 to 75.0 percent.

6 Ordered the preparation and publication by January 1, 1978, of a major revision of the National Airport System Plan (NASP). Last submitted to Congress in 1973, and kept updated since, the NASP comprised more than 4,000 locations, including 649 served by the certificated air carriers.

7 Directed by the initiation of a series of studies having to do with the following: (1) the feasibility of landbank-banking as an expedient in airport development; (2) the case for soundproofing public institutions located near airports; (3) the identification of places in the United States where major new airports would be needed, and alternative approaches to their financing; and (4) the identification of needed airports across the nation, which for economic reasons were threatened with closure, with an analysis in the individual case of what could best be done to keep them open.

8 Authorized the appropriation from the Airport and Airway Trust Fund for the five-year period of fiscal years 1976 through 1980 for disbursement in annual increments of the following sums: (1) up to $1.15 billion to cover the costs of flight checking and maintaining the air navigation facilities of the federal airway system; (2) $1.275 million to assist the states in developing their own general aviation airport standards; and (3) $1.3 billion for the purpose of acquiring, establishing, and improving federal air navigation facilities.

These were the major provisions of the 1976 act as it further amended the Airport and Airway Development Act of 1970. In signing the new legislation, President Ford stated, "The Airport and Airway Development Act of 1976 will make possible the continuing modernization of our airways, airports, and related facilities in communities throughout our fifty states."

Airline deregulation

Passage of the Air Cargo Deregulation Act of 1976, and, more importantly, the *Airline Deregulation Act of 1978*, signaled an end to the 40-year history of economic regulation of the airline industry. The deregulation of airlines was part of a general trend gaining momentum in the 1970s to reduce government regulation of private industry. By this time, many observers in Congress and elsewhere had begun to doubt that federal regulation was encouraging orderly competition and had come to suspect that the regulatory process was imposing unnecessary costs and creating distortions in the marketplace. Even before Congress passed the deregulation acts, the CAB itself had conducted a number of experimental reductions of certain types of regulation in order to encourage competition. With the 1978 act, the market was opened to new firms, and carriers gained much greater freedom to enter or leave markets, to change routes, and to compete on the basis of price. The 1978 act also called for the "sunset" of the CAB by the end of 1984, with transfer of its few remaining essential functions to the DOT and other departments.

Deregulation has had a profound effect on the airport system. Once air carriers were permitted to change routes without CAB approval, they dropped many unprofitable points, confirming the fears of some opponents of deregulation that air service to small communities would suffer. Service to some smaller cities continued under the *Essential Air Service* provisions of the deregulation act, which provides subsidies to the last carrier in a market so as to prevent selected cities from losing service altogether. In many cases, small commuter carriers entered the markets abandoned by larger carriers. In addition, the airlines' new freedom has greatly changed their relationships with airport operators, who can no longer depend on the stability of the carriers serving the airport and who must accommodate new entrants.

Aircraft noise

One of the major issues affecting airport development, especially since the beginning of the jet age, has been aircraft noise. The FAA has responsibility for regulating aircraft noise—in the Federal Aviation Regulations Part 36 (1969) and Part 91 (1976)—and for establishing procedures for airspace use; however, the federal government has not taken on the task of directly regulating the noise level at a given airport, which is considered the province of the airport operator. The *Aviation Safety and Noise Abatement Act*, passed by Congress in 1979, was intended to "provide assistance to airport operators to prepare and carry out noise compatibility programs." It authorizes the FAA to help airport operators develop noise abatement programs and makes them eligible for grants under ADAP.

Airport development in the 1980s and 1990s

Between 1971 and 1980 the trust fund received approximately $13.8 billion, of which $4.1 billion was invested in the airport system through ADAP grants. The Airport and Airway Development Act expired in 1980 and Congress did not agree on reauthorizing legislation until passage of the Airport and Airway Improvement Act of 1982. During fiscal years 1981 and 1982 the taxing provisions of the trust fund were reduced, and revenues were deposited in the General Fund and the Highway Trust Fund. However, Congress continued to appropriate airport aid, $450 million for each of the two years. At least part of the delay in passing new legislation was due to the debate over "defederalization," an action that would have made the nation's largest airports ineligible for federal aid on the grounds that they were capable of supporting themselves financially. Defederalization was dropped from the final version of the legislation, but Congress directed the Department of Transportation to study the matter and to report at a later date.

Airport and Airway Improvement Act of 1982

The *Airport and Airway Improvement Act of 1982* reestablished the operation of the Airport and Airway Trust Fund with a slightly revised schedule of user taxes. Operators of piston aircraft were required to pay 12 cents per gallon for avgas, an increase of 5 cents over the 1970 tax rate. Turbine aircraft operators paid 14 cents per gallon for jet fuel, an increase of 7 cents.

The act authorized a new capital grant program, called the Airport Improvement Program (AIP). In basic philosophy, AIP was similar to the previous ADAP. It was intended to support a national system of integrated airports that recognizes the role of large and small airports together in a national air transportation system. Maximized joint use of underutilized, nonstrategic U.S. military fields was also encouraged.

The 1982 act also contained a provision to make funds available for noise compatibility planning and to carry out noise compatibility programs as authorized by the Aviation Safety and Noise Abatement Act of 1979.

The Airport and Airway Improvement Act has been amended several times. For example, the Continuing Appropriations Act, passed in October 1982, added a section providing authority to issue discretionary grants in lieu of unused apportioned funds under certain circumstances, and the Surface Transportation Assistance Act, passed in January 1983, increased the annual authorizations for the AIP for fiscal years 1983 to 1985. Overall, the Airport and Airway Improvement Act of 1982 authorized a total of $4.8 billion in airport aid for fiscal years 1983 through 1987.

A 1987 amendment, the *Airport and Airway Safety and Capacity Expansion Act of 1987*, extended the authority for the AIP for five years. It authorized $1.7 billion each fiscal year through 1990 and $1.8 billion each year for fiscal years 1991 and 1992. This amendment also authorized a new procedure in which a sponsor is advised of federal intentions to fund long-term high-priority capacity projects as appropriations allow and to reimburse sponsors for certain specified work performed before a grant is received. This procedure is implemented through a letter of intent issued to sponsors. Another provision of the 1987 amendment established a requirement that 10 percent of the funds made available under the AIP be given to small business concerns owned and controlled by socially and economically disadvantaged individuals, known as the Disadvantaged Business Enterprise Program.

The *Aviation Safety and Capacity Expansion Act of 1990* authorized a *Passenger Facility Charge (PFC)* program to provide funds to finance airport-related projects that preserve or enhance safety, capacity, or security; reduce noise from an airport that is part of such system; or furnish opportunities for enhanced competition between or among air carriers by local imposition of a charge per enplaned passenger. This act also established a Military Airport Program for current and former military airfields, which will help improve the capacity of the national transportation system by enhancement of airport and air traffic control systems in major metropolitan areas. It also increased the authorization for 1992 to $1.9 billion.

The *Airport and Airway Safety, Capacity, Noise Improvement, and Intermodal Transportation Act of 1992* authorized the extension of AIP at a funding level of $2.1 billion through 1993. The Act also included a number of changes in AIP funding. The primary changes included the expanded eligibility of development under the Military Airport Program; eligibility for the relocation of air traffic control towers and navigational aids (including radar) if they impede other projects funded under the AIP; the eligibility of land, paving, drainage, aircraft deicing equipment, and structures for centralized aircraft deicing areas; and projects to comply with the Americans with Disabilities Act of 1990, the Clean Air Act, and the Federal Water Pollution Control Act. The Act also increased the number of states that may participate in the State Block Grant Program from three to seven and extended that program through 1996.

The *AIP Temporary Extension Act of 1994* extended the authorization for AIP funding through June 1994. It provided that the minimum amount to be apportioned to a primary airport based on passenger boardings would be $500,000. The act also made modifications to the percentage of AIP funds that must be set aside for reliever airports (reduced from 10 percent to 5 percent), for commercial service, nonprimary airports (reduced from 2.5 percent to 1.5 percent), and for system planning projects (increased from 0.5 percent to 0.75 percent). Eligibility for terminal development was expanded to allow the use of discretionary funds at reliever airports and primary airports enplaning less than 0.05 percent of annual national enplanements.

The *Federal Aviation Administration Authorization Act of 1994* extended AIP funding through September 1996. Significant changes to AIP included increasing the number of airports that can be designated in the Military Airport Program (MAP) from 12 to 15, but required that FAA find that projects at newly designated airports will reduce delays at airports with 20,000 hours of delay or more, expanded eligibility to include universal access control and explosives detection security devices, and required a number of actions by FAA and airport sponsors regarding airport rates and charges and airport revenue diversion.

The *Federal Aviation Reauthorization Act of 1996* extended AIP through September 1998. Various changes were made to the formula computation of primary and cargo entitlements, state apportionment, and discretionary set-asides. Specifically, under primary airport entitlements, the formula was adjusted by changing the credit for the number of enplaning passengers over 500,000 from $0.65 to $0.65 for the passengers from 500,000 up to 1 million and $0.50 for each passenger over 1 million. Cargo entitlements were decreased from 3.5 percent of AIP to 2.5 percent of AIP. The previous cap of 44 percent of AIP for primary and cargo entitlements was removed.

State apportionments were increased from 12 percent of AIP to 18.5 percent, with the previous set-asides for reliever and nonprimary commercial service airports removed. The eligibility for use of state apportionments was expanded to include nonprimary commercial service airports. The system planning set-aside was also eliminated.

The noise and MAP set-aside computations were also changed from 12.5 percent and 2.5 percent of total AIP, respectively, to 31 percent and 4 percent of the discretionary fund. In addition, previously there was a minimum level of $325 million for the discretionary fund after subtraction of the various apportioned funds and set-asides. The new Act changed the minimum level to $148 million over the payments necessary for letters of intent payments (for letters of intent issued prior to January 1, 1996) from the discretionary fund.

Three new pilot programs for innovative financing techniques, pavement maintenance, and privatization of airports were added to the program. Other changes included changes to the MAP in the number of airports under the program, criteria for selection, project eligibility, and permission to extend MAP participants for an additional five-year period. The state block grant program was formally adopted by removing the designation of "pilot" and the number of participant states was increased from seven to eight states in 1997 and to nine states in 1998.

The Act also aligned PFC and AIP to permit both to be used for funding projects to comply with federal mandates and to relocate navigational aids and air traffic control towers. These relocations are eligible only when needed in conjunction with approved airport development using AIP or PFC funding. Finally, new provisions for revenue diversion enforcement were added to FAA's authority.

National Plan of Integrated Airport Systems (NPIAS)

The Airport and Airway Improvement Act also required the secretary of transportation to publish a report on the status of the *National Plan of Integrated Airport Systems (NPIAS)*. The NPIAS emphasizes system planning and development to meet current and future needs; it includes development considered necessary to provide a safe, efficient, and integrated airport system meeting the needs of civil aviation, national defense, and the postal service. An airport must be included in this plan in order to be eligible to receive a grant under the AIP. The latest edition of NPIAS covering 1998–2002 includes a total of 3,344 existing and 217 proposed airports. These airports account for over 90 percent of general aviation and virtually all operations by scheduled air carriers. The NPIAS includes estimates of the type and cost of development that will be required at each airport through 2002. The development recommendations are drawn primarily from plans prepared by state and local agencies responsible for airport planning and development.

The NPIAS includes only development that is eligible for federal aid under the Airport Improvement Program; it does not include hangars, nonpublic areas of terminal buildings, automobile parking facilities, and ground access facilities beyond the airport boundary. Neither does the NPIAS include the effects of inflation on cost estimates. While all of the development in the NPIAS is eligible for federal aid, it is expected that about two-thirds will be accomplished with local and state funds, derived primarily from airport income and user fees.

AIP funding by airport type

Table 1-3 presents AIP funding since it began in 1982. The AIP has provided over $22 billion to airports and local, regional, and state planning agencies over the 16 years from 1982 to 1998. Total authorization levels have been increased steadily over time; however, appropriation levels have been on a downward trend since 1993.

The appropriation levels represent limitations on obligations mandated each fiscal year.

The recent trend of declining AIP funding presents problems when juxtaposed with estimates of the capital needs of the national airport system. Declining funding availability may discourage repair and maintenance of existing infrastructure (the capital costs most dependent on AIP funds) in favor of building new, revenue-generating infrastructure. The funding levels will become problematic if airports have to delay needed repairs and maintenance because of lack of funding, thus raising concerns about efficiency and safety.

AIP funding for primary airports was reduced by 27.3 percent between 1994 and 1998. While all airports have felt the effects of the decrease in the annual AIP appropriation, general aviation and reliever airports may be hit especially hard by the cutbacks. The funds specifically earmarked for general aviation airports have been cut 25.6 percent between 1992 and 1998, while reliever airports have experienced a 29.2 percent drop between 1993 and 1998. This substantial decrease in federal funding for these airports has an even greater effect than cuts at larger airports, since most of these smaller airports cannot effectively implement a profitable PFC to supplement their revenues.

The Airport Improvement Program has been an invaluable source of funding for airports. The infrastructure and capital requirements of our national airport system have been dependent on the receipt of over $22 billion in AIP disbursements since 1982. These disbursements have allowed the system's capacity to grow, airport services to expand and improve, and safe, reliable aviation services to continue to be provided.

The capital requirements of our airport system are not diminishing, however. As funding levels continue their recent decline, discussions within the airport community have centered around the adequacy of the AIP as the primary source of airport funds. The FAA itself has been exploring possibilities for restructuring or streamlining the government funding process for airports. As the FAA continues this introspection, the industry continues efforts to expand its funding base, attempting to qualify for economic development and other potential government-provided funds. In addition, "intermodalism" is the industry buzzword as aviation, maritime, and ground transportation officials seek to take advantage of the synergies between their system and capital requirements. The Intermodal Surface Transportation Efficiency Act of 1991 (see Chapter 10) was only the start of efforts to coordinate better the funding of national infrastructure needs today and into the twenty-first century.

Passenger facility charges (PFCs)

The Aviation and Capacity Expansion Act of 1990 authorized domestic commercial service airports to impose a Passenger Facility Charge (PFC) on enplaning passengers, reversing a 17-year-old policy prohibiting such a charge. Airport head taxes have been widely used outside the United States to fund airport development. In the wake of exponential growth in demand for airport facilities brought about by airline deregulation in 1978, U.S. airport operators and executives pressed the Executive Branch and Congress for a revision of the Anti-Head Tax of 1973 to fund more airport development. Before the 101st Congress, various presidential administrations had supported lifting the prohibition on head taxes, generally as part of a package including defederalization and termination of the federal airport grant program for larger airports.

In 1990, Secretary of Transportation Samuel R. Skinner made enactment of PFCs without elimination of federal funding his top legislative priority. He recognized that there were critical shortages of airport capacity and airport capital development funds across the nation, while the Airport and Airway Trust Fund was increasingly spent on nonairport development expenses, such as FAA operations and airways facilities and equipment and research and development.

In the spring of 1990, Secretary Skinner asked Congress to enact PFC legislation, allowing airport sponsors to impose up to $3-per-passenger charges, as part of legislation extending the Airport and Airway Improvement Act programs. Having identified airport capital needs of $50 billion over the next five years, the Airport Operators Council International (AOCI) and the American Association of Airport Executives (AAAE) mounted a major legislative campaign for PFCs. In November 1990, Congress passed the act authorizing PFCs.

Airport operators seeking to impose a PFC must apply to the Secretary of Transportation for PFC authority, after offering air carriers that use the airport an opportunity for consultation on the projects the airport proposes to include in the application. Airports, and later the FAA, must meet a detailed set of notice and consultation requirements

Table 1-3 AIP funding by airport type (millions), 1982–1998

FY	Congressional authorization	Primary	Appropriations by type of airport				Total appropriations
			Nonprimary commercial	General aviation	Reliever		
1982	$460.0	$312.3	$31.5	$62.4	$48.2		$454.4
1983	800.0	465.0	69.2	155.1	98.7		788.0
1984	993.5	502.8	62.0	146.5	103.6		814.9
1985	987.0	623.4	52.4	154.1	110.1		940.0
1986	1,017.0	542.0	58.9	146.5	100.8		848.2
1987	1,017.2	525.6	72.2	155.8	129.7		883.3
1988	1,700.0	1,082.9	47.7	190.9	135.1		1,456.6
1989	1,700.0	1,013.5	43.9	178.0	171.2		1,406.6
1990	1,700.0	1,010.6	43.7	168.5	138.0		1,360.8
1991	1,800.0	1,210.1	45.5	248.7	211.1		1,715.4
1992	1,900.0	1,203.4	56.4	249.2	166.5		1,675.5
1993	2,025.0	1,296.4	41.2	199.1	180.6		1,717.3
1994	2,070.3	1,316.1	41.4	181.1	133.2		1,671.8
1995	2,161.0	1,166.3	32.5	157.6	85.7		1,442.1
1996	2,214.0	1,025.3	27.8	145.6	105.6		1,304.3
1997	2,280.0	1,209.3	57.7	140.1	114.6		1,521.7
1998	2,347.0	956.7	39.1	185.5	127.8		1,309.1
Subtotal	$27,172.0	$15,461.7	$823.1	$2,864.7	$2,160.5		$21,310.0
		72.6%	3.9%	13.4%	10.1%		100.0%
Planning funds and state block grants, 1982–1998							$754.1
Total							$22,064.1

Source: FAA

designed to elicit the participation of affected airlines, other airport users, and other affected parties at various stages of the process.

Some of the important provisions under the 1990 act were as follows:

1 The airport operator may propose collecting $1, $2, or $3 per enplaned passenger, domestic or foreign. No intermediate amounts (e.g., $2.50) are permitted.

2 The PFCs will be collected by the air carriers.

3 The PFC is limited to no more than two charges on each leg of a round trip at airports at which passengers enplaned aircraft.

4 The PFC revenue must be spent at the designated airport controlled by the same body that imposes the fees.

5 The revenue from PFCs may only be used to finance the allowable costs of the approved projects. This includes bond-associated debt service and financing costs, and the nonfederal share of the costs of projects funded under the federal airport grant program.

6 Revenues can be used for airport planning and development projects eligible for AIP grants such as land acquisition; site preparation; runway, taxiway, and apron construction and repair; roads within airport boundaries; construction and installation of lighting, utilities, and navigational aids; safety and security equipment; snow removal equipment; and limited terminal development. In addition to the AIP development, PFC revenue can be used for the preparation of noise compatibility plans and noise compatibility measures. The final category of projects that can be funded with PFCs is construction of passenger-use areas. Included are loading gates, baggage handling and make-up areas, ticketing areas, security devices, holding areas, waiting rooms, and associated corridors.

7 The legislation requires that AIP funds apportioned to a large or medium hub airport be reduced if a PFC is imposed at that airport. This reduction takes place in the fiscal year following the approval of authority for PFC collections at that airport and continues in each succeeding fiscal year in which the PFC is imposed. The apportionment is reduced by 50 percent of the forecast PFC revenue, but must not exceed 50 percent of the earned apportionments for the fiscal year. The legislation

Table 1-4 PFC expenditures by type of use (millions), 1992–1998

Development/planning	PFC funds authorized
Airside (primarily runway, taxiway, and apron)	$3,848
Landside (primarily terminal)	6,159
Noise	1,292
Access (primarily roads)	$2,682
New Denver airport	2,331
Interest (on bonds)	5,605
Total	$21,917

requires that 25 percent of the revenues obtained through a reduction in these apportioned funds are to be placed in the AIP
discretionary fund, of which one-half is to be used for small hub
airports, and 75 percent is to be used to establish a Small Airports
Fund. One-third of the revenues in the Small Airport Fund is to be
distributed to general aviation (including reliever) airports and
two-thirds to nonhub commercial service airports.

PFC collections and AIP funds are complementary in the overall funding of airport improvements. The majority of PFC-approved projects are
also AIP-eligible, although there is broader eligibility under the PFC program for noise compatibility measures and terminal gates and related
areas. One major use of PFC is as the local "match" funds for AIP grants,
particularly at nonhub primary airports. Table 1-4 illustrates the manner
in which PFC revenues have been used from 1992 through 1998.

As of September 30, 1998, a total of 296 locations had been
approved for PFCs since the program's inception in 1991. Total
authorized PFC collections for these 296 locations totaled over $21.9
billion. Of those primary hub airports eligible to collect PFCs, 81 percent were doing so as of the end of the fiscal year, with 63 percent of
nonhub primary airports collecting PFCs. Participation in the PFC program falls off sharply at the level of nonprimary commercial service
airports, with only 12 percent of these airports collecting PFCs as of
the end of the 1998 fiscal year.

State Block Grant Program

The *State Block Grant Program*, authorized by the 1987, 1990, and
1992 amendments to the Airport and Airway Improvement Act, has

been implemented by Part 156 of the Federal Aviation Regulations. Under this regulation, states assume responsibility for administration of AIP grants at other than primary airports. This program became effective October 1, 1989 with only three states: Illinois, Missouri, and North Carolina. By 1998, the list had been expanded to include nine states: the original three states, Michigan, New Jersey, Pennsylvania, Tennessee, Texas, and Wisconsin.

These block grant states administer funding of nonprimary commercial service, reliever, and general aviation airports. Each state is responsible for determining which locations within its jurisdiction will receive funds and for conducting ongoing project administration. For the period the pilot program has been effective, $503.3 million, including $256.9 million discretionary, has been issued as block grants.

Military Airport Program

The *Military Airport Program (MAP)* was authorized under the Aviation Safety and Capacity Expansion Act of 1990.

The MAP is a special set-aside of the discretionary portion of the Airport Improvement Program to be used for capacity- and/or conversion-related projects at current and former military airports. The MAP allows the Secretary of Transportation to fund capital development at current or former military airports that have been designated as civil commercial or reliever airports in the National Plan of Integrated Airport Systems. Specifically, the criterion requires that approved projects at any MAP location must be able to reduce delays at an existing commercial service airport that has more than 20,000 hours of annual delays in commercial passenger aircraft takeoffs and landings. The designated airports remain eligible to participate in the program for five fiscal years after their initial designation as participants.

At the end of 1998, there were 24 airports in the program. These airports contribute to the capacity of the national air transportation system by enhancing airport and air traffic control system capacity in their respective metropolitan areas, as well as by reducing current and projected flight delays. The projects approved for these airports included land acquisition; security improvements; runway, apron, and taxiway construction and improvements; lighting and terminal development; and other conversion-related projects.

Conversion-related projects are especially important to the newly converting bases. To duplicate this investment in infrastructure with AIP funds would quickly deplete all appropriated funds for many years to come. However, these bases still require significant amounts of AIP funding to be properly retrofitted for civilian use. For example, terminal buildings are not normally found on military bases and must be constructed to provide adequate facilities for movement of passengers at commercial service airports.

The FAA is continuing to pursue a series of initiatives with the Department of Defense (DOD), states, and local governments for joint civil and military use of existing military airfields and the conversion of military airfields being closed by the DOD. There are currently about 44 military airfields closing as a result of the DOD's base closure programs already approved by Congress. It is anticipated that up to 36 of these military airfields will be converted to civil airports. It has been estimated that to replicate the infrastructure at these military airfields would require a total investment of about $36 billion. An AIP investment of $211 million in MAP funds through 1998 has secured this infrastructure for future civil use.

Concluding remarks

In large measure, the system of airports that we have in the United States today owes its existence to federal policy, whose express purpose has been to foster the development of civil aviation. In the earliest years of civil aviation, the government's actions were confined to subsidy of aircraft manufacturers through military purchases and indirect support of aircraft operators by airmail contracts. Because airports were regarded as essentially local enterprises, they did not receive federal aid. But from the beginning, civil aviation was perceived as an adjunct to military aviation in providing national defense, and in the World War II era, this became the rationale for direct federal government assistance to civil airports.

In the years after 1945, the federal government took an even more important step in supporting the civil airport system when it turned over to local authorities hundreds of airports that had been built and operated as military installations but were then deemed surplus. This infusion of capital facilities not only expanded the airport network serving commercial aviation, it also encouraged the purchase and use of general aviation aircraft by ensuring ample landing facilities within reach of nearly everyone in the country.

By 1960, this divestiture of military holdings had largely run its course, and the emphasis of federal policy shifted to upgrading and expansion of major airports to accommodate jet aircraft and to alleviate problems of congestion and delay in airline traffic that were beginning to emerge. Smaller airports were not neglected; between 1960 and 1970, $510 million—about 20 percent of all federal expenditures for airport capital improvements—were directed to small communities and to improving the quality of general aviation facilities. In addition to construction and improvement of runways and airfield facilities, the federal government aided general aviation in other ways. The network of flight service stations was expanded, and the number of airports with FAA-operated control towers grew substantially, with nearly all of the additions coming at smaller airports. Safety of civil aviation was an important motivating factor, but so too was the desire to establish and maintain an extensive system of well-equipped airports serving all classes of civil aviation, providing readily available commercial air transportation, and operating bases for aircraft used for business purposes and private flying.

The passage of the Airport and Airway Development Act of 1970 institutionalized federal airport aid by establishing the Airport and Airway Trust Fund, supported by user fees, which provided a dedicated source of revenue for capital improvement. This act not only committed federal support to the airport system, it also gave the federal government a strong—perhaps dominant—voice in how that system would develop. By identifying the kinds of airports eligible for capital grants, by specifying the types of projects that would be supported, and by establishing formulas for federal, state, and local funding, the Airport Development Aid Program effectively set the pattern of airport development for the 1970s. After a brief period of uncertainty in 1980 to 1982, when Congress allowed the legislative authorization of ADAP to lapse, previous federal policy on airport development was reaffirmed in September 1982 with passage of the Airport and Airway Improvement Act of 1982, which established the Airport Improvement Program.

AIP preserved the general approach to airport aid established under ADAP, with certain revisions to correct what were perceived as imbalances in the allocation of funds and to adjust the shares paid into the trust fund by various classes of airport and airspace users through ticket and fuel taxes. The principal differences between ADAP and the new AIP were in the proportion of federal aid to be allocated to air carrier, reliever, and general aviation airports, the earmarking of 8 percent for noise projects, and extension of federal aid for the first time to privately owned general aviation airports.

Investment of $4.1 billion in federal monies for airport capital projects under ADAP between 1971 and 1980 and $7.9 billion more in state and local funds enabled the airport system to keep abreast of construction needs, but delay problems at a dozen or so major metropolitan airports remained chronic. The capacity gains achieved at major airports were largely offset by growth in passenger traffic, which rose by about 75 percent during the decade.

Between 1980 and 1989, domestic and international air travel demand by scheduled U.S. air carriers, measured in revenue passenger miles (RPMs), increased from 258.6 billion RPMs to 433.8 billion RPMs per year. By 1998 RPMs reached 614.2 billion and the FAA forecasted 830.3 billion RPMs by the year 2005. If this level is attained, air travel demand will have grown by 221 percent over a span of 25 years.

Aircraft operations, a better measure of the load on the airport and airway system, have also increased sharply. Aircraft operations by scheduled U.S. air carriers increased 40 percent between 1980 and 1989, rising from 14.7 million to 20.8 million. By 1998, takeoffs and landings reached 24.4 million and the FAA forecasted 29.1 billion in 2005, almost double the 1980 total. Other indicators of aviation activity (passenger enplanements, fleet size, and hours flown) exhibit similar historical and projected growth.

The boom in air travel during the last two decades has been spurred by several factors: airline deregulation, a robust economy, reduced fares, and an increasing propensity of the public to rely on aviation for trips more than 200 miles. During the 1980s and 1990s, more people flew more often than ever before, and the indications are that the trend will continue into the new millenium.

In accommodating the burgeoning demand, the nation's airports and airways have been severely strained. Congestion and delay have mounted in the airspace, on runways, and in airport terminals. In 1997, 27 major airports experienced more than 20,000 hours of flight delays in air carrier operations. If some way is not found to accommodate growing demand, 31 U.S. airports could be so affected by 2007.

Passenger travel is not the only element of civil aviation that has grown. Air cargo operations and general aviation (private and business flying) also have placed increasing demand on the airport and airway system. The movement of freight and express mail by all-cargo aircraft has expanded rapidly in the past 25 years and is projected to increase at a higher rate than the overall growth of passenger traffic for the next decade. This growth, however, is from a very small base. In 1970, air cargo accounted for less than 1 percent of all commercial aircraft movements. Today, the air cargo share is about 4 percent. By 2010, it might reach 6 percent. At the top 10 hub airports, general aviation (GA) makes up a small part of the traffic, typically less than 8 percent. At other commercial service airports, the GA share is larger; but the overall pattern is that, as air carrier operations increase at an airport, GA traffic declines. Most GA aircraft avoid large airports, and those that do use them are often professionally piloted business or executive-transport aircraft with performance characteristics comparable to large jets.

Accommodating cargo and GA operations at airports and on the airways is an important concern, but it is separable from the problem of providing capacity for commercial passenger transport. In many cases, GA and cargo aircraft can, and do, make use of alternatives, such as reliever airports for GA or airports with a low volume of passenger traffic that can serve as cargo hubs. They also have access to busy metropolitan area airports at off-peak hours. Use of airports by these sectors of civil aviation is not a major driver of the airport capacity problem.

Recent efforts by FAA and local airport authorities have centered on what they perceive to be the major air transport capacity problem: accommodating the rising volume of airline passengers and air carrier operations. FAA has undertaken a multibillion dollar modernization of air traffic control facilities that will allow the system to handle more traffic, not only additional domestic and international passenger traffic but also cargo operations and expected increase in use of the system by private and business GA aircraft.

From 1982 through 1998, FAA allocated about $22 billion in AIP funds for improvements at over 85 percent of the 3,344 airports eligible to receive these funds. Since commercial service airports began collecting PFCs in 1992, 296 of the 538 eligible airports have collected about $22 billion for capital development projects.

The funding mix between AIP and PFCs has changed considerably in recent years. Between 1991 and 1998, AIP funding was reduced by 24 percent, from $1.7 billion to $1.3 billion per year. Funding received by primary airports fell by 21 percent during the same period, from $1.2 billion to $957 million. The total AIP funding between 1992 and 1998 amount to $10.6 billion compared to $21.9 billion for PFC funds.

Commercial service airports have benefited the most from AIP and PFC funds, while AIP funds for other types of airports have decreased. From 1992 through 1998, commercial service airports, representing 16 percent of the airports eligible for AIP funding, received 80 percent of the AIP allocations and all of the PFCs. General aviation and reliever airports, representing 84 percent of the airports eligible for AIP funding, received $2.2 billion, or about 20 percent of all the AIP funds obligated during the same seven-year period. These airports are not eligible to collect PFCs.

The FAA allocated the majority of AIP funds for projects related to airfields' pavement; the airports used their PFC funds for other types of projects. From 1992 through 1998, the FAA directed 74 percent of all AIP funds to projects focusing on the pavements of runways, taxiways, and aprons and on land acquisition. In contrast, on the basis of the PFC-funded projects between 1992 and 1998, airports planned to use 28 percent of the revenues from PFCs for projects to develop terminals or improve airport access. Airports also plan to use $5.6 billion, or 25 percent of the $21.9 billion, for debt servicing costs— costs that are not eligible for AIP funding.

Federal policy since passage of the Airport and Airway Development Act of 1970, and continuing with the Airport and Airway Improvement Act of 1982 and the Aviation Safety and Capacity Expansion Act of 1990 has been on building and expanding airports. Available, efficient, and low-cost air travel stimulates all sectors of the economy. An airport is an important economic resource to a community, both in and of itself and because it can be used to leverage additional highly desirable development. In this sense, aviation is a general boon to the economy, and it can be argued that the federal government's policy is amply justified.

Key terms

Kelly Act of 1925

Air Commerce Act of 1926

Bureau of Air Commerce

Civil Aeronautics Act of 1938

Civil Aeronautics Board (CAB)

Civil Aeronautics Administration (CAA)

Development of Landing Areas for National Defense (DLAND)

Federal Airport Act of 1946

Airways Modernization Act of 1957

Federal Aviation Act of 1958

Federal Aviation Agency

Department of Transportation (DOT)

Federal Aviation Administration (FAA)

National Transportation Safety Board (NTSB)

Airport and Airway Development Act of 1970

Airport and Airway Revenue Act of 1970

Planning Grant Program (PGP)

Airport Development Aid Program (ADAP)

Airport and Airway Development Act Amendments of 1976

Airline Deregulation Act of 1978

Essential Air Service

Aviation Safety and Noise Abatement Act of 1979

Airport and Airway Improvement Act of 1982

Airport Improvement Program (AIP)

Airport and Airway Safety and Capacity Expansion Act of 1987

Aviation Safety and Capacity Expansion Act of 1990

Passenger Facility Charge (PFC)

The Airport and Airway Safety, Capacity, Noise Improvement, and Intermodal Transportation Act of 1992

The AIP Temporary Extension Act of 1994

The Federal Aviation Administration Authorization Act of 1994

The Federal Aviation Reauthorization Act of 1996

National Plan of Integrated Airport Systems (NPIAS)

State Block Grant Program

Military Airport Program (MAP)

Review questions

1 Who established the first airmail service in the United States? How long did it last?

   - What was the primary purpose of the Kelly Act?
   - The Air Commerce Act of 1926?
   - How did the Bureau of Air Commerce become established?

2 When did the federal government first give financial support for the development of airports?

   - Describe the overriding purpose of the Civil Aeronautics Act of 1938.
   - Distinguish between the Civil Aeronautics Board and the Civil Aeronautics Administration.
   - What was the function of DLAND?

3 Discuss some of the recommendations made by a select committee in November 1944 that led to the passage of the Federal Airport Act of 1946. How many dollars were appropriated by the Federal Airport Act during the first seven years? How was the money apportioned?

   - What were some of the provisions that had to be adhered to before federal aid was granted?

4 Describe the state of the air transportation industry during the middle 1950s that led to the passage of the Federal Aviation Act of 1958.

   - What was the purpose of the Curtis Committee?
   - Why was the Airways Modernization Board disbanded?
   - Identify the federal aviation administrator's major responsibilities under the 1958 act.
   - What was the purpose of the Department of Transportation Act of 1966?

5 Discuss some of the factors that led to the passage of the Airport and Airway Development Act of 1970. How were revenues raised under the Airport and Airway Revenue Act of 1970?

   - What are some advantages of the user charge/trust-fund approach?
   - Compare and contrast the provisions of ADAP with the Federal Airport Act.
   - What is the PGP? How does it work?

- Compare the funding for the first five years of ADAP with the 24-year history under the Federal-Aid Airport Program.

6 Discuss some of the important amendments under the Airport and Airway Development Act Amendments of 1976.

- How has the Airline Deregulation Act of 1978 affected the airport system in the United States?
- What is the "Essential Air Service" program?
- What is the purpose of the Aviation Safety and Noise Abatement Act of 1979?
- Discuss some of the major changes under the Airport and Airway Improvement Act of 1982.
- What was the primary purpose of the Airport and Airway Safety and Capacity Expansion Act of 1987?
- What are some of the features of the Aviation Safety and Capacity Act of 1990?
- Discuss some of the changes in AIP funding, State Block Grants, and MAP during the latter half of the 1990s.
- What is included in the NPIAS?

7 Give a brief overview of the AIP funding by airport types from 1982 through 1998.

- Why were Passenger Facility Charges (PFCs) finally approved by Congress? List some of the provisions under the Aviation and Capacity Expansion Act of 1990 pertaining to PFCs.
- What is the State Block Grant Pilot Program? The Military Airport Program?
- How has the tremendous growth in air travel during the 1980s and 1990s affected the airport system?
- What are some of the biggest problems faced by the airport system as we approach the turn of the century?
- How has AIP funding changed during the 1990s? why has PFC funding become so important since 1992? How has this relationship affected funding GA and reliever airports?

Suggested readings

Air Commerce Act of 1926, Public Law 254, 69th Congress, May 20, 1926.
Airport and Airway Development Act of 1970 (Title I) and the Airport and Airway Revenue Act of 1970 (Title II), Public Law 258, 91st Congress, May 21, 1970.

Airport and Airway Development Act Amendments of 1976, Public Law 353, 94th Congress, July 12, 1976.

Airport and Airway Improvement Act of 1982, Public Law 248, 97th Congress, September 15, 1982.

Airway Safety and Capacity Expansion Act of 1987, Public Law 223, 100th Congress, December 30, 1987.

Airway Safety and Capacity Expansion Act of 1990, Public Law 508, 101st Congress, November 8, 1990.

Arey, Charles K. *The Airport*. New York: Macmillan Co., 1943.

Briddon, Arnold E., Ellmore A. Champie, and Peter A. Marraine. *FAA Historical Fact Book: A Chronology 1926–1971*. DOT/FAA Office of Information Services. Washington, DC: U.S. Government Printing Office, 1974.

Civil Aeronautics Act of 1938, Public Law 706, 76th Congress, June 23, 1938.

Department of Transportation Act of 1966, Public Law 670, 89th Congress, October 15th, 1966.

Department of Transportation, Thirteenth Annual Report of Accomplishments under the Airport Improvement Program—Fiscal Year 1994, October 1995.

Federal Airport Act of 1946, Public Law 377, 79th Congress, May 13, 1946.

Federal Aviation Act of 1958, Public Law 726, 85th Congress, August 23, 1958.

Frederick, John H. *Airport Management*. Chicago: Richard D. Irwin, Inc., 1949.

Kelly Air Mail Act of 1925, Public Law 359, 68th Congress, February 2, 1925.

National Plan of Integrated Airport Systems (NPIAS), 1998–2002. Washington, DC: FAA, March 1999.

Richmond, S. *Regulation and Competition in Air Transportation*. New York: Columbia University Press, 1962.

Sixteenth Annual Report of Accomplishments under the Airport Improvement Program, FY 1997. Washington, DC: FAA, May 1999.

Smith, Donald I., John D. Odegard and William Shea. *Airport Planning and Management*. Belmont, California: Wadsworth Publishing Co., 1984.

2

The airport system

Outline

- Introduction
- Classification of airports
- The economic role of airports
- Current issues in airport system development
- Airport information sources

Objectives

When you have completed this chapter, you should be able to:

- Recognize the size and scope of the airport system in the United States.
- Explain the FAA method of classifying airports.
- Discuss the economic role of airports.
- Summarize several major current issues in airport system development.
- Identify 10 prominent airport information sources and briefly describe their primary function.

Introduction

The system of airports in the United States is the largest and most complex in the world. As of January 1, 1998, there were 18,345 civil landing areas (airports, heliports, stolports, and seaplane bases) in the U.S. This includes close to 13,000 private-use airports that were built by individuals or corporations to accommodate their own aircraft and not available to the public. There are 5,357 airports open

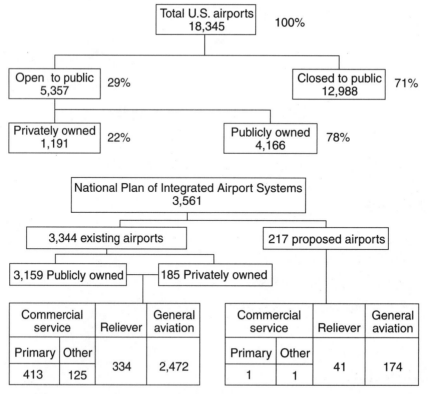

2-1. *Number of airports by ownership and public use as of January 1, 1998.*

for public use, of which 4,166 have at least one paved and lighted runway. There are 3,344 existing and 217 proposed new airports included in the NPIAS. Of the new airports, two will have scheduled air carrier service and 215 will be used primarily for general aviation. Figure 2-1 shows the division of the airports by ownership and availability for public use.

Airport ownership

While only about one-third of the landing areas on record are publicly owned, most of the busier airports are owned by governmental or quasi-governmental bodies. In the U.S., public airports are typically owned by cities and counties, or by semi-independent authorities formed by these jurisdictions. A few states, notably Alaska, Hawaii, and Rhode Island, operate broad airport systems. The federal government's ownership and operation of civil airports is limited to the airport at Pomona (Atlantic City), New Jersey, which is part of the FAA Technical Center.

The transfers of most of these airports, both surplus and those of the World War II programs, were made with provisions that permit the federal government to recapture its interests under certain conditions and also to review and approve any transfer of former federal properties destined for nonairport use. Approximately 600 civil airports have these encumbrances. Army and Air Force Reserve and National Guard units operate out of a number of civil airports, usually under some type of lease arrangements.

Private airports

Many privately owned airports, open to the public, provide access to the air transportation system. When a privately owned airport is shown to be important to national transportation, it is included in the NPIAS. The current NPIAS includes 185 privately owned airports that are eligible to receive federal aid provided the owner is willing to make adequate assurance regarding the continued operation of the airport.

Airport activity

The activity, services, and investment at individual airports vary greatly. They are generally as active as the cities they serve. Indeed, the largest of our airports are almost self-contained cities. Table 2-1 lists the 10 busiest airports in three categories: total commercial passengers, aircraft operations, and cargo handled.

Total passengers is the sum of the enplaning (those who get on aircraft) and deplaning passengers (those who get off). Total passengers is a good indicator, especially of terminal building activity, because airports must provide service for passengers, both before and after they use the aircraft. Total operations is also a good indicator of airport activity, especially the use of the runway system. An aircraft operation is either a takeoff or a landing, including practice touch-and-goes.

Based aircraft is also an important indicator of general aviation activity. At most airports there is a fleet of aircraft that is locally owned, "based," which accounts for a large percentage of total activity. At major airports with airline service, however, there are relatively few based aircraft, most of the activity being transient.

Table 2-1 Activity at the 10 busiest airports

Total commercial passengers CY 1998 (millions)		Total commercial operations CY 1998 (thousands)		Total commercial cargo CY 1998 (million metric tonnes)	
Atlanta	73.5	Chicago-ORD	896.1	Memphis	2.4
Chicago-ORD	72.5	Atlanta	846.9	Los Angeles	1.9
Los Angeles	61.2	Dallas–Ft. Worth	836.1	Miami	1.8
Dallas–Ft. Worth	60.5	Los Angeles	773.6	New York-JFK	1.6
San Francisco	40.1	Detroit	539.1	Chicago-ORD	1.4
Denver	36.8	Miami	536.3	Louisville	1.4
Miami	33.9	Phoenix	519.7	Anchorage	1.3
Newark	32.5	Boston	507.4	Newark	1.1
Phoenix	31.8	Oakland	506.6	Atlanta	0.9
Detroit	31.5	St. Louis	503.7	Dayton	0.9

Source: Avi Airport Council International–North America

Landing areas

The total number of landing areas increases each year, but the number that are open to the public is decreasing. More and more privately owned airports are being closed to the public, often because of insurance costs and liability considerations. Table 2-2 shows how the number of airports available to the public has decreased since 1970.

Classification of airports

Because of the sheer number of airports and the variety of size and function, the term *airport system* has little meaning when applied to all the airports and landing fields in the United States as a whole. Many airports exist only for the convenience of a few aircraft owners and operators and play only a small role in public air transportation. For this reason, FAA has identified a smaller group of airports that serve public air transportation either directly or indirectly and can be deemed of national importance and eligible for federal aid.

Since 1970, FAA has published a list of such airports, classified by size and function, in a planning document known as the National Airport System Plan (NASP). Under the Airport and Airway Improvement Act of 1982, FAA was charged with preparing a new version of this plan, called the National Plan of Integrated Airport Systems (NPIAS). First published in 1986, the latest edition came out in March 1999. A complete discussion of the NPIAS as part of the planning process at the national level is included in Chapter 3.

Table 2-2 U.S. landing areas, 1970–1995

Year	Locations	Public-use	Private-use
1970	11,261	7,084	4,177
1975	13,251	7,005	6,246
1980	15,161	6,519	8,642
1985	16,319	5,858	10,461
1990	17,451	5,598	11,853
1995	18,343	5,474	12,869
1998	18,345	5,357	12,988

Source: FAA

In 1982, FAA revised the method of classifying airports and now lists them in four major categories: commercial service, primary, general aviation, and reliever (see Table 2-3).

Airports with scheduled services

Airports with scheduled passenger service have a number of classifications. *Commercial service airports* are defined as those airports receiving scheduled passenger service and having 2,500 or more annual enplanements; the current total is 538. *Primary airports* are defined as those commercial service airports having 10,000 or more enplanements. Currently there are 413 primary airports among the 538 commercial service airports. Airports with fewer than 2,500 annual enplanements are included under the general aviation category.

Hubs The term *hub* has more than one meaning in air transportation. It was first used by the Civil Aeronautics Board to describe the geographic areas that generate substantial portions of the nation's airline traffic. Later, it was adapted to categorize airports by the amount of passengers enplaned. It is also used to describe an airline route structure in which flights radiate from a major (hub) airport, much like spokes from the hub of a wheel, with the major airport serving as a transfer point for passengers changing flights. The strong competition among airlines in recent years has encouraged the use of such hubs. Urbanization and airline use of transfer hubs tend to concentrate traffic at the nation's largest airports. This point is illustrated in Table 2-4, in which commercial service airports are classified as large, medium, small, or nonhub airports, depending upon the percentage of the total national enplanements for which they account.

Table 2-3. Federal-aid airports by service level, January 1, 1998

Service level	Airports
Commercial service	538
Primary	(413)
Other	(125)
Reliever	334
General aviation	2,472
Total	3,344

Source: FAA

Table 2-4 Airport activity-revenue passenger enplanements, 1998

Hub airport category	Number of airports in category	Percentage of all enplanements at airports	Percentage of active GA aircraft
Large-hub primary	29	67.3	1.3
Medium-hub primary	42	22.2	3.8
Small-hub primary	70	7.1	4.7
Nonhub primary	272	3.3	11.4
Other commercial service	125	0.1	2.1
Relievers	334	0.0	31.5
General aviation	2,472	0.0	37.3
Total NPIAS airports	3,344	100.0	92.1
15,000 low-activity landing areas (non-NPIAS)		0.0	7.9

Source: FAA

Large hubs *Large hubs* are those airports that account for at least 1 percent of the total passenger enplanements. Some enplanements originate in the surrounding community and some consist of passengers transferring from one flight to another. Several large hub airports have very little passenger transfer activity (La Guardia, Ronald Reagan Washington National, and San Diego International—Lindbergh Field) while transfers account for more than half of the traffic at others (Atlanta, Pittsburgh, and St. Louis). Together the 29 large hub airports account for 67 percent of all passenger enplanements. Large hub airports tend to concentrate on airline passenger and freight operations and have limited general aviation activity. Five large hub airports (Salt Lake City, Las Vegas, Honolulu, Miami, and Phoenix) have an average over 343 based aircraft, but the other 24 large hubs average only about 34 based aircraft each. Thus, general aviation plays a relatively small role at most large hubs. The nation's air traffic delay problems are concentrated at the large hub airports.

Medium hubs *Medium hubs* are defined as airports that account for between 0.25 percent and 1 percent of the total passenger enplanements. There are 42 medium hub airports, and together they account for 22 percent of all enplanements. Medium hub airports usually have sufficient capacity to accommodate air carrier operations and a substantial amount of general aviation. Medium hub airports have an average of 176 based general aviation aircraft.

Small hubs *Small hubs* are defined as airports that enplane 0.05 percent to 0.25 percent of the total passenger enplanements. There are 70 small hub airports that together account for 7 percent of all enplanements and 4.7 percent of based aircraft. Less than 25 percent of the runway capacity at small hub airports is used by airline operations, so these airports handle a great deal of general aviation activity., with an average of 130 based aircraft. These airports are typically uncongested and do not account for significant air traffic delays.

Nonhubs Commercial service airports that enplane less than 0.05 percent of all commercial passenger enplanements but at least 10,000 annually are categorized as *nonhub primary airports*. There are 272 nonhub primary airports that together account for 3.3 percent of all enplanements and 11.4 percent of based aircraft. These airports are heavily used by general aviation aircraft, with an average of 81 based aircraft.

Other commercial service Commercial service airports enplaning 2,500 to 10,000 passengers annually are categorized as *other commercial service airports.* There are 125 of these airports in the NPIAS.

The reliever airport system

Reliever airports are a special category of general aviation airports. They are located in the vicinity of major air carrier airports and are specifically designated by FAA as "general aviation type airports which provide relief to congested major airports." To be classified by FAA as a reliever, an airport must have at least 50 based aircraft, or handle 25,000 itinerant operations or 35,000 local operations annually either at present or within the last two years. *Local operations* are aircraft flights that originate and terminate at the same airport. An *itinerant operation* originates at one airport and terminates at another. The reliever airport must also be located in an SMSA with a population of at least 250,000 or where passenger enplanements reach at least 250,000 annually. As the name suggests, reliever airports are intended to draw traffic away from crowded air carrier airports by providing facilities of similar quality and convenience to those available at air carrier airports.

2-2 *General aviation airports play an important role in the air transportation system.* Broward County Aviation Department

They also provide the surrounding areas with access to air transportation. In the early 1960s, special legislation was passed to help develop these airports. By separating them from other general aviation airports, Congress gave them the equivalent of priority funding.

Relievers now account for most of the aircraft landings and takeoffs in major metropolitan areas. Operations at 11 designated reliever airports in the Atlanta area exceed the total at Hartsfield International. Another measure of their importance is the fact that the 334 Relievers base 31.5 percent of all active GA aircraft.

The general aviation system

Communities that do not receive scheduled commercial service may be included in the NPIAS as sites for general aviation aircraft if they account for enough activity (usually at least 10 locally owned aircraft) and are at least 20 miles from the nearest NPIAS airport. The activity criterion may be relaxed for remote locations or other mitigating circumstances. The 2,472 general aviation airports in the NPIAS tend to be distributed on a one-per-county basis in rural areas and are often located near the county seat. These airports, with an average of 29 based aircraft, account for 37.3 percent of the nation's general aviation fleet.

General aviation airports account for the bulk of civil aircraft operations. This system encompasses everything from crop dusting in small aircraft to passenger and cargo charters in the largest aircraft. It includes 96 percent of all registered civil aircraft and 95 percent of all airports; at other than the large and medium hub airports, most of the aircraft activity at commercial service airports is general aviation. Pipeline patrol, search and rescue operations, medical transport, business and executive flying in fixed-wing aircraft and helicopters, charters, air taxi, flight training, personal transportation, and the many other industrial, commercial, and recreational uses of airplanes and helicopters fall in the province of general aviation.

The airports serving general aviation are likewise varied. Typically, they are small, usually with a single runway and only minimal navigation aids. They serve primarily as a base for a few aircraft. There are notable exceptions. A few GA airports located in major metropolitan areas handle extremely high volumes of traffic (particularly business and executive aircraft) and are busier and more congested than all but the largest commercial airports. Such GA airports as Van Nuys, Long Beach, and Santa Ana in California fall into this category.

An important aspect of general aviation airports is that they serve many functions for a wide variety of aircraft. Some GA airports provide isolated communities with valuable links to other population centers. This is particularly true in areas of northern Alaska where communities are often unreachable except by air, but many parts of the Western United States also depend heavily on air transportation. In such areas, the GA airport is sometimes the only means of supplying communities with necessities and is vitally important in emergency situations.

The principal function of general aviation airports, however, is to provide facilities for privately owned aircraft used for business and personal activities. The role of GA airports in providing facilities for business aircraft is of growing importance. The business aircraft fleet is largely made up of twin-engine propeller or jet aircraft, typically equipped with sophisticated avionic devices comparable to those of commercial airliners. General aviation airports serving business aviation play an important role by providing facilities comparable to those at major air carrier airports, thereby permitting diversion of some GA traffic from congested hubs.

Although the general aviation fleet includes transport-type equipment similar to that used by the major airlines, 74 percent of general aviation aircraft are single-engine piston aircraft. Over two-thirds of

2-3 *Cessna Chancellor parked at a general aviation airport.* Federal
Aviation Administration

the single-engine fleet is based at general aviation and reliever airports.

The FAA has established general aviation airport categories based on airport planning considerations. The *Basic Utility (BU) airport* accommodates most single-engine and many of the small twin-engine aircraft, approximately 95 percent of the general aviation fleet. *General Utility (GU) airports* accommodate virtually all general aviation aircraft. Typical runway lengths, at an assumed elevation of 500 feet above mean sea level and at a temperature of 85°F, are 3,200 feet for BU airports and 4,300 feet for GU airports. Other general aviation airport designs are based on transport aircraft or business jets.

Airports not included in NPIAS

The NPIAS includes 3,344 of the 5,357 airports open to the public (Fig. 2-1). There are over 2,000 airports open to the public that are not included in the NPIAS. Approximately 1,000 publicly owned, public use airports do not meet the minimum entry criteria of 10 based aircraft, are within 20 miles of a NPIAS airport, or are located at inadequate sites and cannot be expanded and improved to provide safe and efficient airport facilities. The remaining 1,000 are privately owned, public use airports that are not included because they are located at inadequate sites, are redundant to publicly owned airports, or have too little activity to qualify for inclusion. In addition, more than 12,000 civil landing areas that are not open to the general public are not included in the NPIAS.

The economic role of airports

Transportation is basic to the economy of any region, but little credit is given to the vital role it plays in linking suppliers, manufacturers, and consumers into a productive and efficient pattern of distribution. This is especially true from the aviation standpoint.

Everyone is aware of the contribution of highways to the transportation system because almost everyone drives a car, and almost every 18-wheeler has a sign on the back advertising that "This truck pays $5,000 in taxes every year."

Aviation is a key element in the transportation network, but this fact is not publicized as well. The airlines do a fairly good job of letting the public know the importance of scheduled service at primary airports, but the public is usually unaware of the benefits derived from the general aviation industry.

A transportation link

The local airport is the principal gateway to the nation's transportation system. A community's lack of an airport can be as detrimental to its development as being bypassed by the railroads a century ago, or left off the highway map 50 years ago.

Communities that are not readily accessible to the airways might suffer economic penalties that can affect every local citizen, whether they fly in a general aviation aircraft, use the airlines, or never have occasion to travel at all.

The airlines provide excellent service to many major metropolitan areas of the country, but thousands of smaller cities, towns, and villages also need air transportation service. There are close to 20,000 incorporated communities in the 48 contiguous states and an additional 15,000 unincorporated communities. Because scheduled airlines serve fewer than 5 percent of the nation's 18,000 airports with approximately 7,000 aircraft, a large number of communities and their citizens are without immediate access to the fine airline system.

The role of general aviation airports serving more than 190,000 aircraft, or 96 percent of the total active aircraft in the United States, in providing air access is increasing. By having air access to all the nation's airports, general aviation aircraft can bring the benefits and values of air transportation to the entire country.

Attracting industry

Cities and towns that years ago decided not to build an airport have learned that lack of an airport jeopardizes community progress. Time and again the lack of an airport has proved to be the chief reason why a community has been bypassed as a location for a new plant or a new industry.

While scheduled air service is concentrated in major metropolitan areas, business and industry are moving to less populated areas. Prior to World War II, nine out of 10 new industrial plants were built in metropolitan centers. By the early 1960s, this had shifted to approximately 50/50, and today nine out of 10 new industrial plants are being built in nonmetropolitan areas. Room to expand, lower taxes, and better living and working conditions for employees are just several of the reasons causing this exodus. With branch plants, the source of production is nearer the distribution points—but management is farther away from its responsibilities. Without flexible air transportation provided by corporate aircraft and general aviation airports, management faces the dangers of absentee management—both in the widely spread branches and in the home office because of extended trips.

The airport has become vital to the growth of business and industry in a community by providing air access for companies that must meet the demands of supply, competition, and expanding marketing areas. Communities without airports place limitations on their capacity for economic growth.

Stimulating economic growth

Airports and related aviation and nonaviation businesses located on the airport represent a major source of employment for many communities around the country. The wages and salaries paid by airport-related businesses can have a significant effect on the local economy by providing the means to purchase goods and services while generating tax revenues as well. But local payrolls are not the only measure of an airport's economic benefit to the community. Indirectly, the employee expenditures generate successive waves of additional employment and purchases that are more difficult to measure but nevertheless substantial.

In addition to the local economic activity generated by the regular expenditures of resident employees, the airport also stimulates the economy through the use of local services for air cargo, food catering to the airlines, aircraft maintenance, and ground transportation on and around the airport. Regular purchases of fuel, supplies, equipment, and other services from local distributors inject additional income into the local community. The airport retail shops, hotels, and restaurants further act to recycle money within the local community as dollars pass from one person to another, supporting many people and many businesses. This so-called *multiplier effect* operates in all cities as aviation-related dollars are channeled throughout the community.

Airports provide an additional asset to the general economy by generating billions of dollars per year in state and local taxes. These tax dollars increase the revenues available for projects and services to benefit the residents of each state and community. Whether the extra tax dollars improve the state highway system, beautify state parks, or help prevent a tax increase, airport-generated tax dollars work for everyone.

Cities with good airport facilities also profit from tourist and convention business. This can represent substantial revenues for hotels, restaurants, retail stores, sports and night clubs, sightseeing, rental cars, and local transportation, among others. The amount of convention business varies with the size of the city, but even smaller communities show a sizable income from this area.

Influence on real estate value

Beyond the benefits that an airport brings to the community as a transportation facility and as a local industry, the airport has become a significant factor in the determination of real estate values in adjacent areas. Land located near airports almost always increases in value as the local economy begins to benefit from the presence of the airport. Land developers consistently seek land near airports, and it follows inexorably that a new airport will inspire extensive construction around it.

Current issues in airport system development

In recent years, a number of issues have arisen concerning airport system development where the interests of several parties have come into sharp conflict. One such group of issues relates to the strategic policy of the federal government in development of the airport system. Some have suggested that past federal policy has placed too much emphasis on capital investment in new facilities and not enough on methods to make more effective use of existing facilities.

A second set of issues involves funding. Some observers have suggested that the federal role has become too large and pervasive and that responsibility for airport development should devolve either on the airports and their local sponsors or on state governments. Other industry analysts, pointing to the success of airport privatization in other parts of the world, have suggested that is the way to go in the future.

Other issues arise from the legal and contractual arrangements traditionally concluded between airports and airlines. These arrangements have evolved over several decades, during a period of extensive federal regulation of the airlines. There is some concern that these airport-airline agreements might be inappropriate in a deregulated era, either because they might be too rigid to allow airports and airlines to meet new challenges or because they might have anticompetitive features that do not allow the market to operate freely.

Another issue is the problem of aircraft noise, which has been a growing environmental and political problem for many airports despite technological advances in reducing noise of jet aircraft.

Finally, there are issues surrounding the planning of future airport development, particularly the timing and location of demand growth and the role that the federal government will play in defining and meeting airport needs.

Federal policy and strategy

Historically, federal airport development policy has sought to promote the aviation industry and to accommodate growth of traffic demand. Where forecasts of future traffic demand have exceeded existing airport capacity, the solution has generally been to provide capital aid to build new facilities. The Airport Development Aid Program (ADAP), funded with user fees earmarked for the Airport and Airway Trust Fund, was established in 1970 as a response to the congestion and delay problems that plagued airports in the late 1960s. ADAP provided federal matching grants to airports to pay for certain types of capital improvements, principally construction of new runways, taxiways, and aprons to relieve airside congestion. Federal assistance for capital improvements continues through the Airport Improvement Program (AIP), created by the Airport and Airway Improvement Act of 1982.

FAA projections of future traffic demand indicate that there could be severe airside congestion at a number of major airports over the next 20 years. Although some of the delays might be eased by improved air traffic control technology, the FAA view is that the primary constraint on the growth of the system will be "a lack of concrete" and that there is a need for more runways, taxiways, and ramps.

Thus, basic strategy has been challenged on the grounds that it biases the outcome toward capital-intensive solutions. Critics argue that federal development grants have, in some cases, encouraged airport operators to overbuild. In other cases, the facilities built with federal support are substantially different in form and more expensive than needed to accomplish their intended function. But more fundamentally, the existence of a federal program providing aid for only certain types of capital improvements at airports has distorted investment decisions and led airport operators to build not necessarily what they need, but what the government is willing to help pay for. By accommodating demand wherever and whenever it occurs through increasingly large and complex new capital facilities, more growth is encouraged at precisely those locations where it will be most difficult and expensive to absorb.

Other critics have suggested that projections of traffic growth are too high. Recent changes in the airline industry—such as deregulation, the growth of commuter air carriers, sharp rises in fuel costs, and escalating operating costs—might have caused permanent structural changes in the airline industry such that the great traffic growth of the past four decades will not continue. The general aviation industry has also experienced a sharp downturn in sales since the late 1970s; thus, policies aimed at accommodating high projected levels of growth might lead to overbuilding and excess capacity, and misallocation of resources within the system.

Congestion and delay in the airport system are not evenly distributed, but are concentrated at a few airports, while many others operate far below their design capacity; thus, an alternative strategic response might be to manage or direct growth of air activity in ways that make more productive use of existing, uncrowded airport facilities.

Some observers believe that growth can be managed through administrative or economic means requiring only limited new capital investments. Administrative responses to growth include rules adopted by airport operators or various levels of government to divert traffic from congested airports to places or times where it can be handled more easily. Economic responses rely on market competition to determine access to airport services and facilities. To some extent, both administrative and economic measures for managing demand are already in use at a number of busy airports; however, legal, contractual, and even constitutional barriers might preclude wider use of such techniques. Some of these barriers could be lowered through federal government action. A discussion of possible administrative and economic options is presented in Chapter 8.

Funding issues

Before World War II, the federal government was inclined to the view that airports, like ocean and river ports, were a local responsibility, and the federal role was confined to maintaining the navigable airways and waterways connecting those ports. At the onset of World War II, the federal government began to develop airports on land leased from municipalities. Federal investment was justified on the grounds that a strong system of airports was vital to national defense. After the war, many of these improved airports were declared surplus and turned over to municipalities. Federal assistance to airports continued throughout the 1950s and 1960s at a low level and was aimed primarily at improving surplus airports and adapting them to civil use. Major federal support of airport development resumed in 1970 with the passage of the Airport and Airway Development Act, which was in large part a response to the congestion and delay then being experienced at major airports. This act established the user-supported Airport and Airway Trust Fund and ADAP.

Federal assistance to airports under ADAP was distributed as matching grants for capital improvement projects. There were several formulas for allocation: entitlement (calculated from the number of passengers enplaned at the airport), block grant (based on state area and population), and need (discretionary funds). Over the 10-year life of ADAP, outlays from the trust fund amounted to approximately $4 billion. ADAP expired in 1980, but a similar program of airport development assistance, AIP, was established in 1982. Before AIP was enacted, there was extensive debate about the future direction of federal airport aid, spurred by proposals to withdraw assistance for ("to defederalize") major air carrier airports.

Supporters of *defederalization* advanced two arguments: The federal government is overinvolved in financing airport development and federal assistance is not necessary for large airports because they are capable of financing their own capital development. By excluding large airports from eligibility for federal grants, the government could reduce the overall cost of the aid program and at the same time provide more aid to small air carrier and general aviation airports. The advantage to large airports, as pointed out by supporters of defederalization, would be freedom from many legal and administrative requirements involved in accepting federal assistance.

Opponents of defederalization contended that the proposal was unwise for several reasons. First, it would eliminate federal assistance for the very airports that provide the bulk of passenger service and have the greatest problems of congestion and delay. It is at these airports, the backbone of the national system, where a federal presence can most easily be justified. Further, passengers using large airports pay approximately three-quarters of the taxes supporting the Airport and Airway Trust Fund; thus, defederalization would lead to subsidy of smaller airports by larger ones. Some observers also questioned the ability of many airports to carry out necessary capital improvements without federal participation. While agreeing that federal grants form only a small percentage of total capital budgets at large airports, they argued that it was a needed revenue source for all but the very largest 5 or 10 airports.

In 1990, the Aviation Safety and Capacity Expansion Act was passed authorizing the imposition of passenger facility charges (PFCs) at commercial service airports to make up for the anticipated reduction in federal funding. In recent years Congressional appropriations have been reduced while the number of airports, projects approved by the FAA, and anticipated PFC revenue have increased sharply. It is still too early to assess the success of defederalization, but PFC revenue will no doubt play a significant role in the future, particularly at the primary commercial service airports.

Privatization

Privatization refers to shifting governmental functions and responsibilities, in whole or in part, to the private sector. The most extensive privatizations involve the sale or lease of public assets. Selling or leasing any of the nation's 538 public commercial airports would require the support of local, state, and federal governments. Unlike the air traffic control system, whose assets are owned entirely by the federal government, commercial airports are owned by local governments and, in limited circumstances, states and the federal government. However, commercial airports also receive federal airport development grants, have access to federal tax-exempt financing, and are subject to federal regulatory control. As a result, federal laws can substantially influence whether public owners would choose to sell or lease their airports and whether a private entity would want to be a buyer or lessee.

While no U.S. commercial airport has been sold to a private entity, publicly owned airports have extensive private sector involvement. Most services now performed at large commercial airports, such as airline ticketing, baggage handling, cleaning, retail concessions, and ground transportation, are provided by private firms. Some estimates indicate as many as 90 percent of the people working at 50 of the nation's largest airports are employed by private firms. The remaining 10 percent of the employees are local and state government personnel performing administrative or public safety duties; federal employees, such as FAA air traffic controllers; or other public employees, primarily military personnel. Airports have been increasingly dependent on the private sector to provide services as a way to reduce costs and improve the quality and the range of services offered. In recent years, some public owners have been contracted with private firms to manage their airports; most notably, in 1995, the Indianapolis Airport Authority contracted with a private firm to manage its system of airports, including the Indianapolis International Airport. Six other commercial airports are now operated under a management contract. At the end of 1998, there were nine large GA airports operated under a lease or by management contract.

Similarly, airports are relying more on private financing for capital development. Airports have sought to diversify their sources of capital development funding, including the amount of private sector financing. Traditionally, airports have relied on the airlines and federal grants to finance their operations and development. However, in recent years, airports, especially the larger ones, have sought to decrease their reliance on airlines while increasing revenue from other sources. Nonairline revenue, such as concession receipts, now account for more than 50 percent of the total revenue larger airports receive.

In most other countries, the national government owns and operates airports. However, a growing number of countries have been exploring ways to more extensively involve the private sector as a way to provide capital for development and improve efficiency. These privatization activities range from contracting out services and infrastructure development, in a role similar to private sector activities at U.S. airports, to the sale or lease of nationally owned airports. For example, Mexico passed legislation in 1995 to lease 58 major airports on a long-term basis. Most countries' privatization efforts do not transfer ownership of airports to the private sector, but involve long-term leases, management contracts, the sale of minority shares in individual airports, or the development of runways or terminals by the private sector. Only the United Kingdom has sold major airports to the private sector. To privatize, the United Kingdom sold the government corporation British Airports Authority (BAA) and the seven major airports it operated (including London's Heathrow and

Gatwick Airports) in a $2.5 billion public share offering. Proceeds from this sale were used to reduce the national debt. Even after privatization, the airports have remained subject to government regulation of airlines' access, airports' charges to airlines, safety, security, and environmental protection. The government also maintains a right to veto new investments in or divestitures of airports. BAA has generated profits every year since it assumed ownership of the United Kingdom's major airports in 1987.

Several factors are motivating the current interest in expanding the role of the private sector at commercial airports in the United States. First, privatization advocates believe that private firms would provide additional capital for development. Second, proponents believe that privatized airports would be more profitable because the private sector would operate them more efficiently. For example, the productivity of airports in the United Kingdom increased after they were privatized. However, airports' monopoly power could also be a source for increased profits.

According to analysts who rate airport bonds, some airports face little competition and, if unrestrained, could charge prices above the levels that would prevail in a competitive market. Lastly, advocates believe that privatization would financially benefit all levels of government by reducing demand on public funds and increasing the tax base.

Despite the growing interest in privatization, various legal obstacles have deterred attempts to sell or lease commercial airports in the United States. The primary obstacle stems from the legal assurances airports agree to meet as a condition to obtain federal grants. FAA maintains that airports must continue to adhere to these assurances as part of any transfer of control. Particularly problematic is the assurance regarding the use of airport revenue. Current law generally requires that revenue generated by public airports must be used exclusively to pay for their capital and operating costs and cannot be diverted for nonairport purposes. Because FAA currently considers airport revenue to include any sale or lease proceeds, local and state governments are entitled to recover only their unreimbursed capital and operating costs from these proceeds. Therefore, the financial benefits to local and state governments from privatizing airports would be diminished.

Even if a sale or lease transfer could overcome legal obstacles, the ability of a private airport to operate profitably under current rules and conditions is uncertain. A privately owned airport would not be eligible for federal airport apportionment grants or tax-exempt debt financing and would have to impose another type of fee to replace passenger facility charges. Losing these funding sources would raise financing costs significantly because they generally constitute the majority of an average airport's capital base. Also, a private airport owner or lessee could encounter constraints on its revenue, making recovering its investment costs more difficult. For example, FAA's rules on the rates airports may charge airlines for using their airfields limit the return on investment from these assets. In some cases, a private buyer or lessee would also have to renegotiate the airport's agreements with its tenant airlines to enable the private entity to retain the profits generated at the airport. However, airlines would be reluctant to change their agreements if it meant that their costs would increase.

Airport management issues

Deregulation has led to changes in the relationship between airports and airlines. Airports traditionally maintained long-term use agreements (of 20 to 30 years) with the airlines that served them. These agreements covered such arrangements as landing fees and the leasing of terminal space. As a result of these agreements, airlines have had a strong influence on the creditworthiness of airports in the revenue bond market because their financial stability and continued presence was a guarantee of the long-term economic viability of the airport. In some instances, airlines have been party to airport revenue bonds, agreeing to be jointly and severally liable for payment of debt and interest. In return for such guarantees, airlines have gained approval rights for capital improvement projects to be undertaken at the airport.

Since deregulation, however, air carriers' routes and service points are not as stable, and the airlines themselves have experienced financial difficulties. Long-term contracts written in the era of regulation might now inhibit the carriers' freedom to change routes. Conversely, they may also make it difficult for airports to accommodate new carriers. In some cases, carriers with long-term agreements whose service to the airport has declined might be occupying gate and counter space that a new entrant might be able to use more effectively.

Some observers have questioned whether long-term agreements—especially majority-in-interest clauses—might not have anticompetitive effects in the deregulated environment. They point out that incumbent carriers might make use of their agreements to deny new entrants access to the airport, or at least to place them at a competitive disadvantage with respect to terminal space and facilities. They also point out that carriers often negotiate with airport management as a group in a "negotiating committee" or "top committee" and question whether group negotiations involving competing firms are appropriate in a deregulated market.

It has also been pointed out that a capacity limit at a major airport has the effect of reducing free competition among carriers and works as a form of "reregulation" of the industry. Airport operators must be careful that actions taken to manage or control the growth of traffic at individual airports do not have anticompetitive effects. This issue was raised in connection with two events, the 1981 air traffic controllers' strike and the Braniff bankruptcy, which brought attention to the question of who owns airport operating slots. A *slot* is a block of time allocated to an airport user to perform an aircraft operation (takeoff or landing).

During the strike, FAA imposed quotas on 22 airports, limiting the number of operations that could be performed each hour. Several methods of allocation were tried: administrative assignment, exchanges among incumbent carriers, and, briefly, auction. New entrant airlines complained that all of these methods were unfair.

When Braniff stopped operating, FAA redistributed its slots among other carriers, despite Braniff's claims that the slots were the airline's property for which it should be paid. Throughout this period there was controversy over whether or not a slot should be considered property, and whether the proceeds from a slot sale should go to the airline, the airport, or the federal government.

This issue arose again in connection with slot auctions at Washington National and New York La Guardia. Finally after continued controversy, the FAA granted the airlines the right to buy and sell the slots they held. While the buy-sell slot rule has stabilized the situation somewhat for the airlines, most airport authorities would prefer to see the funds from any sale go toward expanding the capacity of the air transportation system. Authorities also question the rationale for allowing private airlines who obtained federally authorized landing slots at no cost, to sell these slots to other airlines at large profits. New entrant air carriers also claimed that the slot-holding airlines stifle competition. Regional carriers are also concerned about the slots available.

Unquestionably slots represent one of the most significant barriers to entry in the airline business today. Their impact on the industry extends far beyond the few airports where they are imposed because markets critical to many communities either begin or end at one of these facilities.

This question might become particularly acute if problems of delay and congestion spread to more airports, and airport operators seek to employ traffic management techniques. If an airport imposes a quota, it must devise some method for allocating slots to present users and for accommodating new entrants. Until the question of slot ownership is finally resolved, any attempt to use selling or auction as an allocation method is likely to reignite this controversy.

Marketing orientation

As U.S. airports have achieved increasing economic independence, they have also developed an expanded view of their mission. More and more airports see their role not simply as providing needed facilities for airlines, cargo carriers, and passengers, but as ensuring that local residents have a choice of air service to the maximum number of destinations at the lowest possible price. This has led many airports to create air service development departments, whose role is to convince airlines to begin or increase service to the particular airport. While airlines frequently question the need for these departments, they are becoming more and more common at medium and large airports — and are inevitably considered a normal operating expense to be funded by the airlines. Extreme cases include Boston, where the carriers' fees include the amount necessary to fund a London promotional office.

Airports are also increasing their presence in the ground handling area—both because they view this as a profitable opportunity and because they wish to be able to offer the services needed by small operators instead of having the incumbent carrier provide them. The practice is controversial only to the extent that the airport attempts to prevent competition in the area, or engages in accounting practices that create an artificially low cost structure for the captive handler.

The most attractive change for passengers in many airports has been in the concession area. There, airports have realized that airline passengers have above-average spending power and enough time to

2-4 *Spanning 31,000 square feet, the atrium is a focal point of the main terminal at Orlando International Airport. The atrium is the hub of the 450-room, eight-story Hyatt Regency Orlando International Airport Hotel.* Greater Orlando Aviation Authority.

take advantage of buying opportunities. The modern trend in airport design is to provide significant food and beverage and retail space, and to assure that pricing is competitive with stores outside the airport. The theory is that, once passengers conclude that they are not paying a premium to shop at the airport, they will buy in volume. The adjunct to this new theory is that, even if it is possible to generate more income by charging higher prices, airports have a duty to keep prices at reasonable levels.

Airports have also explored use of a "master developer" concept with regard to concessions. Under this concept, a private developer is put in charge of the airport's concessions. The developer generally pays the airport a minimum amount per enplanement, plus a share of the profits. The developer then negotiates its own agreements with various food and retail concessions. Washington National Airport pioneered the concept in 1990. It was then implemented on a larger scare in Pittsburgh's new terminal in 1992.

2-5 *Concourse including retail stores at Ronald Reagan Washington National Airport.* Metropolitan Airports Authority.

Noise and environment issues

Noise has been a major problem at airports since the introduction of the commercial jet aircraft. Recent technological advances in airframe and jet engine design have made new aircraft much quieter, but many industry experts believe that further large-scale reductions in aircraft noise will not be possible.

The public is very sensitive to noise, which has become an emotionally charged political issue. Noise is probably the single most important constraint on the expansion of airports or the building of new ones. The problem is in large part one of land use, and land use decisions are usually beyond the control of FAA and the airport proprietor. Zoning and land use planning are the responsibility of local jurisdictions, and many jurisdictions have not applied land use controls to prevent residential communities from growing up near airports. Often, intergovernmental cooperation is needed because major airports might be surrounded by several municipalities, each with different zoning policies. The federal government has sometimes complicated the issue by financing and approving residential development projects in high-noise areas.

At present, citizens with complaints about airport noise have recourse only to the airport proprietor. While FAA and air carriers have some responsibility for abating aircraft noise, only the airport operator is legally liable. In many cases, airports have had to pay nuisance and damage claims for noise. To reduce their liability and to protect themselves, airports have instituted noise abatement programs that involve restricting aircraft flight paths or hours of operation so as to reduce noise impact on residential areas. Noise abatement procedures can have a detrimental effect on airport capacity, and many airports with serious congestion and delay have found that the need to control noise restricts their freedom of action. In some cases, airports have had to purchase surrounding land or install noise-absorbing insulation in buildings under flight paths.

The federal government pursues a program of aircraft noise control in cooperation with the aviation community. Much of the program is aimed at reducing noise at the source, through quieter engines. The FAA adopted Part 36 of the Federal Aviation Regulations in 1969, establishing noise certification standards for new design turbojet and transport category aircraft. In 1976, the Federal Aviation Regulations were amended to allow U.S. operators until January 1, 1985, to quiet or retire the noisiest (Stage 1) aircraft. In 1977, the regulations were again amended, defining three "stage" levels to categorize aircraft noise emissions and requiring aircraft certificates after March 1977 to meet the more demanding Stage 3 requirement. *The Airport Noise and Capacity Act of 1990* was then enacted, setting December 31, 1999, as the deadline for elimination of Stage 2 aircraft in the contiguous United States weighing more than 75,000 pounds. A schedule for compliance was established under Part 91 of the Federal Aviation Regulations. Each domestic and foreign operator of large civil subsonic turbojet airplanes must submit an annual report reflecting compliance progress as of the end of the calendar year.

A program to encourage noise reduction has supplemented the steady and substantial improvements in noise exposure due to quieter aircraft and compatible land uses in areas around airports. *Part 150 of the Federal Aviation Regulations,* adopted in January 1985, established a system for measuring aviation noise in the community and for providing information about land uses that are normally compatible with various levels of noise exposure. Part 150 encourages airport operators to develop *noise exposure maps* and noise compatibility programs. Noise exposure maps identify noise contours and land use incompatibilities and are useful in evaluating noise impacts and discouraging incompatible development. Once the FAA determines that noise exposure maps have been prepared in accordance with Part 150, the airport operator may submit a noise compatibility program, coordinated with affected parties, outlining measures to improve noise and land use compatibility. An FAA-approved noise compatibility program clears the way for an airport to obtain federal aid for noise projects. Over $2 billion has been granted for airport noise compatibility projects between 1982 and 1998.

The improvement in the noise situation around airports since 1975 has been dramatic, with the estimated population exposed to severe noise declining from 7 million persons to 1.7 million in 1995. This improvement has been remarkable because it took place during a period of substantial growth in air transportation, with enplanements more than doubling. It is projected that the population exposed to severe noise will continue to decline to 600,000 in the year 2000.

Despite the reduction in aircraft noise emissions, public concern and sensitivity are still very high. In recent years, complaints and organized opposition have come from populations exposed to comparatively low levels of noise, sometimes at locations miles from the nearest airport. This will be a factor in future planning for the airport and airspace system and will provide an impetus for further reductions in engine noise emissions.

Planning issues

Many of the difficulties in planning a national airport system arise from its size and diversity. Each airport has unique problems, and each airport operator—although constrained by laws, regulations, and custom—is essentially an independent decision-maker. While airports collectively form a system, it is not a system that is comprehensively planned and centrally managed. FAA's role in planning the system has traditionally been one of gathering and reporting information on individual airport decisions and discouraging redundant development.

Since 1970, the National Airport System Plan and subsequent NPIAS has been prepared by FAA regional offices, working in conjunction with local airport authorities. NPIAS presents an inventory of the project capital needs of more than 3,300 airports "in which there is a potential federal interest and on which federal funds may be spent." Because the funds available from federal and private local sources are sufficient to complete only a fraction of the eligible projects, many of the airport improvements included in NPIAS are never undertaken.

NPIAS has been criticized on three principal points. First, it is not really a plan, in the sense that it does not present time phasing or assign priorities to projects. FAA has attempted to meet this criticism by categorizing projects and needs according to three levels of program objectives: Level I—Maintain the existing system; Level II—Bring airports up to standards; and Level III—Expand the system. Some, however, see this categorization as inadequate.

Second, the criteria for the selection of the airports and projects to be included in the plan have come under criticism. Some have argued that most of the 3,300 airports in NPIAS are not truly of national interest and that criteria should be made more stringent to reduce the number to a more manageable set. On the other hand, there are those who contend that the plan cannot be of national scope unless it contains all publicly owned airports. It is argued that because NPIAS lists only development projects eligible for federal aid and not those that would be financed solely by state, local, and private sources, the total airport development needs are understated by the plan.

A final criticism is that NPIAS deals strictly with the development needs of individual airports, without regard to regional and intermodal coordination.

Airport information sources

Many of the national aviation organizations are deeply interested in helping to develop and preserve airports because of their role in the national air transportation system and their value to the areas they serve. These groups provide facts and figures, films, speakers, and other types of assistance to airport management and other proponents in order to present a strong, positive case to community leaders and others. Many provide publications, which range from mimeographed newsletters and bulletins to first-class magazines. Most are headquartered in the Washington, D.C., area where they compete with hundreds of other lobbying groups for the attention of Congress and federal agencies. Some are frequently called to testify at congressional and federal hearings, where their influence and expertise can be significant.

Each of the organizations is particularly concerned with the interests of their constituents; however, there are numerous times when they close ranks and work together for mutual goals affecting the aviation community in general. The following is a brief listing of the most prominent associations. A complete listing can be found in the *World Aviation Directory* published by McGraw-Hill, Inc. A great deal of information regarding these organizations can be obtained through their Websites.

Aerospace Industries Association (AIA)—1919
1250 Eye Street, NW
Washington, DC 20005
(202) 371-8400
Website: aia-aerospace.org
First called the Aeronautical Chamber of Commerce, it changed its name to Aircraft Industry Association in 1945 and finally to present name in 1959. Member companies represent the primary manufacturers of military and large commercial aircraft, engines, accessories, rockets, spacecraft, and related items.

Aircraft Owners & Pilots Association (AOPA)—1939
421 Aviation Way
Frederick, MD 21701
(301) 695-2000
Website: aopa.org
With over 300,000 members, AOPA represents the interests of general aviation pilots. It provides insurance plans, flight planning, and

other services, and sponsors large fly-in meetings. The Air Safety Foundation is affiliated with AOPA.

Air Line Pilots' Association (ALPA)—1931
1625 Massachusetts Avenue, NW
Washington, DC 20036
(703) 689-2270
Website: alpa.org
Founded in 1931, it is the oldest and largest airline pilots' union.

Airports Council International North America—1948
1775 K Street NW, Suite 500
Washington, DC 20006
(202) 293-8500
Website: aci-na.org
ACI-NA represents approximately 150 state, regional, and local governing bodies that own and operate the principal airports in the United States and Canada. Member airports handle approximately 90 percent of the domestic and virtually all the international air passenger traffic and cargo in North America.

Air Transport Association of America (ATA)—1936
1301 Pennsylvania Avenue, NW
Washington, DC 20004
(202) 626-4000
Website: air-transport.org
Represents the nation's certificated air carriers in a broad spectrum of technical and economic issues. Promotes safety, industrywide programs, policies, and public understanding of airlines.

American Association of Airport Executives (AAAE)—1928
601 Madison Street
Alexandria, VA 22314
(703) 824-0500
Website: airportnet.org
A division of the Aeronautical Chamber of Commerce at its inception, AAAE became independent in 1939. Membership includes representatives from airports of all sizes throughout the United States. The AAAE Foundation was formed in 1957 to encourage education.

Aviation Distributors & Manufacturers Association (ADMA)—1943
1900 Arch Street
Philadelphia, PA 19103
(215) 564-3484

Website: ADMA.org
Represents the interests of a wide variety of aviation firms including FBOs and component part manufacturers. A strong proponent of aviation education.

Experimental Aircraft Association (EAA)—1953
EAA Aviation Center
Oshkosh, WI 54903
(920) 426-4800
Website: eaa.org
EAA, with over 700 local chapters, promotes the interests of home-built and sport aircraft owners. It also hosts the world's largest annual fly-in.

Flight Safety Foundation (FSF)—1947
Suite 300, 601 Madison Street
Alexandria, VA 22314
(703) 739-6700
Website: FlightSafety.org
The primary function of FSF is promoting air transport safety. Its members include airport and airline executives and consultants.

General Aviation Manufacturers Association (GAMA)—1970
Suite 801, 1400 K Street, NW
Washington, DC 20005
(202) 393-1500
Website: generalaviation.org
Originally, a part of AIA, GAMA's members include manufacturers of GA aircraft, engines, accessories, and avionics equipment.

Helicopter Association International (HAI)—1948
1635 Prince Street
Alexandria, VA 22314
(703) 683-4646
Website: rotor.com
Members represent over 1,500 member organizations in 51 countries that operate, manufacture, and support civil helicopters.

International Air Transport Association (IATA)—1945
800 Place Victoria
Montreal, PQ, Canada H4Z1M1
(514) 847-0202
Website: IATA.org
An association of more than 220 international air carriers whose main functions include coordination of fares and operations.

International Civil Aviation Organization (ICAO)—1947
999 University St.
Montreal, PQ, Canada H3C5H7
(514) 954-8219
Website: ICAO.org
A specialized agency of the United Nations with a membership of 185 countries. It fosters the development of international air transport by establishing international standards, procedures, promoting safety, uniformity, and efficiency in air navigation throughout the world. ICAO publishes a wide variety of technical, economic, and legal publications relating to international civil aviation.

National Air Transportation Association (NATA)—1941
4226 King Street
Alexandria, VA 22302
(703) 845-9000
Website: nata-online.org
First called the National Aviation Training Association and later Trades Association, NATA represents the interests of fixed-base operators, air taxi services, and related suppliers and manufacturers.

National Association of State Aviation Officials (NASAO)—1931
Suite 505, 8401 Colesville Road
Silver Spring, MD 20910
(301) 588-0587
Website: nasao.org
Represents departments of transportation and state aviation departments and commissions from 50 states, Puerto Rico, and Guam. Encourages cooperation and mutual aid among local, state, and federal governments.

National Business Aircraft Association (NBAA)—1947
1200 18th Street, NW, Room 200
Washington, DC 20036
(202) 783-9000
Website: nbaa.org
Represents companies that own or operate aircraft flown for corporate purposes. Affiliated with the International Business Aviation Council.

Professional Aviation Maintenance Association (PAMA)—1972
Suite 300, 636 Eye St., NW
Washington, DC 20001
(202) 216-9220

Website: pama.org
Promotes the interest of airframe and powerplant (A&P) technicians

Regional Airline Association (RAA)—1975
Suite 300, 1200 19th Street, NW
Washington, DC 20036
(202) 857-1170
Website: RAA.org
Formerly the Commuter Airline Association, RAA represents the interests of U.S. short- and medium-haul scheduled passenger and cargo airlines.

The Federal Aviation Administration (faa.gov) is also a major resource for airport operators. The most obvious need for coordination with the FAA is in obtaining funds. The regional offices and local airport offices are of considerable assistance in all phases of the procedure. The representatives at those offices know the state and local situations and what must be done to conform with federal policy. The airports' district offices provide a ready source of technical assistance to airport administration. Most importantly, the FAA publishes numerous documents that are designated to assist management in all phases of airport planning and management.

Key terms

commercial service airports

primary airports

hub

large hubs

medium hubs

small hubs

nonhub primary airports

other commercial service airports

reliever airports

local operations

itinerant operations

general aviation airports

basic utility (BU) airport

general utility (GU) airports

multiplier effect

defederalization

privatization

slot

The Airport Noise and Capacity Act of 1990

Part 150 of the Federal Aviation Regulations

Noise exposure maps

Review questions

1 Describe the system of airports in the United States in terms of numbers, significance, and role played by the different types.
   • Identify the leading airports in the United States in terms of enplaned passengers and aircraft operations.
   • Distinguish between primary and commercial service airports; the various classes of hubs.
   • What are the requirements necessary to be classified as a reliever airport?
   • Describe the multifaceted role of general aviation airports.

2 Why is the close proximity to an airport important in attracting businesses to a particular area?
   • The United States has the finest scheduled air transportation system in the world. Why do we need all of these general aviation airports?
   • How do airports stimulate economic growth?

3 Discuss several of the basic criticisms of federal policy and strategy regarding airport development over the years.
   • Give two arguments in favor of and against defederalization.
   • Discuss the growing role of privatization at U.S. airports. What are some of the factors causing this heightened interest?
   • What are some of the obstacles that have deterred attempts to sell or lease commercial airports in the United States?
   • Discuss the future of federal funding in light of the growth in passenger facility charges as a major source of revenue for commercial service airports.

4 How has deregulation led to changes in the relationship between airports and airlines?
  • What are the three principal criticisms of NPIAS?
  • Discuss the controversy surrounding slot allocations at congested airports.
  • How have airports made themselves more marketing-oriented?
  • Discuss the federal role in reducing airport noise around an airport.

5 List and briefly describe the primary role of five national aviation organizations. Where are most of these organizations located? What do they have in common and what is their relationship to airports?

Suggested readings

deNeufville, Richard. *Airport System Planning*. London, England: The Macmillan Press, Ltd., 1976.

Howard, George P., ed. *Airport Economic Planning*. Cambridge, Massachusetts: The MIT Press, 1974.

National Plan of Integrated Airport Systems (NPIAS), 1998–2002. Washington, DC: FAA, March 1999.

Sixteenth Annual Report of Accomplishments under the Airport Improvement Program. FY 1997. Washington, DC: FAA, April 1999.

Wiley, John R. *Airport Administration and Management*. Westport, Connecticut: Eno Foundation for Transportation, 1986.

3

Airport system planning

Outline

- Introduction
- The planning process
- The need for integration among plans

Objectives

When you have completed this chapter, you should be able to:

- Discuss the importance of airport system planning.
- Describe the purpose and some criticisms of the NPIAS.
- Describe the purpose and define the "levels of need" under NPIAS.
- Distinguish between regional and state airport planning.
- Describe the purpose and some criticisms of the SASP.
- Explain what is meant by "Integrated Airport System Planning" as described in the NPIAS.
- List the major objectives of an airport master plan.
- Explain the importance of local coordination in airport system planning.
- Discuss the need for integration among airport system plans at the national, regional, state, and local levels.

Introduction

Considering the high cost and long lead time for building or improving airports, planning is the key in determining what facilities

3-1 *The variety of aircraft shown at this metropolitan airport demonstrates the need for airport systems planning.* Federal Aviation Administration

will be needed and in creating programs for providing them in a timely manner, while making wise use of resources. Planning for airport development requires more than simply scheduling the capital improvements to be made. Airports are public entities, whose managers interact with many other public and private organizations. Airport development plans affect other aspects of community life, such as the land dedicated to aviation use or the noise or automobile traffic that the airport generates. The need for aviation development must thus be weighed against other societal needs and plans. Planning cannot be done for one airport in isolation; each airport is part of a network that is itself part of the national transportation system.

Our attention in the future must be focused on *airport system planning*, not simply airport planning. Airport plans must be developed as part of a system that includes national, regional, state, and local transportation planning.

Determining need and programming development at individual airports has become formalized in a process called *airport master planning*. While master planning in the full sense is practiced primarily by large airports, even the smallest must make use of some elements of the process to prepare for future change. At a level above airport master planning is *regional system planning*, which is concerned with development of all airports in a metropolitan area. It often involves difficult political decisions on development priorities among competing airports. In some cases, this responsibility is assumed by a regional or metropolitan planning agency, but many state governments have also taken on the task of developing a coordinated system plan for airports serving not only major metropolitan regions but also outlying small communities and rural areas within the state. In some cases, state agencies prepare these plans themselves; in others, they provide technical assistance and review for local planning bodies.

The role of the federal government in airport planning includes a broad range of activities. The most comprehensive activity is the National Plan of Integrated Airport Systems (NPIAS) of the Federal Aviation Administration, which summarizes the development needs of roughly 3,600 airports across the country. At the other extreme, FAA has responsibility to approve, on a project-by-project basis, specific development projects for which airport sponsors are seeking federal funds.

This chapter describes airport system planning at various levels, with emphasis on the planning process and the need for integrating planning at all levels.

The planning process
National level

Airport planning at the national level is the responsibility of FAA, whose interests are to provide guidance for development of the vast network of publicly owned airports and to establish a frame of reference for investment of federal funds. These interests are set forth in the *National Plan of Integrated Airport Systems (NPIAS)*, a document required under the Airport and Airway Improvement Act of 1982. The NPIAS is a 10-year plan that is revised every two years and is closely coordinated with the FAA's 10-year capital investment plan to improve the air traffic control system and airway facilities.

NPIAS is not a plan in the fullest sense. It does not establish priorities, lay out a timetable, propose a level of funding, or commit the federal government to a specific course of action. Instead, it is merely an inventory of the type and cost of airport developments that might take place during the planning period at airports eligible for federal assistance. It is a tabular, state-by-state presentation of data for individual airports, listed in a common format, indicating location, role, type of service, and level of activity (enplanements and operations) currently and for 5 and 10 years in the future. Projected costs of airport needs in categories—land, paving, lighting, approach aids, terminal, and other—are shown, also at intervals of 5 and 10 years.

Estimates of need contained in NPIAS are developed by comparing FAA national and terminal area forecasts to the present capacity of each airport. Much of the initial determination of need and the regular updating is performed by FAA regional offices, which monitor changes and developments being carried out at the airports. NPIAS is not a simple compilation of local master plans or state airport system plans, although FAA does draw on these documents as sources in forming judgments about future needs and prospective airport improvements.

NPIAS is not a complete inventory of airport needs. The plan contains only "airport development in which there is a *potential* federal interest and on which federal funds may be spent under the current Airport Improvement Program (AIP) or former Airport Development Aid Program (ADAP) and the Planning Grant Program." There are two necessary conditions in the test of potential federal interest. First, the airport must meet certain minimum criteria as an eligible recipient for federal aid, and second, the planned improvement at that airport must be of a type that is eligible for federal aid. Eligible projects include such projects as land acquisition for expansion of an airfield, paving for runways and taxiways, installation of lighting or approach aids, and expansion of public terminal areas. Improvements ineligible for federal aid are not included in NPIAS: construction of hangars, parking areas, and revenue-producing terminal areas that airports are expected to build with private, local, or state funds.

On the other hand, NPIAS probably overstates the amount that will actually be spent on airport improvements over the 10-year period. Many of the projects whose costs are included in the NPIAS will not receive federal funds and many will not be undertaken at all. Inclusion in the NPIAS does not necessarily represent federal agreement to fund a project or local commitment to carry it out. It is merely FAA's best estimate of likely future need. The goal of NPIAS is to set forth ". . . the type and estimated cost of airport development considered by the secretary to be necessary to provide a system of public airports adequate to *anticipate and meet* the needs of civil aeronautics . . .." If and when local sponsors are ready to undertake projects, they must apply for federal funds.

NPIAS relates airport system improvements to three *levels of need*: Level I—Maintain the airport system in its current condition; Level II—Bring the system up to current design standards; and Level III—Expand the system. Maintaining the system includes such projects as repaving airfields and replacing lighting systems; bringing the system up to standards involves such projects as installing new light systems and widening runways; expanding the system includes construction of new airports or lengthening runways to accommodate larger aircraft.

The classification by three levels of need is a refinement added to subsequent editions of the NPIAS. It moves in the direction of assigning priorities to different types of projects instead of the earlier practice of presenting needs as a single sum. FAA selected this presentation because previous lump sum projections "often did not lend themselves well for use in establishing the funding levels of programs intended to implement their broad findings." The three-level system was developed as a guide to Congress, illustrating how "alternative levels of funding . . . can be based on relating NPIAS development needs to three levels of program objectives."

The classification system is somewhat misleading because it is not as hierarchical as it might appear, and the placement of a type of improvement at a particular program level does not necessarily reflect the priority that will be given a particular project. High-priority projects, those that FAA and a local sponsor agree must be carried out as soon as possible, might not necessarily correspond with "Level I" needs in the NPIAS. An expansion project (Level III) at an extremely congested and important airport might be more urgent than bringing a little-used airport up to standards (Level II); thus, if available funds were limited to 34 percent of total need (the amount needed to cover Levels I and II), it would not be possible, nor would FAA intend, to carry out only Level I and II projects and leave vital Level III projects unfunded. In any given year, the actual grants awarded are used for some projects in each program level.

NPIAS has been criticized for drawing the federal interest too broadly and for being more of a "wish list" than a planning document. Critics have claimed that it is merely a compilation of improvements desired by local and state authorities and that it does not represent a careful assessment of airport development projects that truly serve national airport needs as distinct from those that are primarily local or regional in character. It is true that the plan includes many very small airports of questionable importance to the national system of air transportation. The *criteria for inclusion in the NPIAS* are minimally restrictive. The principal ones are: (1) the airport has (or is forecast to have within five years) at least 10 based aircraft (or engines); (2) it can be at least a 30-minute drive from the nearest existing or proposed airport currently in the NPIAS; and (3) there is an eligible sponsor willing to undertake ownership and development of the airport. Clearly there are many airports that meet these minimum criteria. As of the beginning of 1998, there were 3,561 airports qualifying for inclusion in the NPIAS, roughly a minimum of one airport per county.

Paradoxically, NPIAS has also been criticized for just the opposite reason: It is too exclusive, in that it reflects only FAA's interpretation of national importance and not those of state or regional planning agencies. Approximately 1,000 airports, not listed in the NPIAS, are integral parts of state and regional development plans; and their exclusion means that sponsors or state planning agencies cannot expect federal aid for developing these facilities.

Regional level

Regional airport planning takes as its basic unit of analysis the airport hub, roughly coincident with the boundaries of a metropolitan area. The planner is concerned with air transportation for the region as a whole and must consider traffic at all the airports in the region, both large and small. The practice of regional planning is relatively new and has been instituted to deal with questions of resource allocation and use that often arise when the airports in a region have been planned and developed individually and without coordination among affected jurisdictions. Regional planning seeks to overcome the rivalries and the jurisdictional overlaps of the various local agencies involved in airport development and operation. The goal is to produce an airport system that is optimum with respect to regionwide benefits and costs.

Thus, regional airport planning addresses one critical issue usually not dealt with in an airport master plan: the allocation of traffic among the airports in a region. This can be a sensitive subject.

Questions of traffic distribution involve political as well as technical and economic issues, and they can greatly affect the future growth of the airports involved. One airport might be quite busy while another is underutilized. If traffic were to continue growing at the busy airport, new facilities would have to be constructed to accommodate that growth. On the other hand, if some of the new traffic were diverted to an underutilized airport, the need for new construction might be reduced and service to the region as a whole might be improved.

Although a planning agency might decide that such a diversion is in the interest of a metropolitan region and might prepare forecasts and plans showing how it could be accomplished, it might not necessarily have power to implement these plans. Where airports are competitors, it is probably not reasonable to expect that the stronger will voluntarily divert traffic and revenues to the other. The planning agency would likely have to influence the planning and development process at individual airports so that they will make decisions reflecting the regional agency's assessment of regional needs.

One way to influence planning decisions is through control over distribution of federal and state development grants. Before 1982, regional agencies served as clearing houses for federal funds under the review process required by *Office of Management and Budget Circular A-95*. While the award of federal airport development funds depended mainly on FAA approval of the airport sponsor's application, the A-95 process required that designated regional agencies review projects before the grants were awarded. In particular, the regional agencies were required to certify that the planned improvement was consistent with federal regulations, for example, environmental regulations.

In July 1982, President Reagan issued Executive Order 12372, outlining a new policy for intergovernmental review of direct federal grant programs. The purpose of the new policy: to "strengthen federalism by relying on state and local processes for the state and local government coordination and review of proposed financial assistance and direct federal development . . .." The intent is to give additional weight to the concerns of state and local officials with respect to federally funded development. State and local governments are encouraged to develop their own procedures (or refine existing procedures) for reviewing development plans and grant applications. Under the new policy, agencies are to certify that federal spending is consistent with state and local objectives and priorities, instead of certifying that state and local projects comply with federal guidelines, as they did formerly. Federal agencies, such as FAA, are expected to accommodate recommendations communicated through the state review process or to justify refusal to do so.

Some states may choose to continue using the same regional planning organizations as review agencies, while others may create new procedures and new agencies. The executive order discourages "the reauthorization of any planning organization which is federally funded, which has a federally prescribed membership, which is established for a limited purpose, and which is not adequately representative of, or accountable to, state or local elected officials"; however, states may choose to retain the same regional agencies that were established under state law in the first place, but to change their function to reflect accountability to state and local rather than federal officials.

Much of the regional agency's success depends as much on negotiation and persuasion as on legal or budgetary authority. Often, compromises can be reached on a voluntary basis. For example, the regional airport planning commission worked with the three San Francisco area airports to help each develop a "noise budget" to comply with California's strict environmental laws. Because noise is directly related to the level of aviation activity, the noise budget plan, when completed, will affect future traffic allocation among the airports. Its implementation will most likely require some diversion of new traffic growth from busy San Francisco International to the other bay area airports.

Even where airports in a region are operated by the same authority, allocation of traffic between airports might still be difficult. For example, the Port Authority of New York and New Jersey can implement its planning decision to increase activity at Newark by instituting differential pricing, improved ground access, or other measures to increase use of that airport. Implementation of the policy, however, depends not just on control of airport development expenditures but also on the ability to influence the activities of private parties, the air carriers, and passengers.

Regional airport planning authorities may also, if they have planning responsibility for other transportation modes, plan for the airport as part of the regional transportation system. When multimodal planning responsibility resides in one organization, there is greater likelihood that the planning agency will consider airport needs in relation to other forms of transportation in the region. Also, the regional agency may try to improve coordination between the various modes, so that, for example, airport developments do not impose an undue burden on surrounding highway facilities or so that advantage can be taken of opportunities for mass transit. For this to happen, however, two conditions are necessary: regionwide authority and multimodal jurisdiction.

State level

According to the National Association of State Aviation Officials (NASAO), all 50 state aviation agencies carry out some form of airport planning. A majority of these agencies are subdivisions of the state department of transportation; in the others, they are independent agencies. Several states have an aviation commission in addition to an aviation agency. The commissions are usually appointed by the governor and serve as policy-making bodies. State involvement in airport planning and development takes several forms: preparation of state airport system plans, funding of local master planning, and technical assistance for local planning.

Airport planning at the state level involves issues that are somewhat different from those of local or regional agencies. State governments are typically concerned with developing an airport system that will provide adequate service to all parts of the state, both rural and metropolitan. Development of airports is often seen as an essential tool for economic development or overcoming isolation of rural areas. Some state aviation agencies (in Ohio and Wisconsin, for example), have set a goal to develop at least one well-equipped airport in each county. Usually the allocation of traffic between airports serving the same community is not at issue. Rather, the issue is deciding how to allocate development funds among candidate communities and to maintain a balance between various parts of the state.

Before 1970, very few states conducted extensive or systematic airport planning. An important stimulus to state agencies to initiate comprehensive planning efforts was provided by the Airport and Airway Development Act of 1970, which set aside 1 percent of airport aid monies from the trust fund for this purpose each year. Most states applied for these funds promptly and typically spent from one to four years in developing *state aviation system plans (SASP)* under guidelines issued by FAA, although a few took considerably longer. Most of the states sought assistance from outside consultants in some phase of the planning activity.

State plans typically encompass a planning period of 20 to 30 years; the year 2020 is a common planning horizon. Planning periods are normally divided into short, medium, and long-term segments (usually 5, 10, and 20 years, respectively). In each case, estimates of future needs have been developed by comparing existing facilities with projections of future traffic.

The major feature of the plans, and by far the bulk of each document, is a detailed listing of the actions planned by class of airport and type of improvement. The types of improvements most commonly cited are land acquisition (new sites or expansion of existing airports), pavement repair or improvement (runways, taxiways, aprons, roads, parking), installation of lighting and landing or navigation aids, and building construction (terminals, hangars, administrative facilities).

Although there are surface similarities, SASPs vary greatly in scope, detail, expertise, and planning philosophy. One state system plan might basically be a wish list, prepared primarily because planning funds were available and the state DOT required it. On the other hand, some state agencies regard the SASP as a valuable working document that is kept current and serves as a guide in programming and distribution of state funds.

In many states, programming of funds is somewhat separate from the system planning process. While the SASP might have a long planning horizon of 20 years or more, the actual award of grants to complete particular projects is on a much shorter time scale. Some state agencies have developed methods for keeping current files on local airport projects planned for the near term, say, three years. When airports apply for state aid, or request state assistance in applying for federal aid, the SASP is used to assign priority for a grant award as funds become available. As a rule, only a fraction of the projects outlined in the SASP are undertaken.

Virtually all state plans estimate costs of recommended improvements and identify funding sources. Funding is the primary constraint in implementation of the SASPs. In all states, some sort of consultation, coordination, or review by persons outside the state aviation agency is part of the planning process. Often these are regional economic development or planning agencies created by state government. In many cases, airport planning is part of a general transportation planning process, but methods of interaction and feedback among the modal agencies vary considerably.

Some state agencies are involved in master planning activities for local airports, especially rural or small community airports that do not have the staff to carry out master planning on their own. State agencies might provide technical assistance or actually develop local master plans. Some states also participate in airport planning for major metropolitan areas, although most leave this responsibility with the local airport authority or a regional body. In recent years, state participation in planning at the larger airports has shown some increase, a trend that might be bolstered by current federal policy that earmarks a share of annual trust fund outlays for state aviation planning.

National Plan of Integrated Airport Systems

The Airport and Airway Improvement Act of 1982 reflected a strengthened congressional commitment to airport planning. At the regional and state levels, the law dedicated 1 percent of federal airport development funds for planning. As such, the new law provided an opportunity for state governments and regional agencies to institute or expand their planning efforts.

The act called for refinement of the national airport planning process by instructing the Department of Transportation to develop a *National Plan of Integrated Airport Systems (NPIAS)*. The description of this plan in the legislation makes it clear that the intent is to expand and improve planning at the national level. Specifically, the act calls for *integrated airport system planning,* which it defines:

> . . . *the initial as well as continuing development for planning purposes of information and guidance to determine the extent, type, nature, location, and timing of airport development needed in a specific area to establish a viable, balanced, and integrated system of public-use airports.*

Planning includes identification of system needs, development of estimates of systemwide development costs, and the conduct of such studies, surveys, and other planning actions, including those related to airport access, as might be necessary to determine the short-intermediate-, and long-range demands that the airport must meet.

The policy declaration points out several ways in which the planning effort is to be "integrated":

> . . . it is in the national interest to develop in metropolitan areas an integrated system of airports designed to provide expeditious access and maximum safety . . . [and it is in the national interest to] encourage and promote the development of transportation systems embracing various modes of transportation in a manner that will serve the states and local communities efficiently and effectively.

From this it is evident that the legislation requires a plan that is "integrated" in two ways: (1) geographically, in the sense that all airports in a region are to be considered together; and (2) intermodally, in the sense that planning for the airport should be part of the planning for the regional transportation system as a whole. The requirements of the act bring FAA's airport planning process into closer relation with metropolitan and regional transportation planning than ever before.

Local level

At the local level, the centerpiece of airport planning is the *airport master plan*, a document that charts the proposed evolution of the airport to meet future needs. The magnitude and sophistication of the master planning effort depends on the size of the airport. At major airports, planning might be in the hands of a large department capable of producing its own forecasts and supporting technical studies. At such airports, master planning is a formal and complex process that has evolved to coordinate large construction projects (or perhaps several such projects simultaneously) that can be carried out over a period of five years or more. At smaller airports, master planning might be the responsibility of a few staff members with other responsibilities, who depend on outside consultants for expertise and support. At very small airports, where capital improvements are minimal or are made infrequently, the master plan might be a very simple document, perhaps prepared locally but usually with the help of consultants.

An airport master plan presents the planner's conception of the ultimate development of a specific airport. It effectively presents the research and logic from which the plan was evolved and artfully displays the plan in a graphic and written report. Master plans are

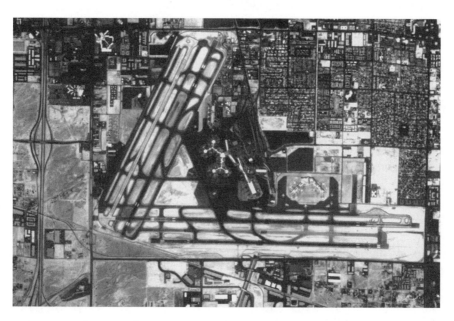

3-2 *Aerial view of McCarran International Airport, Las Vegas, NV.*
Clark County Department of Aviation

applied to the modernization and expansion of existing airports and to the construction of new airports, regardless of their size or functional role.

Objectives of the airport master plan The overall *objective of the airport master plan* is to provide guidelines for future development that will satisfy aviation demand and be compatible with the environment, community development, other modes of transportation, and other airports. Specific objectives within this broad framework are as follows:

- To provide an effective graphic presentation of the ultimate development of the airport and of anticipated land uses adjacent to the airport.
- To establish a schedule of priorities and phasing for the various improvements proposed in the plan.
- To present the pertinent backup information and data that were essential to the development of the master plan.
- To describe the various concepts and alternatives that were considered in the establishment of the proposed plan.
- To provide a concise and descriptive report so that the impact and logic of its recommendations can be clearly

understood by the community the airport serves and by those authorities and public agencies that are charged with the approval, promotion, and funding of the improvements proposed in the airport master plan.

Local coordination The development and operation of an airport impacts on the entire community; therefore, recent emphasis in planning of successful airports has been on integrating the airport into a comprehensive plan. Compatibility with local community goals, residential and commercial land uses, and transportation needs are now considered essential ingredients in airport planning at the local level.

Airports begin with local initiative The local community must decide if it needs a new airport or expansion of an existing one. Planning an airport demands careful consideration of the long-range development goals of the city or town. Effective coordination of planning at the local level requires involvement of individuals that are interested and knowledgeable about the community and the importance of airport development.

A public agency is required in order to qualify for federal airport aid. This group might be the city council, the county board of commissioners or supervisors, or other elected body, state aeronautical commission or agency; port authority, or a specially created airport authority. State legislative approval is generally required if a new authority is created. The airport public sponsor will often seek professional assistance from a consulting firm before planning and obtaining federal funds.

An airport master plan draws widespread interest from the private citizen, community organizations, airport users, area-wide planning agencies, conservation groups, ground transit officials, and aviation and airport concessionaire interests. If these groups are not consulted during the development of the plan, it will likely be unsuccessful when presented to the public; therefore, it is essential that the master plan team coordinate their efforts with and seek the advice of these elements during the critical stages of the plan's development. This coordination will help pave the way for acceptance and, more important, it will permit vital input from organized interests that will lead to the evolution of a well-integrated plan.

Effective coordination between members of the planning teams is also essential to the development of a successful master plan. A balanced effort is not easy to achieve because of the many disciplines involved in the plan's preparation. For large projects, input might be required from economists, financiers, scientists, architects; civil, mechanical, electrical, and traffic engineers; pilots, air traffic controllers, airline and concessionaire advisers; and airport managers. And to put the airport in its proper perspective, the roles of the environmentalist, ecologist, and urban planner must be considered.

This is why the role of the coordinator of the master plan effort is so important. He or she must keep the enthusiasm of advisers in check in order to balance the study efforts and costs of various master plan elements. If successful, the coordinator will develop a salable master plan that will lead to the construction of a functional airport that blends pleasantly into the environment.

An airport doesn't exist in isolation. It is an element of the total transportation availability of an area. Its integration into a whole system is even more important in these days of intermodal shipping than it formerly was. The long-range planning of any form of transportation within an area can most effectively be done in concert with the planning for all modes.

Ground transportation reflects on an airport in at least two ways. First, the less surface transportation there is in an area, especially one of great distances, the more need there is for air facilities. (It costs considerably less to build a runway than to construct 1 mile of interstate highway.) Second, businesses looking to locate in a new community generally require that the airport be fewer than 30 minutes away from the plant location.

A review of access roads, peak-hour traffic patterns, bus and rail transportation, and other nearby airports plays a role in the report that determines whether or not an airport proposal is approved for inclusion in the National Airport System Plan, a prerequisite to federal funding of planning and construction of an airport.

The airport master plan is most applicable to a rather narrow planning problem, the development of a single airport. Coordination efforts required for development of the master plan will be elaborated on for each stage of development of the master plan in the chapters that follow.

The need for integration among plans

Airport planning, as practiced today, is a formalized discipline that combines forecasting, engineering, and economics. Because it is performed largely by government agencies, it is also a political process, where value judgments and institutional relationships play as much a part as technical expertise. On the whole, airport planners have been reasonably successful in anticipating future needs and in devising effective solutions. Still, mistakes have been made—sometimes because of poor judgment or lack of foresight and sometimes because of certain characteristics of the planning process itself. In effect, the process and the methods employed predispose planners toward solutions that might be "correct" for a single airport but perhaps not for the community, region, or airport system as a whole. As a result, airport plans might take on a rigidity that is inappropriate in light of changing conditions or a narrowness of focus that does not make best use of resources.

Airport planning at local, regional, state, and federal levels is not well coordinated and integrated. To some extent, this arises naturally from different areas of concern and expertise. At the extremes, local planners are attempting to plan for the development of one airport, while FAA is trying to codify the needs of several thousand airports that might request aid. Local planners are most concerned with details and local conditions that will never be of interest to a national planning body.

The lack of common goals and mutually consistent approach is also evident between federal and state planning. More than 30 years ago, the federal government recognized the need to strengthen state system planning and provided funds for this purpose under ADAP, and nearly all the state airport systems plans have been prepared with federal funding; however, it does not seem that FAA has always made full use of these products in preparing the NPIAS. The state plans contain many more airports than NPIAS, and the priorities assigned to airport projects by states do not always correspond to those of NPIAS. While it is probably not desirable, or even possible, for NPIAS to incorporate all elements of the state plans, greater harmony between these two levels of planning might lead to more orderly development of the national airport system.

There is also a lack of coordination between airport planning and other types of transportation and economic planning. This is particularly evident in the case of land use, where airport plans are often in conflict with other local and regional developments. Even though the airport authority might prepare a thoroughly competent plan, lack of information about other public or private development proposed in the community (or failure of municipal authorities to impose and maintain zoning ordinances) allows conflicts to develop over use of the airport and surrounding land. This problem can be especially severe where there are several municipalities or local jurisdictions surrounding the airport property.

An additional problem is the lack of integration of airport planning with that for other modes of transportation. An airport is an intermodal transportation center, where goods and people transfer between the ground and air modes. It forms an important link in the total transportation system of a region. The ground transportation system providing access to the airport can be a significant contributor to congestion, delay, and the cost of airport operation. Yet airport operators have little authority or influence over decisions on transportation beyond the airport property line.

Key terms

airport system planning

National Plan of Integrated Airport Systems (NPIAS)

NPIAS levels of need

criteria for inclusion in the NPIAS

regional airport planning

Office of Management and Budget Circular A-95

state aviation system plans (SASP)

integrated airport system planning

airport master plan

objectives of the airport master plan

Review questions

1 "Planning cannot be done for one airport in isolation." Expand on this statement.

• What is NPIAS? Highlight some of the criticisms it has received.

- Describe the three levels of needs under NPIAS.
- Identify the criteria for inclusion in NPIAS.

2 What is regional airport planning?

- Discuss some problems that might arise as a result of coordinating the plans of three airports in one metropolitan area.
- How has the OMB Circular A-95 affected regional airport planning?

3 Discuss some of the concerns of state government regarding airport system planning.

- Why do individual SASPs vary so greatly? What is the major constraint in implementing SASPs?

4 How did the Airport and Airway Improvement Act of 1982 "reflect a strengthened congressional commitment to airport planning"?

5 Summarize the objectives of an airport master plan. Discuss the importance of local coordination in developing an airport master plan and give some examples.

6 Discuss some of the problems in attempting to integrate airport planning at the national, regional, state, and local levels. What can be done to overcome some of these problems?

Suggested readings

deNeufville, Richard. *Airport Systems Planning*. Cambridge, Massachusetts: The MIT Press, 1976.

Howard, George P. *Airport Economic Planning*. Cambridge, Massachusetts: The MIT Press, 1974.

National Plan of Integrated Airport Systems (NPIAS), 1998-2002. Washington, DC, FAA, March 1999.

Schreiver, Bernard A., and William W. Siefert. *Air Transportation 1975 and Beyond: A Systems Approach*. Cambridge, Massachusetts: The MIT Press, 1968.

DOT/FAA advisory circulars

150/5050-3B	Planning the State Aviation System.
150/5050-4	Citizen Participation in Airport Planning.
150/5050-5	The Continuous Airport System Planning Process.
150/5050-7	Establishment of Airport Action Groups.
150/5070-5	Planning the Metropolitan Airport System.
150/5070-6A	Airport Master Plans.

Part II

Planning and funding the airport

4

Airport requirements and site selection

Outline

- Introduction
- Inventories
- Forecasting
- Demand/capacity analysis
- Environmental impact study
- Site selection

Objectives

When you have completed this chapter, you should be able to:

- Define airport master plan and recognize the major components of the first and second phase.
- Describe the five major factors included in the Inventories stage.
- Explain how public hearings can assist the airport sponsor in developing an airport master plan.
- Identify the three basic types of forecasting methods used by airport planners.
- List the five operational activity forecasts needed by airport planners.
- Discuss the purpose of the demand/capacity analysis stage.
- Highlight the major environmental concerns of airport planners.

- List the 10 factors that must be considered by airport planners in preparing an environmental impact statement.
- Discuss the major factors that must be given careful analysis in the evaluation of airport sites.

Introduction

While there is considerable variation in the content of the airport master plan and how it is used, its basic products are a description of the desired future configuration of the airport, a description of the steps needed to achieve it, and a financial plan to fund development. The master planning process consists of four basic phases: airport requirements, site selection, airport layout, and financial planning. This chapter will cover the major considerations included in the first two phases.

The first phase, *airport requirements*, specifies new or expanded facilities that will be needed during the planning period. This involves cataloguing existing facilities and forecasting future traffic demand. The planner compares the capacity of existing facilities with future demand, identifying where demand will exceed capacity and what new facilities will be necessary.

The process of relating future demand to existing facilities and estimating the nature and size of needed improvements is complex. It requires detailed forecasts because sizing depends not only on the number of passengers and aircraft in future years but also on the type of the traffic. For example, traffic consisting mainly of transfer passengers imposes requirements that are different from those where the majority of traffic is origin and destination passengers. Sizing of facilities is also affected by the distribution of activities throughout the day and by the size and operating characteristics of aircraft serving the airport. This process is simplified by the use of standard relationships between general measures, such as annual enplanements, and specific measures, such as peak-hour passenger demand.

The second phase, *site selection*, is most important in the construction of a new airport. When considering the expansion of an existing airport, there is usually less choice about where to locate new facilities. Requirements for safety areas and clear zones around existing runways and taxiways, for example, mean that much apparently "vacant" land at airports cannot be used for other purposes. New facilities can be located only in places where they, and the traffic they generate, will not interfere with existing facilities. The site selection phase for a new airport requires an in-depth analysis of alternative sites, looking closely at such factors as physical characteristics of the site, the nature of surrounding development, land cost and availability, ground access, and the adequacy of surrounding airspace. The final choice of one site over others is often quite subjective. For example, there is probably no objective way to compare the disadvantages of increased noise in some part of the community with the advantages of improved air service for the metropolitan area as a whole. The "right" choice depends on how decision-makers weigh various criteria, and it is often a political rather than a technical choice.

Inventories

The first step in the preparation of an airport master plan for an individual airport is the collection of all types of data pertaining to the area that the airport is to serve. This includes an inventory of existing airport facilities, area planning efforts that might affect the master plan, and historical information related to their development. This review will provide essential background information for the master plan report. It will also provide basic information for the development of forecasts and facility requirements.

Historical review of airports and facilities

The historical review traces the development of a community's airport facilities and the air traffic that they have served. A description of each airport and the date of construction or major expansion is included. Airport ownership is also mentioned. The decision to prepare an airport master plan study of a particular airport and the appropriation of funds for the study will probably have resulted from certain legislative actions and preliminary studies by the airport sponsor such as the airport authority or local governmental body charged with the responsibility of administering airports in the area. These activities are also cited in the historical review of airports and facilities. The results of recommendations by airport committees and local, state, or regional planning groups are also summarized. The dates and amounts of money included in enabling legislation by local, state, and federal authorities are also cited in the review.

The scope of the data collection is generally limited to the area that the master plan airport will serve and to national trends that will affect that area. The planner must carefully research and study data that are available from current sources such as state, regional, and national airport system plans and other local aeronautical studies.

Existing airports and their configurations are shown on a base map. Included are all air carrier, general aviation, and military airports in the area.

Airspace structure and navaids

It is necessary to identify how the airspace is used in the vicinity of each airport and throughout the area, all air navigation aids and aviation communication facilities serving the area, and natural or man-made obstructions or structures that affect the use of the airspace.

The airway and jet-route structures have a significant effect on the utility of existing and future airport locations. The dimensions and configurations of the control zones and transition areas are noted. These segments of controlled airspace are designed to accommodate only specific instrument flight rules (IFR) requirements such as instrument approach, departure, holding, and transition flight maneuvers; thus, the inventory will show the current use of the area's IFR airspace and the balance of the airspace available for future use. Charts that are useful in identifying the airspace structure are the federal and state aeronautical charts, instrument approach and departure charts of Jeppesen Sanderson, Inc., and other aeronautical publications.

Additional maps or overlays showing the existing airspace structure are included in the inventory. Later in the planning process, proposed expansion of new airports can be related to the existing airspace structure and compatibility verified, or adjustment to proposed development made.

Airport-related land use

An inventory of land uses in the vicinity of each existing airport is necessary so that later in the planning process a determination can be made on the feasibility of expansion and whether an expanded airport will be compatible with the surrounding area and vice versa. Current plans that show existing and planned land uses, highways, utilities, schools, hospitals, and so forth are obtained from area-wide agencies and transportation planning agencies that have jurisdiction over the area the master plan airport is to serve. Current land use is also displayed on a map to assist in later steps of the planning process. Also, if feasible, an estimate of the land values is made.

Normally when considering airport-related land use, a survey will be conducted of all ground travel entering or leaving the airport, including the air travelers, employees, suppliers, and visitors. Information might also be collected on parking and commodity movements. Sufficient data is obtained to establish the travel patterns of airport-oriented trips and to develop relationships that will be used to determine future travel patterns.

Copies of zoning laws, building codes, and other regulations and ordinances that might be applicable to the development of an airport master plan are obtained. All of these have an effect on airport-related-land use.

Aeronautical activity

The principal determinant of future airport system requirements is the amount of aeronautical activity that will be generated in the metropolitan area. A record of current aviation statistics as well as a consideration of historical airport traffic data for such elements as passenger and air cargo traffic, aircraft movements, and aircraft mix is necessary to forecast aeronautical activity. The assessment of these aviation statistics, along with consideration of the socioeconomic attributes for the area, forms the basis for forecasts of aeronautical activity for the metropolitan area. The forecasts of aeronautical activity, in turn, form the basis for facilities planning for future requirements.

Aeronautical statistical data include federal, state, and regional statistics as they relate to the master plan airport and the collection of as many local statistics as can be obtained. At the local level surveys and questionnaires are used to supplement data on operations, frequency, and hours of use of aircraft and origins and destinations of travelers. The primary aviation statistics needed are taken up in this chapter's forecasting section.

Socioeconomic factors

The collection and analysis of socioeconomic data for a metropolitan area helps answer the basic questions regarding the type, volume, and concentration centers of future aviation activity in the region. Accordingly, the determinants (what causes a market to be the size it is) of a market for airports are established. What industries need air transportation? Do they have a need for better air transportation facilities? How many people will be available in the future who possess the income to make use of air service? Will the people and industries having the wherewithal to utilize the airport be there? Because people are associated with a multitude of income-earning and income-spending activities at any particular location from and to which they travel, transportation facilities are needed between those points where the future travel is expected to occur.

The primary forces that measure and help determine economic change, and a general rationale for their use in determining air transportation demand, are as follows:

Demography   The size and structure of the area's population and its potential growth rate are basic factors in creating demand for air transportation services. The existing population along with its changing age and educational and occupational distributions can provide a primary index of the potential size of the aviation market and resultant airport employment over short-, intermediate-, and long-range forecast periods. Demographic factors influence the level of airport traffic and its growth, both in terms of incoming traffic from other states, regions, or cities, and traffic generated by the local or regional populations concerned.

Disposable personal income per capita   This economic factor refers to the purchasing power available to residents in any one period of time, which is a good indicator of average living standards and financial ability to travel. High levels of average personal disposable income provide a strong basis for higher levels of consumer spending, particularly on air travel.

Economic activity and status of industries   This factor refers to situations within the area the airport serves that generate activity in business aviation and air freight traffic. A community's population, size, and economic character affect its air traffic generating potential. Manufacturing and service industries tend to generate greater air transport activity than primary and resource industries, such as mining. Much will depend on established and potential patterns of internal and external trade. In addition, other aviation activities such as agricultural and instructional flying and aircraft sales are included in this factor.

Geographic factors The geographic distribution and distances between populations and commerce within the area that the airport serves have a direct bearing on the type of transportation services required. The physical characteristics of the land and climatic differences are also important factors. In some cases, alternative modes of transportation might not be available or economically feasible. Furthermore, physical and climatic attractions assist in determining focal points for vacation traffic and tourism and help in establishing the demand for air services that they generate.

Competitive position The demand for air service also depends on its present and future ability to compete with alternative modes of transportation. Also, technological advances in aircraft design and in other transportation modes, as well as industrial and marketing processes, can create transportation demands that have not previously existed.

Sociological factors The trend toward a more urbanized society, the increased mobility of the population, rising educational levels, and a shorter work week with the resultant increase in leisure time are also major factors in determining demand for air travel.

Political factors The granting of new traffic rights and routes for international air service will influence the volume of traffic at an airport. Demand for air transportation also depends on government

Aerial view of Lindbergh Field at San Diego. Port of San Diego

actions such as the imposition of taxes and other fees. In addition, government might support other modes of transportation, which might result in changes in demand for air transportation services.

Community values

A very important factor in the airport master planning process is the determination of the attitude of the community toward airport development. Poor airport–community relations, unless changed, could influence the ability to implement an airport master plan. On the other hand, a recognition by the community of the need for progress in the development of air transportation can have a positive influence in minimizing complaints; thus, it is necessary to place airport development in its proper perspective relative to community values.

The Airport and Airway Development Act of 1970 established a requirement that airport sponsors must afford the opportunity for public hearings for projects involving the location of an airport, a new airport runway, or a runway extension. Public hearings enable the airport sponsor to:

- Cite examples of nearby communities that have benefited from having an airport. Such examples can point out growth in new and existing businesses and recreational facilities.

- Identify local business and commercial reliance on air transportation.

- Identify the local airport's role in state, regional, and national airport plans.

- Explain how the airport master plan will accommodate potential local environmental problems, immediate and long-range, emphasizing plans for minimizing noise and zoning recommendations for compatible land use.

- Estimate the adverse impact on community growth and economy if the airport project is not carried forward.

- Concentrate on presenting the facts in a positive, comprehensive, and forceful manner, anticipating and rebutting opposition claims.

Recognition of community values and keeping the public apprised of developments will assist in the implementation of the airport master plan.

Forecasting

Airport master plans must be developed on the basis of forecasts. From forecasts, the relationships between demand and the capacity of an airport's various facilities can be established and airport requirements can be determined. Short-, intermediate-, and long-range (approximately 5, 10, and 20 years) forecasts are made to enable the planner to establish a schedule of development for improvements proposed in the master plan.

The inadequacies of past forecasts raise questions as to what the forecasts should encompass to provide proper guidance for the development of a master plan for the individual airport. The planner must go beyond the aviation demand forecast discussed under this section. He or she must study carefully the impacts that social, environmental, economic, and technical forecasts will have on the master plan airport. The planner must incorporate these influences in the development of aviation demand forecasts; however, the necessity to take into consideration a broad-scope analysis of socioeconomic forecasts does not mean that the planner has to develop a mass of far-ranging forecasts as a part of the master plan effort. The planner must first engage in a research of forecasts that exist for the area served by the airport, and then develop only those forecasts that are germane to the development of the master plan. The magnitude of development of forecasts will depend on the size of the community the airport serves and on information that might be available from earlier planning efforts such as state or regional airport system plans.

Forecasting methods

Three basic types of forecasting methods are available to assist planners in the decision-making process: causal models, time-series or trend analysis, and judgmental forecasts. *Causal models* are highly sophisticated mathematical models that are developed and tested by using historical data. The model is built on a statistical relationship between the forecasted (dependent) variable and one or more explanatory (independent) variables. Some models include up to 40 or 50 independent variables. There need not be a cause-and-effect relationship between the dependent and independent variables. A statistical correlation alone is sufficient basis for prediction or forecasting. Correlation is a pattern or relationship between the two or more variables. The closer the relationship, the greater the degree of correlation.

A causal model is constructed by finding variables that explain, statistically, the changes in the variable to be forecast. The availability of data on the variables—or, more specifically, their specific values—is largely determined by the time and resources the planner has available. Prominent independent variables used in forecasting various segments of the air transportation industry include gross domestic product (GDP), disposable personal income (DI), and consumer spending on services.

Another reasonably sophisticated statistical method of forecasting is *time-series analysis or trend extension*, the oldest and in many cases still the most widely used method of forecasting air transportation demand. Time-series models show the dependent variable, time. This method is used quite frequently where both time and data are limited, such as in forecasting a single variable, for example, cargo tonnage, where historical data is obtained for that particular variable.

Forecasting by time-series or trend extension actually consists of interpreting the historical sequence and applying the interpretation to the immediate future. It assumes that the rate of growth or change that has persisted in the past will continue. Historical data is plotted on a graph, and a trend line is drawn. Frequently a straight line, following the trend line, is drawn for the future; however, if certain known factors indicate that the rate will increase in the future, the line might be curved upward. As a general rule, there might be several future projections, depending upon the length of the historical period studied.

Airport authorities keep numerous records of data of particular concern to them (enplanements, aircraft movements, number of based aircraft, and so forth), and when a forecast is needed, a trend line is established and then projected out to some future period. The accuracy of forecasting by historical sequence in time or trend analysis depends on good judgment in predicting those changing factors that might keep history from repeating.

The values for the forecasted variable are determined by four time-related factors: (1) long-term trend, such as market growth caused by increases in population; (2) cyclical variations, such as those caused by the business cycle; (3) seasonal phenomena, such as weather or holidays; and (4) irregular or unique phenomena, such as strikes, wars, and natural disasters.

Judgmental forecasts are educated guesses based on intuition and subjective evaluations. A judgmental forecast is an estimate made by an individual who is closely acquainted with the factors related to the variable being forecast. These factors are weighed and evaluated according to the experience and intuition of the forecaster. This method permits a broad range of information to be brought to bear on the forecast, such as national trends, growth in air travel, political situations, and so forth. It is especially advantageous when used in conjunction with causal models or time-series analysis, or where there are a large number of variables for which relatively little data is available, or when intangible factors are expected to play a major role. The resultant forecasts from use of this method alone are the most difficult to defend under close scrutiny and might be subject to strong bias from the individual involved in the forecasting process.

Forecasts of aviation demand

Forecasts of aviation demand form the basis for facilities planning. There is a need to know (1) the types of civil airport users—certificated air carrier, commuters, general aviation, and the military services where applicable; (2) the types and volume of operational activity—aircraft operations, passengers and cargo, based aircraft, and so forth; and (3) the aircraft mix—jet and large-capacity prop transport aircraft, smaller commercial, corporate, business and pleasure aircraft, future vertical/short takeoff and landing (V/STOL) aircraft, and so forth.

Civil airport users The airport planner must develop forecasts of aviation demand for the following four major *civil airport user categories* as applicable to the airport under construction:

1 Air Carrier. As used here, "air carrier" refers to airline aircraft operators holding certificates of public convenience and necessity issued by the former Civil Aeronautics Board based on the Department of Transportation authorizing them to perform passenger and cargo services. This general air carrier grouping includes the major, national, large, and medium regional air carriers.

2 Commuters. These noncertificated small regionals perform scheduled service to smaller cities and serve as feeders to the

major hub airports. They generally operate aircraft of less than 12,500 pounds maximum gross takeoff weight.

3 General Aviation. As used here, "general aviation" refers to that segment of civil aviation that encompasses all facets of aviation except air carriers and commuters. General aviation includes air taxi operators, corporate-executive transportation, instruction, rental, aerial application, aerial observation, business, pleasure, and other special users.

4 Military. As used here, "military" refers to the operators of all military (Air Force, Army, Navy, U.S. Coast Guard, Air National Guard, and military reserve organizations) aircraft using civil airports.

Operational activity   Annual forecasts of airport traffic (for 5-, 10-, and 20-year periods) form the principal basis for future airport facility requirement planning. It is essential to develop *operational activity forecasts* by the type of major user categories (air carrier, commuter, general aviation, and military) as previously described.

In the development of the operational activity forecasts, an unconstrained approach can be used for most areas. The "unconstrained" forecast represents the potential aviation market in which all of the basic factors that tend to create aviation demand are used, without regard to any constraining circumstances (limited airport expansion capability, airspace, access, and so forth) that could affect aviation growth at any specific airport or location.

Forecasters review and relate national and/or local historical needs and forecast data to the areas under study as a guide for future planning. With this approach, it is possible to determine the theoretical development needs in accordance with the total demand potential. In the exceptionally high activity metropolitan areas, however, potential constraints and alternative methods for their reduction are also considered.

Six major types of operational activity forecasts are considered necessary to determine future facility requirements:

1 *Enplaning Passengers.* This activity includes the total number of passengers (air carrier, commuter, and general aviation) departing on aircraft at the airport. Originating, stopover, and transfer passengers are identified separately.

Influencing factors considered for air carrier passenger traffic, in most forecasting methods, include: historical trends in the national percentage participation rates for both the metropolitan area and its major city-pair markets; local and regional population and socioeconomic trends; and the business/personal composition of the metropolitan area's traffic. These factors are used to develop future participation rates and ultimately to translate national projections into metropolitan area forecasts. Sometimes, two series will be correlated to a degree where one might be capable of measuring the other. For example, some communities' numbers of U.S. international passengers are sufficiently correlated with the domestic passengers to assume that the relationship will continue.

The number of enplaned general aviation passengers is frequently estimated for the area by first developing load factors for the future average number of passengers per plane and then by multiplying these factors by one-half the total number of forecasted general aviation itinerant operations (other than local operations).

2 *Enplaning Air Cargo.* Enplaning air cargo includes the total tonnage of priority, nonpriority, and foreign mail, express shipments, and freight (property other than baggage accompanying passengers) departing on aircraft at an airport, including originations, stopover, and transfer cargo. Where applicable, domestic and international are identified separately.

The air cargo industry (like most industries) depends on population growth, continuing gains in the gross domestic product (GDP), and the export-import increases produced by a free trade market.

Most forecasters make use of both judgment and statistical techniques to develop percentage growth factors derived from such investigative approaches as follows: (1) an extrapolation of past trends of all commerce, with particular attention to air commerce and the metropolitan regions' share of air commerce; (2) a review of national air cargo forecasts by airlines, aircraft manufacturers, governmental agencies, and trade associations; (3) consideration of the effect on the growth of mail by such factors as conflicting mail data, world conflict, changing post office policies and methods, and possible actions of Congress; (4) a projection of air transport cargo lift potential—the impact of new cargo aircraft; (5) the potential air cargo penetration into other transport modes—such as water transport for the overseas market and long-haul common carrier truck transport for the domestic market—due to marketing changes in air cargo transportation; and (6) future costs of ground freight transport as compared with air transport and domestic shipper practices.

Two general methods of forecasting a metropolitan area's air cargo are: using area annual growth rates applied to the area's current cargo base; or calculating a percentage ratio of the area's cargo to the national total and projecting a future trend to apply to an acceptable national forecast of air cargo.

3 *Aircraft Operations* (movements). Aircraft operations include the total number of landings (arrivals) at and takeoffs (departures) from an airport. Two types of operations—local and itinerant—are separately identified: (1) *local operations*—performed by aircraft that (a) operate in the local traffic pattern or within sight of the tower, (b) are known to be departing for or arriving from flight in local practice and flight test areas located within a 20-mile radius of the airport and/or control tower, (c) execute simulated instrument approaches or low passes at the airport; and (2) *itinerant operations*—all aircraft arrivals and departures other than local operations described above. Where applicable, domestic and international itinerant operations should be identified separately.

Air cargo depot located in the southwest corner of Miami International Airport. Metro-Dade Aviation Department

Except for local training flights at some airports, air carrier aircraft movements are itinerant operations. The basic premise underlying the methodology for forecasting air carrier operations by airport is that a relationship exists between the number of enplaned passengers and cargo shipments and the level of service provided. It is assumed that the number of aircraft seats for transiting and enplaning passengers and the number of flights by type of aircraft have been a function of the traffic demand and traffic characteristics of the community as well as the route structure and operating policies and practices of the individual carriers. It is also assumed that these same factors will continue to determine the level of operations in the future.

An often-used forecast method for air carrier operations can be summarized as follows:

The total generated seats at each airport are forecast to increase as a function of the forecast of enplaned passengers.

The analysis and forecast of aircraft mix is an internal part of the methodology to determine the number of air carrier operations because the total forecast seats are distributed among the type of aircraft the carriers are expected to operate at each airport in the forecast year. The seat totals, by aircraft type, are divided by average seating capacities to yield the number of aircraft operations by aircraft type required. Total air carrier operations are determined by summing the operations by aircraft type.

General aviation aircraft movements can be either itinerant or local operations. Because general aviation activity is related to such parameters as population, employment, income, and based aircraft in the metropolitan region, most methods of estimating its future level are centered around historical growth trends and operations per based aircraft. Because trends can be misleading, supporting rationale is often developed before any conclusions are reached after using historical trends. Methods of forecasting general aviation operations at air carrier and general aviation control tower airports in a metropolitan area take into account such factors as: (1) the past trend of general aviation operations at each air carrier airport; (2) the air carrier activity forecast for the airport (this might be large enough to cause general aviation restrictions; any surplus in general aviation activity is allocated to other airports in the area); (3) the number of towers planned or programmed for general aviation in the area; and (4) discussions with airport management and FAA.

Future general aviation activity at air carrier and general aviation control tower airports is generally developed from historical growth trends, considering the above factors and adjusting the trends on the basis of knowledge of the individual airport's potential and the economic expectation of its associated community. An alternate, approximate method for general aviation control tower airports is to determine and project their percent of U.S. towers' operations and apply the derived percentage factors to the FAA's national forecasts of tower operations, adjusted for the addition of new tower airports. (See the FAA publication Aviation Forecasts, which is issued annually.)

One approach to forecasting general aviation activity at general aviation nontower airports is to establish a relationship between operations and based general aviation aircraft, and to apply this relationship to an acceptable forecast of based aircraft. Base norms are determined for the airport's local and itinerant operations per based aircraft. These base norms are then adjusted for normal growth and multiplied by the number of projected based aircraft to obtain future activity.

Future forecasts of military operations can be projected on the basis of past trends and information provided by military sources.

4 *Based Aircraft.* Based aircraft is the total number of active general aviation aircraft that use or might be expected to use an airport as "home base." General aviation based aircraft are separately identified as single-engine, multiengine, piston or turbine, or V/STOL.

Forecasts of general aviation aircraft within the metropolitan area are based upon growth rates reflected for national totals in the FAA annual publication Aviation Forecasts, which establishes an annual percentage increase in based aircraft for single-engine, multiengine, and turbine aircraft. These forecasts are modified to reflect special conditions at each metropolitan area.

5 *Busy-Hour Operations.* Busy-hour operations is the total number of aircraft operations expected to occur at an airport at its busiest hour, computed by averaging two adjacent busiest

hours of a typically high activity day. One definition of typically high activity day would be the average day of the busiest month of the year. The operations are identified by major user category, as applicable.

The operations forecast is translated to reflect the total number of aircraft operations expected to occur at an airport during a busy hour of a typically high activity day. The percent this day of the annual operations is computed from previous records.

Also, the air carrier busy hour is selected. Assuming that this hour and the percent of daily passengers and aircraft operations, together with the percent of annual operations, would remain the same, it is possible to apply these percentages to future passenger and operations forecasts to obtain the busy-hour operations number for the forecast period. Also, a certain percentage of the future estimated annual cargo volumes are translated into all-cargo plane movements, by month, day of week, and hour of day, indicate that only a few of the all-cargo plane movements operate in peak periods; therefore, during the average busy hour of passenger plane movements, only a few all-cargo plane movements are expected.

The annual operations forecast also reflects the total number of general aviation operations at each airport in the metropolitan region during a busy hour of a typically high activity day. In general, the method of forecasting general aviation peak-hour operations follows the steps in forecasting air carrier busy-hour operations. In addition, the number of general aviation operations expected to occur at each airport during the air carrier busy hour is also considered in estimating the total busy-hour operations at each airport.

Military operations are not normally considered in the busy hour because the military services avoid congested time periods at civil airports. At air carrier tower airports, one method of developing military busy hour is to consider that itinerant and local military busy day operations tend toward a constant percentage of annual operations for each category.

6 *Aircraft Mix.* In determining airport requirements, it is necessary to forecast the aircraft mix (types of categories of aircraft) that are to be accommodated at the airport. Airport management must keep abreast of technological advances in aircraft design in order to assure the provision of adequate airfield and terminal design at the airports from which they are to operate.

Forecasts of aircraft mix are summarized into (1) seating capacity groups for air carrier aircraft; and (2) operational characteristics groups for all four of the major airport user categories.

The annual FAA report *Aviation Forecasts* gives national and regional trends in air carrier and general aviation aircraft mix.

Demand/capacity analysis

After aviation demand has been determined, the next step in the airport master planning process is the assessment of facility requirements. The study of the *demand/capacity* relationship involves an estimation of the need to expand facilities and the cost of these improvements. This type of analysis is done in consultation with the airlines and the general aviation community. The analysis is applied to aircraft operations versus airfield improvements; to passenger enplanements versus terminal building improvements; to cargo tonnage versus cargo facility development; to airport access traffic versus access roads and rapid transit facilities; and to other improvements as might be appropriate. Airspace in the vicinity of the master plan airport is also analyzed.

Demand/capacity analysis is normally applied to short-, intermediate-, and long-range developments (approximately 5, 10, and 20 years). The analysis is only an approximation of facility requirements, their costs, and savings that will result from reduced delays to airport users as well as anticipated revenues that might be obtained from proposed improvements; thus, demand/capacity analysis will yield preliminary estimates of the number and configuration of runways, areas of apron, number of vehicle parking spaces, and capacities of airport access facilities. Preliminary estimates of economic feasibility may also be obtained. These approximations will provide a basis for developing the details of the airport master plan and for determining the feasibility of improvements considered in the plan.

Aircraft operational requirements

The forecasts of aviation activity will indicate the kinds of aircraft anticipated to use the master plan airport. The frequency of use, passenger/cargo load factors, and lengths of outbound nonstop flights will also be indicated. From this demand data, the planner can ascertain the required physical dimensions of the aircraft operational areas.

While a capacity analysis provides requirements in terms of numbers of runways/taxiways and so forth, the analysis of aircraft operational requirements allows the determination of runway/taxiway/apron dimensions, strengths, and lateral clearances between airport areas. Of course, both of these analyses are interrelated and are accomplished simultaneously in order to determine system requirements.

Capacity analysis

An analysis of the existing air traffic capacity of the area the master plan airport is to serve will help to determine how much additional capacity will be required at the master plan airport. Four distinct elements require investigation, namely:

Airfield capacity *Airfield capacity* is the rate of aircraft movements on the runway/taxiway system which results in a given level of delay.

Terminal area capacity *Terminal area capacity* is the ability of the terminal area to accept the passengers, cargo, and aircraft that the airfield generates. Individual elements within terminal areas must be evaluated to determine overall terminal capacity. Terminal elements included in the analysis are (1) airline gate positions; (2) airline apron areas; (3) cargo apron areas; (4) general aviation apron areas; (5) airline passenger terminals; (6) general aviation terminals; (7) cargo buildings; (8) automobile parking; and (9) aircraft maintenance facilities.

Airspace capacity The proximity of airports to one another, the relationship of runway alignments, and the nature of operations [IFR or visual flight rules (VFR)] are the principal interairport considerations that will affect *airspace capacity* of the master plan airport. For example, it is not uncommon in a large metropolitan area to have major or secondary airports spaced so closely that they share one discrete parcel of airspace. In such cases there may be a reduction in the IFR capacity for the airports involved due to the intermixing of traffic within the common parcel of airspace. When this occurs, aircraft, regardless of destination, must be sequenced with the proper separation standards. This reduces the IFR capacity for a specific airport.

Ground access capacity   The establishment of capacity requirements for the master plan airport will determine the capacity required for airport access. The airport capacity figures are translated into numbers of movements by people and access vehicles. A preliminary examination of existing and planned highway and mass transit systems allows a judgment as to the availability of *ground access capacity*. In determining the volume of people, it is necessary for the planner to establish the percentage relationship between passengers, visitors, and airport employees. This can vary from one urban area to another and from one site to another.

Facility requirements are developed from information obtained in demand/capacity analysis and from FAA advisory circulars and regulations which provide criteria for design of airport components. Demand/capacity analysis yields approximate number and configuration of runways, number of gates, square footage of terminal buildings, cargo facilities, number of public and employee parking spaces, types of airport access roads, and the overall land area required for the airport. From the mix of aircraft and the number of aircraft operations, general requirements for length, strength and number of runways, spacing of taxiways, layout and spacing of gates, and apron area requirements can be determined. These approximations are used by the planner in developing the details under the airport layout plan (discussed in Chapter 5).

Environmental impact study

Environmental factors must be considered carefully in the development of a new airport or the expansion of an existing one. This requirement was first established in the Airport and Airway Development Act of 1970 and the Environmental Policy Act of 1969. *The National Environmental Policy Act of 1969* requires the preparation of detailed environmental statements for all major federal airport development actions significantly affecting the quality of the environment. The Airport and Airway Development Act of 1970 directed that no airport development project may be approved by the Secretary of Transportation unless he or she is satisfied that fair consideration has been given to the communities in or near which the project may be located.

Studies of the impact of construction and operation of the airport or airport expansion upon accepted standards of air and water quality, ambient noise levels, ecological processes, and natural environmental values are conducted to determine how the airport requirements can best be accomplished. An airport is an obvious stimulus to society from the standpoints of economic growth and the services it offers to the public; however, this generation of productivity and employment might be negated by noise and air pollution and ecological compromises if compatibility between an airport and its environs is not achieved; thus, the airport master plan must directly contend with these problems identified in the studies of environmental qualities so that the engineering of airport facilities will minimize or overcome those operations that contribute to environmental pollution.

Aircraft noise

Aircraft noise is probably the severest environmental problem to be overcome in the development of an airport. Where aircraft noise causes disturbance, it makes an airport unpopular no matter how well the airport serves its community. The resolution of the noise problem requires careful analysis, development of proper land use, and a coordinated approach on the part of the government, aircraft manufacturers, airport operators, and the community.

Improvements in design of engines used on the newer aircraft such as the Boeing 757 and 767 have had a significant effect on reducing noise. Noise abatement procedures and special operational restrictions have resulted in substantial noise reduction from existing airports. Airport layouts that direct the noise away from built-up areas have also been a principal consideration in the development of new airport facilities.

One of the most effective means of reducing noise impact is through the proper planning of land use for areas affected by airport noise. The difficulties that are encountered in establishment of land use plans depend on whether its application is preventive or remedial in nature. Methods of land use control include purchase for direct airport use; conversion to a use compatible with expected noise levels; acquisition of aviation easements; and the establishment of zoning and building codes.

Air pollution

While there is evidence that aircraft engine emission constitutes less than 1 percent of the total air pollutants in a typical metropolitan area, this facet of the environmental impact of airport operations cannot be overlooked in the development of the airport master plan. It is rather evident to the observer on the ground that exhaust smoke does exist and that contaminants are emitted into the environment.

The federal government and industry are keenly aware of the public reaction to engine exhaust emissions and are jointly working toward alleviating the problem. This is an easier problem to resolve from a technical and economic aspect than the noise alleviation problem, and it will probably be eliminated in the foreseeable future as a factor with which the airport planner must deal; however, the anticipated effects of air pollution and considerations given thereto are always reported in the airport master plan.

Natural environmental values

Normally, airport planners will not consider locations for airport development near national parks and wilderness areas or areas designated as wildlife and waterfowl refuges, public recreation areas, and historical monuments. Expansion of existing airports into or adjacent to such areas is avoided where possible.

Water pollution

Although the means of controlling water pollution is probably the best understood aspect of the environmental problem, it is studied carefully in the development of an airport master plan, and means for overcoming water pollution problems are incorporated in the plan. An airport can be a major contributor to water pollution if suitable treatment facilities for airport wastes are not provided. Sources of water pollution are (1) domestic sewage from airport facilities; (2) industrial wastes such as fuel spills; and (3) high temperature water degradation from various power plants at the airport.

Federal environmental policy

Section 4(f) of the Department of Transportation Act requires responsible federal action in assuring the protection of natural environmental values through the following provision:

> It is hereby declared to be the national policy that special effort should be made to preserve the natural beauty of the countryside and public park and recreation lands, wildlife and waterfowl refuges, and historic sites. The Secretary of

Transportation shall cooperate and consult with the Secretaries of the Interior, Housing and Urban Development, and Agriculture, and with the States in developing Transportation plans and programs that include measures to maintain or enhance the natural beauty of the Federal-Aid Highway Act of 1968. The Secretary shall not approve any program or project which requires the use of any publicly owned land from a public park, recreation area, or wildlife and waterfowl refuge of national, State, or local significance as determined by the Federal, State, or local officials having jurisdiction thereof, or any land from an historic site of national, State, or local significance as so determined by such officials unless (1) there is no feasible and prudent alternative to the use of such land, and (2) such program includes all possible planning to minimize harm to such park, recreational area, wildlife and waterfowl refuge, or historic site resulting from such use.

This section represents an important step in an attempt to prevent further encroachment on environmental values. Today there is an awareness at all levels of government, and in the public in general, that our natural resources are being threatened and that this threat must be alleviated.

Another far-reaching federal law to protect our nation's environmental and natural resources was enacted on January 1, 1970. The National Environmental Policy Act of 1969 declares a broad national environmental policy that calls on the federal government to exercise leadership in improving and coordinating federal plans, functions, programs, and use of resources with the goals of preventing damage either to the environment or ecological systems and encouraging mutual productive harmony between man and his environment. The law also established, in the executive office of the president, a council on environmental quality to develop guidelines for agencies affected by the law.

Insofar as airport development is concerned, any required federal actions regarding proposals that significantly affect the quality of the environment must be accompanied by findings concerning:

- The environmental impact of the proposed action.
- Any adverse environmental effects that cannot be avoided should the proposal be implemented.
- Alternatives to the proposed action.

- The relationship between local short-term uses of man's environment and the maintenance and enhancement of long-term productivity.

- Any irreversible and irretrievable commitments of resources that would be involved in the proposed action should it be implemented.

In line with the above guidelines and policy, an airport master plan (including site selection) must be evaluated factually in terms of any proposed development that is likely to:

- Noticeably affect the ambient noise level for a significant number of people.

- Displace significant numbers of people.

- Have a significant aesthetic or visual effect.

- Divide or disrupt an established community or divide existing uses (e.g., cutting off residential areas from recreation or shopping areas).

- Have any effect on areas of unique interest or scenic beauty.

- Destroy or detract from important recreational areas.

- Substantially alter the pattern of behavior for a species.

- Interfere with important wildlife breeding, nesting, or feeding grounds.

- Significantly increase air or water pollution.

- Adversely affect the water table of an area.

Site selection

The site selection process begins after a community has determined that it is feasible to plan for a new airport. Determining the proper site is undoubtedly the most important step in building an airport.

An airport planner will study many factors before recommending sites for the community's new airport. Site selection studies evaluate airspace, environmental factors, community growth, airport ground access, availability of utilities, land costs, and site development costs. The planner also gives preferential ratings to possible sites.

The results of the site selection study are always presented in a positive and persuasive fashion because the actual selection will most likely be decided in the political arena. This is particularly true of airports that serve large urban areas where the citizenry is very sensitive to environmental and socioeconomic factors.

The site selection study is completely integrated with current local and regional comprehensive plans. During the course of study, close liaison is maintained with federal, state, regional, and metropolitan planning agencies having jurisdiction within the area to be served by the airport and with the airlines and other aviation interests operating in the area. The site selection team takes full advantage of data from recent studies that have been developed by these organizations.

The initial investigation of airport sites is the responsibility of the airport sponsor. Preliminary recommendations are presented to the FAA for review. After review, the FAA will confer with the sponsor regarding the preliminary recommendations and will assist the sponsor in evaluating the most desirable sites, if so requested. In some instances, this evaluation will result in a recommendation to the sponsor to study additional sites. When the sponsor has made a final recommendation, or recommendations, the FAA will state in writing its position on the proposed site selection. Grants for phases of an airport master plan that follow site selection will not be made until an airport site has been approved by the FAA.

In its review of proposed airport sites, the FAA will evaluate them from an airspace standpoint. Federal Aviation Regulations Part 157, Notice of Construction, Alteration, Activation and Deactivation of Airports, requires proponents of civil or joint use (civil/military) airport projects to notify the nearest FAA area or regional office before work on the project begins. During the course of the site selection study, the FAA will offer advice to sponsors regarding airspace for sites under consideration.

Factors affecting site selection

The major factors that require careful analysis in the final evaluation of airport sites include:

Airspace analysis In major metropolitan areas, it is not uncommon for two or more airports to share common airspace. This factor might restrict the capability of any one airport to accept IFR traffic under adverse weather conditions. Airports too close to each other can degrade their respective capabilities and create a serious traffic control problem. It is important to analyze the requirements and fu-

Southwest Florida International Airport was certified for operation in May 1983 and, for more than a decade, was the newest commercial air carrier airport in the United States. Lee County Port Authority.

ture needs of existing airports before considering construction sites for a new airport.

Surrounding obstructions   Obstructions in the vicinity of the airport sites, whether natural, existing, or proposed man-made structures, must meet the criteria set forth in Federal Aviation Regulations Part 77, Objects Affecting Navigable Airspace. The FAA requires that *clear zones* at the ends of runways be provided by the airport operator. Runway clear zones are areas comprising the innermost portions of the runway approach areas as defined in FAR Part 77. The dimensions of the clear zones are shown in Fig. 4-1.

The FAA requires that the airport owner have "an adequate property interest" in the clear zone area in order that the requirements of FAR Part 77 can be met and the area protected from future encroachments. Adequate property interest might be in the form of ownership or a long-term lease or other demonstration of legal ability to prevent future obstructions in the runway clear zone.

Expansion   Available land for expansion of the airport is a major factor in site selection; however, it is not always necessary to purchase the entire tract at the start because adjacent land needed for future expansion could be protected by lease or option to buy. The Airport and Airway Development Act of 1970 first established funding for communities to acquire land for future airport development.

Availability of utilities Consideration is always given to the distance that electric power, telephone, gas, water, and sewer lines must be extended to serve the proposed site. Cost of obtaining utilities can be a major influence on the site selection.

Meteorological conditions Sites must be carefully investigated for prevalence of ground fog, bad wind currents, industrial smoke, and smog. A study of wind direction on a year-round basis is always made because prevailing winds will influence the entire design of the airport.

Economy of construction Soil classification and drainage can have an effect on the cost of construction. Similarly, sites lying on submerged or marshy land are much more costly to develop than those on dry land. Rolling terrain requires much more grading than

Category	W_1	W_2	L*
1. Precision instrument runway	1,000	1,750	2,500
2. Nonprecision instrument runway for larger than utility with visibility minimums as low as 3/4 mile	1,000	1,510	1,700
3. Nonprecision instrument runway for larger than utility with visibility minimum greater than 3/4 mile	500	1,000	1,700
4. Visual approach runway for larger than utility	500	700	1,000
5. Nonprecision approach for utility	500	800	1,000
6. Visual approach runway for utility	250	450	1,000

*Length of clear zone is determined by distance required to reach a height of 50 ft. for the appropriate surface.

4-1. *Runway clear zones.* Federal Aviation Administration

flat terrain. The site that is more economical to construct will be a deciding factor in the final selection.

Convenience to population   An airport must be convenient for the people who will use its facilities. Much in the same way that shopping centers derive their success from convenient access and parking, the airport too must be accessible in terms of time, distance, and cost of transportation. As a rule of thumb, the airport should be located no more than 30 minutes from the majority of potential users. Consideration in site selection is always given to the proximity of railroads, highways, and other types of transportation for movement and transfer of cargo and passengers.

Noise   Noise is the most predominant objection raised by opponents to new airports and airport expansion projects. Numerous efforts are being made by industry and government to seek new and better ways to reduce aircraft sound levels. Many of the older jet aircraft are now being retrofitted with noise kits that are designed to reduce noise. Engine manufacturers are exploring new engineering concepts and designs that will reduce this source of noise to an absolute minimum. Pilots of airliners are required to maintain certain power settings and to fly prescribed routes that reduce noise levels in the vicinity of takeoff and landing areas. Noise certification standards have been established by the FAA for new aircraft.

Cost comparisons of alternative sites   A quantitative and qualitative comparison of the aforementioned factors is made from the standpoint of cost. Quantitative analysis includes an evaluation of the costs of land acquisition and easements, site developments, major utilities, foundations, access facilities, ground travel for users, and effects on surrounding areas such as noise, air and water pollution, and safety. Qualitative evaluation considers accessibility to users, compatible land users, expansion capabilities, and air traffic control compatibility.

Key terms

airport requirements

site selection

causal models

time-series analysis or trend extension

judgmental forecasts

civil airport user categories

operational activity forecasts

air carrier passenger traffic

enplaning passengers

enplaning air cargo

aircraft operations

local operations

itinerant operations

based aircraft

busy-hour operations

aircraft mix

airfield capacity

terminal area capacity

airspace capacity

ground access capacity

National Environmental Policy Act of 1969

clear zones

Review questions

1 What is an airport master plan? Describe the first two phases of the airport master plan.

- Why is it important for the planner to make a historical review of airports and facilities in the area?

- What is the chief concern of the planner from the standpoint of airspace structure and navaids when two or more airports serve the area?

2 Discuss some of the socioeconomic factors that airport planners take into consideration during the early development stage. Why is it important that the airport planner involve the public in having hearings throughout the developmental process?

3 Compare and contrast the three methods of forecasting discussed in this chapter.

- List the four major civil airport user categories.

- What are operational activity forecasts? List the six major types.
- Why is the airport planner concerned with aircraft mix?

4 What is the purpose of demand/capacity analysis?
- Discuss the four elements to be investigated under capacity analysis.

5 What are the major environmental concerns in planning an airport?
- How has the problem of noise been addressed in recent years? Describe the guidelines established by the Council on Environmental Quality.
- List the 10 environmental areas that must be evaluated and explained in case of any proposed airport development.

6 Describe the importance of airspace analysis in the site selection phase.
- What is the runway clear zone?
- What is meant by economy of construction?
- Summarize some of the other factors taken into consideration by airport planners in selecting an airport site.

Suggested readings

Ashford, Norman, and Paul H. Wright. *Airport Engineering.* New York: Wiley-Interscience Publications, John Wiley & Sons, 1979.

Deem, Warren H., and John S. Reed. *Airport Land Needs.* San Francisco: Arthur D. Little, Inc., 1966.

Horonjeff, Robert. *Planning and Design of Airports, 4th ed.* New York: McGraw-Hill, 1994.

DOT/FAA advisory circulars

150/5020-1	Noise Control and Compatibility Planning for Airports.
150/5050-4	Citizen Participation in Airport Planning.
150/5070-3	Planning the Airport Industrial Park.
150/5070-5	Planning the Metropolitan Airport System.
150/5070-6A	Airport Master Plans.
150/5060-2	Airport Site Selection.

150/5060-7   Establishment of Airport Action Groups.
FAR, Part 77   Objects Affecting Navigable Airspace.
FAR, Part 151   Federal Aid to Airports.
FAR, Part 153   Acquisition of U.S. Land for Public Airports.
FAR, Part 157   Notice of Construction, Alteration, Activation, and Deactivation of Airports.

5

Airport layout and land use plans

Outline

- Introduction: Phase three of the master plan
- Airport layout plan
- Approach and clear zone layout
- Land use plan

Objectives

When you have completed this chapter, you should be able to:

- Describe the major items included in an airport layout plan drawing.
- Identify the prominent airside facilities.
- Describe the four basic runway configurations.
- Highlight the importance of prevailing wind in planning runways.
- Distinguish between the following runway classifications: visual, nonprecision instrument, and precision instrument.
- Understand the importance of runway lighting and ILS.
- Describe the basic principles involved in laying out taxiways.
- Distinguish between holding areas and holding bays.
- Describe the four basic aircraft parking positions.

- Explain each of the so-called imaginary surfaces described in FAR Part 77.
- Discuss the importance of land use planning on and off the airport.

Introduction: Phase three of the master plan

The third phase of the airport master plan includes four components: the airport layout plan, the land use plan, terminal area plans, and airport access plans. This chapter covers the former two and Chapter 6 the latter two subjects.

Once the airport requirements (phase one) have been determined and the site (phase two), new or existing, has been selected, the master plan process moves on to the development of the airport layout plan. The development of the airport layout plan will establish the actual configuration of runways, taxiways, and aprons, and will set aside areas for the establishment of terminal facilities. Preliminary estimates of facility requirements were made under demand/capacity analysis in phase one of the master plan. The location of air navigation facilities and runway approach zones are also incorporated in the airport layout plan.

The land use plan within the airport boundary sets aside areas for establishment of the terminal complex, maintenance facilities, commercial buildings, industrial sites, airport access, buffer zones, recreation sites, and other possible improvements as may be appropriate to the specific airport situation. The land use plan outside the airport boundary includes those areas affected by obstruction clearance criteria and noise exposure factors.

The development of the terminal area plan and plans for facilities within the terminal area evolve from the airfield configurations and land use criteria established in the airport layout and land use plans. The airport access plan indicates the proposed routings of airport access to central business districts or to points of connection with existing or planned arterial ground transportation systems. Various modes of surface transportation are considered. The sizes of access facilities are based on airport access traffic studies. Because access facilities beyond airport boundaries are normally outside the jurisdiction of airport sponsors, careful coordination is required with other areawide planning bodies.

Airport layout plan

The *airport layout plan* is a graphic presentation to scale of existing and proposed airport facilities and land uses, their locations, and the pertinent clearance and dimensional information required to show conformance with applicable standards. It shows the airport location, clear zones, approach areas, and other environmental features that might influence airport usage and expansion capabilities.

The airport layout plan also identifies facilities that are no longer needed and describes a plan for their removal or phase-out. Some areas might be leased, sold, or otherwise used for commercial and industrial purposes. The plan is always updated with any changes in property lines; airfield configuration involving runways, taxiways, and aircraft parking apron size and location; buildings; auto parking; cargo areas; navigational aids; obstructions; and entrance roads.

Airport layout plan drawing

The *airport layout plan drawing* includes the following items: the airport layout, location map, vicinity map, basic data table, and wind information (Fig. 5-1).

Airport layout The *airport layout* is the main portion of the drawing. It depicts the existing and ultimate airport development and land uses drawn to scale and includes as a minimum the following information:

- Prominent airport facilities such as runways, taxiways, aprons, blast pads, extended runway safety areas, buildings, navaids, parking areas, roads, lighting, runway marking, pipelines, fences, major drainage facilities, segmented circle, wind indicators, and beacon.

- Prominent natural and manmade features such as trees, streams, ponds, rock outcrops, ditches, railroads, powerlines, and towers.

- Revenue-producing non-aviation-related property, surplus or otherwise, are outlined with current status and use specified.

- Areas reserved for existing and future aviation development and services such as for general aviation fixed-base operations, heliports, cargo facilities, airport maintenance, and so forth.

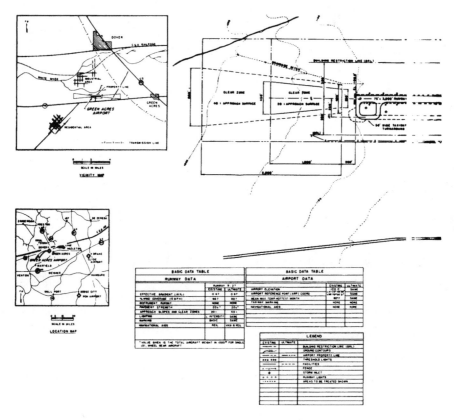

5-1. *Airport layout plan.* Federal Aviation Administration

- Areas reserved for nonaviation development, such as industrial areas, motels, and so forth.

- Existing ground contours.

- Fueling facilities and tiedown areas.

- Facilities that are to be phased out.

- Airport boundaries and areas owned or controlled by the sponsor, including Nvigation easements.

- Approach and clear zone outlines.

- Airport reference point with latitude and longitude given based on U.S. Geological Survey grid system.

- Elevation of runway ends, high and low points, and runway intersections.

- True azimuth of runways (measured from true north).

- North point—true and magnetic.

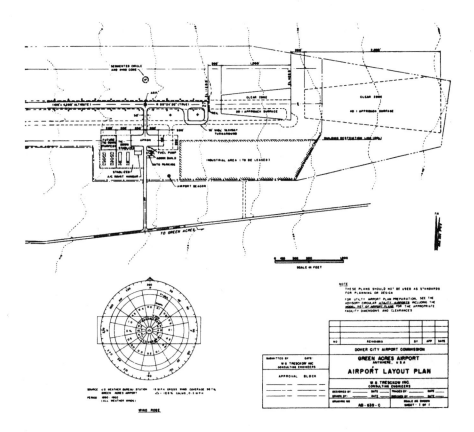

5-1. *Continued.*

- Pertinent dimensional data—runway and taxiway widths and runway lengths, taxiway-runway-apron clearances, apron dimensions, building clearance lines, clear zones, and parallel runway separation.

Location map The *location map* shown in the lower left-hand side of the airport layout plan drawing is drawn to scale and depicts the airport, cities, railroads, major highways, and roads within 25 to 50 miles of the airport.

Vicinity map The *vicinity map* shown in the upper left-hand side of the airport layout plan drawing shows the relationship of the airport to the city or cities, nearby airports, roads, railroads, and built-up areas.

Basic data table The *basic data table* contains the following information on existing and ultimate conditions where applicable:

- Airport elevation (highest point of the landing areas).
- Runway identification such as 9/27.
- Percent effective runway gradient for each existing and proposed runway.
- Percent of wind coverage by principal runway, secondary runway (if applicable), and combined coverage.
- Instrument landing system (ILS) runway when designated, dominant runway otherwise, existing and proposed.
- Normal or mean maximum daily temperature of the hottest month.
- Pavement strength of each runway in gross weight and type of main gear (single, dual, and dual tandem) as appropriate.
- Plan for obstruction removal, relocation of facilities, and so forth.

Wind information   A *wind rose* is always included in the airport layout plan drawing with the runway orientation superimposed. Crosswind coverage and the source and period of data is also given. Wind information is given in terms of all-weather conditions, supplemented by IFR weather conditions where IFR operations are expected.

Airport components

The airport is a complex transportation hub serving aircraft, passengers, cargo, and surface vehicles. It is customary to classify the components of an airport into two major categories: airside facilities and landside facilities (Fig. 5-2).

Airside facilities, sometimes called the *aeronautical surfaces*, or more simply the *airfield*, are those on which aircraft operations are carried out. Principally, they are the runways where aircraft take off and land, the taxiways used for movement between the runway and the terminal, and the apron and gate areas where passengers embark and debark and where aircraft are parked. Because the airspace containing the approach and departure paths for the airfield has an important effect on runway utilization, it is also customary to include terminal area airspace as part of the airside.

The *landside facilities* are essentially those parts of the airport serving passengers, including surface transportation. It includes the terminal buildings, which include passenger loading and waiting areas,

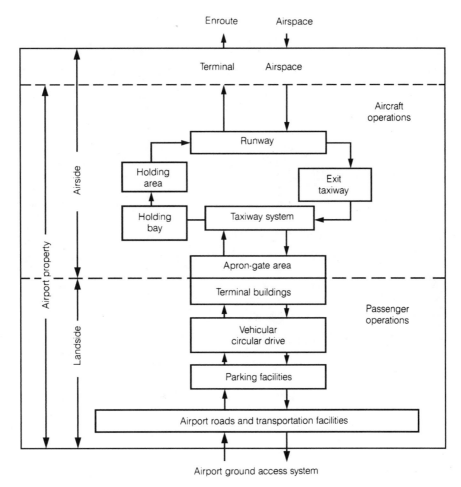

5-2. *Airport Components*

ticket counters, baggage handling facilities, restaurants, shops, car-rental facilities, and the like. Loading, handling, and storage areas for air cargo and mail, often separately located, are also part of the terminal complex.

The landside also includes the vehicular circular drive, parking facilities, and, in some cases, rail rapid transit lines and stations that are part of a larger urban mass transit system. Customarily, only roadways and transportation facilities on the airport property are considered part of the landside, even though they are actually extensions of, and integral with, the urban and regional transportation network.

The discussion that follows will focus in on the airside facilities and land use plan. Landside facilities will be taken up in the next chapter.

An aerial view of Greensboro/High Point/Winston-Salem Airport showing airside and landside facilities. Reynolds, Smith, and Hills

Airside facilities

Prominent airside facilities include runways including their classifications, marking and lighting, instrument landing system, taxiways, holding areas and bays, ground control, and parking.

Runways There are many airport runway configurations. The FAA includes 22 different layouts in their advisory circular 150/5060-5, Airport Capacity Criteria Used in Long-Range Planning. The basic runway configurations are (1) single runway; (2) parallel runways; (3) open-V runways; and (4) intersecting runways (Fig. 5-3).

   1 *Single runway.* The single runway is the simplest of the configurations. Under VFR conditions it can accommodate up to 99 predominantly light twin-engine and single-engine piston aircraft (type D&E) operations per hour. The capacity under IFR conditions is reduced to 42 to 53 operations per hour depending on the aircraft mix and navigational aids available at the particular field.

Runway configuration					PHOCAP(3)	
	FAA layout	Description	Aircraft mix (1)	PANCAP (2)	IFR	VFR
Single A		Single runway (arrivals = departures)	1	215,000	53	99
			2	195,000	52	76
			3	180,000	44	54
			4	170,000	42	45
Parallel B	Less than 2,500'	Close parallels	1	385,000	64	198
			2	330,000	63	152
			3	295,000	55	108
			4	280,000	54	90
C	2,500' to 4,300'	Intermediate parallels	1	425,000	79	198
			2	390,000	79	152
			3	355,000	79	108
			4	330,000	74	90
D	4,300' or more	Far parallels	1	430,000	106	198
			2	390,000	104	152
			3	360,000	88	108
			4	340,000	84	90
H	4,300' or more	Dual-lane runway	1	770,000	128	396
			2	660,000	126	304
			3	590,000	110	216
			4	560,000	108	180
Open-V K_1		Open V, dependent operations away from intersection	1	420,000	71	198
			2	335,000	70	136
			3	300,000	63	94
			4	295,000	60	84
K_2		Open V, dependent operations toward intersection	1	235,000	57	108
			2	220,000	56	86
			3	215,000	50	66
			4	200,000	50	53
L_1	Direction of OPS	Two intersecting at near threshold	1	375,000	71	175
			2	310,000	70	125
			3	275,000	63	83
			4	255,000	60	69
Intersecting L_2		Two intersecting in middle	1	220,000	61	99
			2	195,000	60	76
			3	195,000	53	58
			4	190,000	47	52
L_3	Direction of OPS	Two intersecting at far threshold	1	220,000	55	99
			2	195,000	54	76
			3	180,000	46	54
			4	175,000	42	57

				Percentage			
Key: (1) Aircraft mix			1	2	3	4
Type A - 4 engine jet and larger			0	0	20	60
Type B - 2 and 3-engine jet, 4-engine piston, and turbo prop			0	30	40	20
Type C - executive jet and transport type twin-engine piston			10	30	20	20
Type D & E - light twin engine piston and single-engine piston				40	20	0

(2) PANCAP - Practical Annual Capacity
(3) PHOCAP - Practical Hourly Capacity

5-3. *Airport runway configurations.*

2 *Parallel runways.* There are basically four types of parallel runways: (1) *close* [less than 2,500 feet between runways], (2) *intermediate* [2,500 to 4,300 feet between runways], (3) *far* [more than 4,300 feet between runways], and (4) *dual-lane* [two close parallel runways separated by 4,300 feet or more]. The capacities of parallel runway configurations vary considerably depending upon the number of runways and the spacing. With an aircraft mix of predominantly type D and E, operations per hour vary under IFR conditions between 64 for close parallels to 128 for a dual-lane configuration.

3 *Open-V runways.* Runways that diverge from different directions and do not intersect are classified as open-V runways. When there is little or no wind, both runways can be used simultaneously. Open-V runways revert to a single runway when winds are strong from one direction. Operations increase significantly when takeoffs and landings are made away from the V. When the operations are toward the V, the hourly capacity is reduced by almost 50 percent for Type D and E aircraft during VFR conditions.

4 *Intersecting runways.* Two or more runways that cross each other are referred to as intersecting runways. An intersecting runway configuration is utilized when there are relatively strong winds during the year from more than one direction. Like open-V runways, intersecting runways revert to a single runway when the winds are strong from one direction. If winds are relatively light, both runways can be used simultaneously. The capacity of intersecting runways greatly depends upon the location of the intersection and the way the runways are operated. The highest capacity is achieved when the intersection is close to the takeoff end and landing threshold as shown in layout L_1.

From a planning standpoint, a single-direction runway configuration can achieve greater capacity and ease air traffic control. Routing aircraft in a single direction is less complex than routing in multiple directions. In general, an open-V configuration will yield higher capacities than intersecting configurations.

An analysis of the prevailing wind is essential in planning runways. The primary runway should be oriented as closely as possible to the direction of the prevailing winds. Aircraft that are landing and taking off can maneuver on a runway as long as the wind direction at right angles to the direction of travel (crosswind) is not excessive. The maximum allowable crosswind depends on the size of aircraft and the condition of the pavement surface. Large jet aircraft can maneuver in crosswinds as high as 40 knots, but it is difficult to do so, and consequently, lower values are used for planning purposes.

For all runways other than utility (constructed and intended for propeller-driven aircraft weighing 12,500 pounds or less), the FAA requires that "runways should be oriented so planes may be landed at least 95 percent of the time with crosswind components not exceeding 15 mph (13 knots)." For utility airports, the crosswind component is reduced to 11.5 mph (10 knots). The "95 percent" criterion required by the FAA is applicable to all conditions of weather.

Runway classifications and markings The FAA classifies runways as visual, nonprecision instrument, and precision instrument. A *visual runway* is intended solely for the operation of aircraft using visual approach procedures, with no straight-in instrument procedure and no instrument designation indicated on an FAA-approved layout plan. A *nonprecision instrument runway* is one having an instrument approach procedure using air navigation facilities with only horizontal guidance for which straight-in nonprecision instrument approach procedure has been approved. A *precision instrument runway* is one having an instrument approach procedure using an instrument landing system (ILS), or a precision approach radar (PAR). Figure 5-4 shows the standard markings required by the FAA for all visual and nonprecision instrument runways. Markings common to all runways include (1) centerlines (2) designator and (3) holding indications. Additional markings for a nonprecision instrument runway include: (4) threshold marking and (5) fixed distance marker.

Figure 5-5 shows the detailed markings of a precision instrument runway. Additional markings for this runway include: (6) touchdown zone markers; and (7) side stripes.

Figure 5-6 shows the markings for a *displaced threshold* (available for takeoff or rollout but not for touchdown) and a *relocated threshold* (area preceding arrows unusable for takeoff or landing). Figure 5-7 shows the markings for intersecting runways. Figures 5-8 and 15-9 show the markings for closed runways and heliports.

Visual runway

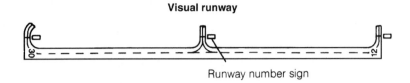

Runway number sign

Nonprecision instrument runway

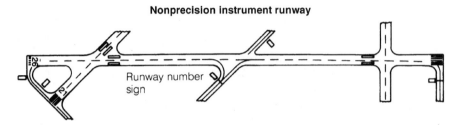

Runway number sign

5-4. *Visual and nonprecision instrument runways.*
Federal Aviation Administration

Detail of precision instrument runway

2. Designator—runway is within 5° of 200° magnetic; "L" indicates left runway of a parallel set

5. Fixed distance marking—1000 feet from approach end; aiming point marker for jets

7. Side stripes—solid line shows lateral usable runway pavement.

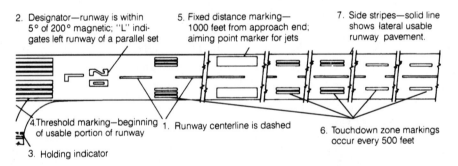

4. Threshold marking—beginning of usable portion of runway

1. Runway centerline is dashed

6. Touchdown zone markings occur every 500 feet

3. Holding indicator

5-5. *Detail of precision instrument runway.* Federal Aviation Administration

Runway lighting Runway lighting is extremely important for a pilot who might have flown for long hours in darkness. Sophisticated lighting systems are also essential for a rapid alignment check during daytime approaches if visibility is poor. For a pilot breaking out of low clouds, high-intensity approach lights are the only visual clue that the ground is near. In fog, even approach lights might hardly be visible, and the bright runway lights will guide the pilot after touchdown.

Fog-plagued airports might have individual lights that peak at an intensity of 30,000 candelas (twice the illumination of a set of car headlights). To prevent disorientation, they can be dimmed—from 100 percent for sunlight or fog, to 1 percent for a clear night.

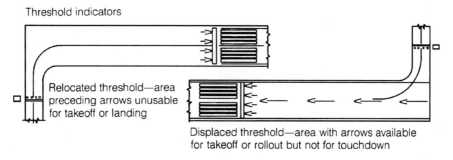

Threshold indicators

Relocated threshold—area preceding arrows unusable for takeoff or landing

Displaced threshold—area with arrows available for takeoff or rollout but not for touchdown

5-6. *Displaced and relocated thresholds.* Federal Aviation Administration

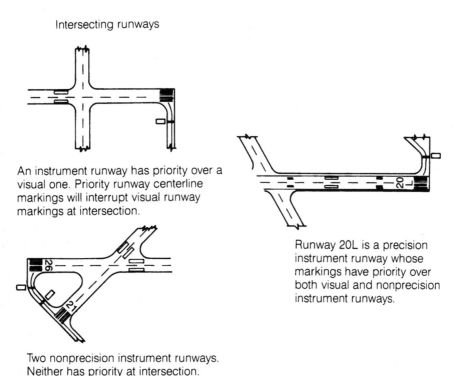

Intersecting runways

An instrument runway has priority over a visual one. Priority runway centerline markings will interrupt visual runway markings at intersection.

Runway 20L is a precision instrument runway whose markings have priority over both visual and nonprecision instrument runways.

Two nonprecision instrument runways. Neither has priority at intersection.

5-7. *Intersecting runway markings.* Federal Aviation Administration

Failure of the electricity supply could be catastrophic to a landing jet, so most civil airports have emergency systems that switch automatically within 15 seconds of a failure, and those with all-weather facilities have a standby system that switches within 1 second. Figure 5-10 shows the lighting system for a precision instrument runway.

Instrument runway landing system The guidance system for approach and landing now in use is the *instrument landing system (ILS)*, which has been the standard system in the United States since 1941

Closed
runways

5-8. *Closed runways.*
Federal Aviation Administration

Temporarily closed runway sign is a simple cross at both ends. A permanently
closed runway will have the "x's" at intervals along its length. Closed taxiways
have the same symbols but smaller and in
yellow.

Civil heliport

Military heliport

5-9. *Heliport markings.*
Federal Aviation Administration

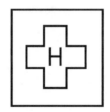

Recommended for
hospitals

and is widely used by civil aviation throughout the world. ILS provides guidance by radio beams that define a straight-line path to the
runway at a fixed slope of approximately 3 degrees and 5 to 7 miles
from the runway threshold. All aircraft approaching the airport under ILS guidance must follow this path in single file, spaced at intervals dictated by standards for safe longitudinal separation and the
need to avoid wake turbulence (Fig. 5-11).

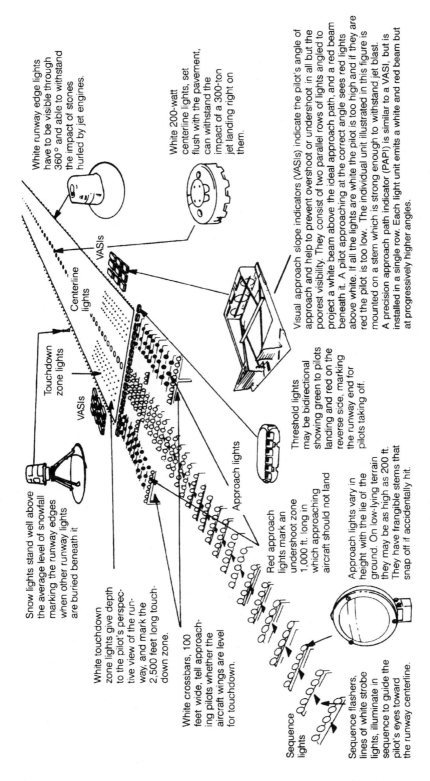

White runway edge lights have to be visible through 360° and able to withstand the impact of stones hurled by jet engines.

White 200-watt centerline lights, set flush with the pavement, can withstand the impact of a 300-ton jet landing right on them.

Snow lights stand well above the average level of snowfall marking the runway edges when other runway lights are buried beneath it

White touchdown zone lights give depth to the pilot's perspective view of the runway, and mark the 2,500 feet long touchdown zone.

White crossbars, 100 feet wide, tell approaching pilots whether the aircraft wings are level for touchdown.

VASIs

Centerline lights

Touchdown zone lights

VASIs

Approach lights

Threshold lights may be bidirectional showing green to pilots landing and red on the reverse side, marking the runway end for pilots taking off.

Red approach lights mark an undershoot zone 1,000 ft. long in which approaching aircraft should not land

Approach lights vary in height with the lie of the ground. On low-lying terrain they may be as high as 200 ft. They have frangible stems that snap off if accidentally hit.

Sequence lights

Sequence flashers, lines of white strobe lights, illuminate in sequence to guide the pilot's eyes toward the runway centerline.

Visual approach slope indicators (VASIs) indicate the pilot's angle of approach and help to prevent overshoot or undershoot in all but the poorest visibility. They consist of two parallel rows of lights angled to project a white beam above the ideal approach path, and a red beam beneath it. A pilot approaching at the correct angle sees red lights above white. If all the lights are white the pilot is too high and if they are red the pilot is too low. The individual unit illustrated in this figure is mounted on a stem which is strong enough to withstand jet blast. A precision approach path indicator (PAPI) is similar to a VASI, but is installed in a single row. Each light unit emits a white and red beam but at progressively higher angles.

5-10. *Precision instrument runway lighting.* Federal Aviation Administration

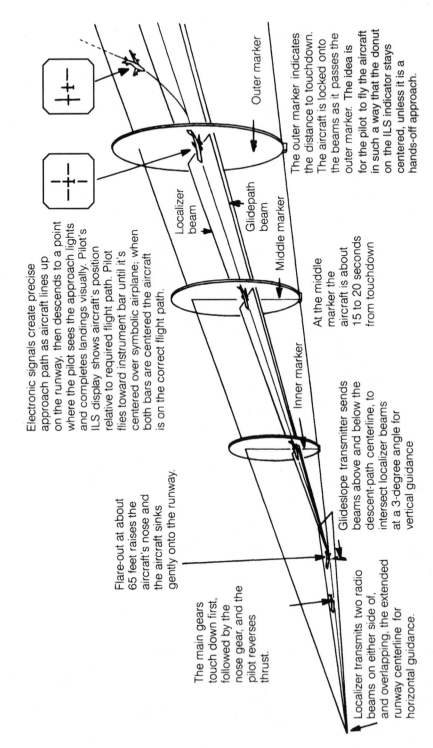

Electronic signals create precise approach path as aircraft lines up on the runway, then descends to a point where the pilot sees the approach lights and completes landings visually. Pilot's ILS display shows aircraft's position relative to required flight path. Pilot flies toward instrument bar until it's centered over symbolic airplane; when both bars are centered the aircraft is on the correct flight path.

Outer marker

Localizer beam

Glidepath beam

Middle marker

The outer marker indicates the distance to touchdown. The aircraft is locked onto the beams as it passes the outer marker. The idea is for the pilot to fly the aircraft in such a way that the donut on the ILS indicator stays centered, unless it is a hands-off approach.

At the middle marker the aircraft is about 15 to 20 seconds from touchdown

Inner marker

Glideslope transmitter sends beams above and below the descent-path centerline, to intersect localizer beams at a 3-degree angle for vertical guidance

Flare-out at about 65 feet raises the aircraft's nose and the aircraft sinks gently onto the runway.

The main gears touch down first, followed by the nose gear, and the pilot reverses thrust.

Localizer transmits two radio beams on either side of, and overlapping, the extended runway centerline for horizontal guidance.

5-11. *Instrument landing system.* Federal Aviation Administration

148

The ILS consists of a *localizer beacon* beam radiating along the straight line of approach to the runway that activates a needle on the aircraft's ILS signal receiver and guides the pilot in the direction toward the runway centerline. This signal can be considered as an electronic extension of the centerline of the runway. The *glideslope transmitter*, set approximately 450 feet to one side of the runway, sends out a different electronic signal that activates a second needle on the same ILS receiver and guides the pilot downward on a sloping path to the runway. This beam, angled at approximately 3 degrees to the horizontal, guides the aircraft down at a steady rate of descent.

By checking a map or chart when nearing the airport, the pilot can navigate to a point or fix close enough to receive both these signals, which will activate the two needles on the ILS receiver. The pilot then begins the descent. The needles will show how far to the right or left or how much above or below the aircraft is in relation to the precise electronic path the pilot must follow at the center of the intersection of the localizer and glideslope signals. The pilot's job is to fly the plane so as to keep the needles on the ILS receiver as close as possible to their center positions on the instrument's face.

As the aircraft descends on the glideslope, it will pass through two electronic markers. The markers transmit vertical beams that penetrate the localizer and glideslope beams and identify precise lateral positions.

The first or *outer marker* is located from 5 to 7 miles from the end of the runway. Its vertical beam activates a rapidly flashing blue light on the marker beacon receiver when the plane passes through. The outer marker also has an audio signal—two dashes per second at a low tone to further alert the pilot to the aircraft's position on the glideslope.

About 3,500 feet from the runway, the *middle marker* vertical beam flashes an amber light on the marker beacon receiver. This marker's audio signal is a series of alternating dots and dashes at a high tone. Just seconds after passing through the middle marker, depending upon the decision height of landing category, the pilot should see the approach lights. The *decision height* is the point where the pilot has to decide whether it is safe to land, or whether to pull up and abort the landing.

Another approach is the *microwave landing system (MLS)*, which has been in the development stage for a number of years. This system transmits a radio beam from left to right and right to left across the sky. By automatically timing the intervals between successive interceptions of the sweeping beam, the landing system can accurately calculate an aircraft's position relative to the runway. It is cheaper than the ILS to install at airports (although the aircraft equipment is more costly) and, because the beams spread more widely, it offers a number of alternative approach paths. In 1995, the FAA canceled the MLS contract and further installations after installing only several units.

The application of satellite technology holds the greatest opportunity to enhance the current landing system. It also should improve aviation system capacity, efficiency, and safety. The foundation for this optimism is the *global positioning system (GPS)*, a satellite-based radio-navigation system operated and controlled by the United States Department of Defense (DoD). In December 1993, DoD declared GPS to be in initial operational capability with 24 satellites in orbit, available, and usable for satellite navigation.

GPS achieves significantly better accuracies than most existing land-based systems because the system provides velocity information and because the satellite signals are propagated independently of the ground (thus, the system is less prone to ground-derived errors). Furthermore, because the satellite signals are available worldwide, GPS represents a unique opportunity for the international aviation community to start converging toward the goal of a single, integrated global navigation and landing satellite system. This will eventually allow aviation users to reduce the number of different types of receivers required for navigation services for all phases of flight. Coupled with satellite communications, GPS will contribute to increased safety and efficiency of international civil aviation by supporting real-time surveillance of aircraft and reducing the separation requirements and increasing the number of flights possible on busy transoceanic flights.

Taxiways The major function of taxiways is to provide access to and from the runways to other areas of the airport including the terminal area in an expeditious manner. *Exit and entrance taxiways* are generally located at the ends of the runway and constructed at right angles to the runway. At busy airports where taxiing traffic moves simultaneously in different directions, *parallel* one-way taxiways are often provided. Taxiways are planned with the following principles in mind:

1 Aircraft that have just landed should not interfere with aircraft taxiing to take off.

2 Taxi routes should provide the shortest distance between the terminal area and the runways.

3 At busy airports, taxiways are normally located at various points along runways so that landing aircraft can leave the runways as quickly as possible. These are also referred to as *exit taxiways* or *turnoffs*.

4 A taxiway designed to permit higher turnoff speeds reduces the time a landing aircraft is on the runway.

5 When possible, taxiways are planned so as not to cross an active runway.

At busy airports, blue edge lights mark the sides of the taxiway and sometimes green center lights mark the route to the active runway. Red stop bars might appear when another aircraft crosses its path. Standard taxiway markings are shown in Fig. 5-12.

Holding areas   *Holding areas* (commonly referred to as *run-up areas*) are located at or very near the ends of runways for pilots to make final checks and await final clearance for takeoff. These areas are generally large enough so that if an aircraft is unable to take off, another aircraft can bypass it. The holding area normally can accommodate two or three aircraft and allow enough space for one aircraft to bypass another.

Holding bays   *Holding bays* are apron areas located at various points off taxiways for temporary storage of aircraft. At some airports where peak demand results in full occupancy at all gate positions, ground control will often route an aircraft to a holding bay until a gate becomes available. Some holding bays, each the size of a football field, are located as close as 250 feet from the active runway. During peak hours, aircraft are held in the bay until given a takeoff position at which time they move to the holding area. See Fig. 5-13 for an example of a holding area and holding bay.

Ground control and parking   An aircraft landing at a major metropolitan airport might have to negotiate a mile or more of taxiways to reach the parking apron area. Pilots normally have a map of the airport layout, and taxiways are marked with lights and other signals. If a pilot loses the way despite the radioed instructions from controllers in the tower giving the route to be taken, an airport truck with a large "Follow Me" sign might be sent to lead the pilot onto the parking apron area.

Taxiways

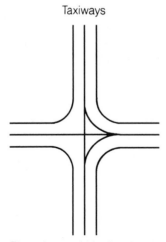

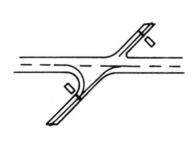

There is no priority for direction of travel at intersecting taxiways. Turns at taxiway intersections may be made safely only if centerlines curve in desired direction.

There is no priority for direction of travel at intersecting taxiways. Turns at taxiway intersections may be made safely only if centerlines curve in desired direction.

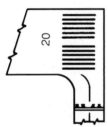

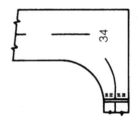

Taxiway markings extend beyond holding indications. However, aircraft must hold short of these lines before taxiing onto the runway unless prior clearance has been received from air traffic control.

Taxiways leading to visual runways at uncontrolled airports may also have hold lines. Pilots should hold here and check for traffic on final approach before turning onto runway.

5-12. *Taxiway markings.* Federal Aviation Administration

Lines painted on the concrete parking apron adjoining the taxiways lead the airline pilot to the final positioning. Linemen will greet the incoming aircraft and direct the pilot with appropriate parking signals (Fig. 5-14). The pilot will attempt to keep the aircraft's nosewheel on the appropriate line while following the lineman's instructions. The aircraft's stopping point must be precise if the jetways (the telescopic walkways joining aircraft to terminal) are to reach the door and be in the correct position. Various optical or electrical devices assist in this maneuver.

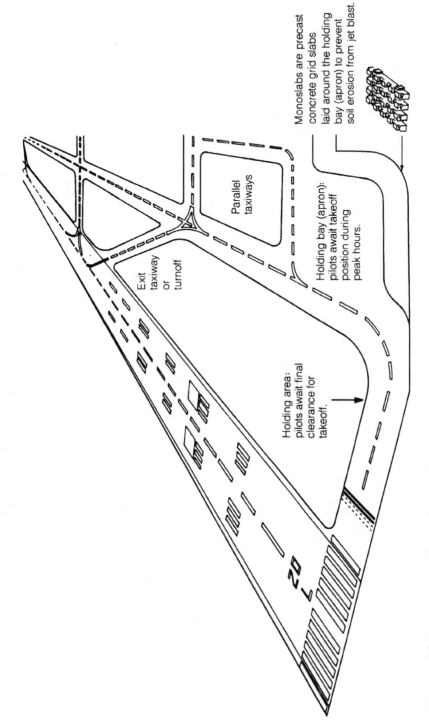

Monoslabs are precast concrete grid slabs laid around the holding bay (apron) to prevent soil erosion from jet blast.

Parallel taxiways

Holding bay (apron): pilots await takeoff position during peak hours.

Exit taxiway or turnoff

Holding area: pilots await final clearance for takeoff.

20 L

5-13. *Holding areas and bays (aprons).* Federal Aviation Administration

Parking apron.

Aircraft can be positioned at various angles with respect to the terminal building, but the nose-in parking position is the most frequently used at major airports (Fig. 5-15). Normally, an aircraft will maneuver into the *nose-in* parking position under its own power; however, in order to leave the gate position, it has to be towed out a sufficient distance to allow it to proceed under its own power.

The nose-in parking position requires the smallest gate area per aircraft. It also causes lower noise levels and there is no jet blast toward the terminal building. Parking close to the building also facilitates passenger loading and unloading.

Aircraft can also be parked in *angled nose-in, angled nose-out,* and *parallel* positions (Fig. 5-16). Generally, these positions are used at smaller airports with less traffic and fewer facilities and equipment. The big advantage of these positions is the ability of the pilot to maneuver in and out of gate positions without the need for towing.

Airport layout plan report

The airport layout plan drawing is normally accompanied by a written report that documents the following items:

1 Reasoning behind the design features such as demand/capacity analysis and so forth.
2 Basis and/or computation for the runway length design.
3 Basis for runway orientation if not aligned for maximum wind coverage.
4 Low visibility wind data where available.

Approach and clear zone layout

The *approach and clear zone layout* is a graphic presentation to scale of the following items:

1 Areas under the imaginary surfaces as defined in FAR Part 77, Objects Affecting Navigable Airspace.
2 Existing and ultimate approach slopes and any height or slope protection established by local zoning ordinance.
3 A plan and profile of the clear zones and approach areas showing the controlling structures and trees therein (usually the tallest object within a cluster) and their elevations. Also, roads, railroads, and pipelines that cross clear zones and approach areas are shown.

5-14. *Lineman signals.* Federal Aviation Administration

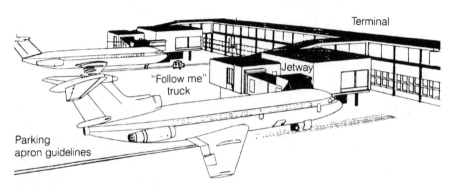

5-15. *Nose-in parking.*

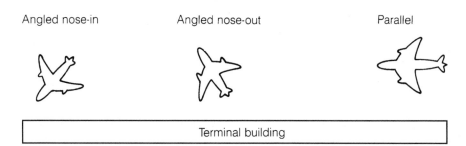

Angled nose-in   Angled nose-out   Parallel

Terminal building

5-16. *Aircraft parking positions.*

4 Location and elevation of obstructions exceeding criteria in FAR Part 77.

5 For airports serving jet aircraft and within the boundaries defined by the imaginary surfaces given in FAR Part 77, an outline of all areas with present or potential concentrations of people is shown on the drawing. The primary type of development in these areas includes industrial developments, residential areas, ballparks, schools, and hospitals. For other airports, this information is shown for the areas under the approach surfaces and at least 1,000 feet to either side of each runway or 500 feet from the nearest aircraft operational area.

6 In the approach areas, tall smokestacks, television, and radio transmission towers, garbage dumps, or other areas attracting a large number of birds, and any other potential hazard to aircraft flight.

FAR Part 77

Obstruction clearance requirements at or near airports are contained in *FAR Part 77*, Objects Affecting Navigable Airspace. An object that protrudes above the imaginary surfaces specified in this part is considered an obstruction to air navigation. If the airport planner finds that there is an obstruction to air navigation, the planner must contact the airport services section of the FAA and seek advice.

In order to determine whether an object is an obstruction to navigable airspace, several imaginary surfaces are established with relation to the airport and to each runway. The size of the imaginary surfaces depends upon the type of approach planned for that runway: visual, nonprecision instrument, and precision instrument.

Northeast Orient 747 parked nose-in at Seattle-Tacoma
International Airport.

The principal imaginary surfaces defined in FAR Part 77 are shown in Fig. 5-17:

1 A surface longitudinally centered on a runway is called a *primary surface*. When the runway has a specially prepared hard surface, the primary surface extends 200 feet beyond each end of that runway, but when the runway has no specially prepared hard surface, or planned hard surface, the primary surface ends at each end of that runway.

2 A *horizontal surface* is a horizontal plane 150 feet above the established airport elevation, the perimeter of which is constructed by swinging arcs of specified radii from the center of each end of the primary surface of each runway of each airport and connecting the adjacent arcs by lines tangent to those arcs.

3 The *conical surface* extends outward and upward from the periphery of the horizontal surface at a slope of 20 horizontal to 1 vertical for a horizontal distance of 4,000 feet.

4 A surface longitudinally centered on the extended runway centerline and extending outward and upward from each end of the primary surface is called the *approach surface*.

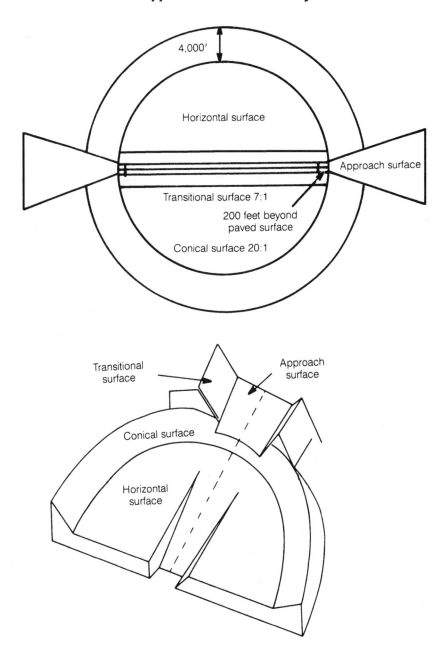

4,000'

Horizontal surface

Approach surface

Transitional surface 7:1

200 feet beyond
paved surface

Conical surface 20:1

Transitional
surface

Approach
surface

Conical surface

Horizontal
surface

5-17. *Imaginary surfaces.* Federal Aviation Administration

5 The *transitional surfaces* extend outward and upward at right angles to the runway centerline and the runway centerline extended at a slope of 7-to-1 from the sides of the primary surface and from the sides of the approach surfaces.

The dimensions of the imaginary surfaces are shown in Table 5-1. FAR Part 77 specifies dimensions for each category of runway coded A, B, C, and D.

Land use plan

The airport *land use plan* shows on-airport land uses as developed by the airport sponsor under the master plan effort and off-airport land uses as developed by surrounding communities. The work of airport, city, regional, and state planners must be carefully coordinated. The configuration of airfield runways, taxiways, and approach zones established in an airport layout plan provides the basis for development of the land use plan for areas on and adjacent to the airport. The land use plan for the airport and its environment in turn is an integral part of an area-wide comprehensive planning program. The location, size, and configuration of the airport needs to be coordinated with patterns of residential and other major land uses in the area, as well as with other transportation facilities and public services. Within the comprehensive planning framework, airport planning, policies, and programs must be coordinated with the objectives, policies, and programs for the area that the master plan airport is to serve.

Land uses on the airport

The amount of acreage within the airport's boundaries will have a major impact on the types of land uses to be found on the airport. For airports with limited acreage, most land uses will be aviation-oriented. Large airports with a great deal of land in excess of what is needed for aeronautical purposes might be used for other uses. For example, many airports lease land to industrial users, particularly those who use business aircraft or whose personnel travel extensively by air carrier or charter. In many cases, taxiway access is provided directly to the company's facility. In some instances, railroad tracks serving the company's area, company parking lots, or low-level warehousing can be located directly under runway approaches (but free of clear zones). Companies that might produce electronic disturbances that would interfere with aircraft navigation or communications equipment or cause visibility problems due to smoke are not compatible airport tenants.

Some commercial activities are suitable for locating within the airport's boundaries. Recreational uses such as golf courses and picnicking ar-

Table 5-1 Imaginary surface dimensions FAR Part 77 (in feet)

| | Visual runway | | Nonprecision instrument runway | | | Precision instrument runway |
| | A | B | A | B | | |
				C	D	
Width of primary surface and approach width at inner end	250	500	500	500	1,000	1,000
Radius of horizontal surface	5,000	5,000	5,000	10,000	10,000	10,000
Approach surface width at end	1,250	1,500	2,000	3,500	4,000	16,000
Approach surface length	5,000	5,000	5,000	10,000	10,000	*
Approach slope	20:1	20:1	20:1	34:1	34:1	*

Categories   **Description**

A   Utility runway—constructed for and intended to be used by propeller-driven aircraft weighing 12,500 lb or less.

B   Runways larger than utility.

C   Visibility minimums greater then ¾ mile.

D   Visibility minimums as low as ¾ mile.

*   Precision instrument approach slope is 50:1 for inner 10,000 feet and 40:1 for an additional 40,000 feet.

Source: FAA

Hangar facilities at Greater Pittsburgh International Airport.
Fred Dupin, Allegheny County Photography

eas are quite suitable for airport land uses and might in effect serve as good buffer areas. Certain agricultural uses are appropriate for airport lands, but grain fields that attract birds are avoided.

Although lakes, reservoirs, rivers, and streams might be appropriate for inclusion within the airport's boundaries, especially from the standpoints of noise or flood control, care is normally taken to avoid those water bodies that have in the past attracted large numbers of waterfowl. Dumps and landfills that might attract birds are also avoided.

Land uses around the airport

The noise problem is the biggest objection voiced by people in areas near the airport. The responsibility for developing land uses around the airport so as to minimize the impact of noise and other environmental problems lies with the local governmental bodies. The more political entities involved, the more complicated the coordination process becomes.

In the past, the most common approach to controlling land uses around the airport was zoning. Airports and their surrounding areas become involved in two types of zoning. The first type of zoning is *height and hazard zoning*, which protects the airport and its approaches from obstructions to aviation while restricting certain elements of community growth. FAR Part 77, Objects Affecting Navigable Airspace, is the basis for height and hazard zoning.

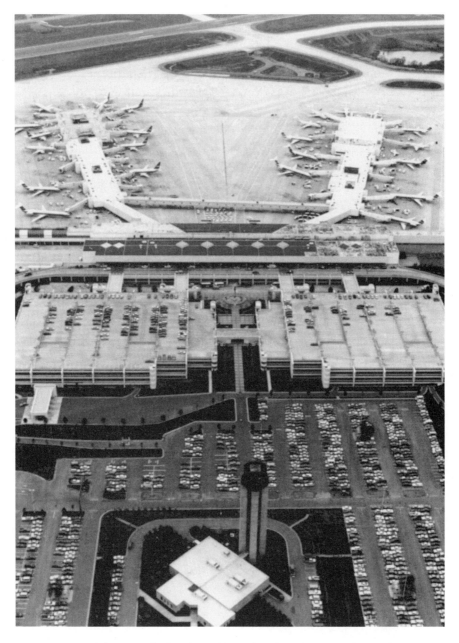

A symmetrical view of Charlotte/Douglas International Airport showing the airport's twin parking decks, terminal building, and four concourses. The 150-foot FAA control tower is in the foreground and a 15-foot sculpture of Queen Charlotte, whom the city was named after, is centered between the twin parking decks.

The second type of zoning is *land use zoning*. This type of zoning has several shortcomings. First, it is not retroactive and does not affect preexisting uses that might conflict with airport operations. Secondly, jurisdictions with zoning powers (usually cities, towns, or counties) might not take effective zoning action. This is partly because the airport might affect several jurisdictions and coordination of zoning is difficult. Or the airport might be located in a rural area where the county lacks zoning powers and the sponsoring city might not be able to zone outside its political boundaries. Another problem is that the interest of the community is not always consistent with the needs and interests of the aviation industry. The locality might want more tax base, population growth, and rising land values, all of which are not often consistent with the need to preserve the land around the airport for other than residential uses.

Another approach to land use planning around the airport is *subdivision regulations*. Provisions can be written into the regulations prohibiting residential construction in intense noise exposure areas. These areas can be determined by acoustical studies prior to development. Insulation requirements can be made a part of the local building codes, without which the building permits cannot be issued.

Finally, another alternative in controlling land use around the airport is the relocation of residences and other incompatible uses. Often urban renewal funds are used for this purpose.

Key terms

> airport layout plan
> airport layout plan drawing
> airport layout
> location map
> vicinity map
> basic data table
> wind rose
> airside facilities (aeronautical surfaces)
> landside facilities
> single runway

parallel runways

open-V runways

intersecting runways

visual runway

nonprecision instrument runway

precision instrument runway

displaced threshold

relocated threshold

instrument landing system (ILS)

localizer beacon

glideslope transmitter

outer marker

middle marker

decision height

microwave landing system (MLS)

global positioning system (GPS)

exit and entrance taxiways

parallel taxiways

holding areas

holding bays (aprons)

nose-in, angled nose-in, angled nose-out, and parallel parking

approach and clear zone layout

FAR Part 77

primary surface

horizontal surface

conical surface

approach surface

transitional surfaces

land use plan

height and hazard zoning

land use zoning

subdivision regulations

Review questions

1 What is an airport layout plan drawing? Describe the information included in the airport layout section of the drawing. What other items are included in the drawing?

2 Define airside facilities. Describe the four basic runway configurations.

- What is the FAA's requirement with regard to runway orientation and the prevailing wind? Is it the same for utility and nonutility airports?

- Describe the following runway classifications: visual, nonprecision instrument, and precision instrument. What is meant by a displaced threshold? A relocated threshold?

- Describe the lighting system for a precision instrument runway.

3 How does the ILS work?

- What is the microwave landing system (MLS)? The global positioning system (GPS)?

- Describe the basic principles in laying out taxiways. Distinguish between holding areas and holding bays.

- What are the four basic aircraft parking positions? Which is the most popular at major airports? Why?

- What is the airport layout plan report?

4 What is the approach and clear zone layout? Describe the "imaginary surfaces" described in FAR Part 77. What is a utility runway?

5 What nonaviation land uses would be compatible with aviation activities within the airport boundary? Which would not?

- What is the biggest problem when residential communities are built adjacent to the airport? Discuss some possible solutions to this problem.

- Which type of businesses might be appropriate airport neighbors?

Suggested readings

Doganis, Rigas. *The Airport Business.* New York: Routledge, Chapman and Hall, Inc., 1992.

Horonjeff, Robert, and Francis McKelvey. *Planning and Design of Airports,* 4th Ed. New York: McGraw-Hill, 1994.

DOT/FAA advisory circulars

70/7460-1H	Obstruction Marking and Lighting
70/7460-2I	Proposed Construction or Alteration of Objects That May Affect the Navigable Airspace
150/5020-1	Noise Control and Compatibility Planning for Airports
150/5070-3	Planning the Airport Industrial Park
150/5070-6A	Airport Master Plans
150/5300-13	Airport Design Standards
150/5320-5B	Airport Drainage
150/5050-2	Compatible Land Use Planning in the Vicinity of Airports
150/5100-5	Land Acquisition in the Federal-Aid Airport Program
150/5190-3	Model Airport Zoning Ordinance
150/5340-1G	Standards for Airport Markings
150/5340-4C	Installation Details for Runway Centerline Touch-down Zone Lighting Systems
150/5340-14B	Economy Approach Lighting Aids
150/5340-5B	Segmented Circle Airport Marker System
150/5340-17B	Standby Power for Non-FAA Airport Lighting Systems
150/5340-18C	Standards for Airport Sign Systems
150/5340-19	Taxiway Centerline Lighting System
150/5340-21	Airport Miscellaneous Lighting Visual Aids
150/5340-24	Runway and Taxiway Edge Lighting System
150/5340-26	Maintenance of Airport Visual Aid Facilities
150/5345-28D	Precision Approach Path Indicator
150/5345-39B	FAA Specification L-853, Runway and Taxiway Centerline Retroreflective Markers
150/5345-44F	Specification for Taxiway and Runway Signs
150/5345-46A	Specification for Runway and Taxiway Light Fixtures
150/5345-50	Specification for Portable Runway Lights
150/5370-10A	Standards for Specifying Construction of Airports
150/5370-2C	Operational Safety on Airports During Construction

Federal Aviation Regulations (FARs)

Part 77	Objects Affecting Navigable Airspace
Part 153	Acquisition of U.S. Land for Public Airports
Part 157	Notice of Construction, Alteration, Activation, and Deactivation of Airports

6

Terminal area and airport access plans

Outline

- Introduction: Continuation of phase three
- Terminal area plans
- Airport access plans

Objectives

When you have completed this chapter, you should be able to:

- Define "terminal area."
- Describe the primary objective of the terminal area plans.
- Discuss some of the factors taken into consideration by airport planners in selecting a terminal area concept.
- Summarize the advantages and disadvantages of the centralized and decentralized passenger processing systems.
- Distinguish between the four terminal building design concepts.
- Explain what is meant by the passenger handling system and identify the processing links.
- List some of the terminal building facilities occupied by airport operations and management, airline operations, and government agencies.
- Describe the flow of domestic, international, and transfer passengers through the terminal.

- Define "general concept evaluation" and "criteria for design and development."
- Identify the steps involved in determining space requirements.
- Describe the purpose of the airport access plans.

Introduction: Continuation of phase three

This chapter completes phase three of the airport master plan with a discussion of the terminal area and airport access plans. The development of the terminal area plan, plans for components within the terminal area, and airport access plans evolve from demand/capacity analysis and from the airfield configurations and land use criteria established in the airport layout and land use plans. This does not mean that the terminal area concept that is selected for a particular airport will not have a vital impact on the airport layout plan. The airfield configuration and the terminal area configuration must fit together and adjustments in both layouts must be made as the master plan evolves. Regardless of these necessary design adjustments, the details of the terminal area plan will follow the development of the airport layout plan.

The *terminal area* is the area used or intended to be used for such facilities as terminal and cargo buildings; gates, hangars, shops, and other service buildings; automobile parking, airport motels, restaurants, garages, and vehicle service—facilities used in connection with the airport; and entrance and service roads used by the public within the boundaries of the airport.

The airport terminal—the building itself and the paved areas surrounding it on the airside and the landside—is the zone of transition for passengers, providing the link between surface and air transportation. Design and operation of the terminal have an influence on both airside capacity and ground access and the overall rate at which aircraft can be handled. The basic relationship, illustrated in Fig. 6-1, dictates the design of the terminal complex.

Terminal area plans

The primary objective of the terminal area plans is to achieve an acceptable balance between passenger convenience, operating effi-

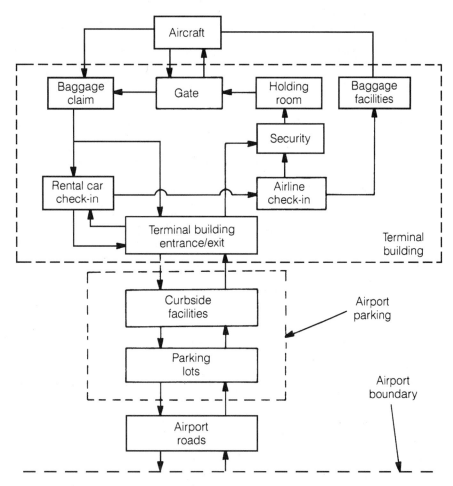

6-1 *Airport landside functional flow.*

ciency, facility investment, and aesthetics. The physical and psychological comfort characteristics of the terminal area should afford the passenger orderly and convenient progress from automobile or public transportation through the terminal to the aircraft and back again.

One of the most important factors affecting the air traveler is walking distance. It begins when the passenger leaves the ground transportation vehicle and continues on to the ticket counter and to the point at which he or she boards the aircraft. Consequently, terminals are planned to minimize the walking distance by developing convenient auto parking facilities, convenient movements of passengers through the terminal complex, and conveyances that will permit fast and efficient handling of baggage. The planner normally establishes objectives for average walking distances from terminal points to parked aircraft. Conveyances for passengers such as moving walks and baggage handling systems are also considered.

The functional arrangement of the terminal area complex with the airside facilities is designed so as to be flexible enough to meet the operating characteristics of the airline industry for handling passengers and for fast ground servicing of aircraft so that minimum gate occupancy time and maximum airline operating economy will be achieved.

The final objective of the terminal area plans is to develop a complex that provides all necessary services within an optimum expenditure of funds from the standpoints of capital investment and maintenance and operating costs. This takes into account flexibility and costs that will be required in future expansions of the terminal area.

Terminal area factors

In the selection of a terminal area concept, the following factors are taken into consideration by airport planners:

A Passengers

    1 Adequate terminal area curb space for private and public transportation.

Tom Bradley International Terminal at Los Angeles International Airport.

2 Minimum walking distance—automobile parking to ticket counter.

3 Minimum walking distance—ticket counter to passenger holding area and holding area to aircraft.

4 Passenger transportation—where long distances must be traversed.

5 Pedestrian walkways to aircraft—as backup to mechanical transportation systems for passengers.

6 Efficiency of passenger interline connection.

7 Baggage handling—enplaning and deplaning.

8 Convenient hotel-motel accommodations.

9 Efficient handling of visitors and sightseers at the airport.

B Passenger vehicles

1 Public automobile flow separation from service and commercial traffic.

2 Public transportation to and from the airport.

3 Public parking—long-term (3 hours or more) and short-term (less than 3 hours).

4 Airport employee parking.

5 Airline employee parking.

6 Public auto service area.

7 Rental car parking and service areas.

C Airport operations

1 Separation of apron vehicles from moving and parked aircraft.

2 Passenger flow separation in the terminal building (departing and arriving).

3 Passenger flow separation from apron activities.

4 Concession availability and exposure to public.

5 Airfield security and prevention of unauthorized access to apron and airfield.

6 Air cargo and freight forwarder facilities.

7 Airport maintenance shops and facilities.

8 Airfield and apron drainage.

9 Airfield and apron utilities.

10 Utility plants, and heating and air conditioning systems.

11 Fire and rescue facilities and equipment.

D Aircraft

1 Efficient aircraft flow on aprons and between terminal aprons and taxiways.

2 Easy and efficient maneuvering of aircraft parking at gate positions.

3 Aircraft fueling.

4 Heliport areas.

5 General aviation areas.

6 Noise, fumes, and blast control.

7 Apron space for staging and maneuvering of aircraft service equipment.

E Safety

1 Enplaning and deplaning at aircraft.

2 Elevators, escalators, stairs, and ramps as to location, speed, and methods of access and egress.

3 People-mover systems as to location, speed, methods of access and egress.

4 Road crossings as to protection of pedestrians.

5 Provisions for disabled persons.

The planner must also take into consideration expansion capabilities to accommodate increasing passenger volumes and aircraft gate positions. In addition, the planner must provide a proper balance between capital investment, aesthetics, operation, and maintenance costs, and passengers and airport revenues.

Specific planning criteria are developed for the aforementioned factors and for major terminal area components. Information for terminal requirements is obtained from the air carriers, general aviation interests, airport concessionaires, airport management, and special technical committees. The criteria are analyzed and agreed upon by all parties involved before it is incorporated in the master plan. It is essential that coordination with airport interests and users be effected before the final selection of a terminal area concept is made.

Terminal building design concepts

Airport terminal buildings can be categorized as either centralized, decentralized, or a combination of the two (hybrid). *Centralized passenger processing* means all the facilities for ticketing, baggage check-in, security, customs, and immigration are all done in one building and used for processing all passengers using the building. Advantages and disadvantages of a centralized passenger processing terminal are as follows:

Advantages

1 Centralizes airline, airport, and international processing personnel, thus reducing costs.
2 Facilitates control of passengers—transfers and security.
3 Provides for simplified vehicular and pedestrian information systems.
4 Centralizes passenger services and amenities.

Disadvantages

1 Generates vehicular congestion at curbside.
2 Creates pedestrian congestion at check-in processing areas.
3 Develops long walking distances from parking areas to processing areas.
4 Limits expansion.

Decentralized passenger processing means the passenger handling facilities are provided in smaller units and repeated in one or more buildings. Advantages and disadvantages of a decentralized passenger processing terminal are as follows:

Advantages

1 Optimizes the level of service/convenience for passengers.
2 Minimizes walking distances.
3 Clarifies circulation, providing direct passenger flow.
4 Disperses vehicular circulation for curbside drop-off and parking.
5 Provides potential for growth through modular construction.
6 Accommodates diverse modes of transportation for passenger access/egress.

Disadvantages

1 Necessitates decentralization of personnel for airline, airport, and governmental processing activities.
2 Increases capital costs per gate.
3 Increases operating and maintenance costs.

There are four terminal building design concepts, each of which can be used with varying degrees of centralization: (1) gate arrival; (2) pier finger; (3) satellite; and (4) transporter. These concepts are shown in Fig. 6-2.

Gate arrival The *gate arrival* concept is a centralized layout that is aimed at reducing the walking distance by bringing the automobile as close as possible to the aircraft. The most fundamental type of gate arrival concept is the *simple terminal*. It consists of a single common waiting and ticketing area with several exits onto a small aircraft parking apron. It is adaptable to airports with low airline activity and is also adaptable to general aviation operations whether it is located as a separate entity on a large airline-served airport or is the operational center for an airport used exclusively by general aviation. Where the simple terminal serves airline operations, it will usually have an apron that provides close-in parking for three to six

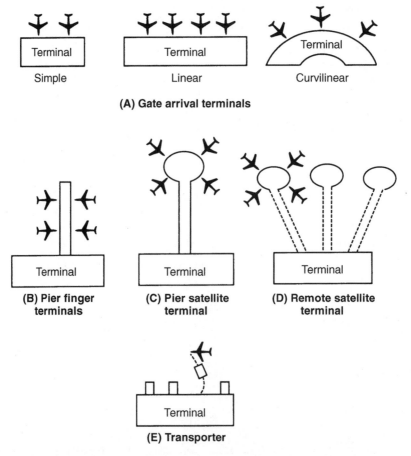

(A) Gate arrival terminals

(B) Pier finger terminals

(C) Pier satellite terminal

(D) Remote satellite terminal

(E) Transporter

6-2 *Terminal building design concepts.*

commercial transport aircraft. Where the simple terminal serves general aviation only, it is within convenient walking distance of aircraft parking areas and adjacent to an aircraft service apron. The simple terminal normally consists of a single-level structure where access to aircraft is afforded by a walk across the aircraft parking apron. The layout of the simple terminal takes into account the possibility of linear extension for terminal expansion.

The *linear* or *curvilinear terminal* concept is merely an extension of the simple terminal concept—that is, the simple terminal is repeated in a linear extension to provide additional apron frontage, more gates, and more room within the terminal for passenger processing. The more sophisticated linear terminals often feature a two-level structure where enplaning passengers are processed direct from curb to aircraft on one level while the other level is used by deplaning passengers for baggage claim and access to ground transportation. Passenger walking distance from curb through terminal to aircraft is short, usually 75 to 100 feet. The linear configuration also lends itself to the development of adequate, close-in public parking. Ample curb frontage for loading and unloading ground transportation vehicles is provided with each extension of the linear terminal and there is a direct relationship of enplaning or deplaning curb frontage to departing or arriving aircraft. Linear terminals can be expanded with almost no interference to passenger processing or aircraft operations. Expansion may be accomplished by linear extension of the existing structure or by developing two or more linear terminal units.

The linear concept does not require long concourses, fingers, satellites, or service buildings, but it does not lend itself to common facilities such as waiting rooms, concessions, ticket counters, or hold rooms. These facilities are usually repeated with each linear extension. At large airports, the concept can also require an extensive system of directional signs because enplaning passengers must not only be directed to the correct airline area but also to the correct passenger processing module within that area. Another problem with the concept is that on a return flight to the airport, passengers might find that the deplaning module is located a long distance from where they parked the cars at the enplaning module. These factors must be taken into account in comparing the operating and construction costs of the linear terminal with other concepts. The configuration of the space occupied by the linear concept must also be compared with the space and configurations of other concepts in determining their compatibility with particular airport situations.

Pier finger The *pier finger terminal* concept evolved in the 1950s when gate concourses were added to simple terminal buildings. Since then, very sophisticated forms of the concept have been developed with the addition of hold rooms at gates, jetways, and aircraft loading bridges, and vertical separation of the ticketing check-in function from the baggage claim function; however, the basic concept has not changed in that the main terminal building is used to process passengers and baggage while the finger or pier provides a means of enclosed access from the central terminal to aircraft gate. Aircraft are parked at gates along the pier, as opposed to the satellite concept, where they are parked in a cluster at the end of a concourse.

Walking distances through finger terminals are long, averaging 400 feet or more. Curb space must be carefully planned because it depends on the length of the central terminal and is not related to the total number of gates afforded by fingers. This is particularly true of deplaning curbs near centralized baggage claim facilities.

Although the finger concept has afforded one of the most economical means of adding gate positions to existing terminals, its use for expansion is limited because it takes valuable apron space. Planners also must be aware not to add new pier fingers without providing adequate space for passenger processing in the main terminal.

Satellite terminals The primary feature of the *satellite terminal* concept is the provision of a single terminal (with all ticketing, baggage handling, and ancillary services) that is connected by concourses to one or more satellite structures. The features of the satellite concept are very similar to those of the finger concept except that aircraft gates are located at the end of a long concourse rather than being spaced at even intervals along the concourse. Satellite gates are usually served by a common hold room rather than individual hold rooms. Another feature is that the concourse can be located underground (*remote satellite*), thereby providing space for aircraft taxi operations between the main terminal and the satellite.

The distance from the main terminal to a satellite is usually well above the average distance to gates found with the finger concept; therefore, people-mover systems are provided between terminal and satellite at many airports to reduce walking distances.

One of the advantages of the satellite concept is that it lends itself to a compact central terminal with common areas for processing passengers.

International terminal lobby at San Francisco International Airport.
San Francisco International Airport

In some instances where terminal area space is limited, structural parking is provided above the central terminal building.

Aircraft maneuvering areas are required around satellites so that push-out tug operations do not cause aircraft to block active taxiways. Wedge-shaped aircraft parking positions around the satellite also tend to crowd the operation of aircraft servicing equipment.

Terminals developed under the satellite concept are difficult to expand without reducing ramp frontage or disrupting airport operations; therefore, increases in terminal capacity are usually effected by the addition of terminal units rather than expansion of an existing unit.

Mobile lounge or transporter The *mobile lounge or transporter* concept is in use at a number of airports including Dulles International and Tampa International airports. It is sometimes called the *remote aircraft parking* concept. Aircraft parking aprons are remote from the terminal building. The mobile lounges transport passengers from the building to aircraft and can be used as hold rooms at terminal building gate positions. In this concept, the aircraft gate positions are placed in parallel rows at required spacings with mobile lounge and service vehicle roads running between the parallel rows

Vehicular circular drive at the Greater Pittsburgh International Airport. Fred Dupin, Allegheny County Photography

of aircraft. Several sets of parallel aircraft parking rows can be provided for ultimate development of gate positions. Airline operations buildings must be provided adjacent to aircraft parking aprons.

With the mobile lounge concept, walking distances are held to a minimum because the compact terminal building contains common passenger processing facilities and curb frontage can be located directly across the terminal building from mobile lounge gates. Building and curb length, which is established in part by the number of mobile lounge gates, must be carefully planned to provide adequate frontage for enplaning and deplaning passengers.

The concept has good expansion capability in that capacity can be increased by the addition of mobile lounges and the main terminal and aprons can be expanded without the addition of extensive concourses, fingers, or satellites. With the mobile lounge concept, additions can be made with little impedance to airport operations and aircraft movements.

Aircraft maneuvering capability is excellent with this concept. Remote aircraft parking can reduce taxi time and distance to runways and avoid aircraft congestion next to terminal building facilities. This also removes the aircraft noise and jet blast problem from the building area. Mobile lounges must be capable of mating with various aircraft sill heights and terminal building floor heights.

In comparing the mobile lounge concept with other concepts, the cost of independent terminal and service buildings and the purchase, operation, and maintenance of mobile lounges must be considered. The time required to move passengers between terminal and aircraft by mobile lounge also has to be taken into consideration by the planner.

These concepts are embodied in pure form only at a few airports that have been built on entirely new sites, such as Dallas-Fort Worth (Fig. 6-3). At most airports the design of the terminal building has evolved and been modified in response to traffic growth and local conditions, giving rise to a hybrid that incorporates features of two or more of the basic

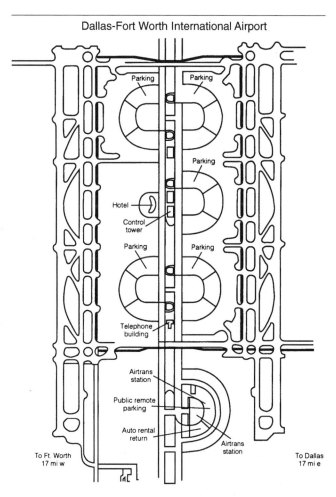

6-3 *Pure concept (curvilinear gate arrival).*

concepts (Figs. 6-4 and 6-5). At airports with land available adjacent to the existing facility, the design has tended to evolve into a pier finger arrangement, sometimes with separate unit terminals for commuter airlines or groups of new air carriers for whom there is not room in the main terminal. At airports where the terminal has grown to the limits of available land area, satellite terminals and remote parking have typically developed. Transporter and satellite terminal concepts utilizing people-moving equipment have been adopted at some airports to enhance the attractiveness of the terminal for passengers because they eliminate the extreme walking distances associated with long piers extending from central terminals.

Overestimation or underestimation of traffic volume or the type of service to be provided can sometimes render even a well-conceived design inefficient or inappropriate. Dallas-Fort Worth Airport, for example, was planned with the expectation that origin-destination traffic would predominate. Since airline deregulation, the growth of hub and spoke net-

La Guardia Airport

Lower level

Baggage claim area
Buses
Car rental
Hotel/motel reservation phones
Limousine service
Lounges
Baggage service no flights
from LGA

Upper level

Approximate walking
distance from one end of
the terminal to the other is
1300 feet

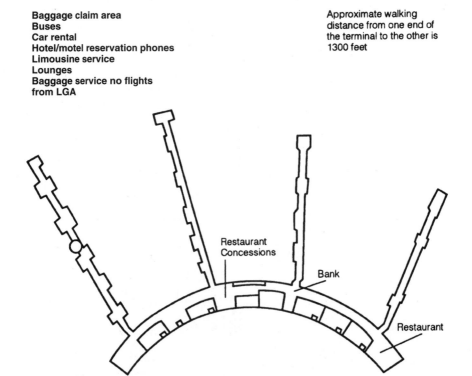

6-4 *Hybrid concept (separate concourses with transporters).*

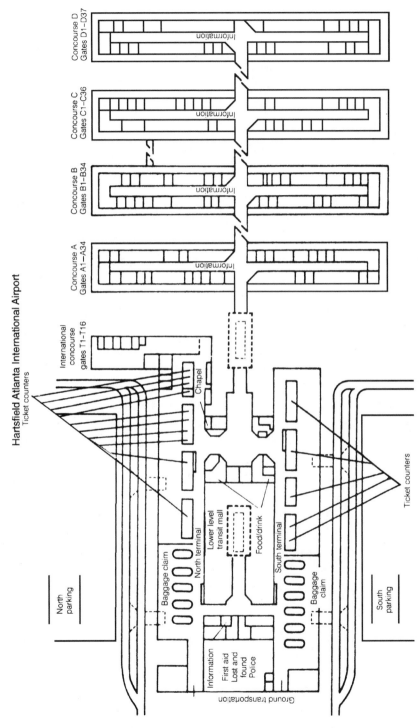

Hartsfield Atlanta International Airport

Ticket counters

Concourse A Gates A1–A34

Concourse B Gates B1–B34

Concourse C Gates C1–C36

Concourse D Gates D1–D37

Information

International concourse gates T1–T16

Chapel

Lower level transit mall

Food/drink

North terminal

South terminal

Baggage claim

Baggage claim

Information

First aid

Lost and found

Police

Ticket counters

North parking

South parking

Ground transportation

6-5 *Hybrid concept (separate concourses with transporters).*

works, which typically requires passengers to change planes at the airport, has thwarted the effectiveness and convenience of the design. At Chicago O'Hare Airport, the need to adapt the concourses for passenger security screening has created long and circuitous routes for transferring passengers. Efforts to encourage greater use of Dulles Airport in Virginia for short- and medium-length domestic flights have been hindered by the design of the terminal because the need to go from apron to terminal and back again by mobile lounges greatly increases the time and inconvenience of interline connection. New York Kennedy Airport, planned with separate terminals for major airlines, is well suited for origin-destination passengers and for transfers to flights on the same airline, but very inconvenient for interlining domestic passengers and those coming in on international flights and continuing to other U.S. destinations.

Clearly, no single design is best for all circumstances. Traffic patterns, traffic volume, and flow characteristics (peaking), the policies of individual carriers using the airport, and local considerations (esthetics and civic pride) dictate different choices from airport to airport and from one time to another. The airport planner, who is required to anticipate conditions 10 to 15 years in the future, must often resort to guesswork. Even if the guess is correct initially, conditions change and result in a mismatch between terminal architecture and the traffic to be served. To guard against this, airport planners now tend to favor flexible designs that can be expanded modularly or offer the opportunity for low-cost, simple modifications as future circumstances might demand.

The passenger handling system

The *passenger handling system* is a series of links and processes that a passenger goes through in transferring from one mode of transportation to another. These processes include (1) access/egress; (2) access/processing interface; (3) processing; and (4) flight interface.

Access/egress The *access/egress* link includes all of the ground transportation facilities, vehicles, and other modal transfer facilities required to move the passenger to and from the airport. Included are:

1 Highways.
2 Rail and metropolitan train service.
3 Autos, taxicabs, buses, and limousine service.
4 V/STOL facilities.
5 Transfer stations—off- and on-airport parking sites and rail stations.

Access/processing interface The next link or process is the *access/processing interface,* in which the passenger makes the transition from the vehicular mode of transportation to pedestrian movement into the passenger processing activities. Activities here include loading and unloading of passengers from vehicles at curbside and pedestrian circulation from surface and parking facilities. Facilities include:

1 Vehicular circular drive for loading and unloading passengers.

2 Sidewalks, shuttle buses, and other automated conveyance systems to and from parking facilities.

3 Bus stops, taxi stands, and limousine stops.

Passenger processing The *passenger processing link* accomplishes the major processing activities required to prepare the passenger for using air transportation. Primary activities include ticketing, baggage check-in, security, and passport check on the enplaning cycle, and baggage claim, passport check, and customs check on the deplaning cycle. Facilities include:

1 Ticketing and baggage check-in counters.

2 Counters for security, customs, health, and immigration.

3 Terminal waiting lobbies.

4 Baggage claim area.

Flight information Display Systems (FIDS) at the entrance to the west wing of the D gates at McCarran International Airport, Las Vegas, NV. Clark County Department of Aviation.

International Satellite Terminal at Miami International Airport.
Metro-Dade Aviation Department

Pier finger with loading bridges at Baltimore-Washington International Airport. Federal Aviation Administration

Spanning 31,000 square feet, the atrium is a focal point of the main terminal at Orlando International Airport.
Greater Orlando Aviation Authority.

5 Visitor departure and arrival waiting areas.

6 Space for passenger movement and circulation.

7 Visitor observation area and lounges.

8 Public service areas including restrooms, baggage lockers, first aid facilities, lost and found, nursery, TV lounge, hotel-reservation desks, post office, and place of worship.

9 Information booths and displays for flight schedules and other flight-related announcements, and for giving directions for movement within the terminal building.

10 Eating and drinking facilities including snack shops, coffee shops, bars, restaurants, private banquet rooms, kitchens, automatic food dispensers, and water fountains.

11 Concessions, including news/flowers/gifts/books/candy, beauty, and barber shops, cleaning/valet, banks, car rental agencies, insurance, and duty-free shops, currency exchange services, tourist information/accommodation services (at international airports).

Flight interface The *flight interface* provides the link between the passenger processing activities and the flight. Facilities include:

1 Gate lounges and counters.

2 Moving sidewalks, buses, and mobile lounges (transporters).

3 Loading facilities including jetways, nose bridges, stairs, and escalators.

4 Facilities for transferring between flights including corridors, waiting areas, and mobile conveyance facilities.

Facilities for airport operations and management

The terminal building normally houses the facilities for airport operations and management. These include:

1 Office space for airport administrative and operations personnel.

2 Storage facilities for maintenance supplies, materials, tools, and equipment.

3 Repair shops and offices.

4 Mechanical/utility system space such as air conditioning and heating, boilers and water supply, electrical service and equipment, elevator-escalator machinery rooms, emergency equipment (generators), and communications (telephones and radio).

5 Employee lounges, food and beverage facilities, and restrooms.

6 Fire, crash, and rescue facilities.

Facilities for airline operations

Space in the terminal building must be available for the following airline operations:

1 Operations offices adjacent to passenger handling counters.

2 Control/dispatch offices for such flight-related activities as flight planning and associated administrative duties.

3 Hospitality/VIP lounges.

4 Employee/aircrew lounges.

5 Telecommunications facilities.

6 Baggage handling facilities, including conveyors, sorting equipment, and baggage carts.

Facilities for government agencies

While government agencies might not necessarily be housed in the terminal building, space for their functions must be provided near the passenger handling system. These include the FAA, weather service, postal service, customs, immigration and naturalization, agriculture, health, and security services.

Passenger flow through the terminal

A terminal building is designed around the passengers' needs and wants. By locating passenger processing points conveniently and in a logical order, terminal designers aim to keep passengers moving through the system in a smooth flow with a minimum of delay; however, passenger traffic follows an irregular pattern, peaking at certain times of the day and year, so public areas must be large enough to accommodate peak crowds including friends and relatives.

Passengers can be divided into three primary groups: (1) domestic; (2) international; and (3) transfer.

Domestic passengers   The domestic long-haul or short-haul business traveler generally arrives at the terminal shortly before departure, frequently alone and with relatively little baggage. Business travelers prefer fast service. They are generally familiar with the airport and need to be processed quickly.

Leisure passengers generally arrive at the airport an hour or so before departure, bringing much more luggage than the average business traveler. They are generally unfamiliar with the airport layout, which means more time spent in the terminal. These passengers, plus their friends and relatives, frequent the concessions to a greater degree than do business travelers.

A domestic departure passenger would enter the general concourse (which is A in Fig. 6-6) and proceed to the ticket counter, where tickets are verified and baggage loads totalled. The passenger would then proceed to the security checkpoint (B) and onto the gate serving his or her flight. A domestic arrival would depart the aircraft, leave the gate area, go to the baggage claim area (C) to pick up luggage, and depart the airport terminal via the general concourse (A).

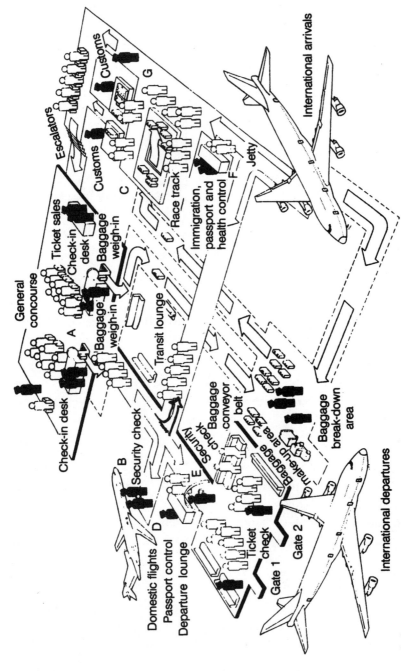

General concourse

Check-in desk

Ticket sales

Check-in desk

Baggage weigh-in

Baggage weigh-in

Escalators

Customs

Customs

Transit lounge

Immigration, passport and health control

Race track

International arrivals

Jetty

Security check

Security check

Baggage conveyor belt

Baggage make-up area

Baggage break-down area

Domestic flights

Passport control

Departure lounge

Ticket check

Gate 1

Gate 2

International departures

A B C D E F G

6-6 *Passenger flow through the terminal.*

190

Skyride, Miami International Airport. Metro-Dade Aviation Department

International passengers International flights are similar to long-haul flights and possess many of the characteristics of those flown by leisure passengers. Passengers tend to check in early because processing time for international flights is longer. Consequently, they tend to utilize the concessions and other facilities to a great degree. An international departure follows a pattern similar to that of the domestic departure. The traveler proceeds from the general concourse (A), after ticket verification and baggage check-in to passport control (D), then through security (E) on to a specific concourse (area between the general concourse and gate area), and then to a gate area.

An international arrival leaves the aircraft and goes directly to immigration, passport, and health control (F). The arrival passenger then proceeds to the baggage claim area (C). The passenger then goes to the customs area (G) for an inspection of luggage and then on to the general concourse (A) to leave the terminal.

Transfer passengers A transfer passenger is one who transfers from one flight to a connecting flight. The domestic transfer passenger simply proceeds from one specific concourse to the boarding gate of the next flight. The transfer passenger flow is somewhat complicated when domestic and international flights are mixed. A domestic arrival passenger transferring to an international departure must go to the airline ticket counter for a passport verification before proceeding to the international gate.

Loading bridges are part of the flight interface. USAR

An international arrival passenger goes through immigration and the baggage claim area after departing the aircraft. The traveler then proceeds through customs for an inspection check and on to the general concourse to purchase a ticket for the domestic departure. An international traveler transferring to another international flight generally goes directly to an international transit lounge, then proceeds to the international departure gate for the connecting flight.

Vertical distribution of passenger flow

Many of the larger airports distribute the passenger flow over several levels within the airport terminal. The primary purpose of distributing passenger processing activities over several levels is to separate the flow of arriving and departing passengers. The question of how many levels a terminal building should have depends primarily on the volume of passengers. It is also influenced by the type of passengers: domestic, international, and transfer.

Figure 6-7 shows a cross section of the major functional areas in a multilevel passenger terminal. Departing passengers park their vehicles (1) and proceed via the bridge level (3) into the terminal or are dropped off at the vehicular circular drive (enplane drive) (5). Ticketing lobby (6), concourse (11), and gate area (14) are all on the first level. Arriving passengers proceed from the gate area (14) through the concourse (11) to the baggage claim area (7). After claiming their baggage, they proceed to the parking facility (1) via the bridge level

The underground transit mall at Hartsfield Atlanta International Airport links the terminal buildings with the four domestic concourses. It offers three modes of transportation for passengers and visitors: walk, step onto a moving sidewalk, or use the automated train system. Hartsfield Atlanta International Airport

(3) or are picked up at the ground level (deplane drive—4). Notice that the airport offices (10), mechanical, storage and maintenance facilities (8) and service vehicle drive (2) are located above or below the passenger flow. Transit shuttles (9) and satellite transit tunnel (13) leading to a satellite terminal (normally for long-haul domestic or international flights) are located on the lower level.

Variations in this basic design might occur when traffic volumes or type of traffic requires. For example, at large airports where intra-airport transportation systems operate, a special level might be needed to provide access to these systems.

Terminal building space requirements

The terminal building is a complex major public-use facility serving the needs of passengers, the air carriers, visitors, airport administration and operations, and concessionaires. Clearly, different objectives and space requirements are sought by each of these groups of users. Conflicts in objectives and space requirements often arise in planning passenger handling systems. Because the main users of the system are the passengers and the air carriers, it is important to recognize the objectives that are sought in planning space requirements from the viewpoints of these two user groups:

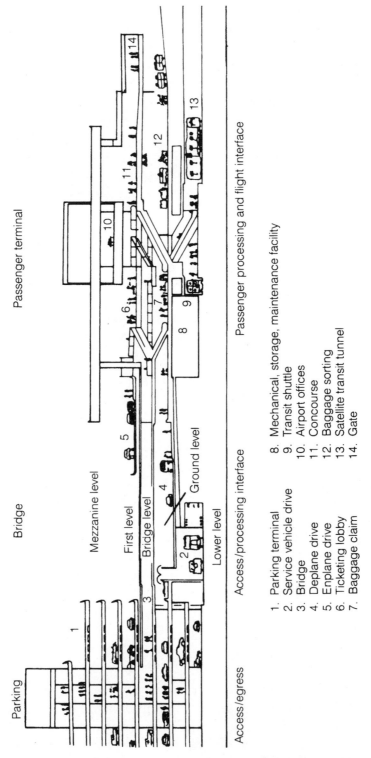

Parking

Bridge

Passenger terminal

Mezzanine level

First level

Bridge level

Ground level

Lower level

Access/egress

Access/processing interface

Passenger processing and flight interface

1. Parking terminal
2. Service vehicle drive
3. Bridge
4. Deplane drive
5. Enplane drive
6. Ticketing lobby
7. Baggage claim

8. Mechanical, storage, maintenance facility
9. Transit shuttle
10. Airport offices
11. Concourse
12. Baggage sorting
13. Satellite transit tunnel
14. Gate

6-7 *Vertical distribution of passenger flow through multilevel terminal.*

For the passengers

1 Minimization of delays in processing.

2 Minimization of walking distance.

3 Protection from the elements: weather, noise, jet blast, and so forth.

4 Simplification of orientation and provision of comfort and convenience.

For the air carriers

1 Minimization of operating costs per passenger handled.

2 Maximization of capacity per dollar invested.

3 Minimization of delays in operations.

4 Provision for sufficient capacity to handle expected demand.

The above lists include only the major objectives for two users. Planning objectives are established for other user groups; however, the space requirements are largely determined from the aforementioned objectives. A planner must consider these objectives in establishing criteria for space requirements.

It has been recognized in airport planning that two sets of space criteria are needed. One is a set of criteria that can be used for *general concept evaluation*. This is a set of general considerations that the planner uses to evaluate and select among alternative concepts in a preliminary fashion prior to any detailed design and development. The other set of space criteria is the actual *criteria for design and development*. In this set, specific performance measures are needed in order to evaluate the likely operation of well-developed plans.

While general concept evaluation criteria can be developed on the basis of experience and observation of existing terminal buildings, the more specific design and development criteria require the use of a number of analytic techniques for their generation. These include network models, critical path method (CPM), queuing models, and simulation models. A complete discussion of these techniques can be found in *Planning and Design of Airports* by Robert Horonjeff and Francis X. McKelvey.

The most important general concept evaluation criteria for space requirements are:

Adequate space to accommodate passengers is exemplified in this picture showing a portion of the terminal lobby at Jacksonville International Airport. Reynolds, Smith, and Hills

1 Ability of the facility to handle expected demand.

2 Compatibility with the expected aircraft fleet mix.

3 Flexibility for growth and response to advances in technology.

4 Compatibility with ground access systems.

5 Compatibility with the airport master plan.

6 Delay potential caused by the physical layout of the building.

7 Cost considerations.

8 Sociopolitical and environmental considerations.

The most important specific design and development criteria for space requirements are:

1 Processing costs per passenger.

2 Walking distances for various types of passengers.

3 Passenger delays in processing.

4 Occupancy levels for lounges and corridors.

5 Aircraft maneuvering delays and costs.

6 Construction costs.

7 Operating and maintenance expenses.

8 Estimated revenues from concessionaires.

Steps involved in determining space requirements Once the sets of criteria have been established, the next determination is the actual space requirements for the various users. The following is a general outline of the major steps involved in this process:

1 Number of passengers and types. The first step involves a forecast of the annual passenger volume. Next is a determination of the approximate hourly volume. Planners refer to this figure as the *typical peak-hour passenger volume* or *de-*

A moving sidewalk at Miami International Airport. Metro-Dade Aviation Department

Baggage claim area at McCarran International Airport, Las Vegas, NV. Clark County Aviation Department

sign volume. The peak hour of an average day in the peak month is commonly used as the hourly design volume for terminal space. This figure is generally in the range of 3 to 5 percent of the annual volume.

The type of passenger is broadly classified as domestic, international, or transfer. A further breakdown by type would include such items as: (a) arriving or departing, (b) with or without checked baggage, (c) mode of access to or egress from the airport—automobile, bus, limousine, train, or helicopter, (d) scheduled, charter, or general aviation flight, and (e) any other characteristics that might be relevant to the particular airport.

The forecasted volume of passengers is then broken down by type, including subcategories.

2 Passenger type by facility. A matrix is developed matching passenger types and volumes with the various facilities in the terminal. These would include such areas as the ticket lobby, restrooms, baggage claim area, waiting rooms, eating facilities, and so forth. Areas for servicing international passengers would include public health, immigration, customs, agriculture, and visitor waiting areas. By summing the volume of passengers in rows corresponding to the facilities, it is possible to approximate the total load on each facility.

3 Determining space requirements. The actual space requirements are determined by multiplying the estimated number of passengers using each facility with an empirical factor to arrive at the approximate area or capacity of the facility required. The empirical factor or constant is based upon experience acquired by planners and contemplates a reasonable level of service and occupancy. See Table 6-1.

Baggage handling services

Baggage handling services include a number of activities involving the collection, sorting, and distribution of baggage. An efficient flow of baggage through the terminal is an important element in the

Table 6-1 Terminal building space requirements (hypothetical)

Facility (example)	Space required in 1,000 square feet per 100 typical peak-hour passengers (empirical factor)	Typical peak-hour passengers	Area required (square feet)
Ticket lobby	1.5	400	6,000
Fast food facilities	0.8	250	2,000
Customs	2.6	300	7,800
Baggage claim	1.4	275	3,850

passenger handling system. Much of the passenger delay in the terminal can be attributed to the baggage flow (Fig. 6-8).

Departing passengers normally check their baggage at one of a number of sites including curbside check-in and at the ticket counter in the terminal building. The bags are then sent to a central sorting area, where they are sorted according to flights and sent to the appropriate gate to be loaded aboard the departing aircraft. Arriving baggage is unloaded from the aircraft and sent to the central sorting area. Sorted bags are sent to another flight (transfer passenger), to storage for later pickup, or to the baggage claim area.

Airport access plans

The *airport access plans* are an integral part of the master planning process. These plans indicate proposed routing of airport access to the central business district and to points of connection with existing or planned ground transportation arteries. All modes of access are

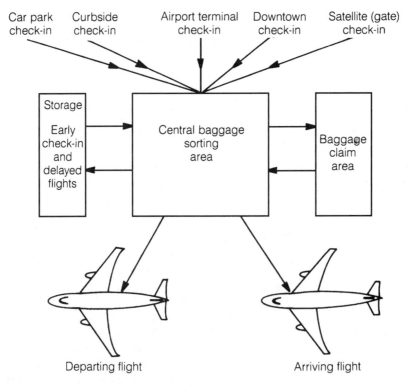

6-8 *Baggage flow.*

Baggage handling.

considered, including highways, rapid transit, and access by vertical and short takeoff and landing (V/STOL) aircraft. The estimated capacity requirement for the various modes considered is determined from forecasts of passengers, cargo, and aircraft operations. The airport access plans normally are general in nature because detailed plans of access outside the boundaries of the airport will be developed by highway departments, transit authorities, and comprehensive planning bodies.

Segments of airport access

Airport access is usually divided into two major segments:

1 Access from the central business district and suburban areas via highway and rapid transit systems to the airport boundary.

2 Access from the airport boundary via airport roads and rapid transit to parking areas and passenger unloading curbs at the terminal building.

The first segment is a part of the overall regional or urban transportation system and serves general and airport traffic. State and local highway departments and local transit authorities will bear the

New 4,900-space parking garage at Fort Lauderdale-Hollywood International Airport. Broward County Aviation Department

major responsibility for the administration, design, and construction of this segment. Airport sponsors are responsible for developing the requirements of airport traffic that must be served within the first segment. They are also responsible for promoting the development of facilities to serve that demand. Regional, state, and local planning bodies are relied upon to bring together the general needs of urban transportation and the specialized needs of airports by the development of comprehensive transportation plans for metropolitan or regional areas as a whole. At the federal level, the Department of Transportation and the Department of Housing and Urban Development provide national inputs through programs such as the Federal Highway Grants-in-Aid Program, and urban transportation planning funds. With this diversification of responsibility, careful coordination is required if the first segment of the airport access problem is to be effectively resolved.

The second segment of airport access, from the airport boundary to the parking area and terminal building unloading curbs, is primarily the responsibility of airport management. They plan and construct the second segment of access, although they are often assisted by the air carriers in this effort. Airport sponsors must take special care in planning on-airport access, although they are often assisted by the air carriers in this effort. Airport sponsors must take special care in planning on-airport access to ensure that it is compatible with off-airport ground transportation plans and with ultimate terminal area development.

The biggest problem concerning access stems from the fact that airport travel tends to peak in the same morning and afternoon periods as does general urban and suburban travel. The first segment of access traffic is made up of general urban travelers, and airport passengers, visitors, and employees. General urban travelers drop out after the first segment, leaving only the airport traffic in the access system. Because most visitors ride in the same vehicle with passengers during access, they do not add to the peaking problem except for congestion within the terminal building. Airport-based employees do add to the peaking problem because they ride in separate vehicles. Airport access facilities are designed on the basis of typical peak-hour traffic. At some of the busiest airports, congestion rises in the morning, remains almost constant throughout the day, and does not taper off until evening.

Rapid transit is an alternative to relieve access problems to some of the most congested airports. An example is in Cleveland, where an extension of the city subway line carries passengers from downtown to Cleveland Hopkins International Airport. In conjunction with the existing access highway system, it is a quick and practical airport access mode.

Vehicle parking

Parking facilities at or near the airport must be provided for (1) airline passengers; (2) visitors accompanying passengers; (3) spectators; (4) people employed at the airport; (5) car rentals and limousines; and (6) people having business with the airport tenants.

A separate parking facility is normally provided for employees. At some of the major airports, an employee parking lot is often several miles from the terminal area. Employees are bused to the airport from the outlying facility. Buses run on a regular schedule around the clock.

The car-rental parking area is normally close to the terminal building in order to minimize the passenger walking distance. Normally this close-in facility will only accommodate cars that have been reserved. Other rental cars are often parked in a special area away from the terminal building and driven to the car-rental area upon request.

Departing passengers normally deposit rental cars in the special area and are bused to the terminal area. This is a common arrangement at many large airports.

Public parking facilities are provided for airline passengers, visitors, and spectators. The major goal here is to locate this area as close as possible to the terminal building in order to minimize walking distance.

Most of the major airports have separate parking facilities for short-term and long-term parkers. Surveys at a number of major airports indicate that a large number (75 percent or more) park 3 hours or less and a much smaller group parks from 12 hours to several days or longer; however, short-term parkers typically represent only about 20 percent of the total maximum vehicle accumulation. Consequently, many airports designate the most convenient (closest area) spaces to short-term parkers, who represent the highest number of users.

At some very busy airports, long-term parking is provided off the airport property at reduced rates by private concessionaires who provide shuttle transportation to the airport for their customers.

Key terms

terminal area
centralized passenger processing
decentralized passenger processing
gate arrival
simple terminal
linear or curvilinear terminal
pier finger terminal
satellite terminal
mobile lounge or transporter
passenger handling system
access/egress link
access/processing interface
passenger processing link
flight interface

general concept evaluation

criteria for design and development

typical peak-hour passenger volume (design volume)

airport access plans

Review questions

1 What is included in the "terminal area?"

- Discuss the primary objective of the terminal area plans.

- Describe the factors taken into consideration by airport planners in selecting the terminal area concept.

2 What are the advantages and disadvantages of the centralized and decentralized passenger processing system?

- Describe the four basic terminal building design concepts including their advantages and disadvantages. How can some of the best plans be thwarted by the realities of present airport-airway systems?

3 Describe the four components of the passenger handling system. What facilities are required for the following: airport operations and management, airline operations, and government agencies.

- Why is the terminal building primarily designed around passenger needs and wants? Describe the passenger flow (arriving and departing) through the terminal building for the following passengers: domestic, international, and transfer.

- What is the primary purpose of the vertical distribution of passenger flow?

4 List the primary objectives in planning space requirements for the passengers and the air carriers.

- Define *general concept evaluation* and *criteria for design and development.*

- Discuss the steps involved in determining space requirements.

- Describe the baggage flow through the terminal building for arriving and departing passengers.

5 Why must airport management and planners work very closely with other governmental bodies in developing airport access plans?

- What are the two segments of airport access?
- What is the biggest problem concerning access roads?
- Describe the parking facilities required at a major airport.

Suggested readings

Airport Access—A Planning Guide. DOT/Federal Highway Administration, Transmittal 113, Vol. 20, Appendix 55. Washington, DC: GPO, October 1971.

Airport Ground Access. Report of the Secretary of Transportation to the United States Senate Committee on Appropriations pursuant to Senate Report No. 95-268. Washington, DC: GPO, May 1975.

Airport Land Banking. DOT/FAA/Office of Aviation System Plans, FAA Report #ASP-77-7. Washington, DC: GPO, August 1977.

Airport Landside Capacity. Special Report 159. Washington, DC: Transportation Research Board, 1975.

Airport Landside Planning and Operations. Special Report 1373. Washington, DC: Transportation Research Board, 1992.

Airport Terminal and Landside Design and Operation. Special Report 1273. Washington, DC: Transportation Research Board, 1990.

Doganis, Rigas. *The Airport Business.* New York: Routledge, Chapman and Hall, Inc., 1992.

Hart, Walter. *The Airport Passenger Terminal.* Malabar, FL: Krieger Publishing Co., 1991.

Horonjeff, Robert, and Francis X. McKelvey. *Planning and Design of Airports.* New York: McGraw-Hill, Inc., 1994.

Measuring Airport Landside Capacity. Special Report 215. Washington, DC: Transportation Research Board, 1987.

DOT/FAA advisory circulars

150/5320-14	Airport Landscaping for Noise Control Purposes
150/5360-9	Planning and Design of Airport Terminal Facilities at Non-Hub Locations
150/5360-11	Energy Conservation for Airport Buildings
150/5360-12	Airport Signing and Graphics
150/5360-13	Planning and Design Guidelines for Airport Terminal Facilities
150/5360-9	Planning and Design of Airport Terminal Facilities at Non-Hub Locations
150/5070-6	Airport Master Plans

150/5360-6   Airport Terminal Building Development With Federal Participation
150/5360-7   Planning and Design Considerations for Airport Terminal Building Development
150/5070-3   Planning the Airport Industrial Park

7

Financial planning

Outline

- Financial plan
- Financing methods
- Completing the financial plant

Objectives

When you have completed this chapter, you should be able to:

- Describe the purpose of the financial plan.
- Distinguish between nondepreciable and depreciable investment.
- List and briefly describe five potential airport revenue sources.
- Distinquish between the various federal funding programs.
- List and briefly describe the approved project categories for AIP funding.
- Describe the eligible projects for which PFC revenue may be used.
- Distinguish between general obligation bonds, self-liquidating general obligation bonds, and revenue bonds as alternate financing methods.
- List and briefly describe the factors that are considered in analyzing the quality of airport bonds.
- Discuss the importance and types of private financing used by airports.

Financial plan

The fourth and final phase of the airport master plan includes the financial plan. The *financial plan* is an economic evaluation of the entire plan of development. It looks at the activity forecasts of the first phase from the point of view of revenues and expenditures, analyzing the airport's balance sheet over the planning period to ensure that the airport sponsor can afford to proceed. A corollary activity in this phase is the consideration of funding sources and financing methods for the proposed development. Questions to be addressed include which portions will be funded through federal grants-in-aid; the size and timing of bond issues; and the revenue from concessionaire rents, parking fees, landing fees, and so on.

Economic evaluation

Although the primary objective of the airport master plan is to develop a design concept for the entire airport, it is essential to test the economic feasibility of the plan from the standpoints of airport operation and individual facilities and services. Economic feasibility will depend on whether the users of the airport improvements programmed under the plan can produce the revenues (as might be supplemented by federal, state, or local subsidies) required to cover annual cost for administration, operation, and maintenance. This must be determined for each stage of development scheduled in the master plan. This consideration includes the cost of capital to be employed in financing the improvement, the annual operating costs of facilities, and prospective annual revenues.

The schedule of improvements proposed in the master plan, as well as the cost estimates are developed by stages (Table 7-1).

This preliminary cost estimate for each of the proposed improvements provides the basic capital investment information needed for evaluating the feasibility of the various facilities. Estimated construction costs are adjusted to include allowance for architect and engineering fees for preparation of detailed plans and specifications, overhead for construction administration, allowance for contingencies, and allowance for interest expenses during construction. Estimated costs of land acquisitions as well as the costs of easements required to protect approach and departure areas are included. If the master plan provides for the expansion of an existing airport, the cost

Table 7-1 Preliminary master plan cost estimates by stage
(in thousands of dollars—hypothetical)

Description of improvement	First	Second	Third	Total
Airfield (includes lights):				
Runway	$400	$90	$1,200	$1,690
Taxiways	800	400	1,000	2,200
Aprons	200	150	900	1,250
Roads:				
Terminal and service	150	100	800	1,050
Parking lot	50	—	150	200
Buildings:				
Expansion of existing terminal	1,130	400	—	1,530
New terminal	—	—	8,500	8,500
Fire/crash	—	—	200	200
Airport maintenance	—	—	150	150
Relocation:				
Fixed base operator	200	—	—	200
National Guard	40	100	—	140
Airport maintenance	35	—	—	35
Miscellaneous:				
Electrical	140	25	90	255
Utilities	40	—	200	240
Drainage	30	20	225	275
Landscaping	—	—	175	175
Fencing	10	—	50	60
Site preparation	300	150	800	1,250
Total estimated construction	$3,525	$1,435	$14,440	$19,400
Legal, administrative, engineering	800	250	2,800	3,850
Total project	$4,325	$1,685	$17,240	$23,250
Land acquisition	2,800	—	—	2,800
Total estimated cost	$7,125	$1,685	$17,240	$26,050

of the existing capital investment might be required to be added to the new capital costs.

The airport layout plan also indicates the stage development of the proposed facilities. The drawings are normally legended to indicate staging shown on the plan, either on single or separate sheets. Charts that show the schedule of development for various items of the master plan are developed for inclusion in the master plan report.

Break-even need The annual amount that is required to cover cost of capital investment and costs of administration, operation, and maintenance can be called the *break-even need*. The revenues required to produce the break-even need are derived from user charges, lease rentals, and concession revenues produced by the airport as a whole. In order to make sure that the individual components of the airport are generating a proper share of the required annual revenues, the airport can be divided into cost areas to allow allocation of costs to such areas following generally accepted cost accounting principles. Carrying charges on invested capital include depreciable and nondepreciable items.

Nondepreciable investment *Nondepreciable investment items* are those that have a permanent value even if the airport site is converted to other uses. Nondepreciable investment items include the cost of land acquisition, excavation and fill operations, and road relocations that enhance the value of the airport site. The annual cost of capital invested in nondepreciable assets depends in the first instance on the source of capital used. If revenue or general obligation bonds have been issued to acquire the asset, the total of the principal and interest payments and required reserves or coverage payments called for by the bonds is used. Assets acquired with airport operating surpluses of prior years, general tax revenues, or gifts do not ordinarily impose a cash operating requirement and the treatment of these investments will require a decision by the operator based upon legal considerations and financial operating objectives of the airport. Interest or depreciation charges are not required to be recovered on amounts secured by the airport under the Airport and Airway Improvement Act of 1982 or previous acts. Treatment of funds acquired under state grants-in-aid programs are governed by the terms of the act involved.

Depreciable investment The annual cost of capital invested in plant and equipment (as distinguished from land) can be regarded as *depreciable investment*. The annual charge for depreciation depends on the useful life of the asset and the source of capital used in acquiring the asset. If payments of principal and interest on bonds issued to pay for the asset are required over a shorter period than the useful life of the asset, this schedule would govern and form the basis for depreciation charges unless other revenues are available to service the debt. Depreciation charges for capital assets acquired with operating surpluses of prior years, general tax revenues, or gifts do not ordinarily impose a cash operating requirement on the operator, and the treatment of this investment will require a policy decision by the operator. Interest or depreciation charges are not required to be recovered on amounts secured under the Airport and Airway Improvement Act of 1982 or previous acts. Funds obtained under state grants-in-aid are governed by the terms of the act involved.

Expenses for administration, operation, and maintenance
Estimated expenses for administration, operation, and maintenance are developed for each airport cost area on the basis of unit costs for direct expenses. For nonrevenue areas, these expenses are forecasted separately and distributed to various airport operations. For utility expenses, the net amount expected to be owed from utility purchase, after sale of utility services, is forecast.

Potential airport revenue The sum of the estimated annual carrying charges on invested capital and the estimated average annual expenses of administration, operation, and maintenance establishes the break-even need for each revenue-producing facility and for the airport as a whole. The next step in establishing economic feasibility is to determine if sufficient revenues (that might be supplemented by federal, state, and local subsidies) can be expected at the airport to cover the break-even needs; therefore, forecasts are prepared for revenue-producing areas. These areas include:

1 Landing area. This area includes runways and related taxiways and circulation taxiways. Flight fee revenue determination is distributed between scheduled airlines, other air carrier users, and general aviation. Flight fee amounts should provide sufficient revenues to cover the landing area break-even need.

2 Aircraft aprons and parking areas. Revenues to obtain the break-even need for airline terminal aprons and cargo aprons are assigned to the scheduled airlines. Those for general aviation ramps are assigned to private aircraft. Apron and parking area fees should provide sufficient revenues to cover the break-even needs for specific aircraft aprons and parking areas.

3 Airline terminal buildings. Revenues for concessionaires and ground transportation services are usually based on a percentage of gross income with a fixed-rate minimum for each type of service. Space for scheduled airlines and other users is paid for on a fixed-rental basis. In order to establish rental rates, forecasts of potential revenue from concessions and ground transportation must be established. Rental rates are based on the break-even need of the terminal building after giving credit for forecasted revenues from concessions and ground transportation.

4 Public parking areas. Public parking is usually operated on a concessionaire basis with revenues obtained from rentals based on a percentage of gross income with a fixed-rate minimum. The revenue amount required to meet break-even needs will depend on whether parking facilities are constructed by the airport owner or under provisions of the concessionaire contract. These revenues apply to public parking for both airline and general aviation terminals. Revenues in excess of the break-even need for public parking is allocated to the break-even need for the airport as a whole.

5 Cargo buildings. Rentals are usually charged on a rate per square foot and cover investments in employee parking, and truck unloading docks, as well as building space. Rates are established to meet break-even needs.

6 Aviation fuel. Fees charged to aviation fuel handling concessionaires are established to cover the costs of fuel storage areas and associated pumping, piping, and hydrant systems.

7 Hangars. Rentals are usually based on a rate per square foot and cover investments in associated aircraft apron space and hangar-related employee parking. Hangar office space is charged on a similar basis and covers office-related employee parking.

8 Commercial facilities. Airport office buildings, industrial facilities, and hotels are usually operated on a lessee-management basis with revenues obtained from rentals on a square foot basis. The facilities are often financed by private capital. Revenues in excess of the break-even need are allocated to the break-even need of the airport as a whole.

9 Other usable areas. Various uses of ground space for activities such as gasoline stations, service facilities for rental car operators, and bus and limousine operators usually obtain revenues on a flat rate basis. Those facilities are often financed by private capital. Revenues in excess of the break-even need are allocated to the break-even need of the airport as a whole.

Final economic evaluation After analysis of the break-even needs for individual components of the master plan has been made, economic feasibility is analyzed on an overall basis. The goal of overall analysis is to determine if revenues will equal or exceed the break-even need. This determination requires an evaluation of the scope and phasing of the plan itself in terms of the users' requirements and their ability to make the financial commitment necessary to support the costs of the program. If this review indicates that revenues will be sufficient, revisions in the scheduling or scope of proposed master plan developments might have to be made, or recovery revenue rates for airport cost areas might require adjustment. These factors are adjusted until the feasibility of the master plan is established; this is to say, airport revenues (as might be supplemented by federal, state, or local subsidies) will match capital investment throughout the master plan forecast period. When the economic feasibility of improvements proposed in the master plan has been established, capital budget and a program for financing those improvements is developed.

Financing methods

The establishment of the airport master plan's economic feasibility (the balance between annual cost of capital investment and airport revenues) is vital to the financing for the improvements proposed in the plan. The implementation of the airport master plan will depend largely on the proper financing of those capital improvements. The primary responsibility for financing the development plans rests with local operating agencies or authorities. Public financing of airport development can be accomplished many ways. Financing might be raised from taxes, general obligation bonds, revenue bonds, private financing, government assistance, passenger facility charges (PFCs), or a combination thereof.

Federal funding

The federal government initiated a grants-in-aid program shortly after the end of World War II to promote the development of a system of airports to meet the nation's needs. This early program, the Federal-Aid Airport Program (FAAP), was established with the passage of the Federal Airport Act of 1946 and funded from the general fund of the Treasury (see Chapter 1).

A more comprehensive program was established with the passage of the Airport and Airway Development Act of 1970. This act provided for grant assistance for airport planning under the Planning Grant Program (PGP) and for airport development under the Airport Development Aid Program (ADAP). The source of funds for these programs was a new Airport and Airway Trust Fund, into which revenues were deposited from several aviation user taxes on such items as airline fares, air freight, and aviation gasoline. The act, after several amendments and a one-year extension, expired on September 30, 1981.

The successor grant program, the Airport Improvement Program (AIP), was established by the Airport and Airway Improvement Act of 1982. It provided assistance under a single program for airport planning and development through funding from the Airport and Airway Trust Fund. The Airport and Airway Improvement Act has been extended several times over the years, providing increasing funding authorizations throughout the 1990s.

The Airport Improvement Program AIP funds are used for four general purposes: airport planning, airport development, airport capacity enhancement, and noise compatibility programs. The trust fund relies on user fees and taxes assessed on those who benefit from the services made possible by AIP grants, such as:

- A 10 percent airline ticket tax.
- A 6.25 percent tax on freight waybills.
- A $6.00 international departure fee assessed per passenger.
- A $0.15 per gallon general aviation gasoline tax.
- A $0.175 per gallon jet fuel tax.

An airport must be a part of the National Plan of Integrated airport Systems (NPIAS) to be eligible for AIP funding. The purpose of the plan is to identify those public-use airports that are essential to providing a safe and efficient air traffic system to support civil aviation, the military, and the U.S. Postal Service. The sponsor must also meet several legal, financial, and miscellaneous requirements. These requirements are necessary to ensure that the sponsor is capable of fulfilling the provisions stipulated in the grant obligations.

Approved AIP uses The sponsor must meet specific project categories for approval of AIP funding. The categories of projects approved for AIP funding are airport planning, airport development, airport capacity enhancement and preservation, and noise compatibility programs.

Airport planning   Eligible airport planning projects can be conducted on either an area-wide or individual airport basis. Area-wide planning includes preparation of integrated airport system plans for states, regions, or metropolitan areas. Grants for integrated airport system planning are made to the planning agency with jurisdiction over the entire region under study. Airport system planning addresses the current and future air transportation needs of the region as a whole. Individual airport planning addresses the current and future needs of an individual airport through the airport master planning process, aviation requirements, facility requirements, and potential compatibility with environmental and community goals. Individual airport planning also includes the preparation of noise compatibility plans.

Airport development   Eligible airport development projects may include the construction, improvement, or repair (excluding routine maintenance) of an airport. These projects may include land acquisition, site preparation, navigational aids, or the construction of terminal buildings, roadways, runways, and taxiways. For AIP funding purposes, airport development grants cannot be used for the construction of hangars, automobile parking areas, buildings not related to the safety of persons on the airport and art objects or decorative landscaping.

Airport capacity enhancement and preservation   The Airport and Airway Safety and Capacity Expansion Act of 1987 allows for AIP funding of projects that significantly enhance or preserve airport capacity. Increasing airport capacity allows the national system to better accommodate its service demand and also reduces aircraft delays, particularly at the largest primary airports. Considerations for airport capacity funding include the project's cost and benefit, the project's effect on overall national air transportation system capacity, and the financial commitment of the airport sponsor to preserve or enhance airport capacity.

Noise compatibility programs   Federal Aviation Regulations Part 150 outlines the eligibility criteria for an airport noise compatibility program. Sponsors receiving noise compatibility related grants can include the owners and operators of a public-use airport or local governments surrounding the airport.

AIP funding   Funds granted to airports by the AIP are provided in three different funding categories: apportionment, set-aside, and discretionary funds. *Apportionment funds* represent the largest funding category, making up approximately half of all AIP funding. Apportionments to primary airports are based on those airports' annual enplanements. In addition, apportionment funds for cargo operations at these airports are based on aggregate landed weight of all cargo aircraft. *Set-aside funds* are available to any eligible airport sponsor and are allocated according to congressionally mandated requirements for a number of different set-aside subcategories. Set-aside distributions include:

- Allocations to all 50 states, the District of Columbia, and the insular areas based on land area and population.
- Funds specifically for the insular areas.
- Minimum funding levels for Alaska for purposes such as reliever airports, nonprimary commercial service airports, airport noise compatibility programs, integrated airport system plans, and the Military Airport Program.

Discretionary funds are grants that go to projects that address goals established by the Congress, such as enhancing capacity, safety, and security or mitigating noise at all types of airports.

Other federal funding   While the AIP is the primary form of federal funding for airports, two additional programs are available. They are the Facilities and Equipment (F&E) Program and Federal Letters of Intent (LOI).

Facilities and Equipment Program   The *Facilities and Equipment Program (F&E)* provides funding for airports for the installation of navigational aids and control towers, as necessary. It funds 100 percent of the costs of these requirements in the interest of navigation, air traffic control, and safety. Eligible projects under the F&E Program include site preparation for navigational aids, the installation of navigational aids, and the construction of control towers.

Federal Letters of Intent   *Federal Letters of Intent (LOI)* represent another means of receiving government funding for airport capital improvements. In general, the Airport and Airway Improvement Act of 1982 prohibited the use of AIP funds for projects begun before an AIP grant had been formally issued. However, the Airport and

Airway Safety and Capacity Expansion Act of 1987 allowed the issuance of LOI. In writing LOI, the FAA states its intent to appropriate future funds to the approved project. The FAA issues LOI for projects that will significantly enhance systemwide airport capacity.

In 1994, the FAA issued new regulations stating that it would consider LOI for primary and reliever airports only for airside development projects with significant capacity benefits. The three main criteria for determining which airports will receive LOI for certain projects are:

- The effect of the project on the overall capacity of the airport system.
- Project benefit and cost.
- Project sponsor financial commitment or timing.

The FAA evaluates the use of LOI in terms of "aircraft delay savings," measured as the avoided cost of operating delayed flights and the value of passenger hours wasted during delays. The best project candidates are new airports, new runways, or existing runway extensions in metropolitan areas with current forecasted delays of over 20,000 hours per year. Projects are prioritized according to their function:

- Airport safety and security.
- Preservation of existing infrastructure.
- Aid compliance with governmental standards (e.g., noise migration).
- Upgrade of service.
- Increase in airport system capacity.

The use of LOI has been a subject of great interest and concern to the airport community. A number of issues limit the use of LOI as a stand-alone, tangible revenue stream. First, LOI are not a legal pledge to provide funds; the letters clearly state that the FAA is not committing funds to a proposed project. Second, LOI bear the risk that Congress may delay or even fail to grant re-authorization of AIP funding in any given year. Third, future federal budget cuts may limit the amount of AIP discretionary fund. Fourth, apportionments are based on the number of enplanements; failure to attain projected enplanement levels could result in reduced funding. In the words of the General Accounting Office (GAO), the potential for using "LOI disbursements exclusively to leverage investment-grade bonds would be undermined if the disbursements are not made in full, as scheduled."

Passenger facility charges

In 1972 the Supreme Court ruled in *Evansville-Vanderburgh Airport v. Delta Air Lines* that tolls charged to enplaning and deplaning passengers were constitutional. This ruling prompted several airport operators to collect such tolls. However, in 1973 Congress enacted the Anti-Head Tax Act, which stated that the user-fee and tax revenues collected for the Airport and Airway Trust Fund would be sufficient to fund airport development, and banned airport tolls, or head taxes.

Some years later, critical shortages of airport capacity and the associated capital to finance airport development prompted major legislative campaigns for *passenger facility charges (PFCs)*. In response to these shortages, Congress authorized domestic airports to assess PFCs on enplaning passengers as part of the Aviation Safety and Capacity Expansion Act of 1990. Publicly owned commercial service airports are permitted to assess a $1, $2, or $3 PFC on domestic, territorial, or international revenue passengers enplaned at the airport. The PFC must be assessed uniformly across all of an airport's passengers. A maximum of two charges may be imposed on a passenger traveling to and from an airport (either one-way, round trip, connecting, or origin/destination).

The PFC revenue may be used only to fund eligible projects that satisfy statutory goals. Projects eligible for PFC funding include those that meet one of the following three criteria:

- Preserve or enhance the capacity, safety, or security of the national air transportation system.
- Reduce noise resulting from an airport.
- Furnish opportunities for enhanced competition between or among air carriers.

The PFC revenue can finance the entire allowable cost of a project or can be used to pay debt service or related expenses for bonds issued to fund an eligible project. A PFC is considered local revenue and may be used to meet the nonfederal share of projects funded under the AIP.

If a sponsor of an airport that accounts for at least 0.25 percent of total annual U.S. enplanements imposes a PFC, then that airport will lose a fraction of its AIP apportionment. This amount is equal to 50 percent of the projected PFC revenues per year. However, the reduction may not exceed 50 percent of the AIP apportionment funds (not including discretionary or set-aside funding) anticipated for that airport in that fiscal year.

The PFC revenue may also be leveraged as a revenue stream to support a bond issue. The PFCs can be a fairly stable revenue stream, assuming that enplanements do not fluctuate greatly in the short run. However, several risks are associated with leveraged PFC revenue, including:

- The failure to generate the amount needed for annual debt service payments (including coverage) because enplanements, and subsequently PFC revenues, were lower than projected.
- Interruption in the flow of PFC revenues if, for example, an airline that is collecting PFCs declares bankruptcy.
- Expiration of authority to collect PFC revenue due to failure to obtain project approval.
- Termination of PFC authority for failure to comply with necessary assurances or for a violation of federal noise regulations.
- Requirement of FAA approval of amendments to an approved PFC application.

Airport bonds

Another major funding source available to airports for capital improvements and additions is the issuance of debt in the form of bonds. Perhaps the toughest test of an airport's financial strength is its success in competing with other municipal enterprises for private investment capital in the bond market. While the financially stronger airports are the ones most active in the bond market, even financially weaker airports can attract private capital, though often they must use the taxing power of the local government as security for bond financing.

Airports raise millions of dollars annually in the bond market. Most municipal bonds are exempt from federal income tax, a key feature that makes this financing less expensive than most other sources of private money. Predictably, the vast majority of airport debt capital is raised in the tax-exempt bond market.

The role of bond financing in overall investment varies greatly according to an airport's size and type of air traffic served. In terms of total dollar volume of bond sales, large and medium airports are by far the most prominent in the bond market. Of the total amount of municipal debt sold for airport purposes during the last two decades, 90 percent was for large and medium airports, in contrast to only 9 percent for small commercial airports. GA airports accounted for a little more than 1 percent of total airport bond sales.

Types of bonds   The vast majority of airport debt is issued in the form of revenue bonds. Used predominantly by large and medium-sized commercial airports, revenue bonds are secured solely by the operations of the airport and are not backed by any additional governmental subsidy or tax levy. Other debt instruments used by airports include local or state general obligation bonds backed by the taxing authority of the issuer (i.e., the locality or state) and debt backed by sales tax. Smaller airports tend to rely on this source of debt financing. In addition, airports may issue special facility bonds, a hybrid of a revenue bond and an industrial development bond that is issued to finance a specific facility on behalf of a specific carrier that directly secures the debt.

General obligation bonds   *General obligation bonds* are issued only by states, municipalities, and other general-purpose governments. The payments (interest and principal) to bondholders are secured by the full faith, credit, and taxing power of the issuing government agency. An advantage of general obligation bonds is that, because of the community guarantee, they typically can be issued at a lower interest rate than can other types of bonds; however, most states limit the amount of general obligation debt that a municipality may issue to a specified fraction of the taxable value of all property within its jurisdiction. In addition, many states require voter approval before using general obligation debt.

Fiscal pressures on local governments for all manner of activities have been especially great in recent years. The need for school construction and other essential public works has required a considerable volume of general obligation bond financing. In numerous cases, local governments have reached statutory bond limits or desire to reserve whatever margin is left for more general functions of government. It is becoming increasingly difficult to obtain taxpayer approval for general obligation bond issues for airports.

Self-liquidating general obligation bonds *Self-liquidating general obligation bonds* are also secured by the full faith, credit, and taxing power of the issuing government body; however, there is adequate cash flow from the operation of the facility to cover the debt service and other costs of operation of the facility. In other words, they are self-liquidating (self-sustaining). The debt is not legally considered as part of the community's debt limitation; however, because the credit of the local government bears the ultimate risk of default, the bond issue is still considered, for purposes of financial risk analysis, as part of the debt burden of the community; therefore, this method of financing generally means a higher rate of interest on all bonds sold by the community. The amount of interest rate generally depends in part upon the degree of "exposure risk" of the bond. Exposure risk occurs when there is insufficient net operating income to cover the level of debt service plus coverage requirements, and the community is therefore required to absorb the residual.

Revenue bonds The debt service on *revenue bonds* is payable solely from the revenue derived from the operation of a facility that was constructed or acquired with the proceeds of the bonds. Revenue bond financing for airport improvements has become the most common financing method. Financing with revenue bonds presents an opportunity to provide those improvements without direct burden to the taxpayer.

Airports in the municipal bond market

After World War II, larger airports began switching from general obligation bonds to revenue bonds as a method for financing new construction and improvements to existing fields. The first airport revenue bond in the United States was a $2.5 million issue sold in 1945 by Dade County, Florida, to buy what is now Miami International Airport from Pan American World Airways.

In the 1950s, the city of Chicago and the airlines that serve it worked out what has become the basic pattern for revenue bonds underwritten by airlines in the agreement that set up the financing for O'Hare International Airport. The airlines pledged that if airport income fell short of the total needed to pay off the principal and interest on the bonds, they would make up the difference by paying a higher landing fee rate. The historic *O'Hare Agreement* demonstrated that airports, backed up by the airlines that use them, could raise the money they need in the financial market without depending on general tax funds, and airport revenue bonding became the accepted way to raise money for construction and expansion.

The revenue bonds are usually issued for 25- or 30-year terms, in contrast to the customary 10- or 15-year terms for general obligation bonds. Interest rates run slightly higher on revenue bonds than on general obligation bonds.

A bond issue can be sold competitively, with the airport accepting bids and selling the issue to the bond house that offers to buy it for the lowest interest rate, or the interest rate can be negotiated between the seller and a single buyer. Often airport sponsors use the services of a bond counsel, who advises on the best way to market a particular bond issued. After a bond house buys a bond issue, it resells the bonds to commercial banks, insurance companies, pension funds, and other large investors.

Bond ratings   The perceived credit quality of an airport is the product of its performance in a number of analytical areas. Different analyses may place varying emphasis on these issues, but, generally, the following are considered: financial and operational comparables, nature of airline rates and charges, local economic base, airport current financial situation or debt level, strength of airport management, and airport layout.

Financial and operational factors   Standard financial ratios can be developed that represent median performance for airports of varying size, geographic location, and passenger mix. Analysis of an airport's position with respect to these medians is a useful starting point for bond rating analysts. It develops a benchmark of airport financial and operational performance. The following is a representative list of ratios that might be analyzed in the development of a bond rating for a particular airport:

- Traffic ratios, such as total origin and destination (O&D) passengers to transfer passengers.
- Annual increase in originating and transfer passenger traffic.
- Annual increase in cargo traffic.
- Aeronautical and nonaeronautical revenue per enplaned passenger.

- Local per capita income, gross product, and total employment.
- Debt per enplaned originating and transfer passenger.
- Debt service coverage.
- Percentage of traffic generated by the airport's two primary carriers.

Airline rates and charges   Airline rates and charges generate a significant portion of total airport revenues. Since airport revenues are the sole backing for revenue bonds, the nature of airline rates and charges has a significant impact on an airport's credit rating. The fact that lease agreements can vary also makes analysis through comparisons of traditional financial ratios difficult, as these ratios do not indicate the relative flexibility of an airport's rate structure. Instead, analysts often consider whether the type of lease agreement seems appropriate given local circumstances.

More important, however, is the fact that the rate-setting methodology affects the airport's control over its capital spending decisions. Under residual approaches in which the airlines assume the risk and guarantee revenues necessary to keep the airport operational, airlines can exercise control over capital spending through majority-in-interest (MII) lease provisions, which give signatory carriers the right of approval for airport capital spending. These provisions may allow existing carriers to resist capital projects designed to create facilities for new airlines. The debt of airports operating under such provisions is often considered less favorable by bond rating analysts.

Community economic base   The strength and diversity of the local economy in which the airport operates is a critical factor considered in airport bond rating. Economic strength results in greater demand for air transportation. Economic diversity protects the airport from economic fluctuations, resulting in more consistent enplanement levels. In addition, several nonairline revenue sources such as parking and ground transportation (which contribute to the airport's financial viability) are closely linked to the economy in the local service area. These services represent a constant, dependable source of revenue (in that they are not subject to volatility in hubbing arrangements) as long as the local economy remains strong. Thus, airports located in economically booming areas may receive higher ratings than those in areas suffering from an economic downturn.

Current financial status and debt level   Credit analysts evaluate airports in the context of their capital plans and financial forecasts. An airport's overall level of indebtedness and need to generate future revenues affects its credit quality. However, the unique context in which each airport operates makes it difficult to develop simple comparative measures of the relative indebtedness of airports because of growth, changes in the air carrier industry, and varied service demand. While there is usually a strong relationship between airport size and indebtedness, even this relationship can be skewed by the airport's stage in capital planning, debt issuance, and use of debt financing. Thus, although figures such as "debt per enplaned passenger" can be calculated, they are not always useful.

Airport management   Analysts review the managerial and administrative performance of airport operators and believe that well-run airports are generally better risks. Clearly, airport management's ability to negotiate favorable rates and charges and tenant agreements is a positive indication of managerial control, as is general ability to manage financial and other resources during traffic declines. Both of these criteria may indicate the airport's likelihood of operating effectively in the future. Similarly, management's success in planning existing capital programs and implementing debt issuances demonstrates managerial quality.

Airport layout   An airport's layout obviously affects the need for certain capital improvements and development. Layout also has implications for operating costs and revenues. For example, a hub that has concessions located in a central terminal building loses potential revenues from connecting passengers who never leave a particular concourse. Also, newer airports with multilevel access roads can reserve a level for buses, car rental, hotel limos, or taxis, and thereby collect a user fee from these businesses. Moreover, airports with midfield terminals reduce taxi times and distances for carriers, thus saving fuel and maintenance costs for airlines. To assess the relative strength or weakness of the airport layout, credit analysts evaluate the airport master plan.

Final rating   The final bond rating, which reflects the reliability of the bond, results from the airport's performance measured by these and other criteria. This rating determines the perceived risk potential investors associate with the bond issue and therefore affects the

*Master planned on nearly 15,000 acres, this arial view of Orlando
International Airport shows separated landslide and airside design
which are connected by automated people mover systems.*
Greater Orlando Aviation Authority.

interest rate or terms attached to the debt issuance, which is important
to the financial feasibility of the proposed project to be financed.

Bond ratings, interest cost, and defaults

The major investor services (such as Moody's and Standard & Poor's)
grade bonds according to investment quality. The top ranked bonds
are as follows:

1 Best grade. Bonds rated Aaa (by Moody's) or AAA (by Standard & Poor's) are graded best. Their exceptionally strong capacity to pay interest and repay principal offers the lowest
   degree of risk to investors in bonds.

2 High grade. Bonds rated Aa1 or Aa (by Moody's) or AA+ or AA (by Standard & Poor's) have very strong ability to pay interest and repay principal, but they are judged to be slightly less secure than best-grade bonds. Their margins of protection might not be quite so great, or the protective elements might be more subject to fluctuation.

3 Upper-medium grade. Bonds rated A1 or A (by Moody's) or A+, A, or A- (by Standard & Poor's) are well protected, but the factors giving security to interest and principal are deemed more susceptible to adverse changes in economic conditions or other future impairments than for bonds in the best and high-grade categories.

4 Medium grade. Bonds rated Baa1 or Baa (by Moody's) or BBB+, BBB, or BBB- (by Standard & Poor's) lack outstanding investment characteristics. Although their protection is deemed adequate at the time of rating, the presence of speculative elements might impair their capacity to pay interest and repay principal in the event of adverse economic conditions or other changes.

Although investors have considerable confidence in airport bonds, ratings vary between the top and medium grades. A medium grade means that rating firms see the investment as carrying a measure of speculative risk. General obligation bonds generally draw the best ratings. Under this form of security, ratings are determined by the economic vigor of the municipality or the entire state, and airports have little or no influence on the rating. Revenue bonds, on the other hand, draw ratings according to the fiscal vitality of the airport itself. Because more than 90 percent of all airport bonds (in terms of dollar volume) are secured with airport revenues, the criteria used by investor services to rate such bonds are central to the marketability of such bonds.

Airline deregulation, which has freed air carriers from virtually all obligation to serve particular airports, has caused some shift in the relative weight credit analysts give to these different factors. In response to deregulation, the investor services today place greater emphasis on local economic strength than on airport use agreements and the financial stability of the airlines serving an airport. The rationale is that if one airline withdraws service, a strong local economy would attract other airlines to pick up the travel business.

In view of the methods adopted by the investor services, it is not surprising that large airports—with their comparatively stronger financial showings—tend to draw the best revenue bond ratings. During the 1990s, credit analysts were far more likely to assign medium-grade revenue bond ratings to issues for medium and small airports than for large airports. In fact, over that period not a single large airport issuing debt was rated below the upper-medium category.

Since deregulation, bond rating organizations have emphasized that passengers are an airport's true customers and that sufficient passenger demand will provide financial incentives for some airlines to offer service over the long term. In particular, for origin-destination airports (those at which most passengers either begin or end their journeys) in strong travel markets, the financial failure of one carrier might have no influence on the airport bond rating.

Interest costs Interest costs represent the payments by airports to attract investors relative to what other municipal enterprises pay. The difference between interest costs paid by airports and by other public enterprises indicates that airports generally hold a strongly competitive position in the municipal bond market.

Like municipal bonds in general, airport bonds are sold and traded at prices that reflect both general economic conditions and the credit quality of the airport or (in the case of general obligation bonds) the creditworthiness of the issuing government. Rated revenue bonds are offered for sale in one of two ways. Under competitive bidding, the airport selects the lowest bid and thus obtains funds at the lowest cost of borrowing. Under a negotiated sale, the bond purchaser consents at the outset to purchase the bond issue at an agreed price. In either case, the entire bond issue is usually purchased by an underwriter (commonly, an investment brokerage company), or an underwriter team, which in turn markets the bond to institutional and individual investors.

In deciding the price of a particular bond issue, underwriters identify a "ballpark" interest rate on the basis of general market conditions and then refine this estimate according to the credit standing of the airport in question. General market conditions represent by far the most important determinant of interest costs on airport revenue bonds, and in this respect airports have little control over the cost of capital.

Within the range of interest costs dictated by market conditions, underwriters refine their bids on airport revenue bonds on the basis of the credit standing of the individual airport. Two factors have greatest importance here: the airport's basic fiscal condition (including its prospects for traffic growth and the strength of the local economic base), and the presence of special pressures on the airport to expand capacity, thereby necessitating extensive capital development. On average, larger airports pay lower interest costs than smaller airports, allowing for differences in types of security and average maturities of issues.

Defaults Defaults refers to the frequency with which a given type of enterprise has defaulted on a bond issue. This history of an enterprise, or of an entire industry, with regard to the number of defaults is an important index of investment value. By this measure, the record of airports is particularly strong. The airport industry has never suffered a single default, a fact noted by several credit analysts in citing the premium quality of airports as credit risks.

Private financing

As the need for airport development has grown during the past two decades, and traditional financing sources have become more difficult to obtain, airports have begun to consider innovative forms of financing. Many of these include some form of private capital, either through public-private partnerships or complete privatization. Privatization can be structured in a number of ways. When assessing expanded private sector involvement in airports, two major financial issues must be examined:

- The profitability of the arrangement.
- The ultimate costs of the arrangements and where the risks are borne.

There are a number of potential airport revenue sources as mentioned earlier in the chapter. These include air carrier rates and charges and airport concessions. With regard to profitability, pro forma operating statement analysis can determine if these revenue streams can sustain the cost of the transaction and who will ultimately bear the burden of the transaction price and any new costs, including taxes. In assessing the costs of the arrangements, it may be found that government outlays and subsidies are not required, and therefore government costs are reduced and the government's exposure to financial risk is removed. The risk may not fall to zero if the public sector takes ultimate responsibility for the success of the venture.

Both internationally and domestically, privatization has become a popular way for government entities to finance new and existing infrastructure projects. In developing countries, governments are turning to the private sector as an alternative source of capital to build much needed infrastructure or to improve the existing infrastructure. In more developed countries, the private sector is bringing efficiencies to traditionally government-run projects. Finally, government entities are turning to the private sector to provide innovation in service provision and operation. All of these factors have made privatization an attractive option for financing infrastructure projects, including the building and operating of airports.

Operation and management contracts Most airports in the United States currently use private sector involvement to their advantage through some type of external contract for service provision. Operation and management contracts can be given for any service at the airport, including fire and rescue services, fuel farms, and concessions. By

Opened in June, 1998 and known as the Philadelphia Marketplace at the airport, this terminal includes ticketing and baggage claim facilities, moving sidewalks, and a 45,000 square foot retail mall with 33 shops and eateries, featuring name brands and local favorites. Philadelphia International Airport

providing any of these services through a management contract, government entities are able to benefit from the efficiency, innovation, and expertise of the private sector without losing any control over the airport or airport services.

Long-term lease agreements   A long-term lease agreement is a more aggressive form of privatization than a management contract. The lease arrangement allows a government entity to realize many of the benefits associated with complete privatization without losing control over the airport assets. In a long-term lease (usually lasting from 20 to 40 years), the government allows the private sector company or consortium to manage the airport, including operations, strategic decisions, and development. In return, the government receives a lease payment (usually a revenue percentage).

In addition to a lease payment, the government is able to capture the efficiencies and innovation of the private sector. The private sector entity has the advantage of complete control over the airport; yet in many cases, the private sector firm also has the added benefits of access to tax-free financing and exemption from property taxes.

Sale of the airport   The final basic form of airport privatization is the sale of the entire airport or partial interest in the airport. This form of privatization is prominent internationally but has not occurred domestically. Under the terms of complete sale, the government gives up all rights of ownership to the private entity; however, the government often maintains its regulatory authority.

State funding

State funding has become an important source in financing airport development at GA and reliever airports. Virtually all states provide some financial assistance for airport improvements. The state participation varies, depending on whether federal funds are involved and whether this aid is channeled through the state agency. Fuel taxes are the major revenue source of state funds with other incomes derived from aircraft, airport, and pilot registration fees, sales taxes on the purchase of general aviation or air carrier fuel, highway or transportation funds or bond issues, and the general fund.

The exact amount of state funding varies considerably. For example, in Alaska and Hawaii, where most publicly owned airports are owned and operated by the state, the support from the state is considerable. Some of the smaller states, such as Delaware and West Virginia, provide little financial support for their airports.

Completing the financial plan

The development of a financial plan is the final step in the airport master plan process. Thereafter, the overall master plan must be accepted by the airport sponsor and by the public. Once the plan has been adopted and the financing has been obtained, the final design and construction of improvements proposed in the master plan can be implemented.

With a determination of the projects to be constructed and their timing, a capital budget is prepared to show on an annual basis the requirement for capital funds and the source of funds. This analysis also permits an accurate estimation of the amount of interest to be earned on capital funds held from the sale of bonds prior to the need to commit such funds for construction purposes.

The future

The financial plan is not a static model. It must be continually reviewed and adjusted. As air traffic and freight continue to expand and new technology develops, existing airport facilities in the United States will require expansion and improvement, and new facilities will need to be built. The current limitations on AIP funding may mean that airports will not receive significant federal aid, even if they qualify for it. As a result, the structure of airport rates and charges and PFCs becomes increasingly important, as does an airport's perceived credit in the bond market. Airports will continue to employ traditional financing, largely in the form of revenue bonds. However, greater numbers of capital projects will require financing and private funding may become a major solution.

Key terms

financial plan
break-even need
nondepreciable investment items
depreciable investment

apportionment funds

set-aside funds

discretionary funds

facilities and equipment program (F&E)

federal Letters of Intent (LOI)

passenger facility charges (PFCs)

general obligation bonds

self-liquidating general obligation bonds

revenue bonds

O'Hare Agreement

Review questions

1 What is included in the fourth phase of the airport master plan? Why are preliminary cost estimates needed for each stage of the master plan?

- What is the "break-even need"?
- Distinguish between nondepreciable investment items and depreciable investment.
- Forecasted potential revenue-producing sources are required in determining the break-even need. List and briefly describe five of these areas.

2 AIP funds are used for four general purposes. Briefly describe each of these purposes or project categories.

- Distinguish between apportionment funds and set-aside funds.
- What is the purpose of the Facilities and Equipment Program?
- What are the main criteria for determining which airports will receive federal Letters of Intent? Why are LOI of concern to the airport community?

3 What are passenger facility charges (PFCs)? How are they applied and for what projects may they be used?

4 Compare general obligation bonds and self-liquidating obligation bonds. Why have revenue bonds become so popular in recent years?

- What is the O'Hare Agreement?
- What are the factors on which the credit quality of an airport is determined for bond ratings?

5 Why do larger airports rely on the bond market more than smaller airports?

- Explain the bond ratings system used by the major investor services.
- Why do general obligation bonds generally draw the best ratings?
- What is the most important determinant of interest costs? What are defaults?

6. What type of facilities are financed privately?

- Distinguish between a management contract and a long-term lease agreement as they relate to private financing.
- What type of airports rely on state funding?

Suggested readings

"Airport Financing—Comparing Funding Sources with Planned Development," GAO, March 1998.

"Airport Financing—Funding Sources for Airport Development," GAO, March 1998.

Ashford, Norman, and Clifton A. Moore. *Airport Finance.* New York: Van Nostrand Reinhold, 1992.

"Better Management Needed for Funds Provided Under Letters of Intent," GAO, February 1994.

Bollinger, Lynn L., Alan Passen, and Robert E. McElfresh. *Terminal Airport Financing and Management.* Boston: Harvard University Press, 1970.

Doganis, Rigas. *The Airport Business.* London: Rutledge, 1992.

Horonjeff, Robert, and Francis X. McKelvey. *Planning and Design of Airports*, 4th ed. New York: McGraw-Hill, Inc., 1994.

Howard, George P., ed. *Airport Economic Planning.* Cambridge, Mass.: M.I.T. Press, 1974.

Introduction to the Airport Improvement Program (*Amended 1987, 1990, 1992*), U.S. Department of Transportation, Federal Aviation Administration, Office of Airport Planning and Programming, June 1993.

"Moody's on Airports: A New Look at Airport Debt in a Changing Environment," Moody's Public Finance Department, September 1991.

Transportation Quality, Vol. 46, No. 1, January 1992 (99-114).

Whitlock, Edward M. "Financing Airport Facilities." Westport, Conn.: Eno Foundation for Transportation, Inc. *Transportation Quarterly*, Vol. 46, No. 1, January 1992 (99-114).

Wiley, John R. *Airport Administration and Management.* Westport, Conn.: Eno Foundation for Transportation, Inc., 1986.

Part III

Managing growth

8

Airport capacity and delay

Outline

- Introduction
- Capacity, demand, and delay
- Factors affecting capacity and delay
- Measuring delay
- Approaches to reducing delay

Objectives

When you have completed this chapter, you should be able to:

- Understand the relationship between capacity, demand, and delay.
- Describe the factors affecting capacity and delay.
- Discuss the methods of measuring delay.
- Recognize some of the problems inherent in new airport development during the 1990s and beyond.
- Discuss some of the advantages and problems associated with conversion of military airfields and intermodalism.
- Compare the "administrative management" and "demand management" approaches to reducing delay.
- Summarize five administrative management approaches to controlling demand.
- Describe how demand management relies on the price mechanism in determining airport access.

- Discuss some of the factors affecting the use of demand management alternatives.

Introduction

The performance of the airport system is affected by many factors, including the layout of individual airports, the manner in which airspace is organized and used, operating procedures, and application of technology. A major concern in airport system planning is the adequacy of runways to handle anticipated aircraft operations. If air traffic demand exceeds runway capacity, air traffic is delayed, causing expense to airlines, inconvenience to passengers, and increased workload for the FAA air traffic control system.

Most airports are uncongested because they serve small communities and a single runway is able to handle over 200,000 operations annually, which is approximately the amount of activity that would be generated by a city with 350,000 inhabitants. When a city becomes so large that it generates more than 10 to 12 million originating passengers per year, a second commercial service airport may be warranted. A number of large cities with primary service airports fall into this category including Chicago, Los Angeles, Miami, San Francisco, and Washington, D.C.

The concentration of traffic at an airport can result in congestion and delay. *Delay* is defined as the difference between the time an operation actually takes and the time that it would have taken under uncongested conditions without interference from other aircraft. Flights cannot be started or completed on schedule because of the line of aircraft awaiting their turn for takeoff, landing, or use of taxiways and gates at terminal buildings. These delays translate into increased operating costs for airport users and wasted time for passengers. The cause for delay is commonly referred to as a *lack of capacity,* meaning that the airport does not have facilities such as runways, taxiways, or gates in sufficient number to accommodate all those who want to use the airport at peak periods of demand.

In 1997, approximately 245,000 flights were delayed 15 minutes or more, a decrease of 9.6 percent from 1996. The overall decrease in delay was primarily a result of fewer weather-related delays. Twenty-seven airports in the U.S. had more than 20,000 hours of annual delay in 1997, and, if no significant capacity enhancements are made, this number is expected to increase to 31 airports by 2007.

Capacity and delay will become an increasing problem at large-hub airports during the twenty-first century. Federal Aviation Administration

Of the 29 large hub airports, Newark International Airport had the highest average delay per operation in 1997.

The solutions generally advocated by airport operators, airlines, and the FAA are to build additional facilities at crowded airports or to find ways to make more efficient use of existing facilities. The latter course is viewed as attractive because it requires less capital investment and avoids many of the problems associated with increasing the size of the airport and infringing on the surrounding communities. A third course advocated by some is not to increase capacity but to manage demand by channeling it to off-peak times or to alternative sites. The rationale underlying all these approaches is that capacity and demand must somehow be brought into equilibrium in order to prevent or reduce delay.

The relationship of capacity, demand, and delay is considerably more complex than the foregoing suggestions. Before addressing solutions, it is necessary to look more closely at matters of definition and to examine how and where delays occur. It is also necessary to look at specific airports where delays are now being encountered to obtain a clearer picture of the severity of the problem and the points at which it could be attacked.

Capacity, demand, and delay

Capacity generally refers to the ability of an airport to handle a given volume of traffic (demand). It is a limit that cannot be exceeded without incurring an operational penalty. As demand for the use of an airport approaches this limit, lines of users awaiting service begin to develop, and they experience delay. Generally speaking, the higher the demand in relation to capacity, the longer the lines and the greater the delay.

Figure 8-1 shows that delay is not a phenomenon occurring only at the limit of capacity. Some amount of delay will be experienced long before capacity is reached, and it grows exponentially as demand increases. The term *congestion*, referring to the condition where demand approaches or exceeds capacity, is not commonly defined in the technical literature and is used in this chapter only as a descriptor of a situation where demand is high in relation to capacity.

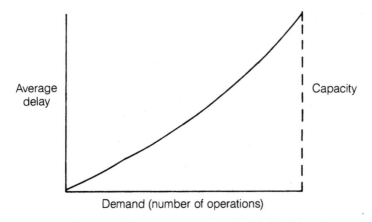

8-1 *Theoretical relationship of capacity and delay.*

Capacity

There are two commonly used definitions of airfield capacity: "*throughput*" and "practical capacity." The *throughput* definition of capacity is the rate at which aircraft can be brought into or out of the airfield (handled), without regard to any delay they might experience. This definition assumes that aircraft will always be present waiting to take off or land, and capacity is measured in terms of the number of such operations that can be accomplished in a given period of time. *Practical capacity* is the number of operations (takeoffs and landings) that can be accommodated with no more than a given amount of delay, usually expressed in terms of maximum acceptable average delay. Practical hourly capacity (PHOCAP) and practical annual capacity (PANCAP) are two commonly used measures based on this definition. PANCAP, for example, is defined as that level of operations that results in not more than 4 minutes average delay per aircraft in the normal peak 2-hour operating period.

Delay

Delays occur on the airfield whenever two or more aircraft seek to use a runway, taxiway, gate, or any other airside facility at the same time. One must wait while the other is accommodated. If all users of the airfield sought service at evenly spaced intervals, the airfield could accommodate them at a rate determined solely by the time required to move them through the facility.

Aircraft arrive and leave not at a uniform rate but somewhat randomly, which means that delay can occur even when demand is low in relation to capacity. Further, the probability of simultaneous need for service increases rapidly with traffic density, so that the average delay per aircraft increases exponentially as demand approaches throughput capacity. When demand exceeds capacity, there is an accumulation of aircraft awaiting service that is directly proportional to the excess of demand over capacity. For example, if the throughput capacity of an airfield is 60 operations per hour and the demand rate is running at 70 operations per hour, each hour will add 10 aircraft to the line awaiting service and 10 minutes to the delay for any subsequent aircraft seeking service. Even if demand later drops to 40 operations per hour, delays will persist for some time because the lines can be depleted at a rate of only 20 aircraft per hour.

Figure 8-2 indicates the relationship between practical and through-put capacity. As demand approaches the limit of throughput capacity, delays increase sharply and, theoretically, become infinite when demand equals or exceeds throughput capacity. Practical capacity, which is always less than throughput capacity, is that level of airfield utilization that can be attained with no more than some acceptable amount of delay.

The acceptability of delay is the key to the concept of practical capacity. Unlike throughput capacity, which can be objectively determined by analysis of airfield components and traffic patterns, practical capacity is a value judgment—a consensus among airport users and operators—about how much delay they can tolerate.

Although practical capacity is usually stated in terms of an average figure, the acceptability of delay is actually determined not so much by the average but by the probability that the delay for a given aircraft will be greater than some amount. Just as demand tends to be nonuniformly distributed, so too is delay.

Figure 8-3 shows a typical distribution of delays encountered by aircraft at a particular level of demand. Note that most delays are of short duration, and that even though the average delay is low (5 minutes), there are a few aircraft encountering relatively long delays of 15 minutes or more; thus, while practical capacity is usually specified as that level of operations that—on average—will result in a given amount of delay, it is understood that the average implies that some percentage of delays will be considerably longer.

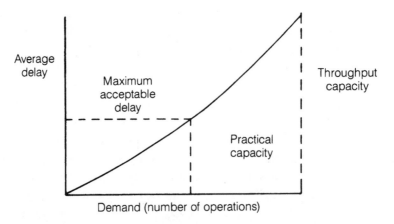

8-2 *Relationship between throughput and practical capacity.*

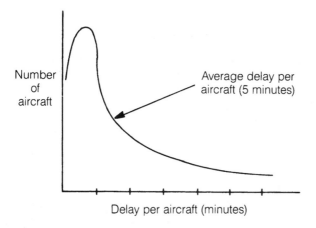

8-3 *Typical probability distribution of aircraft delay.*

How much delay is acceptable? This is a judgment involving three factors. First, it must be recognized that some delay is unavoidable because it occurs for reasons beyond anyone's control—wind direction, weather, aircraft performance characteristics, the randomness of demand for service. Second, some delay, though avoidable, might be too expensive to eliminate, for instance, the cost of remedial measures might exceed the potential benefit. Third, even with the most vigorous and successful effort, the random nature of delay means that there will always be some aircraft encountering delay greater than some "acceptable" length; thus, acceptable delay is essentially a policy decision about the tolerability of delay being longer than some specified amount, taking into account the technical feasibility and economic practicality of available remedies.

Factors affecting capacity and delay

The capacity of an airfield is not constant over time; it might vary considerably during the day or the year as a result of physical and operational factors such as airfield and airspace geometry, air traffic control rules and procedures, weather, and traffic mix. When a figure is given for airfield capacity, it is usually an average based either on some assumed range of conditions or on actual operating experience.

It is the variability of capacity, rather than its average value, that is more detrimental to the overall operation of an airfield. Much of the strategy for successful management of an airfield involves devising ways to compensate for factors that, individually or in combination, act to lower capacity or to induce delay. These factors can be grouped in five categories: (1) airfield characteristics, (2) airspace characteristics, (3) air traffic control, (4) meteorological conditions, and (5) demand characteristics.

Airfield characteristics

The physical characteristics and layout of runways, taxiways, and aprons are basic determinants of the ability to accommodate various types of aircraft and the rate at which they can be handled. Also important is the type of equipment (lighting, navigation aids, radar, and the like) installed on the airfield as a whole or on particular segments. For any given configuration of runways and taxiways in use, capacity is constant; however, capacity varies as configurations change.

Airspace characteristics

The situation of the airfield in relation to other nearby airports and in relation to natural obstacles and features of the built environment determines the paths through the airspace that can be taken to and from the airport. Basically, the airspace geometry for a given airfield does not change over time; however, when there are two or more airports in proximity, operations at one airport can interfere with operations at another, causing the acceptance rate of one or both airports to suffer or requiring aircraft to fly circuitous routes to avoid conflict. In some cases, the interdependence of approach and departure paths for nearby airports can force one to hold departures until arrivals at the other have cleared the airspace or necessitate that each leave gaps in the arrival or departure streams to accommodate traffic at the other.

Air traffic control

The rules and procedures of air traffic control, intended primarily to ensure safety of flight, are basic determinants of airfield capacity and delay. The rules governing aircraft separation, runway occupancy, spacing of arrivals and departures, and the use of parallel or converging runways can have an overall effect on throughput or can induce delays between successive operations. ATC rules and procedures have an especially important influence on capacity and delay at airfields where two or three runways might be in use at the same time or where there might be several arrival streams that must be merged on one final approach path.

A related factor affecting delay is the noise-abatement procedures adopted by FAA and by local airport authorities. These usually take the form of restrictions on flight paths over noise-sensitive areas or reduction (or outright prohibition) of operations during certain hours. These noise-control measures can have an adverse effect on capacity. For example, the runway configuration with the highest capacity might not be usable at certain times because it leads to un-acceptably high noise levels in surrounding areas. Similarly, some noise-abatement procedures involve circuitous flight paths that may increase delays. The airport must thus make a trade-off between usable capacity and noise control, with the usual result being some loss of capacity or increase of delay.

Meteorological conditions

Airport capacity is usually highest in clear weather, when visibility is at its best. Fog, low ceilings, precipitation, strong winds, or accumu-lations of snow or ice on the runway can cut capacity severely or close the airport altogether. Even a common occurrence such as a wind shift can disrupt operations while traffic is rerouted to a differ-ent pattern; if the new pattern is not optimum, capacity can be reduced for as long as the wind prevails. A large airport with multi-ple runways might have 30 or more possible patterns of use, some of which might have a substantially lower capacity than the others.

For most airports, it is the combined effect of weather, runway con-figuration, and ATC rules and procedures that results in the most severe loss of capacity or the longest delay lines. Much of the effort to reduce delays at these airports, through airfield management strategy and installation of improved technology, is aimed at minimizing the disparity between visual meteorological conditions (VMC) and instru-ment meteorological conditions (IMC) capacity. *Visual meteorological conditions* are those in which atmospheric conditions permit pilots to approach, land, or take off by visual reference and to see and avoid other aircraft. *Instrument meteorological conditions* are those in which other aircraft cannot be seen and safe separation must be ensured solely by ATC rules and procedures. Under IMC, pilots must also rely on instruments for navigation and guidance to the runway.

Demand characteristics

Demand—not only the number of aircraft seeking service, but also their performance characteristics and the manner in which they use the airport—has an important effect on capacity and delay. The basic relationship among demand, capacity, and delay described earlier is that as demand approaches capacity, delays increase sharply. But for any given level of demand, the mix of aircraft with respect to speed, size, flight characteristics, and pilot proficiency will also determine the rate at which they can be handled and the delays that might result. Mismatches of speed or size between successive aircraft in the arrival stream, for example, can force air traffic controllers to increase separation, thus reducing the rate at which aircraft can be cleared over the runway threshold or off the runway.

For any given level of demand, the distribution of arrivals and departures and the extent to which they are bunched rather than uniformly spaced also determines the delay that will be encountered. In part, this tendency of traffic to peak at certain times is a function of the nature of the flights using the airport. For example, at airports with a high proportion of hub-and-spoke operations, where passengers land at the airport only to transfer to another flight, the traffic pattern is characterized by closely spaced blocks of arrivals and departures. Accommodating this pattern can cause much greater delays than if arriving and departing flights are spread and more uniformly intermixed.

Measuring delay

Currently, the FAA gathers delay data from two different sources. The first is through the *Air Traffic Operations Management System (ATOMS)*, in which FAA personnel record aircraft that are delayed 15 or more minutes by specific cause (weather, terminal volume, center volume, closed runways or taxiways, and NAS equipment interruptions). Aircraft that are delayed by less than 15 minutes are not recorded in ATOMS.

The second source of delay data is through the *Consolidated Operations and Delay Analysis System (CODAS)*. CODAS is a new FAA database and reporting system containing delay information by phase of flight for U.S. domestic flights. CODAS is developed by merging the former Airline Service Quality Performance (ASQP) database with the FAA's Enhanced Traffic Management System (ETMS). In addition, CODAS contains flight schedule information from the Official Airline Guide (OAG) and weather data from the National Oceanic and Atmospheric Administration (NOAA). CODAS contains actual times for gate out, wheels off, wheels on, and gate in. From this information, gate delays, taxi-out delays, airborne delays, and taxi-in delays as small as 1 minute are computed. CODAS measures delay where it occurs, not where it is caused. The principal purpose of CODAS is to support analytical studies and not the day-to-day management of the ATC system. CODAS will not replace ATOMS, which will continue to be the official FAA delay reporting system.

The delay data reported through ATOMS is not without its problems. It reports only delays of 15 minutes or more; it aggregates flight delays, thus making it impossible to determine if a particular flight was delayed; and it reports only flight delays due to an air traffic problem (i.e., weather, terminal, volume, center volume, closed runways or taxiways, and NAS equipment interruptions). ATOMS is based on controller reports, and the quality and completeness of reporting vary considerably with controller workload. In addition, it measures delay against the standard of flight times published in the OAG. This, in all probability, results in an overestimation of delay because there is wide variation in the "no-delay" time from airport to airport and, at a given airport, among various runway configurations. Many operations, when measured against a single nominal standard, are counted as delays but are within the normal expectancy for a given airport under given circumstances. There might also be a distortion in the opposite direction. Most airline schedules, especially for flights into and out of busy airports, have a built-in allowance for delay. In part, this is simply realistic planning, but there is also a tendency to inflate published flight times so as to maintain a public image of on-line operation. Finally, ATOMS incorporates whatever delay might be experienced en route. Delays en route might not be attributable to conditions at the airport, and including them in the totals for airports probably leads to overestimation.

Approaches to reducing delay

Commercial service airports, particularly in large metropolitan areas, are experiencing congestion and delays on the airfield, in the terminals, and in ground access to the airport itself. In many cases, airport sponsors are unable to expand to develop the additional facilities needed to continue to provide quality service to air travelers and the airlines. Without additional capacity, the increasing aircraft operations and passenger growth forecast for the future will result in greater delays, more costly operations, and less efficient passenger service. In addition, airfield pavement designs will require capacity improvements and strengthening to accommodate the increasing number of larger, heavier aircraft in the air carrier and general aviation fleet. System planning studies have been conducted by many metropolitan areas and state planning organizations in attempts to identify new sites for the construction of new airports or for capacity development at existing airports.

New airport development

Historically, the development of new airports and the construction of new runways and runway extensions at existing airports has offered the greatest potential for increasing aviation system capacity. These options for achieving major capacity increases are becoming more difficult because of surrounding community development, environmental concerns, shortage of available adjacent property and funding required, lack of public support, rival commercial and residential interests, and other competing requirements. The new Denver International Airport (DIA), for example, will increase capacity and reduce delays not only in the Denver area but also throughout the aviation system. However, at a cost of over $5 billion for a new airport like Denver, it will remain a challenge to finance and build others. Opened in 1995, DIA is the only major new commercial service airport constructed in the past 10 years. Studies in other areas including San Diego, Orange County south of Los Angeles, Seattle, Chicago, New York, Boston, and Miami have not resulted in identifying new airport sites, or in developing public support for the project.

As environmental, financial, and other constraints continue to restrict the development of new airport facilities in the United States, an increased emphasis has been placed on the redevelopment and expansion of existing airport facilities. The construction of new runways and extension of existing runways are the most direct and significant actions that can be taken to improve capacity at existing airports. Large capacity increases, under both visual flight rules (VFR) and instrument flight rules (IFR), come from the addition of new runways that are properly placed to allow additional independent arrival/departure streams. The resulting increase in capacity is from 33 percent to 100 percent (depending on whether the baseline airport has a single, dual, or triple runway configuration).

Of the top 100 U.S. airports, 18 completed runway construction projects between 1995 and 1998, eight airports are currently constructing new runways or runway extensions, and 59 airports have proposed runway construction projects.

Conversion of closed military airfields

Recent changes in the world's political and military situation, combined with efforts to reduce the nation's deficit, have resulted in plans to close a number of military airfields and provided a one-time opportunity for state and local governments. Conversion of these military airfields into civil airports would provide significant aviation capacity gains with relatively small additional investments by the state and local governments. Most of these military airfields are designed to accommodate heavy wide-body aircraft and already have the 8,000 to 13,000 foot runway lengths necessary to support long-haul operations.

Many of these airfields are conveniently located in the vicinity of congested metropolitan areas where the search for major new airports has been under way for years. Examples include the Miami area where Homestead Air Force Base (AFB) has become available; Bergstrom AFB near Austin, Texas, where the city had previously been planning to replace the Robert Mueller Municipal Airport with a new airport; Williams AFB near Phoenix; Pease AFB located 60 miles north of Boston Logan, where it could provide service to the metropolitan area north of Boston; and Norton AFB near San Bernardino in the Los Angeles area. Some of the smaller military airfields available for conversion are ideal for use as reliever airports, relieving small/slow aircraft operations from the nearby commercial airports serving scheduled air carrier operations.

In addition to military airfield conversions to civil airports, there are a number of military airfields now in operation accommodating joint civil and military use. For the most part, these joint-use airfields provide primary service to the communities and have a modest impact on system capacity. For example, in South Carolina, Charleston AFB provides primary commercial service for Charleston. Similarly, Myrtle Beach AFB, which is now the Myrtle Beach International Airport, previously provided primary commercial air service through joint use to a community that might not otherwise have had air carrier access to the commercial system. Also, Dillingham Army Airfield (AAF), Hawaii, and Rickenbacker Air National Guard (ANG) Base, Columbus, Ohio, provide congestion relief to the airports at Honolulu International and Port Columbus International Airports, respectively.

To assist in transitioning military airfields to civilian airports, the *Military Airport Program (MAP)*, established as a funding set aside under the Airport Improvement Program (AIP), provides grant funding of airport master planning and capital development. The MAP allows the Secretary of Transportation to designate current or former military airfields for participation in the program. To participate, eligible airport sponsors apply to the FAA. In determining whether or not to designate a facility, the FAA considers (1) proximity to major metropolitan air carrier airports with current or projected high levels of delay; (2) capacity of existing airspace and traffic flow patterns in the metropolitan area; (3) the availability of local sponsors for civil development; (4) existing levels of operation; (5) existing facilities; and (6) any other appropriate factors.

There are currently about 44 military airfields closing as a result of the Department of Defense's base closures programs approved in 1988, 1991, 1993, and 1995. By 1998, a total of 20 major military airfields have been converted to civil use, and this number could reach as high as 36. In addition, there are about 20 existing joint-use agreements and 18 long-term leases executed by the DOD that allow civil airport sponsors to operate at active military airfields and surplus military facilities. Under the MAP, airports receive funding for airport capital development, including rehabilitating airport pavements, terminals, lighting systems, improving access roads, automobile parking facilities, airport master plan studies, and other eligible projects necessary to convert a military airfield to an active civil airport.

The most important step in converting a closing military airfield or setting up a joint-use facility is to establish the state or local government sponsorship for the proposed civil aviation operation. The conversion or joint use of military airfields is not a panacea for aviation system capacity problems, but it is an important component in the strategy of the state and local governments and the FAA to maximize the safe utilization of the nation's aviation system.

Intermodalism

Aviation is a part of the national transportation system. Each mode of transportation within the system has specific strengths and weaknesses. The transportation system cannot work effectively if critical segments are not connected. No matter how good the individual parts of the system may be, the effectiveness of the overall system depends on the connections a passenger or consignment of cargo can make in getting from origin to destination.

Intermodalism is a goal fostered under National Transportation Policy and the Intermodal Surface Transportation Efficiency Act enacted in 1991. Its purpose is to improve the speed, reliability, and cost-effectiveness of the country's overall transportation system. One initial objective is to devise an integrated transportation strategy to promote intermodal exchanges among highway, railway, waterway, and air transportation. Intermodalism is not intended to bypass the airports but to bring passengers to and from the airport and their point of origin and destination.

In the past, the emphasis at most airports has been on ground access for passengers via roads and highways. Airport planning studies should begin to investigate the feasibility of subway or train stations on the airport with easy access to passenger terminals and of cargo-handling facilities that enable quick, easy transfer among trucks, trains, and airplanes.

High-speed passenger trains, which will reach speeds of 150 to 200 miles per hour, have been recommended or are being studied for use in several densely populated intercity transportation corridors, for example, Washington–Philadelphia–New York–Boston in the Northeast; Portland–Seattle–Vancouver in the Pacific Northwest; Dallas–Fort Worth–Houston–San Antonio in Texas; and San Francisco–Los Angeles–San Diego on the Pacific coast. High-speed rail appears to be a reasonable transportation alternative, especially for densely populated urban corridors and distances of less than 450 miles, that would serve to reduce airport congestion at many delay-problem airports.

On the one hand, high-speed rail represents another competitive force for short-haul air traffic and can be seen as a threat to air carrier markets for trips shorter than 500 miles. Commercial air already provides rapid intercity mass transportation system. On the other hand, high-speed rail is ideally suited for short-haul intercity trips and as a feeder for major hub airports, especially in the future when new airports might have to be built in outlying locations. These high-speed trains could replace many of the short-haul and feeder flights that add to the congestion and delay at the major hub airports.

In fact, the airlines themselves may be partners in operating such trains, much as in Europe. Intercity high-speed rail systems would be designed for immediate access to the airport, with rail stations "inside" passenger terminals. In large metropolitan areas, high-speed rail could also provide the connection among multiple airports serving the region, carrying passengers during the peak hours of the day and perhaps carrying cargo to and from the airports during the off-peak hours at night.

Growth in air travel, congestion of urban highways, and environmental concerns will continue to draw increased attention to the adequacy of ground access to airports, particularly major airports in large metropolitan areas. The Federal Highway Administration (FHWA) and the FAA developed, in December 1996, a report entitled Intermodal Ground Access to Airports: A Planning Guide. The report provides policy guidance, rules of thumb, data, and analytical techniques related to airport access. It is intended for use by airport operators, local government, metropolitan planning organizations, consultants, and others involved in the identification and resolution of access problems.

Most air travel is between a few major airports and at certain times of the day. Chronic delay is limited to a very few specific times and places, and one of the principal causes is peaking of traffic flow. One approach is to manage the demand to fit within existing capacity.

Administrative and Demand Management

Two basic approaches to managing demand have the same objective: to ease congestion by diverting some traffic to times and places where it can be handled more promptly or efficiently. This might be done through *administrative management*; the airport authority or another governmental body might allocate airport access by setting quotas on passenger enplanements or on the number and type of aircraft operations that will be accommodated during a specific period. The alternative approach is economic—to structure the pricing system so that market forces allocate scarce airport facilities among competing users; thus, *demand management* does not add capacity, it promotes more effective or economically efficient use of existing facilities.

Any scheme of demand management denies some users free or complete access to the airport of their choice. This denial is often decried as a violation of the traditional federal policy of freedom of the airways and the traditional "first-come, first-served" approach to allocating the use of airport facilities. Economists reject this argument on the grounds that it is a distortion of the concept of freedom to accord unrestricted access to any and all users without regard to the societal costs of providing airport facilities. Attempts to manage demand are also criticized for adversely affecting the growth of the aviation industry and the level of service to the traveling public. Nevertheless, as growth in traffic has outstripped the ability to expand and build airports, some forms of demand management have already come into use, and many industry observers have taken the position that some form of airport use restrictions will become increasingly important in dealing with delay and in utilizing existing airport capacity efficiently.

Administrative management

Several administrative management approaches are being adopted to manage demand at individual airports or for a metropolitan region. Among these are (1) required diversion of some traffic to reliever airports; (2) more balanced use of metropolitan air carrier airports; (3) restriction of airport access by aircraft type or use; (4) establishment of quotas (either on the number of operations or on passenger enplanements); and (5) "rehubbing" or redistributing transfer traffic from busy airports to underused airports.

Diversion of traffic In some metropolitan areas, the shortage of airport capacity might not be general, but confined to one overcrowded airport. Perhaps other airports in the region could absorb some of the demand. The FAA lists 27 airports in the Chicago area, 51 in Los Angeles area, and 53 in the Dallas-Fort Worth region. The vast majority of these airports are small and suited only for general aviation (GA) aircraft, but in some cases there is also an underutilized commercial service airport.

The best regionwide solution to the problem of delay at a major airport might be to divert some traffic away from the busy airport to either a general aviation reliever airport or a lightly used commercial airport. To some extent, this can occur as a result of natural market forces. When delays become intolerable at the busy airport, users begin to divert of their own accord. While those who choose to move to a less crowded facility do so for their own benefit, they also reduce somewhat delays incurred by users that continue to operate at the crowded airport. Public policy might encourage this diversion through administrative action or economic incentives before traffic growth makes conditions intolerable or necessitates capital investment to accommodate peaks of demand at the busy airport.

Diversion of general aviation from busy air carrier airports is often an attractive solution. GA traffic, because it consists mostly of small, slow-moving aircraft, does not mix well with faster, heavier air carrier traffic. GA operators—especially those flying for recreational or training purposes—want to avoid the delays and inconveniences (and sometimes the hazards) of operating at a major airport. These fliers are often willing to make use of GA airports located elsewhere in the region if suitable facilities are available.

Diversion of GA traffic from commercial air carrier airports has been taking place for many years. As air carrier traffic grows at a particular location, it almost always tends to displace GA traffic. FAA has encouraged this trend by designating approximately 334 airports as "relievers" or "satellites" to air carrier airports, and earmarking funds especially for developing and upgrading these airports. Many other airports, although not specifically designated as relievers, serve the same function; they provide an alternative operating site for GA aircraft well removed from the main commercial airport of the region.

To be attractive to a broad spectrum of GA users, a reliever airport should be equipped with instrument approaches and provide runways capable of handling the larger, more sophisticated GA aircraft. In addition, users need facilities for aircraft servicing, repair, and maintenance, as well as suitable ground access to the metropolitan area.

Not all GA aircraft can make use of reliever airports. Some might be delivering passengers or freight to connect with commercial flights at the air carrier airport. Others might be large business jets that require the longer runways of a major airport.

In general, airport authorities do not have the power to exclude GA as a class, although this has been attempted on occasion. For example, in the late 1970s, the airport management and city government of St. Louis attempted to exclude all private aircraft from Lambert Airport. This ordinance was overturned by the courts as discriminatory.

Where they have had any policy on the matter, local airport authorities have attempted to make GA airports attractive to users by

Corporate aircraft and commercial jet prepare for takeoff.

offering good facilities or by differential pricing schemes. This approach is most effective where the commercial airport and the principal reliever are operated by the same entity. The state of Maryland, owner of Baltimore-Washington International Airport, operates a separate GA airport, Glenn L. Martin Field, and has a specific policy of encouraging GA traffic to use it rather than the main airport. The master plan for Cleveland Hopkins International Airport depends on the availability of the city-owned Lakefront Airport as a reliever. If that airport should for some reason cease operation as a GA reliever, Hopkins would experience a great increase in traffic, which might necessitate additional construction that is not now planned.

Most local airport authorities, however, do not operate their own GA relievers. Some large airport authorities plan and coordinate activities with nearby reliever airports operated by other municipalities or private individuals, but this has not been the general case. The system of relievers in each region has tended to grow up without any specific planning or coordination on the regional level.

Development of GA relievers is not without problems. These airports are also subject to complaints about noise, and they experience the same difficulties as commercial airports in expanding their facilities or in developing a new airport site. Further, because many GA airports are small and function just on the ragged edge of profitability, problems of noise or competing land use can actually threaten the airport's existence. The number of airports available for public use in the United States has been declining. Between 1980 and 1998, for example, the number of public-use airports declined from 6,519 to 5,357. Although most of the airports that closed were small, privately owned facilities, some industry observers worry that the nation is irrevocably losing many potential reliever airports just as it has become clear that they are vital.

Balanced use of large airports   At the largest commercial service airports, GA activity consists primarily of flights by large business and executive aircraft. This type of GA traffic accounts for approximately 10 to 20 percent of the use of major airports, a figure that many consider the "irreducible minimum." The delays that persist at these airports are primarily the result of air carrier demand that can be satisfied only by another commercial service airport. In several metropolitan areas, it is clear that the commercial airports are not used in a balanced manner. For example, San Francisco International is experiencing delay problems while nearby Oakland airport is underutilized. Washington National is overcrowded while Dulles International and Baltimore-Washington International are looking for business. Orlando-Sanford and Daytona Beach International are underutilized compared with busy Orlando International.

Similar pairs exist in Chicago (O'Hare and Midway), Dallas (Dallas-Fort Worth and Love Field), and Houston (Houston Intercontinental and Hobby). A policy designed to divert traffic from busy to under-utilized airports would have a generally positive effect on the ability of metropolitan areas to accommodate air traffic. Further, it might obviate the need for expansion or expensive technological improvements designed to reduce delays at the busy airport.

Diverting air carrier traffic to alternative airports is not a simple solution; there are a number of problems. One is simply the habits of the traveling public. People are accustomed to using the busier airport. They probably prefer the better ground access, the larger choice of flight times and destinations, the greater variety of carriers, and other advantages that the busy airport offers.

Air carriers, sensitive to public preferences, tend to concentrate their service at the busier airport, where they perceive a larger market. It is in the carrier's economic interest to serve the airport where passengers want to go. The busier airport is a known and viable enterprise, while the underutilized alternative airport is a risk. Air carriers are justifiably reluctant to isolate themselves from the major market by moving all their service to the less popular airport. On the other hand, serving both airports imposes an economic burden that carriers seldom choose to bear, as they would incur the additional expense of setting up and operating duplicate ground services. In addition, splitting their passengers between two airports might make scheduling of flights more complicated and lead to inefficient utilization of aircraft.

These obstacles have sometimes been overcome in locations where airport operators have the authority to encourage a diversion of traffic from one airport to another. For example, in the New York area, the Port Authority of New York and New Jersey operates all three air carrier airports. In theory, this gives the port authority the ability to establish regulatory policies or economic incentives to encourage the diversion of some traffic to Newark. In practice, however, measures adopted to promote traffic redistribution have not been fully effective. The recent growth of traffic at Newark has been due primarily to new carriers entering the New York market and not diversion of established carriers.

In contrast, San Francisco and Oakland airports are operated by separate sponsors. San Francisco, despite severe problems of delay, would rightly be reluctant to encourage passengers and air carriers to move to Oakland. Even though more balanced regional airport use might be achieved and the long-range need for expansion at San Francisco reduced, the short-range effect would be that San Francisco would lose revenues to a competitor. There is no regional authority with the power to promote this reallocation of traffic.

Restriction of access by aircraft type One means of diverting certain traffic from a busy airport to one with unused capacity is to restrict access to the busy airport on the basis of aircraft type or use. Restriction of aircraft access to airports by size or performance characteristics might affect airport capacity and delay in several ways. First, the mix of aircraft using a runway system helps to determine capacity. When aircraft are of similar size, speed, and operating characteristics, runway acceptance rate is greater than when performance characteristics vary widely. Similar aircraft can be more uniformly and accurately spaced on approach and departure, thereby smoothing out irregularities in the traffic stream, which is a major factor causing delay; thus, at airports where the bottleneck is in the runway system, restrictions that narrow the range of aircraft using that system might have a beneficial effect. Diversion of small GA or commuter aircraft to other airports or construction of a separate short runway dedicated to their use could improve the ability of the airport to handle larger transports or the overall traffic mix.

A second implication of limiting access to specific aircraft types is that it might reduce the need for capital improvements required to accommodate a larger variety of aircraft. For example, Washington National Airport does not accept jumbo jet aircraft. Allowing larger aircraft into National would probably necessitate changes in runways, taxiways, aprons, and gates. In addition, the larger number of passengers per aircraft would put additional strain on National's already congested terminal and landside facilities, making a number of collateral improvements necessary.

Quotas One technique of administrative management now in use at a few airports is the quota system—an administratively established limit on the number of operations per hour. Because delay increases exponentially as demand approaches capacity, a small reduction in the number of hourly operations can have a significant effect on delay. This makes the quota an attractive measure for dealing promptly (and inexpensively) with airport congestion.

Examples of airports with quotas are O'Hare, La Guardia, JFK, and Washington National, airports covered by the *FAA high-density rule*. The quotas at these airports were established by FAA in 1973 on the basis of estimated limits of the air traffic control (ATC) system and airport runways at that time. An example of a locally imposed quota is John Wayne Airport in Orange County, California, which limits scheduled air carrier operations to an annual average of 41 operations per day. This quota is based on noise considerations as well as limitations on the size of the terminal and gate areas.

During busy hours, demand for operational slots typically exceeds the quota. At the airports covered by the high-density rule, the slots are allocated among different user classes. For example, at National, where there are 60 slots available per hour, 37 are allotted to air carriers, 11 to commuter carriers, and 12 to general aviation. During visual meteorological conditions, more than 60 operations can be handled, and aircraft without assigned slots may be accommodated at the discretion of air traffic controllers and the airport manager.

At airports where the quota system is in force, slots may be allocated in various ways: a reservation system, negotiation, or administrative determination. The GA slots are generally distributed through a reservation system—the first user to call for a reservation gets the slot.

However, for commuters and air carriers, the slots at the high-density rule airports are still subject to a great deal of controversy. In

1986, FAA declared the slots the property of the airlines holding them by allowing carriers to sell or lease slots to other airlines. A few available slots were also distributed by lottery.

Under airline regulation, when the number of carriers and routes was fairly stable, airline scheduling committees would meet under antitrust immunity to negotiate the flights to be allotted to each user, which meant the incumbent carriers. From 1979 to 1986, the committees had to accommodate new entrants and the changing market strategies of incumbent carriers. On several occasions during this period, negotiations between carriers concerning available slots nearly broke down, which would have necessitated that the FAA use administrative means to distribute the slots.

Rehubbing A systemwide response to alleviate delays at busy airports is redistribution of operations to other, less busy airports in other regions. Some air carriers, especially those with a high proportion of interconnecting flights, might voluntarily move their operations to underutilized airports located at some distance from the congested hub. Transfer passengers account for a large percentage of traffic at some large airports. About three-fourths of passengers at Atlanta and nearly half of passengers at Chicago, Denver, and

Rehubbing would relieve congestion as shown in this photo of Bush International Airport, Houston, TX. Houston Airport System

Dallas-Fort Worth arrive at those airports merely to change planes for some other destination. There is an advantage for carriers in choosing a busy airport as a transfer hub—they can offer passengers a wide variety of possible connections; however, when the airport becomes too crowded, the costs of delay might begin to outweigh the advantages of the large airport, and carriers might find it attractive to establish new hubs at smaller, less busy airports.

This rehubbing of the airport system is already a trend. Redistribution of operations has certainly been facilitated by the deregulation of the airline industry, which allowed carriers greater freedom in restructuring their routes. Medium-size airports have received increased air carrier activity since deregulation, and some carriers have shifted their transfer operations to these less-congested facilities. For example, US-Air has developed Charlotte (North Carolina), Dayton (Ohio), and Baltimore-Washington (Maryland) as regional hubs.

In addition to relief from congestion, carriers who have moved to less busy airports find another perhaps more compelling advantage. Because there is often little service by competing carriers at those locations, the hubbing carrier has greater control of passengers, who can transfer only to departing flights of the airline that brought them, not to a competitor's.

While it is doubtful that rehubbing has actually reduced delay problems at major airports, it does seem clear that development of transfer hubs at medium-size airports has allowed for growth that might not have been possible had the carriers sought to concentrate their activities at the major hubs. Further, rehubbing has taken advantage of a certain "overcapacity" in the national airport system by making greater use of the facilities available at medium-size airports.

Demand management

Administrative management of airport use—whether by restricted access for certain types of aircraft, by demand balancing among metropolitan area airports, or by imposition of quotas—offers the promise of immediate and relatively low-cost relief of airport congestion. As long-term measures, these solutions might not be as attractive. Administrative limits tend to bias the outcome toward maintenance of the status quo when applied over a long period of time. Because the economic value of airport access is not fully considered in setting administrative limits, incumbents cannot be displaced by others who would place a higher value on use of the airport. Further, incumbents and potential new entrants alike have no way to indicate the true economic value they would place on increased capacity. Economists contend that a vital market signal is missing and that airport operators and the federal government cannot obtain a true picture of future capacity needs. Administratively limiting demand, they say, creates an artificial market equilibrium that—over the long term—distorts appreciation of the nature, quality, and costs of air transportation service that the public requires. Economists, therefore, favor a scheme of allocating airport access by demand management which relies on the price mechanism.

At present, price plays a rather weak role in determining airport access or in modulating demand. Access to public use airports, except for the few large airports where quotas are imposed, is generally unrestricted so long as one is willing to pay landing fees and endure the costs of congestion and delay. Landing fees, most often based solely on aircraft weight and invariant by time of day, make up a very small fraction of operational cost—typically 2 to 3 percent for air carriers and even less for GA. Further, landing fees are not uniform from airport to airport. In many cases, landing fees are set so that, in the aggregate, they make up the difference between the cost of operating the airport and the revenues received from other sources such as concessions, leases, and automobile parking fees.

This leads economists to the conclusion that landing fees are somewhat arbitrary and do not reflect the costs imposed on the airport by an aircraft operation. Economists suggest that by including airport costs and demand as determinants of user fees, delay could be significantly reduced. The two most commonly advocated methods of achieving this are differential pricing and auctioning of landing rights.

Differential pricing Many economists argue that weight-based landing fees are counterproductive because they do not vary with demand, and consequently provide no incentive to utilize airport facilities during off-peak hours. Further, they do not reflect the high capital costs of facilities used only during peak hours. Thus, economists contend, a more effective pricing method would be to charge higher user fees during peak hours and lower fees during off-peak hours. Theoretically, the net effect of such a pricing policy would be a more uniform level of demand.

Much of the traffic moved away from peak hours by higher landing fees would probably be GA. Correspondingly, the benefits of peak-hour fees would be greater at airports with a high proportion of GA activity. But peak-hour fees could also be structured so as to affect the pattern of air carrier activity. These charges would have to be fairly high because landing fees represent only a small fraction of air carrier operating costs and because increases can be passed on to passengers.

Despite increases in landing fees, carriers would want to continue to use the airport at peak times, either to have access to a large number of passengers or because long-haul scheduling problems require them to serve a particular airport during certain hours; thus, they would absorb some increase in landing fees—just as they absorb the cost of delays—as part of the cost of doing business; however, some flights might be moved to off-peak hours if the charges were high enough. It is possible that properly structured peak-hour prices, if they were reflected in fares, could have an effect not only on the airline's scheduling patterns but on passengers' travel habits as well. If significant savings were possible, some passengers would choose to travel during off-peak hours.

It is difficult to project accurately the changes in patterns of airport use that might be brought about by peak-hour surcharges. Some analysts estimate that peak-hour surcharges, along with improvement of the ATC system, would reduce anticipated air carrier delay significantly in the future. Others argue that although expansion might be inevitable at many airports, peak-hour surcharges could significantly delay the need for expansion and reduce financial pressure at a number of airports. Another important aspect of peak-hour surcharges noted by the Congressional Budget Office (CBO) is that even if they do not reduce traffic levels at peak hours to the desired levels, they could provide airports with increased revenues to expand facilities and, consequently, to reduce delays.

Some observers reject this line of reasoning. They contend that to be effective in shifting demand to slack periods, peak-hour charges would have to be set so high that they would be politically unacceptable. Further, there is no assurance that airlines would not average the higher costs of peak-hour access at certain airports with the lower cost at other times and places and pass this along to all passengers as a general fare increase. Airlines would thus create an internal cross-subsidy in their fare structure to cover the higher costs of access to some airports. Because the average fare increase would likely be small, the economic signal to the public would be diminished and have scant effect on travel behavior.

A major problem with the concept of peak-hour surcharges is how to determine the level of surcharge. One widely advocated method is to charge the airport user the full marginal costs of airport facilities. In other words, each airport user pays a share of the additional capital and operating costs to the airport authority of providing service at the time demanded. For example, if a user lands at an airport during a period of peak demand where two or more runways are necessary to handle the traffic, the charge should include a contribution to the cost of building, operating, and maintaining those additional runways. On the other hand, if the user lands during an off-peak hour, when the one runway in use is not sought by others, there would be no additional charge. While both on-peak and off-peak users would pay fees to cover maintenance, wear and tear, or other costs, only peak-hour users would pay the additional costs associated with the time of use. The resulting user fees would be directly related to the levels of airport activity, producing the desired effect of higher fees during peak hours and a strong price signal to use the airport at off-peak hours.

Some contend that a system of marginal cost pricing should be based on the delay costs that each peak-hour user imposes on other users. For example, during peak hours, airport users would be charged a fee based on the delay costs associated with their operations. This creates a system of user fees where the fees become progressively larger as delays increase. Proponents contend that using marginal delay costs as the basis for pricing airport access provides a stronger incentive for off-peak airport use than a scheme based on marginal facility costs alone.

Implementing a policy of differential pricing—whether based on marginal facility cost, marginal delay cost, or some purely arbitrary scheme—is difficult. It is likely that a significant increase in airport user fees will raise questions of equity. Higher fees might be more burdensome for small airlines and new entrants than for established carriers. There are a number of examples where airport operators have attempted to increase user fees and have been challenged by air carriers and general aviation. In some cases, air carrier landing fees are established in long-term contracts that cannot be easily changed.

GA users often contend that differential pricing is discriminatory because it favors those with the ability to pay, and illegal because it denies the right to use a publicly funded facility. Economists rebut this argument by pointing out that time-of-use price is neither discriminatory nor illegal so long as price differences reflect cost differences and that it is fair and just to set prices on the basis of the costs that each user imposes on others and on society generally.

In general, peak-hour surcharges represent an attempt to manage demand by charging cost-based landing fees. Access to airports is not limited except by the user's willingness to bear the additional cost imposed during peak hours. Another method of reducing peak-hour airport activity involves limiting airport access through a process by which landing rights (slots) are auctioned to the highest bidder. The auction is a hybrid process—partly administrative, partly economic—in which access is regulated, but the right of access is distributed through a market-oriented mechanism.

Slot auctions Slot auctions have been advocated as the best method of allocating scarce airport landing rights on the grounds that if airport access must be limited, it should be treated as a scarce resource and priced accordingly. The method to accomplish this is a system whereby the price of airport access is determined by demand. Slot auctions allow peak-hour access only to those users willing to pay a market-determined price. However, as operations increase, there might not be enough extra capacity in the traditional off-peak time periods to accommodate additional operations without significant delays. At this point, slot allocations will only be able to reduce delay by effectively "capping" the total number of operations at the airport. This program can be cumbersome to execute both equitably and efficiently. Its use within this country has been restricted to the four high-density traffic airports, Washington National, Chicago O'Hare, New York La Guardia, and New York Kennedy, where delays have historically affected the performance of the National Airspace System (NAS).

It was mentioned earlier that in 1986 the FAA granted the right to the airlines to buy and sell the slots that they held. While the buy-sell slot rule has stabilized the situation somewhat for the airlines, airports strongly argue that the funds should go toward the air transportation system, not the few air carriers who obtained the slots for free.

Critics also contend that the current slot sale process gives an advantage to the airlines already operating at the airport and denies access to competitors, providing the existing users with virtual monopolies and a financial windfall. Slot holders know that without a slot, no competitor can enter a market, and consequently, slots represent one of the most significant barriers to entry in the airline business today. Their impact on the industry extends far beyond the few airports where they are imposed because markets critical to many communities either begin or end at one of these facilities.

The carriers that control the slots contend that the system is fair because they took the risk necessary to develop the market and, as a result, they should be rewarded by retaining the slots. Contrary to FAA's expectations, the slot sale plan has not fostered an active market; available slots are scarce and expensive.

Factors affecting the use of demand management alternatives

The demand management techniques enumerated above could—in theory—reduce delay. Some have actually been tried, with mixed results; however, there are factors that might affect the ability of airport operators or the federal government to implement them on a wide scale.

Some argue that regulations restricting airport access are unconstitutional because they interfere with interstate commerce and abridge the right of access for some users. Many industry observers shudder to think that the kinds of access restrictions in effect at National Airport might become common at major airports. Determination of whether they would be an undue burden is a delicate matter that must be decided on a case-by-case basis, depending on the parties involved, the location of the airport, and its importance to the national system. FAA itself does not appear to encourage the spread of quotas and other restrictions imposed by airports.

Deregulation has made the allocation of slots through negotiation or sale a more difficult process, as the scheduling committees must constantly accommodate new entrants or changes in incumbent carriers' levels of service.

Policies to encourage development of reliever airports or more balanced utilization of airports in metropolitan regions are unlikely to be implemented in locales where airports are competitors and not operated by the same sponsor. Congress has attempted to address the regional implications of airport development in its mandate for FAA to develop a National Plan of Integrated Airport Systems. It remains to be seen whether this planning document—or any other action at the federal level—can improve regional coordination of airport facilities.

The basic theory of demand-related airport access fees and the general principle that fees should be proportional to marginal delay costs are well understood. It is also commonly acknowledged that the present scheme of pricing services, especially at congested airports, is far from economically efficient; however, market-related approaches such as peak-hour pricing and congestion surcharges might be difficult to implement, and they are likely to encounter stiff opposition from some classes of users, especially GA.

Despite the theoretical attractiveness of marginal-cost pricing, it might be difficult in practice to determine the true marginal cost of a landing or a takeoff. There are analytical problems and policy issues to be resolved, as well as the underlying question of whether economic efficiency should be a primary goal of airport management. Several years of experimentation might be needed to establish the most effective fee structure for controlling delay and covering airport costs.

There are some dangers inherent in these experiments. It is possible that in a deregulated environment where carriers are frequently changing routes and levels of service, airports would be unable to determine the effects of their experiments or to guard against unpredictable (and undesirable) side effects on the airline industry or on other airports. The process of diverting air carrier operations to off-peak might be self-defeating for some airports. Rather than schedule operations in slack hours at airports that they perceive as marginal, carriers might prefer to move out of the airport altogether. While this might be a desirable effect from the system perspective, it would be the opposite for the airport operator, who would lose revenue.

Further, in order to be effective in shifting air carrier traffic to off-peak hours, landing fees during peak hours might have to be raised substantially. In many cases, use agreements between air carriers and airports would prevent such radical changes in fees. If it were determined to be in the national interest for airport operators to make such changes in their fee structures, the federal government might have to take action to abrogate or modify existing use agreements. On the other hand, some believe it is unwise for the federal government to become so directly involved in the pricing decisions of individual airports.

Economic policies or administrative actions to reduce GA traffic at congested major airports could have two effects. The intended effect would be diversion of some GA traffic to other nearby landing places; however, for some types of aircraft and for some GA users, there will be no other facility as suitable as the main air carrier airport, and they would have to pay the cost if they wish to continue using it. Alternatively, some users might find the monetary cost or inconvenience too high and choose to use commercial flights rather than continuing to operate their own aircraft.

While programs to redistribute demand might be less expensive to the airport owner than physical improvements, any actions that significantly raise the cost of air travel or limit the ability of the airlines to offer air service in response to passenger demand can have far-reaching implications on the region's economy. Air travel is not an economic product in itself, but a utility used for other purposes, e.g., business or pleasure. When the cost of this utility increases, or its efficiency diminishes, those economic activities that depend on air travel will be negatively affected. Therefore, any analysis of demand management strategies has to carefully consider these impacts prior to its implementation.

The critical question is whether the premium prices that result directly or indirectly from demand management are sufficiently offset by savings in the costs associated with delay and congestion. The answer to this deceivingly simple question is usually quite complex and further complicated by the issue of who pays and who benefits.

Key terms

delay

capacity

congestion

throughput

practical capacity

visual meteorological conditions (VMC)

instrument meteorological conditions (IMC)

Air Traffic Operations Management System (ATOMS)

Consolidated Operations and Delay Analysis System (CODAS)

Military Airport Program (MAP)

intermodalism

administrative management

demand management

FAA high-density rule

Review questions

1 Compare throughput capacity and practical capacity. Define PHOCAP and PANCAP. How much delay is acceptable?

2 Discuss how the following factors affect capacity and delay: (1) airfield characteristics, (2) airspace characteristics, (3) air traffic control, (4) meteorological conditions, and (5) demand characteristics.

3 What are the two primary databases used in measuring delay? What are some of the difficulties encountered in using ATOMS? How will the new CODAS system improve the process of reporting delay?

4 What are some of the problems encountered in developing new airports or expanding existing ones?

- Discuss some of the advantages and problems associated with the conversion of closed military airfields.

- What is the Military Airport Program (MAP)?

- How might intermodalism be utilized to alleviate the problem of delay?

5 Distinguish between the administrative management and demand management approaches to reducing delay.

- Describe the various administrative management techniques to reduce delay.

- What are some of the problems associated with differential pricing? slot auctions?

Suggested readings

deNeufville, Richard. *Airport Systems Planning*. Cambridge, Mass. The MIT Press, 1976.

Airfield and Airspace Capacity/Delay Policy Analysis, FAA-APO-81-14, Washington, DC: FAA, Office of Aviation Policy and Plans, December 1981.

Airport Capacity Enhancement Plan. Washington, DC: FAA, October 1998.

Airport Congestion: Background and Some Policy Options. Washington, DC: Congressional Research Service, The Library of Congress, May 20, 1994.

Airport System Capacity-Strategic Choices. Washington, DC: Transportation Research Board, 1990.

Airport System Development. Washington, DC: U.S. Congress, Office of Technology Assessment, August 1984.

Report and Recommendations of the Airport Access Task Force. Washington, DC: Civil Aeronautics Board, March 1983.

Policy Analysis of the Upgraded Third Generation Air Traffic Control System. Washington, DC: Federal Aviation Administration, January 1977.

9

Airside technological improvements

Outline

- Introduction
- Airport and airspace technology
- Airspace development
- Operational procedures
- Capacity enhancing technologies
- Airport surface utilization

Objectives

When you have completed this chapter, you should be able to:

- Describe the purpose of the National Airspace Redesign.
- Discuss the principal NAS modernization changes affecting capacity.
- Discuss several procedural initiatives designed to improve pilots' ability to plan and fly direct routes.
- List and briefly describe several capacity-enhancing technologies under the following areas: communications, navigation, surveillance, weather, and air traffic management.
- Distinguish between Airport Surface Detection Equipment (ASDE-3) and Airport Movement Area Safety System (AMASS).

- Give several examples of ground surveillance and control technologies designed to improve airport surface utilization.

Introduction

The airport system in place in the United States today is extensive and highly developed; in general, it serves the nation well. Still, there are problems of congestion and delay at the busiest airports, where facilities are not adequate to accommodate demand at all times and in all conditions of weather and visibility. The FAA forecasts that growth of commercial and private aviation could be constrained by lack of airport capacity, which it considers to be the most serious problem facing civil aviation through the first decades of twenty-first century.

Recent policy statements by FAA acknowledge that, with a few exceptions, the direct solution of building new airports and expanding existing ones might not be practical because of lack of suitable new airport sites, physical limitations of present facilities, and concerns about environmental impacts of aviation on surrounding communities. Similar views have been expressed in other studies of airport capacity, and there is a widely held opinion that while the airport system is expandable in the broad sense, there is little hope of creating major new facilities in those key metropolitan areas where air travel demand and aviation activity continue to outstrip available airport capacity unless airport planners can persuade surrounding communities that airports can be good neighbors.

For this reason, the aviation community and FAA have sought technological solutions that will ease congestion by allowing fuller and more efficient use of the airports we already have. This technology includes new equipment for surveillance, navigation, and communication, and revised procedures for using the airspace and airport facilities. In this way, it is hoped that additional demand can be absorbed within the infrastructure now in place without adversely affecting surrounding communities.

Chapters 9 and 10 examine *technological improvements*—either currently available or under development—that could be employed to relieve congestion and delay. These chapters provide a survey of

United jet taking off from Seattle-Tacoma International Airport.
Port of Seattle

possible improvements in airport technology, with emphasis on the circumstances in which this technology would be applicable, the extent to which it could increase the amount of traffic handled, and the prospects for development and deployment over the coming years.

In aviation, the term *technology* typically brings to mind sophisticated electronic and mechanical devices used for navigation, surveillance, communication, and flight control. Such devices are clearly of interest, but for the purposes of these chapters, technology is interpreted in a broader sense. As used here, technology refers not only to new devices and equipment but also to new operational concepts and procedures that they make possible. Also, many in the aviation community draw a distinction between technology (meaning equipment and sometimes procedures) and civil engineering (referring to the design and construction of physical components of the airport—the concrete, so to speak). While recognizing that different engineering disciplines and techniques are involved, these chapters do not make such a distinction but consider the design and construction of improved physical components such as runways, taxiways, and terminal buildings as simply one more form of technology that will add to airport capacity or permit more effective and economical use of the airport as a whole.

Airport and airspace technology

Technological approaches to expanding airport capacity or reducing delay fall into three broad categories. First are improved devices and procedures that will expedite the flow of air traffic into and out of the airport—essentially, techniques that will augment airside capacity or mitigate aircraft delay by increasing the runway operation rate. This portion of the chapter will be covered under three headings: airspace development, operational procedures, and capacity enhancing technologies.

The second category includes techniques to facilitate movement of aircraft on the airport surface. The purpose of these technologies is to move aircraft from the runway to the passenger loading gates and back again as expeditiously as possible, thereby shortening the taxi-in and taxi-out components of delay and easing congestion on taxiways, aprons, and loading ramps.

The third category embraces techniques that can be used to aid the transit of passengers through the terminal building and the flow of vehicles on airport circulation and access roads. In contrast with the first two categories, where the aim is to alleviate aircraft delay, the third category is intended to facilitate the movement of people and to reduce that part of delay incurred in getting to and from aircraft. The third category is examined in chapter 10.

The discussion that follows addresses the broad question of airport capacity, not just airside capacity or aircraft delay. The intent is to examine ways to improve the overall adequacy and efficiency of the airport as a transportation hub. The underlying proposition is that delay—*any* form of delay—ultimately affects the passenger through the loss of time and increased cost of air transportation service. In this sense, it is parochial to speak only of aircraft delay because the basic purpose of the air transportation system is to move people from origin to destination, in safety, with minimum expenditure of time and money. All measures taken at airports to shorten travel time, to lower travel cost, or to lessen inconvenience are of equal importance, regardless of whether they apply to the airside or landside.

Airspace development

Airspace development studies strive to reduce delays by determining how to restructure airspace and modify arrival, departure, en route, and terminal flow patterns. In mid-1998 the FAA initiated the *National*

Airspace Redesign, a large-scale analysis of the national airspace structure that began by identifying problems in the congested airspace of New York and New Jersey. Additional FAA airspace studies are ongoing in Chicago, northern and southern California, Salt Lake City, the Southern Region (from Florida to Atlanta), and the Caribbean. The goal of the National Airspace Redesign is to ensure that the design and management of the national airspace system (NAS) is prepared as the system evolves towards free flight. The National Airspace Redesign will consist of incremental changes to the national airspace structure consistent with evolving air traffic technologies and avionics and operational concepts. Environmental issues will be addressed in parallel with capacity and efficiency analyses.

The capacity of today's national airspace system is constrained by rules, procedures, and technologies that require pilots and air traffic controllers to conduct operations within narrow, often inefficient guidelines. As air traffic continues to grow, these inefficiencies and their associated costs are compounded. Responding to these limitations, the FAA and the aviation industry are working together on two major, interdependent capacity initiatives—free flight and NAS modernization.

Free flight   *Free flight* is a concept for safe and efficient flight operating capability under instrument flight rules (IFR) in which the operators have the freedom to select their path and speed in real time. Air traffic restrictions are imposed only to ensure separation, to preclude exceeding airport capacity, to prevent unauthorized flight through special-use airspace, and to ensure the safety of flight. Restrictions are limited in extent and duration to correct the identified problem. Any activity that removes restrictions represents a move toward free flight. The transition to free flight requires changes in air traffic philosophies, procedures, and technologies.

The principal philosophical change required for free flight is a shift from the concept of air traffic control (ATC) to air traffic management (ATM). ATM differs from ATC in several ways: the increased extent of collaboration between users and air traffic managers, greater flexibility for users to make decisions to meet their unique operational goals, and the replacement of broad restrictions with user-determined limits and targeted restrictions only when required.

The procedural changes required for free flight correspond directly to the change in philosophy from ATC to ATM. Under the current air traffic system, aircraft are frequently restricted to ATC-preferred routes, which may not be the routes preferred by the pilot or airline. Air traffic controllers direct pilots to change their direction, speed, or altitude to avoid adverse weather or traffic congestion. In contrast, free flight will grant pilots substantial discretion in determining their routes. Many decisions will be collaborative, taking advantage of the best information available to the pilot and air traffic manager to ensure safe, efficient flights.

A joint government–industry workgroup in free flight is presently working on procedural and technical recommendations for moving toward free flight.

NAS modernization   To achieve the free flight concept and accommodate projected increases in air traffic, the FAA is modernizing and replacing much of the equipment, computers, and software used to manage air traffic and assure safe operations. Modernization of the NAS will give users new abilities such as flexible departure and arrival routes and increased usage of preferred flight trajectories. Ultimately, NAS modernization will increase the flexibility and efficiency of the NAS, improve traffic flow and weather predictability, and reduce user operating costs. The schedule and interdependencies of the many technological advances required for NAS modernization and free flight are outlined in the NAS Architecture. The FAA must balance the need to sustain and replace critical ATC infrastructure with the desire to provide new capabilities to NAS users. The NAS Architecture process is an integrated approach to modernization that matches expected FAA funding levels.

The principal NAS modernization changes affecting capacity are categorized into five functional areas: communications, navigation, surveillance, weather, and air traffic management. The transition between the current and future NAS and the new capabilities created by this change are described below.

Communications   In the future, communication between aircraft and ground facilities will require less radio voice communication and greater use of electronic data transmitted to and from the flight deck via digital data link technology. Changes in the communication system will create the following capabilities:

- Integration of voice and data communications.
- More efficient use of the frequency spectrum.
- Improved quality and clarity of ATC messages to aircraft.

- Better flight and traffic information services, such as weather graphics and proximity traffic data.
- Seamless communications across all operational domains (airport, terminal, en route, and oceanic).
- Information sharing with all NAS users.
- An effective interchange network to support dynamic airspace usage.

Navigation Navigation will become increasingly reliant on the satellite-based *Global Positioning System (GPS)*. Existing ground-based stations will be decommissioned as new ground-based systems designed to augment the accuracy of GPS are deployed. An augmented GPS system will create the following capabilities:

- Increased prevalence of user-preferred routing.
- Increased access to airports under instrument meteorological conditions (IMC) through more precision approaches.
- Reduced separation standards.
- Decommissioning of some costly ground-based navigation and landing systems.

Surveillance In the future, replacing verbal aircraft position reports with an onboard system known as *Automated Dependent Surveillance (ADS)* will enhance surveillance coverage and accuracy. ADS transmits position information that will be combined with radar images to ensure the system's accuracy. Analog radar will be replaced by digital radar. The implementation of ADS and digital radar will create the following capabilities:

- Continuous surveillance of all positively controlled aircraft.
- More precise monitoring of aircraft separation and flight progression in oceanic airspace.
- Enhanced airport surface surveillance.

Weather Today's fragmented weather gathering, analysis, and distributions systems will be enhanced by a more harmonized, integrated system. Incremental improvements in weather detection sensors, processors, dissemination systems, and displays will also occur. Improved weather technologies will allow the following advancements:

- Common situational awareness among service providers and users through the use of integrated weather products.

- NAS-wide availability of distributed weather forecast data.
- Improved accuracy, display, and timeliness of weather information to service providers and users.
- Better separation of aircraft from convective weather.
- Integrated weather information into associated air traffic automation systems.

Air traffic management Managing air traffic and airspace utilization will be increasingly augmented with computer-based decision support systems. These systems will improve the efficiency and effectiveness of NAS-wide information, enhancing all phases of surface and flight operations. The use of advanced automation and decision support systems will enable the following capabilities:

- Greater collaboration on problem resolution through dynamic airspace management.
- More efficient use of airports through improved sequencing and spacing of arrival traffic and assigning aircraft to runways.
- Improved acquisition and distribution of flight-specific data.
- More information from static and dynamic data (e.g., route structures, NAS infrastructure status, special-use airspace restrictions, aircraft position and trajectories).
- Improved accommodation of user preferences through improved traffic flow management, conflict detection and resolution, sequencing, and optimal trajectories.
- More flexible airspace structure by reducing boundary restrictions and creating dynamic sectors.

Operational procedures

A cost-efficient alternative to airport and airspace development is modifying air traffic control procedures to improve the flow of aircraft in the en route and terminal area. Examples of initiatives in the en route environment are the National Route Program (NRP) and the 3D User Preferred Trajectories Flight Trials Project, which are decreasing restrictions and allowing pilots to fly more direct routes. In the oceanic environment, reduced horizontal and vertical separation minima will provide pilots with more flexibility and efficient routing. Additionally, less restrictive instrument approach procedures are being developed for the terminal environment as the accuracy of landing aids improves.

En route procedures

Several procedural initiatives will improve pilots' ability to plan and fly direct routes. These direct routing procedures allow increased system capacity, efficiency, and economy. A few of these procedures, as well as other en route procedures, are described below.

Area navigation (RNAV) *RNAV* is a generic term that refers to any instrument navigation performed outside of conventional routes defined by the ground-based navigational aids or by intersections formed by two navigational aids. Technologies such as flight management systems (FMSs), LORAN-C, and inertial guidance systems have offered RNAV capability to aircraft, especially commercial carriers, for nearly two decades. With the introduction and widespread acceptance of the Global Positioning System (GPS) to civilian aviation in the 1990s, even more aircraft have acquired this capability.

While RNAV offers the potential for more flexibility and greater airspace efficiency, its use is often restricted by air traffic control procedures that are based on established route structures. This is the case in high-density terminal airspace where air traffic controllers rely on the use of departure procedures and standard terminal arrival routes to align and sequence traffic. It is often difficult for controllers to simultaneously accommodate nonstandard RNAV arrival and departure procedures with traditional departure procedures and standard terminal arrival routes procedures. For this reason, RNAV arrival and departure routes are typically restricted to periods of low traffic.

To make greater use of RNAV capabilities in terminal airspace, the FAA has begun to develop RNAV arrival and departure procedures for the top 50 airports.

The National Route Program The *National Route Program (NRP)* gives airlines and pilots increased flexibility in choosing their routes. Aircraft operating under the NRP are not subject to route restrictions such as published preferred IFR routes, letter of agreement requirements, and standard operating procedures. NRP flights are subject to route limitations only within a 200 nautical mile (nm) radius of takeoff or landing. This flexibility allows airlines to plan and fly the most cost-effective routes and increases the efficiency of the aviation system. NRP operations are currently authorized at or above FL290 across the contiguous United States. The FAA accommodates all flights that want to take advantage of the NRP.

The FAA estimates that approximately 1,200 flights per day participated in the NRP in 1997, saving the aviation industry as much as
$65 million, or about $150 per flight. As of February 1998, an average of 1,500 flights a day (more than 7 percent of eligible flights)
participated in the NRP, with a peak day numbering 1,967. Participation rates are higher on longer flights.

***Three-Dimensional User-Preferred Trajectories Flight Trails
Project*** The purpose of the *3D UPT Flight Trials Project (3D UPT)*
is to quantify the savings associated with unrestricted flight. The 3D
UPT Project differs from the NRP in that it allows unrestricted climb
and descent. Under the 3D UPT procedures, the airline operations
center plans the route for each phase of flight to maximize efficiency
and cost savings. The 3D UPT route includes priority initial departure, unrestricted climb to cruise altitude, and priority descent. After
reaching an initial cruise altitude, the pilots fly within a block altitude of 2,000 feet and are free to fly at optimal altitudes based on favorable winds and aircraft performance information.

Increasing civilian access to special-use airspace Commercial
and general aviation users seek access to *special use airspace (SUA)*
in order to fly more fuel-efficient routes. The FAA is working with
the Department of Defense (DOD) and NAS users to develop procedures that will permit greater civilian access to SUA. For these procedures to be effective, more real-time information on SUA
availability is needed. Providing civilian users with this information
requires the development of software for recording SUA time and altitude availability and ensuring that users have access to the data.
Other initiatives to increase access to SUA include cooperative decision-making between the DOD and the FAA on which hours SUA
will be active and redefining some SUA boundaries.

Elimination of unnecessary ATC-preferred routes While the
NRP has increased flexibility for aircraft that fly at higher altitudes
and longer distances, flexibility in flights that traverse lower altitudes
is also critical to system capacity. ATC-preferred routes are important
tools that help air traffic controllers organize traffic flows around major airports and at lower altitudes. There are currently 1,975 ATC-preferred routes. It is estimated that, during a given day, pilots using the
low-altitude system (below 18,000 feet) add approximately 125,000
miles of extra distance to their flight plans as a result of published
ATC-preferred routes. In an effort to reduce this inefficiency, the FAA
plans to eliminate unnecessary routes.

The primary goal of the published preferred route reduction program (also called P2R2) is to evaluate and validate ATC-preferred routes. Routes found unnecessary will be eliminated, while necessary routes will be maintained or altered.

Oceanic en route procedures Oceanic separation standards are based on limits in the capability of ATC to determine the position and altitude of aircraft. Procedures implemented more than 40 years ago required 2,000-foot separation above FL290 because altimeters in use at that time were less accurate at higher altitudes. The current oceanic ATC system uses filed flight plans and position reports to track an aircraft's progress and ensure horizontal separation is maintained. Position reports, created by using high frequency (HF) radio, are infrequent (approximately one report per hour) and require the use of radio operators to relay the messages between pilots and controllers. HF communication is also subject to interference. These deficiencies in communications and surveillance have necessitated horizontal separation minima of 60 to 100 nm laterally, and 15 minutes longitudinally.

The separation minima currently in effect on many oceanic routes limits the ability of controllers to grant preferred wind-efficient routes or preferred altitudes during peak traffic periods. With anticipated increases in air traffic congestion, the associated delays and unavailability of desired routes will only escalate. As a result of improved navigational capabilities made possible by highly accurate altimeters, advanced navigation, satellite communications, and collision-avoidance systems, however, oceanic separation minima are being incrementally reduced.

Reduced vertical separation minima (RVSM) The goal of RVSM is to reduce the oceanic vertical separation between FL290 and FL410 from the current 2,000-feet minimum to 1,000-feet minimum. Operational trials of RVSM began in the North Atlantic airspace from FL330 to FL370, inclusive, in March 1997. The trials have shown that fewer flight tracks are required as users take advantage of the available flight levels on prime tracks. Full implementation for FL290 to 410 is planned to be completed by the year 2001.

RVSM improves system efficiency by increasing the number of available altitudes, allowing aircraft to operate closer to optimum altitudes. It also allows users more flexibility in choosing their desired altitude. Fuel savings from aircraft flying more optimum routes due to RVSM in the North Atlantic are projected to range from 13 to 18 million gallons annually, depending on traffic density.

Reduced horizontal separation minima (RHSM) In April 1998, oceanic lateral separation standards were reduced from 100 nm to 50 nm in the Anchorage airspace of the North Pacific. Longitudinal separation minima were also reduced in the North Pacific in 1998 from the time-based standard of 15 minutes to 50 nm. The FAA expanded the 50-nm lateral and longitudinal separation standards to the Central Pacific airspace for all qualified aircraft in December 1998.

The reduced lateral and longitudinal separation minima will provide increased opportunities for altitude changes to achieve optimum altitudes, fuel efficiency, and time savings. There are also proposed initiatives to further reduce lateral separation minima to 30 nm. However, there is currently no funding for the enhanced automation and technology required to support separation reduction initiatives beyond 50 nm lateral and 50 nm longitudinal

Terminal area/approach procedures

A number of visual and electronic landing aids at or near airports assist pilots in locating the runway, particularly during IFR weather conditions. Approach procedures have been based on the type and accuracy of landing aids available, geography, traffic, and many other factors. Some of these approach procedures are discussed below.

Removal of 250-knot speed limit for departing aircraft in Class B airspace Aircraft are currently restricted to 250 knots below 10,000 feet mean sea level (MSL). This restriction can constrain capacity by limiting departure rates from busy terminal areas. In June 1997, the FAA began to field-test removing the 250-knot speed restriction for departures from Houston Class B airspace. In that field test, controllers were given the authority to remove the speed restriction. American Airlines reviewed a month of efficiency data for 405 Houston departures that participated in the field trial. They found significant savings of approximately half a minute and 100 pounds of fuel per flight.

The results of that test were evaluated in terms of the impacts on air traffic controllers, flight crews, and aircraft noise on the ground. The evaluation found that a substantial number of controllers removed the speed restriction for departures when authorized to do so. The evaluation also found that the vast majority of the controllers interviewed believed that it is operationally acceptable for departures to fly faster than 250 knots below 10,000 feet in Class B airspace. All of the pilots interviewed during the test also found the concept operationally acceptable. There were no noise impacts from removing the speed limit that were perceived by the community surrounding the airports within the Class B airspace.

The one concern raised by the test was an apparent increase in the number of aircraft exiting the Class B airspace below 10,000 feet at speeds greater than 250 knots. It was found that aircraft traded altitude for speed during the test and tended to exit the Class B airspace at lower altitudes. Thus, aircraft exited through the side of the Class B airspace rather than the top of the Class B airspace, which had previously been the case. Procedures for ensuring that the faster aircraft exit the Class B airspace at or above 10,000 feet are now being developed.

Simultaneous converging instrument approaches (SCIA) Under existing approach procedures, converging runways can be used for independent streams of arriving aircraft only when the ceiling is at least 1,000 feet and visibility is at least 3 statute miles. This requirement decreases runway capacity in instrument meteorological conditions (IMC) and causes weather-related delays. Simultaneous approaches cannot be conducted under IMC if the converging runways intersect. However, a new missed-approach procedure, requiring a 95° turn and a flight management system in the cockpit, may enable use of SCIA at 650-foot minimums. Following validation and further flight testing, these minimums could be reduced to as little as 500 feet.

In 1997, the Converging Approach Standards Technical Work Group (CASTWG) continued to work toward increasing operational efficiency for users by refining and applying new converging approach procedures. Much of the CASTWG's efforts focused on applying SCIA at Chicago O'Hare's Runways 4R and 9R. This application of SCIA would not have increased arrival capacity, but would have removed arrival traffic from the north side of the airport, greatly increasing departure capacity and reducing departure delays. However, SCIA will not be applied at O'Hare until concerns about the controller's visual contact with aircraft flying FMS-based missed approaches in the busy Chicago airspace are resolved. Efforts to apply SCIA are also being directed toward sites other than Chicago O'Hare.

Simultaneous offset instrument approaches (SOIA) A new combination of technology and procedures called *simultaneous offset instrument approaches* is now under development. This combination has the potential to increase airport capacity and reduce delays at airports with closely spaced parallel runways. Using a precision runway monitor, an offset ILS localizer and glideslope, and a new procedure, it may be possible to significantly reduce the minimums for simultaneous approaches to parallel runways with centerlines as close as 700 feet. This procedure, illustrated in Figure 9-1, could be applied at San Francisco International Airport and could reduce approach minimums to a ceiling of 1,600 feet and visibility of 4 miles from the current minimums of 3,000 feet and 5 miles.

In the SOIA procedure, pilots on the offset approach would fly a straight-but-angled instrument (and possibly autopilot) approach until descending below the cloud cover. At that point, they would have a period of time to visually acquire the traffic on the other approach until they reach the missed approach point (MAP). If, as expected, the pilots visually acquire the traffic on the other approach before the aircraft reaches the MAP, they would switch to a visual approach and hand-fly the aircraft to the runway.

Capacity enhancing technologies

Over the next two decades significant capacity enhancements will be gained from increased capabilities in the areas of communication, navigation, surveillance, weather, and air traffic management (ATM) decision-support systems. Digital communications systems, combined with augmentations to the Global Positioning System (GPS), Automated Dependent Surveillance (ADS), improved decision support tools for controllers, and improved weather prediction and dis-

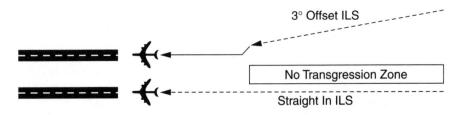

9-1. *Independent and dependent parallel approaches.*
FAA Aviation Capacity Enhancement Plan, 1994.

semination systems will lead to the more efficient use of airspace and airports and greater operational flexibility.

This section is divided into five areas: communications, navigation, surveillance, weather, and air traffic management. For each area, the characteristics of the current system, planned enhancements, and the key technologies that will make those enhancements possible are described.

Communications

The exchange of information is vital to all flight operations. This is especially true for large commercial operations that require continual interaction with flight planning and ATC facilities to obtain weather forecasts, clearances, taxi instructions, expected delays, position reports, air traffic advisories, airport information, etc. Problems in the communication system, such as frequency congestion and interference, impact the overall efficiency of operations. Planned improvements to the communications systems will greatly improve the quality, clarity, and amount of information exchanged among and between aircraft and ground facilities.

Current communication capabilities

In domestic airspace, information is typically transmitted and received by using voiced air/ground ultrahigh-frequency (UHF) and very high frequency (VHF) radio. As the number of aircraft operations has grown and the demand for information exchange continues to rise, frequency congestion has become an increasing problem, especially within terminal airspace. This congestion limits the effectiveness of communication, increases controller/pilot workload, creates delays, and increases the likelihood of missed or misinterpreted information. Frequency congestion is largely a result of increased demand for the spectrum available to the FAA. Los Angeles, Chicago, New York, and Atlanta airspace are already out of available channels. As early as 2004, the FAA will be unable to provide additional channel assignments.

In oceanic airspace, long-range air/ground communication is performed through third-party high-frequency (HF) radios—a communication system that is often hampered by lengthy delays and is subject to atmospheric interference. The shortcomings inherent in the HF radio system make position reports and ATC approvals for routine pilot clearance requests (i.e., altitude changes for favorable

winds) difficult to obtain because of communication delays and uncertainties concerning the location of nearby air traffic.

Planned communication enhancements

Between 1998 and 2003, the NAS will add digital communication capabilities through the expanded use of VHF, HF, and satellite data
links. As a result of this transition, the volume of information transmitted among aircraft and ground facilities will increase while frequency congestion, interference, delays, and misunderstandings are
minimized. Data, especially in the form of text and graphical information, will constitute a much larger portion of all air/ground communications than today.

Aeronautical data link systems The term "data link" refers to the
overall system for entering, processing, transmitting, and displaying
voice, alphanumeric, and graphic information between aircraft and
ground facilities. Conceptually, a data link can be thought of as an
information pipeline. Many systems connect with this pipeline, including ground automation, avionics, applications, subnetworks,
and transmission equipment.

Today's analog-based data link system—a technology developed
over 20 years ago—remains widely in use by airlines for text mes-
saging to aircraft. While useful, the analog system has many technical and capacity limitations because of its slow data transmission
rate. To improve data link capabilities, the FAA has adopted the VHF
digital link (VDL). VDL, being digital, can transmit data at a much
higher rate, with greater frequency spectrum efficiency, and with
less interference than existing analog systems. The development of
VDL is vital to the free flight concept, as it supports advances being
made in communications, navigation, surveillance, and decision
support technologies.

Technical improvements made possible by advanced data link systems and associated services will encompass all domestic operational environments, from the airport surface through all phases of
flight. In the oceanic environment, a satellite data link network will
be combined with a high-frequency data link (HFDL) to improve the
exchange of voice and data messages in oceanic airspace. The satellite and HFDL technologies will vastly improve communications coverage, surveillance capabilities, and flexibility in requesting course
changes over the ocean.

These new systems will allow for greater on-demand access to important aeronautical information such as airport arrival, departure, and taxi clearance schedules; airborne and surface traffic surveillance information; NAS infrastructure status; and real-time weather. Expanded use of data link technologies in the cockpit will increase the effectiveness of pilot and air traffic controller communications, situational awareness, and collaborative decision making. These changes will improve capacity by reducing congestion on the voice channels and improving airspace usage by allowing more efficient routing, spacing, and sequencing of traffic.

Controller-to-Pilot Data Link Communications *Controller-to-Pilot Data Link Communications (CPDLC)* is a data link service that will improve the speed, quality, and reliability of controller/pilot communications in the terminal and en route environment. To achieve this, the CPDLC will replace sets of controller/pilot voice messages with data messages displayed in the cockpit. By permitting more timely and effective communication of ATC messages, CPDLC will improve airspace use and capacity by reducing frequency congestion and operational errors resulting from verbal miscommunication.

The initial version of CPDLC, which uses a combination of analog and digital data link technologies and supports four uplink messages with corresponding pilot response messages, provides an incremental step for implementing en route data links. CPDLC is a free flight phase technology that will be tested in the en route airspace of the Miami Air Route Traffic Control Center (ARTCC). Initial operating capability is expected at Miami by the end of 2001, and national availability by 2003.

The final version of CPDLC, expected in the year 2011, will be an all-digital system that will be fully integrated with air traffic management decision support systems.

Next-Generation Air/Ground Communication System (NEXCOM) Demand for air-to-ground communication frequency assignments is expected to increase 4 percent annually, a rate unsustainable under the current communications system. If the frequency spectrum is exhausted, overall NAS system expansion will be constrained. To illustrate this, an analysis by the FAA Joint Research Council indicates that, of 21 airports planning new runways, 16 will have insufficient frequency spectrum to support them unless communications systems are improved.

In addition to frequency shortages, other deficiencies of the current, analog-based communication system include a lack of data link capability, an inability to overcome channel blockage, and a lack of security against unauthorized users. If not resolved, these deficiencies will increase delays and prevent implementation of new services, or will lead to a curtailment of existing services. Moreover, investment in NAS modernization will not yield expected productivity and efficiency gains.

Next-Generation Air/Ground Communication (NEXCOM) is a digital radio system designed to alleviate the problems of the current system while meeting future requirements. NEXCOM radios will be compatible with existing analog radios. When fully operational, NEXCOM will:

- Increase the number of available voice circuits.
- Provide for simultaneous use of frequency for both voice and data communications.
- Increase capacity within the available VHF frequency spectrum.
- Provide new data link communications capability to all users.
- Enable new operational capabilities of advanced digital technologies.
- Reduce frequency change errors.
- Reduce air/ground radio-frequency interference.
- Provide consistent voice quality over a range of operating conditions.

In May 1998, the FAA Joint Resources Council approved the first implementation segment of the NEXCOM program. In this initial segment (2002–2008), ground-based analog radios currently used to transmit voice communications between pilots and controllers will be replaced with new radios installed for communication with aircraft in high and superhigh en route airspace. Communications with aircraft flying in the remaining airspace will transition to the new radios in later program segments. Full operational capability is planned for 2015.

Flight Information Service (FIS) and Cockpit Information System (CIS) The *Flight Information Service* (*FIS*) will use a ground-based data server and data links to provide a variety of non-operational control information to the cockpit such as weather products, traffic information, special use airspace (SUA) status, notices to airmen, and obstruction updates. The *Cockpit Information System (CIS)* will process and display FIS information and integrate it with navigation, surveillance, terrain, and other data available in the cockpit. When fully operational, the CIS will also be capable of sending and receiving route requests via data link to the air traffic controller. Weather information will be obtained via data link from a ground-based source or from other aircraft. SUA information may be stored prior to flight or may be updated in real time while in flight. The primary capacity benefits of FIS/CIS technology are enhanced situational awareness leading to greater flexibility and predictability, and reduced delays resulting from improved planning and more direct routes made possible by current and accurate traffic, environmental, terrain, and NAS resource information. The FAA does not expect to provide significant FIS until deployment of NEXCOM.

Navigation

Aviation navigation systems in use today vary considerably in terms of accuracy, coverage, reliability, and capabilities. The current navigational airways structure and most approach and landing charts are designed principally around the geographic location and technical characteristics of ground-based navigational aids. Future initiatives will enhance the current navigation system by using a more flexible satellite-based system augmented by ground-based systems.

Current navigation capabilities

The primary means of aircraft en route navigation in the United States today is the VHF omnidirectional range (VOR)—a system made up of a series of ground stations that broadcast directional signals. These signals are used by aircraft to determine bearings to or from VOR stations. If the VOR and aircraft are equipped with distance measuring equipment (DME), the signals can also be used to determine the distance to VORs. Navigating by using VORs typically consists of flying airways (specific radials connecting VOR stations). The location of VOR stations often leads to indirect, inefficient flight paths between an aircraft's origin and destination. However, some avionics is capable of interpreting VOR and/or DME signals to provide area navigation (RNAV), allowing for more direct routing of flights. Most new large commercial aircraft are equipped with a flight management system (FMS) having multiple DMEs that improve RNAV VOR accuracy.

Landing navigational systems are similar to and in some cases the same as en route systems. Landing aids are classified as precision and nonprecision. Precision landing aids refer to systems that can, with a high degree of accuracy, align an aircraft's vertical and horizontal path with a runway to allow for low visibility landings. The instrument landing system (ILS) is the primary system used for precision navigation today. The capabilities of instrument landing systems are defined in three categories, with Category I being the least accurate and Category III being the most accurate.

The satellite-based U.S. Global Positioning System (GPS), managed by DOD, is an alternative to land-based navigation systems that has been steadily gaining in popularity among civil aviation users for much of the last decade. The current GPS available to civilian users, while not as accurate as many of the ground-based navigational aids, offers several advantages such as RNAV capability, ease of use, worldwide coverage, and horizontal and vertical position information—a capability lacking in ground-based navigational aids (with the exception of certain precision landing aids). These combined attributes offer pilots more flexibility in determining routes and provide for nonprecision approach to any runway. GPS has been extensively tested and is already being used as a primary means of navigation in the oceanic environment.

Planned navigation enhancements

The GPS navigation system in use today will become more prevalent, accurate, available, and will have greater integrity. Current GPS capabilities will be further augmented by ground facilities that will allow for precision approaches available during instrument meteorological conditions. On the ground, innovative navigation technologies will assist in efficiently and safely guiding aircraft during low-visibility operations. Many existing ground navigation systems will be phased out as these advanced GPS systems come on line.

GPS Wide Area Augmentation System (WAAS) The *Wide Area Augmentation System (WAAS)* is an augmentation of GPS that includes integrity broadcasts, differential corrections, and additional ranging signals; its primary objective is to provide the accuracy, integrity, availability, and continuity required to support all phases of flight. In doing this, WAAS will allow GPS to be used for en route navigation and nonprecision approaches throughout the NAS, as well as for making Category (CAT) I approaches to selected airports. WAAS will allow a pilot to determine a horizontal and vertical position within 6 to 7 meters, compared to 100-meter accuracy available from basic GPS service. The wide area of coverage for this system includes the entire United States and some outlying areas.

WAAS consists of a network of ground reference stations that monitor GPS signals. Data from these reference stations are data-linked to master stations, where the validity of the signals from each satellite is assessed and wide area corrections provide a direct verification of the integrity of the signal from each satellite in view. The signals broadcast from the WAAS geostationary satellites act as additional sources of GPS ranging signals, thereby improving the availability of the GPS WAAS system.

The last of 25 initial WAAS reference stations was installed in June 1998. Operational and testing activities in preparation for initial WAAS system commissioning was completed in July 1999, with full operational WAAS certification expected by December 2001. Most IFR aircraft are expected to equip with GPS/WAAS receivers by 2005, at which time the FAA plans to begin reducing VOR/DME, NDB, and ILS service on the basis of the anticipated decrease in the use of these conventional ground-based navigational aids.

Until WAAS is certified as a sole-means precision approach aid, CAT I ILSs will be installed at newly qualifying runways only if there is a clear indication that the benefits exceed the costs. Once GPS/WAAS is available to support CAT I approaches, no new CAT I ILSs will be installed.

GPS Local Area Augmentation System (LAAS) The *Local Area Augmentation System (LAAS)* is a differential GPS (DGPS) system that provides localized measurement correction signals to basic GPS signals to improve navigation accuracy, integrity, continuity, and availability of GPS. With these increased capabilities, LAAS will allow for stringent CAT II/III precision landing minimums. The system also provides accurate navigation signals for aircraft and vehicles on the airport surface.

The LAAS system relies on precisely surveyed ground stations, called pseudolites, which are located within the airport area and are used to calculate differential correction and integrity information. This corrected information is transmitted to aircraft within a radius of 25 to 30 nm. One LAAS system can provide service for multiple runways as long as the runway approaches are within the LAAS operational range. By making precision approach procedures available to more airport runways and by extending precision navigation to the airport surface, the LAAS will improve the safety, efficiency, and capacity of airports and surrounding airspace.

An FAA Joint Resources Council decision in January 1998 approved the development and acquisition of 143 LAAS systems (31 CAT I and 112 CAT III systems). In 1998, the FAA began performing specification validation testing of a prototype LAAS ground station located at the FAA Technical Center. Acquisition of LAAS systems is planned to begin in 2003, with full operational capability expected by 2006.

Surveillance

Knowing the position and intended path of aircraft relative to other aircraft—both on the ground and in the air—is necessary to ensure safe separation. The accuracy and certainty with which aircraft positions can be tracked determines the procedures and spacing allowed into maintaining safe operations. Enhancing surveillance improves the efficiency of airspace usage by allowing for reduced separation requirements. In order to realize reduced separation standards, the free flight concept imposes particularly high demands on the ability to accurately and reliably locate and track the movement of aircraft with greater precision and at a faster update rate than is used today.

Current surveillance capabilities

Separation is ensured today by visual confirmation, radar imaging, and pilot position reports. Visual separation is common in both general aviation and commercial air transport operations, though its use is limited to clear weather conditions. Radar imaging allows air traffic controllers to see a wide view of aircraft movements and makes it possible to monitor and sequence large numbers of aircraft. Pilot position reports are used particularly in areas where radar coverage is poor or absent and where visual contact cannot be assured.

Planned surveillance enhancements

Surveillance coverage and accuracy will be enhanced by incorporating aircraft navigation information with existing radar. This information will be translated into 4-D (three dimensional position plus time) information and made available to pilots and controllers to enhance situational awareness, improvement efficiency of aircraft spacing, allow for greater route flexibility, and heighten conflict avoidance capabilities.

External view of Airport Surveillance Detection Equipment Radar in use at many airports today. Federal Aviation Administration.

Automated Dependent Surveillance To augment existing surveillance procedures and radar, a new system known as *Automated Dependent Surveillance* (*ADS*) will be used. Unlike radar, which tracks aircraft by using interrogating radio signals, ADS transmits position reports based on onboard navigational instruments. ADS relies on data link technologies to transmit this information. At present, there are two forms of ADS: ADS-Address (ADS-A) and ADS-Broadcast (ADS-B). The ADS-A system exchanges point-to-point information between a specific aircraft and air traffic management facility, while the ADS-B system broadcasts information periodically to all aircraft and all air traffic management facilities within a specified area. The primary objective of ADS-A and ADS-B technology is to improve surveillance coverage, particularly in areas having poor or no radar coverage.

ADS-B will enable transmission of GPS position information, aircraft identification, altitude, velocity vector, and intent information. Airborne surveillance will be obtained using the Cockpit Display of Traffic Information (CDTI) system that will show pilots the relative position and movement of ADS-equipped aircraft in their vicinity. Air traffic controllers will verify ADS positions by superimposing them over primary radar reports. In areas not covered by radar, ADS-B will allow separation requirements for participating aircraft to be reduced from current procedural separation standards, providing greater capacity and increasing the number of approvals for user-preferred routes and altitudes.

In the oceanic environment, where separation is now maintained through pilot position reports, the use of ADS-B will have a particularly beneficial impact. Optimum altitudes and speeds will be achieved through the expanded use of oceanic in-trail climb and descent procedures, and aircraft will have the flexibility to change routes midflight if winds are not as forecast. Because separation requirements will be reduced, more efficient merging of traffic from multiple oceanic tracks onto arrival routes will be possible.

On the airport surface, ADS-B will be used to assist in taxi operations. ADS-B equipped aircraft will be displayed directly to flight crews and air traffic controllers on an appropriate overlay map. This capability will give the flight crew information to better evaluate the potential for runway and taxiway incursions, especially at night or in poor visibility, than is available today. The FAA plans to add ADS-A capabilities in Oakland and New York oceanic airspace in the year 2000. With deployment of Standard Terminal Automation Replacement System (STARS) and replacement of the host computer, the FAA can begin initially to use interrogation of aircraft to receive the ADS-B information, then add additional ground stations to increase surveillance coverage. A fully operational ground system is not scheduled until 2008.

Weather

Weather is the single largest contributor to delay in the civil aviation system and is a major factor in aircraft safety incidents and accidents.

Short-term forecasts and timely, accurate weather information on hazardous weather are critical to ensure safe flight and to plan fuel and time-efficient flight plans.

Many of the inefficiencies in today's weather system can be attributed to limitations in the accuracy, predictability, analysis, transmission, coordination, and display of weather data. To mitigate these issues, the FAA will incorporate technologies and procedures to improve the dissemination of consistent, timely, and user-friendly aviation weather information in graphical format available to all users of the aviation system, both ground and airborne. Further, weather information will be improved through the use of better sensors, sophisticated computer modeling, and new automatic systems.

Current weather capabilities

The timeliness, reliability, and clarity of weather information available to pilots and air traffic controllers is largely determined by the degree of communication and coordination among the many organizations and technical systems that gather and disseminate that information. Weather information is not always accessible to all parties when needed, especially real-time, route-specific information. Even when weather can be predicted accurately and reliably, the air traffic system cannot operate with the same efficiency as in good weather conditions. To maintain safe separation in poor visibility, for example, procedures require that spacing between aircraft be increased because of limitations of current communication, navigation, and surveillance technologies. These procedures create delays both on the ground and in the air.

Planned weather enhancements

The FAA is working in conjunction with other agencies such as NASA, National Weather Service (NWS), and the National Oceanic and Atmospheric Administration (NOAA) to improve NAS capacity through better forecasting, detection, and dissemination of adverse weather conditions. Other weather-related technology enhancements include new information systems designed to integrate a wide range of weather data into a single database where it can be analyzed by using new models. The output of these analytic tools will be displayed in the form of enhanced graphics on new display systems in ATC facilities and in the aircraft cockpit. Data link will be an essential element in the timely dissemination and coordination of weather information to flight crews.

Integrated Terminal Weather System (ITWS) The *Integrated Terminal Weather System (ITWS)* is a fully automated weather-prediction system installed at ARTCCs that will give both air traffic personnel and pilots better information on near-term weather hazards in the airspace within 60 NM of an airport. ITWS will work by integrating data from radar, weather sensors, and automatic aircraft reports and present the information in easily understood graphics and text. ITWS can generate predictions of weather phenomena such as microbursts, gust fronts, storm cell movements, and runway winds up to 30 minutes in advance. ITWS can also display data on the presence of lightning, hail, and tornadoes.

Additionally, the system will display weather data in tower cabs, Terminal Radar Approach Control (TRACONs), and Air Route Traffic Control Center (ARTCCs) to facilitate coordination among air traffic control personnel. ITWS will free controllers from the labor-intensive task of manually interpreting data from the various weather sensors and will allow them to concentrate on controlling air traffic. Airline dispatchers will receive ITWS data and pilots will receive a simplified version of the ITWS products via the Terminal Weather Information for Pilots program.

ITWS will improve the FAA's ability to minimize the delays caused by localized, hazardous weather, and will increase the margin of safety. Additionally, ITWS will improve traffic flow because of earlier warnings of weather impacts to an airport. By providing accurate, predictive wind information, ITWS will enhance the capabilities of decision-support tools that rely on making accurate aircraft trajectory predictions. Having better wind information will also improve the merging and sequencing of aircraft in the terminal area.

ITWS testing began in 1999. On completion of these tests, ITWS will be installed at 34 operational sites covering 45 airports with significant weather hazards. The first system is scheduled to be operational at Memphis in November 2001, with the last installation becoming operational at Dayton, Ohio, in February 2003.

Weather and Radar Processor (WARP) Meteorologists working in the weather units of ATC centers do not have an integrated system for collecting and displaying multiple weather sensor inputs, but instead rely on time-consuming and inefficient human interpretation of these weather sources. The *Weather and Radar Processor (WARP)* will collect and process weather data from Low-Level Windshear Systems (LLWAS), Next Generation Weather

Radar (NEXRAD), Terminal Doppler Weather Radar (TDWR), and surveillance radar and disseminate this data to controllers, traffic management specialists, pilots, and meteorologists. In addition to the radar information, meteorological observations, warnings, forecasts, lightning strikes, satellite data, and oceanographic information will be received by WARP. Information that is significant to operations will be sorted and overlaid on ATC displays as they monitor flights. By providing a mosaic of weather information to advanced display systems, WARP will assist meteorologists in analyzing rapidly changing weather conditions and ATC in managing and minimizing weather-related delays.

Air traffic management

Air traffic management requires gathering and processing large volumes of data to make effective decisions according to ever-changing conditions. The development of automatic decision-support systems will improve the effectiveness of air traffic information and yield more efficient use of airspace.

Current air traffic management capabilities

Air traffic controllers today use a combination of procedures and automatic systems to separate traffic. The decision-support systems in use today, however, provide only limited assistance to air traffic controllers. Most routine decisions are based on the training, experience, and judgment of the individual controllers, who must follow a set of narrowly defined air traffic procedures. As the volume of air traffic increases and as procedures allow greater pilot discretion, the efficient management and monitoring of air traffic will require the use of more advanced decision-support systems.

Planned air traffic management enhancements

Numerous technologies are being developed to ensure the efficient and effective collection, transfer, and display of information. Decision-support systems will augment these initiatives by coordinating information (e.g., flight plans, weather forecasts, infrastructure status, traffic densities, etc.) from multiple ground-, air-, and space-based sources and processing this information to improve, with minimum intervention, the effectiveness of flight planning, conflict checking and resolution, and traffic flow management. Graphical output from these analytic tools will assist users in decision-making. Advanced decision-support systems will enable controllers throughout the system to simultaneously provide greater flexibility, reduce delays in congested airspace, and enhance overall safety.

Standard Terminal Automation Replacement System and display system replacement (DSR) The *Standard Terminal Automation Replacement System (STARS)* will replace outdated air traffic control computers with twenty-first century systems at nine large consolidated TRACONs and approximately 173 FAA and 60 DOD terminal radar approach control sites across the country. STARS will support radar target identification and separation, traffic and weather advisory services, and navigational assistance to aircraft. STARS will also provide safety functions such as conflict alert and minimum safe altitude warning. Improvements, such as better weather displays, will be introduced on the STARS platform to support air traffic management decision-support functionality. STARS will also provide the platform for data link communications and Center-TRACON Automation System (CTAS) and Final Approach Spacing Tool (FAST).

The STARS counterpart for en route airspace is the display system replacement (DSR). DSR will provide air traffic controllers with a modern digital display system capable of processing and providing information in a fast, reliable manner. DSR will support a conflict probe capability.

Collaborative decision-making *Collaborative Decision-Making (CDM)* is a joint FAA–industry initiative designed to improve traffic flow management through increased interaction and collaboration between airspace users and the FAA. Through improved communication and more efficient use of airline schedules, CDM reduces the use of ground delay programs (GDPs) and gives NAS users more flexibility in responding to airport arrival constraints. The FAA runs the GDPs at major airports when weather, air traffic control (ATC), system outages, airport operational status, and other factors are affected to the point where restricting the flow of aircraft into or out of affected airports is required.

The *Flight Schedule Monitor (FSM)*, a primary component of CDM, is a support tool that collects and displays arrival information, retrieves real-time demand and schedule information, monitors ground delay performance, and provides "what if" analyses capable of projecting arrival rates, slot availability, and departure delays. The FSM is shared among CDM participants and is updated as schedules change.

FSM works by giving participants notice of actual and potential delay issues that can be mitigated or avoided through schedule adjustments.

For example, when a GDP is proposed for an airport expected to encounter bad weather, airlines using FSM can cancel a flight and move another aircraft, delayed by the GDP, to arrive at the slot opened by the canceled flight. This process is known as slot swapping.

Another mechanism FSM uses for reducing delays is schedule compression which moves participating flights into newly available slots, thereby compressing the departure schedule and reducing assigned delay. In this process, one airline cancels a flight and offers this open slot to another airline expecting or experiencing a flight delay. The slot opened by the moved flight is then offered back to the original airline for its use, and then to other airlines if it cannot be used by the original airline. Schedule compression and slot swapping activities cascade through the flight schedules and benefit all participating airlines, leading to overall reductions in GDP delays.

When adjusting schedules using FSM, airlines can make decisions concerning individual slot assignments or they can have the FSM software perform these substitutions automatically. In either case, the FSM flight schedule and the supporting database are continually updated to reflect the results of schedule changes. Operational testing of the FSM prototype was completed in March 1997.

Another component of CDM is the *Airline Operations Center Network (AOCNet)*. AOCNet is a private intranet that provides an enhanced capability for the FAA and airline operations control centers to rapidly exchange and share a single integrated source of CDM-related aeronautical information concerning delays and constraints in the NAS. This network allows airlines to access FAA GDP and aircraft situation display-to-industry (ASDI) data. ASDI data includes near-real-time position and other relevant flight data for every IFR aircraft operating within the NAS subject to traffic flow management planning. Using information provided through the AOCNet, airlines can better manage flight delays by making informed operational decisions in real time. Implementation of AOCNet was completed in March 1997.

CDM is in use at four airports: Newark, New York La Guardia, San Francisco, and St. Louis. Participating airlines include American, Continental, Delta, Southwest, TWA, United, and US Air. Current efforts in the CDM project are being directed toward improving the database of flight information shared between the FAA and the airlines.

Center Terminal Radar Approach Control Automation System (CTAS), Traffic Management Advisor (TMA), and Passive Final Approach Spacing Tool (pFAST)

The *Center Terminal Radar Approach Control Automation System* (*CTAS*) will provide users with airspace capacity improvement, delay reductions, and fuel savings by introducing computer automation to assist controllers in efficiently descending, sequencing, and spacing arriving aircraft within 200 nm of an airport. CTAS will provide two major functional capabilities in the near term: Single Center *Traffic Management Advisor* (*TMA*), and *Passive Final Approach Spacing Tool* (*pFAST*). The TMA will provide en route controllers and traffic management coordinators with automation tools to manage the flow of traffic from a single center into selected major airports. It will result in estimated delay reductions of 1 to 2 minutes per aircraft during peak periods. The pFAST tool will help controllers select the most efficient arrival runway and arrival sequence within 50 NM of an airport, resulting in increased arrival throughout. The CTAS and FAST technologies are part of NASA's Advanced Aircraft Technology Transfer (AATT) program.

Long-term improvements for CTAS include: multicenter TMA capability, required when multiple ARTCCs meter arrivals into a single terminal; descent advisor, which will provide optimized descent point and speed advisories to controllers based on aircraft type; and active FAST, which will help controllers determine how to vector aircraft onto final approach.

Initial Conflict Probe (ICP)   The *Initial Conflict Probe* (*ICP*), formerly called the User Request Evaluation Tool, provides controllers with the ability to identify potential separation conflicts up to 20 minutes in advance, and to do this with greater precision and accuracy than possible today. By estimating current position and predicted flight paths, ICP checks for potential loss of separation at current and future times. This system can be triggered automatically or manually.

The ICP display supports the strategic planning function and reduces the use by air traffic controllers of manual flight strips. Other potential benefits of ICP include conflict detection in oceanic airspace, greater route flexibility during weather changes, relaxed boundary restrictions, and more efficient routings provided well in advance of, rather than close to, the conflict. A primary capacity benefit of ICP is that it enables more efficient routings that reduce the frequency and magnitude of course changes.

Airport surface utilization

An airport is an interconnected set of physical facilities and components. For it to function efficiently, the capacities of each of these elements must be matched. Relief of a bottleneck in one part of the airport will not have the desired effect on overall throughput unless other parts are capable of absorbing a greater influx of traffic. Indeed, a common experience is that enlargement of one part of the airport complex simply shifts the delay elsewhere, to the next most constraining element.

Nowhere is this more evident than on the airport surface. Measures to augment runway capacity or to increase the flow of traffic through the airspace might be of little practical benefit unless aircraft are able to move expeditiously on and off runways and to and from the terminal building. It is on airport taxiways and aprons that aircraft are closest together and that their speed is lowest. If the movement of aircraft on the airport surface is constrained by runway and taxiway design and layout, by operational procedures, or by poor visibility, the effect ripples throughout the airport and airspace, and delays accumulate.

This section examines three types of technology deployed on the airport surface: surveillance and control systems, taxiway design and lighting, and equipment used at parking aprons and gates. In general, new airport surface utilization technologies will not lead to major increases of airside capacity, which is largely determined by available runways and airspace use procedures. The primary capacity benefits are indirect—increased safety, especially during inclement weather, and relief of operational impediments to making efficient use of the airside.

Surveillance and control

Surveillance and control of aircraft movement on the airport surface is accomplished largely by visual means. During periods of low visibility caused by conditions such as rain, fog, and night, the surface movement of aircraft and service vehicles is drastically reduced. To improve the safety and efficiency of ground movement operations in low visibility, controllers require improved monitoring of traffic and early warnings of potential conflicts. Two systems currently being deployed have been designed to meet this objective: *Airport Surface Detection Equipment* (*ASDE-3*) and *Airport Movement Area Safety System* (*AMASS*).

Federal Aviation Administration controllers at the air traffic control tower at North Philadelphia Airport. Federal Aviation Administration

ASDE-3 is a high-resolution ground mapping radar that provides surveillance of taxiing aircraft and service vehicles at high activity airports. AMASS enhances the function of the ASDE-3 radar by providing automated alerts and warnings to potential runway incursions and other hazards. AMASS can visually and aurally prompt tower controllers to respond to situations that potentially compromise safety. Combined, ASDE-3 and AMASS allow for more efficient and safer airport surface movement operations during low-visibility conditions, which are currently responsible for numerous airport delays.

The ADS-B system, using the navigational accuracy of GPS LAAS and combined with upgrades to AMASS, will eventually display accurate surface movement information to pilots and controllers, which may eliminate the need for ADSE-3. To further improve the efficiency of low-visibility operations, NASA's Taxi Navigation and Situation Awareness (T-NASA) system combines ADS-B and GPS LAAS technology with advanced visual displays and an audible ground-collision-avoidance system. Early simulations of T-NASA technology have shown that taxi speeds can be safely increased by as much as 25 percent in low-visibility operations. Eventually, T-NASA and other surface surveillance technologies being researched by NASA may replace or augment AMASS/ASDE-3capabilities.

Another program called the *Surface Movement Advisor* (*SMA*) is a system developed by FAA and NASA to promote the sharing of dynamic information among airlines, airport operators, and air traffic controllers in order to control the efficient flow of aircraft and vehicles on the airport surface. The system provides prediction capabilities to controllers to assist them with increased airport capacity and to help them manage operational resources more efficiently.

SMA uses a decentralized airport situational awareness tool that presents the effects that previous, current, and future arriving and departing aircraft have had and are having on the airport system. It provides help to air traffic controllers, supervisors, and coordinators in selecting optimum airport configurations and specifics on each aircraft before an aircraft leaves the gate. SMA also gives airlines and airport officials touchdown, takeoff, and taxi time predictions.

The SMA software and architecture interfaces with NAS data, airline data, electronic *Official Airline Guide* (*OAG*), and airport/ramp tower "pushed-back" and/or "blocked-in" data. The real-time data provided by SMA has potentially huge tactical and monetary value. Results of the SMA prototype evaluation at the Hartsfield Atlanta International Airport in 1997 show a reduction in taxi times of more than 1 minute per operation, or over 1,000 minutes per day. These taxi time savings can be translated into commercial airline savings that could potentially be passed on to the customer. Another beneficial result from the SMA prototype was the increased sharing of information that the system facilitated among airport users.

Taxiways

The design and layout of taxiways—particularly those that provide egress from runways—have an important effect on *runway occupancy time* (*ROT*). Runway occupancy time is measured from the time an approaching aircraft crosses the threshold until it turns off the runway or from the time a departing aircraft takes the active runway until it clears the departure end. Current ATC rules prohibit two aircraft from occupying the runway at the same time.

The placement of exit taxiways, where landing aircraft turn off the runways, and the angle at which these taxiways intersect the runways can be crucial. Poorly placed exit taxiways prolong runway occupancy by forcing incoming aircraft to taxi at low speed for some distance before clearing the runway. Taxiways that leave the runway at right angles force the aircraft to come almost to a complete stop before turning. Because the runway occupancy rule (with a few exceptions in VMC) does not allow an approaching aircraft to cross the runway threshold while the preceding aircraft remains on the runway, longer runway occupancy either forces the air traffic controller to increase arrival spacing or causes some approaching aircraft to execute a go-around, both of which are disruptive of throughput.

At some airports, relocating taxiways so that aircraft with shorter stopping distances can leave the runway sooner would lower ROT by as much as 20 to 30 percent. At others, providing a drift-off area alongside the runway or redesigning taxiways so that they diverge from the runway gradually and allow aircraft to turn off at higher speeds (sooner after landing) would have much the same effect; however, translating reduced ROT into a corresponding throughput gain is not straightforward because it depends on whether the runway layout, the airspace geometry, and the ATC procedures will permit closer arrival spacing to take advantage of the shorter runway occupancy.

Marking and lighting of taxiways can be as important as their design and physical layout in expediting ground movement of aircraft. For runway exits to be used to their full potential, pilots must be able to detect their location and identify the one they are to use with ample lead time. This is especially critical at night and during periods of poor visibility. A taxiway marking and lighting system that conveys the necessary information to pilots in a clearly understandable fashion promotes more efficient utilization of airfield pavements.

Research and development are in progress on several aspects of marking and lighting. For exit taxiways, the major efforts are to improve the lighting pattern and the configuration, spacing, and orientation of components in a way that promotes ready identification of the exit and provides visual guidance for safe and prompt transition from the runway to the taxiway. Among the areas under study are improved lighting and signing for taxiway intersections, traffic control signals and lighting systems for ground guidance, and methods for controlling lighting patterns and intensity from the tower. Development is also proceeding on new lighting techniques such as lights that use low-voltage electricity, light-emitting diodes, and electroluminescent components to relieve some of the deficiencies of present lighting, which pilots characterize as "the blueberry pie maze."

To optimize the use of airport pavements and to make proper decisions related to safety, pilots and controllers must have accurate and up-to-date information on surface conditions that affect aircraft ground movement and stopping characteristics. Perhaps the most noticeable changes in these characteristics are aircraft braking and stopping distance on wet or icy pavement, which are important not only from a safety standpoint but also because of the effect on capacity.

One major effort is to devise pavement designs and surface treatments that will improve traction. Research is also being conducted on means to provide information that will allow pilots and controllers to predict aircraft stopping capability and skid risk more accurately under various runway surface conditions. Items such as pavement sensors that continuously monitor pavement condition and coefficients of friction are being examined. Attention is also directed at development of better methods to convey this information to the pilot and, ideally, to provide braking guidance or warning of specific hazardous conditions and locations. The primary concern is safety, but better information about pavement condition and aircraft performance when traction is reduced would also yield a capacity benefit in that a more accurate delineation of safety limits might make it possible to relax some of the present conservative rules governing aircraft movement on the surface in slippery conditions.

Apron and gate facilities

Aircraft parking positions are designed to accommodate the particular dimensions of specific types of aircraft and may thus be unavailable to other aircraft with significantly different dimensions. If the apron area is not large enough to allow safe maneuvering of aircraft under established FAA, airline, and airport standards, capacity may be constrained. If a parking position is not available at the terminal building, the aircraft may be accommodated at a hardstand, an apron parking position made relatively permanent by installation of ground power and sometimes fueling facilities. During periods of very high demand, commercial service aircraft may have to be parked and serviced at remote parking positions.

Although airlines typically lease gates, they may own the passenger loading bridge and aircraft service equipment installed at the gates. These aircraft gates may be operated on an exclusive-use basis, under which a single airline has complete use and control of a gate. Lease agreements may give the airport operator the right to renegotiate for underutilized gates, but day-to-day assignment of aircraft to gates under the exclusive-use arrangement is usually an airline decision. Because of differences in schedules, a flight may arrive to find all of its company's gates occupied and have to wait for gate access, even though the nearby gate of another airline with a different pattern of arrivals is empty.

Some airports provide preferential and joint-use gate strategies. Under the preferential gate use strategy, a gate is leased to a particular airline but the airport operator retains the right to assign it to other airlines when it is not in use by the leasing airline. Under the joint-use gate strategy, gates are usually rented to more than one airline. This strategy is similar to exclusive use in that the airport operator is not typically involved in day-to-day gate assignment decisions. Except where very large numbers of daily flight operations occur, gates operated under preferential and joint-use strategies normally serve more flights than gates operated under an exclusive gate use strategy.

Some airports normally operate gates on a common-use basis, in which the assignment of aircraft to gates is entirely an airport operator's decision. This type of operation is common at small commercial service airports.

Beyond the required basic physical compatibility between each airline's aircraft fleet and an airport's gates, hardstands, and remote temporary apron parking locations, the principal measure of service level for aircraft parking positions and gates is the time an aircraft and its passengers may be delayed by gate area congestion. Although data on aircraft delays due to airside problems are available, information on delay due to landside problems such as gate access or departure-gate holds is not. Such data are needed to define service levels. Some airport professionals believe that apron configuration is one of the principal characteristics influencing airport landside capacity.

Demand and operating factors influencing service level and capacity of aircraft parking positions and gates are given in Table 9-1. Because of typical gate service or turnaround time, capacity over the short term, normally a period of 0.5 to 2 hours, is typically one aircraft per parking position and gate.

However, 100 percent gate utilization might not be achievable because of incompatibility between parking and ramp configuration or gate equipment and types of aircraft seeking access. Over the course of a full operating day, the patterns of arrivals and departures as well as airline ground operations, community factors, and weather deter-

Table 9-1 Demand and operating factors influencing service level and capacity of aircraft parking positions and gates

Factor	Description
Number of parking positions and physical layout	Controls the total number of air craft at gate at one time, should include hardstands and apron parking
Utilization	Ratio of time gate is effectively occupied (service, layover, and recovery) to total service time available (hours of operation), depends on flight turnaround time, including time for recycling between successive flight operations (a function of aircraft type and airline scheduling practices)
Hours of operation (especially noise restrictions)	Limits number of operations that can be handled per gate in a given day
Flight schedule and aircraft mix	Determines whether gates are likely to be available when needed, taking into account uncertainty in actual operation times compared with schedule; gates must be physically compatible with type of aircraft scheduled (see Utilization)
Airline leases and operating practices, airport management practice	Gate use strategy controls gate availability and utilization

mine the average number of operations per gate that can be served over the course of a year and whether a group of gates can accommodate additional flights.

Opportunities to relieve airport surface congestion extend up to the parking spaces at the gates. Aircraft docking is typically accomplished by a ramp agent with flashlights and hand signals guiding the flight crew for proper parking of the aircraft and ensuring that the wingtips have safe clearance from buildings, ground equipment,

Jet aircraft parked on the ramp area preparing for departure. USAir

and other aircraft. New optical, electrical, electronic, and mechanical devices are being developed to provide flight crews with positive visual guidance that will permit more rapid and accurate docking. This technology will allow apron space to be used more efficiently and help prevent the delays that arise when aircraft must be repositioned in order to mate with fixed ground support systems and passenger loading bridges.

While needs and procedures vary by airline and by airport, the aircraft servicing functions commonly performed at an airport include fueling, engine start, galley and cabin service, electrical ground power, towing, passenger stair or loading bridge operation, and handling of baggage, mail, and cargo. In addition, various routine or special aircraft maintenance functions are conducted.

Several technological advances offer reductions in servicing time and cost. At some airports, ground power is now being provided by fixed systems mounted on the passenger loading bridge or in underground pits. Similarly, fixed pneumatic systems are being developed to provide ground power and aircraft engine start. These installations ease the congestion caused by mobile units clustered around aircraft on the ramp and provide for a more efficient servicing operation. Auxiliary power units now provided on most newer aircraft alleviate congestion by replacing ground equipment needed for electric service, air start, and air conditioning. These self-contained units also assist in quick turnaround, thereby reducing gate occupancy time. Special pallets and handling equipment provide for efficient transfer and loading of bags and cargo. While use of this technology saves time at the gate, the loading and unloading of the pallets themselves can sometimes be time-consuming because of mechanical problems and alignment difficulties.

These improvements in technology help ease surface congestion in two ways. Those that speed turnaround lessen gate delays and enhance throughput. Those that reduce the apron space needed for service vehicles and equipment allow more aircraft to be parked in a given area, thereby directly increasing apron capacity and helping to ease airport surface congestion in general.

Key terms

technological improvements

National Airspace Redesign

free flight

Global Positioning System (GPS)

RNAV

National Route Program (NRP)

3D UPT Flight Trials Project

special-use airspace (SUA)

simultaneous offset instrument approaches

Controller-to-Pilot Data Link Communications (CPDLC)

Next-Generation Air/Ground Communication (NEXCOM)

Flight Information Service (FIS)

Cockpit Information System (CIS)

Wide Area Augmentation System (WAAS)

Local Area Augmentation System (LAAS)

Automated Dependent Surveillance (ADS)

Integrated Terminal Weather System (ITWS)

Weather and Radar Processor (WARP)

Standard Terminal Automation Replacement System (STARS)

Collaborative decision-making (CDM)

Flight Schedule Monitor (FSM)

Airline Operations Center Network (AOCNet)

Center Terminal Radar Approach Control Automation System (CTAS)

Initial Conflict Probe (ICP)

Airport Surface Detection Equipment (ASDE-3)

Airport Movement Area Safety System (AMASS)

Surface Movement Advisor (SMA)

Runway Occupancy Time (ROT)

Review Questions

1. Why has there been more attention directed to better utilization of existing facilities in recent years?

- Why not simply build more airports?
- What is meant by "technological measures" as used in this chapter? Technological approaches to expanding airport capacity or reducing delay fall into three broad categories. Explain.

2. What is the National Airspace Redesign? Free flight? How does air traffic control differ from air traffic management?

- Describe several NAS modernization changes falling under each of the following functional areas: communications, navigation, surveillance, weather, and air traffic management.
- Define Global Positioning System and Automated Dependent Surveillance.

3. Discuss the following en route procedural initiatives designed to improve pilots' ability to plan and fly direct routes: The National Route Program (NRP); increasing civilian access to special-use airspace, and elimination of unnecessary ATC-preferred routes.

- What is the purpose of 3D Flight Trials Project?
- Describe how oceanic separation standards are being reduced incrementally.
- Describe several changes in approach procedures that are designed to increase capacity.

4. Describe several of the planned improvements in communication systems that will take place during the next 5 years.

- What are some of the advantages of digital communications versus analog-based data link systems?

- What is NEXCOM?

- What is the purpose of the Cockpit Information System (CIS)?

5. How will future navigation systems enhance accuracy, coverage, and reliability?

- Distinguish between the Wide Area Augmentation System (WAAS) and the Local Area Augmentation System (LAAS).

- Why has GPS been gaining in popularity over ILS?

6. How does Automated Dependent Surveillance (ADS) differ from traditional radar? Distinguish between ADS-Address and ADS-Broadcast.

7. Discuss several initiatives taken by the FAA in recent years to improve weather forecasting, detection, and dissemination of adverse weather conditions.

8. What is the purpose of the STARS program? How will the Flight Schedule Monitor (FSM) and Airline Operations Center Network (AOCNet) enhance the joint FAA-industry Collaborative Decision-Making (CDM) initiative?

- Describe the Center Terminal Radar Approach Control Automation System (CTAS).

- What is the purpose of the Initial Conflict Probe (ICP)? How will it affect capacity?

9. The primary capacity benefits from airport surface technologies are really indirect. Do you agree with this statement? Why?

- Describe two systems currently being deployed to improve the safety and efficiency of ground movement operations during periods of low visibility.

- What is the purpose of the Surface Movement Advisor (SMA) system?

- How can runway occupancy time be shortened?

- What new technologies are being employed in the apron and gate area to permit more rapid and accurate docking? To ease congestion caused by mobile units clustered around an aircraft? To load cargo and baggage more efficiently?

Suggested readings

Airport Capacity and Operations. Washington, DC: Transportation Research Board, 1991.

Airport Capacity Enhancement Plan. Washington, DC: FAA, December 1998.

Airport System Capacity: Strategic Choices. Washington, DC: Transportation Research Board, 1990.

Airport System Development. Washington, DC: U.S. Congress, Office of Technology Assessment, August 1984.

Airport and Air Traffic Control System. Washington, DC: U.S. Congress, Office of Technology Assessment, January 1982.

Capital Investment Plan. Washington, DC: FAA, December 1990.

Improving the Air Traffic Control System: An Assessment of the National Airspace System Plan. Washington, DC: Congressional Budget Office, August 1983.

Nagid, Giora. Simultaneous Operations on Closely Spaced Parallel Runways Promise Relief from Airport Congestion, ICAO Journal, Montreal, Canada, ICAO Journal, April 1995, pp. 17–18.

National Airspace System Plan, revised edition. Washington, DC: FAA, April 1983.

Parameters of Future ATC Systems Relating to Airport Capacity/Delay. Washington, DC: Federal Aviation Administration, June 1978.

Report of the Industry Task Force on Airport Capacity Improvement and Delay Reduction. Washington, DC: Airport Operators Council International, September 1982.

Response to the Industry Task Force on Airport Capacity Improvement and Delay Reduction. Washington, DC: Federal Aviation Administration, FAA Management Steering Group, May 1983.

Soaring Demand and Lagging Capacity: A Formula for Delay. Washington, DC: Partnership for Improved Air Travel, 1988.

Swatek, Phillip M. Talking Capacity. FAA World, Washington, DC: FAA, May 1990.

Thompson, Stephen J. Airport Congestion: Background and Some Policy Options. Washington, DC: Congressional Research Service. The Library of Congress, May 1994.

Woolley, David. Capacity Fears Not Soothed by Airport Construction. *Airline Executive*. Atlanta, GA: Communication Channels, Inc., May 1991, pp. 10–12.

10

Landside technological improvements

Outline

- Introduction
- Terminal facilities and services
- Landside access
- Applications of technology to airport problems

Objectives

When you have completed this chapter, you should be able to:

- Identify several demand and operating factors influencing service level and capacity for the terminal circulation and passenger waiting areas.
- Describe several technologies designed to improve passenger movement through the terminal.
- Define "computerized ticket systems" and "computerized aircraft manifest."
- List three ways to expedite the baggage handling process.
- Describe how passenger security screening may affect service levels and what might be done to enhance capacity.
- Explain how the Federal Inspection Service (FIS) is improving the process of clearing passengers and cargo through customs, immigration, and agriculture.
- Discuss several management techniques designed to improve landside access.

- Describe the pros and cons of rail transit as a solution to the airport access problem.

Introduction

The terminal and associated landside facilities such as the parking areas and access roads provide the zone of transition for passengers, providing the link between surface and air transportation. Basically, the landside facilities are long-term installations with relatively stable use. They are largely independent of the specialized aircraft and activities that occur on the airside. In contrast, the airside is characterized by short-term, impermanent use that is closely tied to changing aircraft technology with a useful life of about 10 to 15 years. The principal effect of the terminal on the airside is through the design of aprons and gates, which determines the number of aircraft that can be accommodated at one time and the turnaround time for passenger boarding and aircraft servicing. As seen in the previous chapter, gate and apron operations can also have a wider—though not major—effect on airside throughput capacity.

Overall, the influence of the terminal on the functional requirements and performance of airside facilities is relatively small compared with the inverse effect that the airside exerts on the terminal. The primary purpose of the terminal is to transfer passengers and their baggage between surface and air transportation with minimum time, confusion, and inconvenience. The functional requirements and choice of design for a terminal complex must take into account the passenger and baggage flows resulting from aircraft size, traffic mix, schedules of operation, and type of service provided (origin-destination or connecting flights). As a design task, this involves the integration of three major parts of the terminal: airside gates, passenger collection and service areas, and landside access and egress. Because these parts are highly interactive, it is important that the separation between them be kept to a minimum and that traffic flows smoothly among the parts.

This would be a fairly straightforward task were it not for the need to design the airside interface so that it can be adapted to accommodate continually changing aircraft technology, airline service patterns, and traffic volumes. At some large hubs, the steadily increasing size of aircraft and their fixed-point servicing requirements, when coupled with growing passenger and automobile traffic, have led to terminal complexes of a size that imposes inconvenience and delay on passengers. In response, airport designers have been forced to add an intermediate transportation mode within the terminal itself (moving sidewalks, transport buses, fixed rail systems, and other such people movers) to aid passengers in transferring between the airside and the landside.

This chapter discusses the various landside technological improvements that are aimed at facilitating passenger movement or to reduce passenger inconvenience and delay. It should be recognized that these aspects of design and operation will have little, if any, effect on airside capacity and throughput even though they might lead to substantial reductions in the overall trip time for air travel. It should also be recognized that such matters have been of little interest to FAA or to policymakers in the federal government. They are, of course, keenly important to airport operators and to a lesser extent airlines because they constitute investment needs that must be balanced against airside capacity expansion in the overall program of capital improvements for airports.

Terminal facilities and services

Many airports will continue to suffer from inappropriate or outdated designs that lead to congestion and delay in passenger areas and diminish the overall utility of the airport as a transportation hub. For such airports, an alternative to a new or expanded terminal as an avenue of relief from congestion is to correct specific features that cause bottlenecks by applying improved technology that will compensate for design inadequacies. Some of these partial technological remedies are discussed in the following sections.

Terminal circulation

Generally speaking, the total time it takes for a passenger to move through the airport's landside is the sum of the time waiting for service and being served at each of the functional components used along the way, such as check-in or baggage claim, plus the time required to travel between components. If only the travel time is added, the sum represents an estimate of the time it takes to travel through the landside without stopping. A business traveler with all tickets and boarding passes in hand and with no luggage to check or retrieve might allow just this much time plus time for brief delays at the security screening, at the gate awaiting departure, and at ground transportation for the terminal portion of the trip. Except at airports where individual airlines exercise complete control over unit terminals, virtually all aspects of this terminal circulation component are the responsibility of the airport operator.

The principal demand and operating factors influencing service level land capacity for the terminal circulation component are given in Table 10-1. These same factors may be cited for their influence on general circulation. For elevators and people movers, details may also be required on the dimensions and operating characteristics of the specific mechanical system.

Passenger demand within this component is determined primarily by patterns of passenger arrival at the airport before scheduled flight departures, by the paths passengers take going between gates and the terminal curb, and by speeds at which both arriving and departing passengers make this trip. The rate at which passengers move through the landside depends on such characteristics as age, purpose for the travel, and time available before the flight or following the arrival; on the degree of crowding encountered along the way; and on the geometry of the path traveled.

Table 10-1 Demand and operating factors influencing service level and capacity of terminal circulation

Factor	Description
Terminal configuration	Space available for people to move freely without conflict of flows; availability of alternative paths; placement of seating, commercial activity, stairs, escalators
Passenger characteristics	Amount of hand luggage, mobility, and rate of arrival before scheduled departure influence demand loads and service time
Flight schedule and load	Basic determinant of number and direction of people on concourse

Note: These same factors affect circulation on elevators and people movers; specific mechanical systems, however, may differ.

Although terminal building design determines what routes may be available to passengers, airport operators and airline personnel can use partitions and signs to direct passenger traffic and improve overall terminal circulation in an attempt to optimize the path a passenger must take through the terminal building. Escalators and elevators may become bottlenecks but generally improve service levels. Reduction of the degree of physical obstruction and likelihood of intersection of pedestrian paths going in different directions tends to improve pedestrian travel speeds and reduce congestion.

Passengers normally do not take the shortest route through the terminal. In a study of Vancouver International Airport, for example, Transport Canada found that actual walking distances of travelers were 1.3 to 2.1 times longer than the ideal shortest-path route. In two sections of the terminal, the ratio exceeded a factor of 5. Concessions, rest rooms, and pay telephones located along corridors typically create some congestion and slow general travel speeds as well as increase the path lengths of the passengers who use these facilities.

The time spent traveling between curb and gate is the principal measure of service level and a determinant of capacity. Number of level changes and how complicated the pathway appears to the passenger may also affect service levels. Very little generally comparable data have been collected for describing circulation service levels at typical airports.

Passenger waiting area

The number of passengers waiting for flight departures and arrivals depends primarily on the number of aircraft served by the waiting area, aircraft seating capacity, aircraft passenger load factors, degree to which passengers are accompanied by family or friends, passenger arrival time at the airport, and the length of time between commencement of boarding of a flight and its departure. Interdependence among components might have a substantial impact on the number of passengers waiting in various areas of the terminal. For example, delays at a passenger security screening device might delay passengers' arrival at waiting areas, and thereby reduce the number waiting to board. Variations in aircraft departure times might increase the number of passengers waiting. For example, almost half of the departing passengers at New York's JFK International arrive two or more hours in advance of their scheduled departure times. Such behavior, related at least in part to the predominantly long-haul flight schedule at this airport, substantially increases the number of passengers waiting in the terminal. Final steps in processing enplaning passengers, including seat assignment and ticketing, might impose delays and generally increase the length of time during which passengers occupy waiting areas as well as the number of people waiting.

Airlines normally seek to avoid crowding in their exclusive-use areas. However, during the 15 to 20 minutes before departure when about 70 to 90 percent of the passengers are in the vicinity of the gate, crowding is sometimes unavoidable. Design of a common waiting area for several gates is used at some airports to avoid severe crowding.

Demand and operating factors influencing service level and capacity in waiting areas are given in Table 10-2. Service levels and service volumes over the short run—typically a period of one-half to three-quarters of an hour—are determined primarily by comparing areas available to passengers, the number of passengers waiting and the amount of baggage they have with them, and targets for available space per person. The number of passengers waiting is determined by flight schedules and passenger behavior, including the length of time it takes for passengers to pass through the other components of the landside. The number of waiting passengers in an area generally is greater when passengers arrive at the airport early for their flights and decreases when more time is required for check-in or transfer. Waiting areas such as gate lounges serve originating and transfer passengers, whereas terminal lobbies accommodate originating passengers and their nontraveling companions. When weather or air traffic conditions disrupt flight operations schedules, corridors and airline passenger service counters may become important passenger waiting areas and help to maintain higher service levels throughout the terminal as the number of waiting passengers increases.

Demand is frequently expressed as the percentage of departing passengers arriving at the waiting area in discrete intervals of time before scheduled flight departure. Rules of thumb have been proposed to generalize this relationship, but direct observation of conditions at a particular airport remains the only reliable way of describing demand patterns.

Peak demand levels are likely to occur during periods when all gates in a terminal concourse are occupied by flights with closely scheduled departure times. Airline hub-and-spoke operations, with their limited

**Table 10-2 Demand and operating factors influencing service level
and capacity of passenger waiting areas**

Factor	Description
Waiting and circulation area (lounge and accessible corridor)	Space available for people to move around and wait for departing flights; depends on terminal configuration; for example, waiting areas may be shared by passengers on several departing flights or restricted to single gate.
Seating and waiting-area geometry	Seated people may occupy more space but are accommodated at higher service levels.
Flight schedule; aircraft type, passenger load, and gate utilization	Larger aircraft typically mean higher passenger loads; areas used jointly to serve simultaneous departures.
Boarding method	Availability and type of jetways, stairs, and doors from terminal to aircraft affect rates at which passengers board as well as airline passenger handling procedures.
Passenger behavioral characteristics and airline	How soon before scheduled departure should people arrive at gate service characteristics areas, amount of carry-on baggage, knowledge of system, and percentage of special needs passengers (families with small children; elderly, handicapped, first class, and business travelers); airline passenger service policy, seat assignment and boarding pass practices.

scheduling windows, are likely to exhibit sharp peaking of waiting-area occupancy levels. Effective design is the primary means for ensuring adequate service levels in waiting areas. Some of the more frequently used design space standards for gate lounges and other terminal waiting areas are given in Table 10-3. These standards appear to be generally upheld in current practice, except perhaps at

Table 10-3 Typical space standards used in planning and design

Design situation	Space standard (square feet-person)
IATA design standard for departure lounges	8.5 per aircraft seat
IATA suggested breakdown level of service in holdrooms	> 6.5 for more than 15 minutes
IATA suggested breakdown level of service in waiting and circulation areas	> 10.8 for more than 15 minutes
Unofficial FAA minimum-space guidelines for departure lounge design	6.7–10.0 per aircraft seat; 15 per seated waiting passenger
Architectural reference standard for adequate waiting and circulation space with baggage	13
Design loading of urban transit vehicles	3–4

Note: IATA = International Air Transport Association.

those airports where introduction of larger aircraft or a new airline hub-and-spoke operation has produced larger passenger loads per gate than was anticipated in design. Service-level targets for lounges may differ among airlines and among airports but are typically based on market conditions. For example, the management of New York City's La Guardia Airport tries to maintain 10 square feet per person in gate lounges, whereas planning for JFK International, with its different passenger mix, was based on a figure of 15 square feet per passenger.

Transporter vehicles used in some airports to connect the terminal to remote apron parking areas are a special case. The transporter vehicle serves as an extension of the gate lounge during the time between commencement of boarding and transporter departure. Standards within the transporter vehicle are generally lower than those for gate lounges and may approximate those used in design of urban transit vehicles (Table 10-3). Capacity is generally determined by manufacturers' standards.

In analyzing the capacity of passenger waiting areas, service levels are usually indicated by the ratio of the number of people in the area and the size of that area. Targets for this ratio may vary with the time passengers wait for boarding, but in many cases, only a space standard is stated. Airlines may also employ standards for the number of seats that should be available for a given number of passengers.

Transfer passengers

Transfer passengers must travel with their carry-on baggage from one gate to another by walking or with the aid of buses or other mechanical devices, sometimes moving between separate terminal buildings, possibly leaving and reentering secure areas, and sometimes using check-in and other facilities along the way. Arriving international passengers must pass through customs and immigration and claim and recheck their luggage.

When an on-line connection is made (between two flights operated by the same airline), the airline will typically try to ensure that the passenger is assisted with the transfer. Airline hub-and-spoke operations depend on the ability of passengers to make the transfer quickly and easily. Transfer passengers arriving and departing on flights operated by different airlines must make an interline transfer. Typical problems encountered by transfer passengers making transfers at some airports include long distances to be traversed, obstacles such as changes in elevation and unprotected areas separating terminals, and poor information on where the next flight's gate is located.

Standard minimum connection times listed in the Official Airline Guide (OAG) and agreed on by airlines and reported to the travel industry are generally based on access time for passengers and 100 percent transfer of baggage.

The principal demand and operating factors influencing service level and capacity for passenger transfers are given in Table 10-4. These factors influence how long it may take for passengers to make the transfer, which is the primary basis for judging service level and estimating capacity.

Transfer passenger traffic in general varies with the number of flight arrivals and departures scheduled within a period of 60 to 120 minutes. On-line connecting passengers usually have a short journey for their transfer. However, rapid growth in activity at airports where airline

Table 10-4 Demand and operating factors influencing service level and capacity for passenger transfer

Factor	Description
Terminal configuration	Distance between gates, information for connecting passengers, intervening security screening
Ground transport	Connecting passenger assistance systems, baggage transfer systems
Passenger characteristics	Fraction needing assistance for ground transport, intergate travel speeds, baggage loads
Flight schedule and load factors	Basic determinant of number of people making peak-period connections

hub-and-spoke operations are centered has sometimes led to widely separated on-line gates and subsequently longer connection times.

If an airline operates a route hub at a particular airport, the number of interline passengers will be reduced, although total transfer traffic may be high. Large airlines have in recent years formed associations with small commuter carriers in which flight times of the major carrier's long-distance flights are coordinated with those of the commuter carrier, so that the latter serves as the feeder to the hub. Often the two carriers share terminals and gate space, making transfers easier for passengers on those particular airlines.

At some large airports, the passengers of interest should also include originating and terminating passengers who might have an automobile parked near the terminal of an airline other than the one on which they are currently traveling and who then use the airport's interline transfer system to reach their vehicle. Some analysts have observed that the number of these "phantom transfers" might become relatively significant.

The physical design of the airport's terminal facilities is the principal variable influencing service provided to transfer passengers. However, effective signing and other assistance to aid the transfer passenger may influence their ability and perceptions of service offered and mitigate some difficult aspects of making a transfer.

In many airports, interline transfer passengers have no choice but to walk from one airline's area to another's. But in some large airports, systems are available to aid the passenger in this movement, such as moving walkways, people movers, and interterminal buses. Buses, however, are subject to congestion on airport roadways and at the terminal curb. Collection of fares for buses and people movers makes these facilities less effective and desirable from the passenger's point of view.

The time that passengers require for transfer will depend on the characteristics of the passengers as well as the design of the airport. Some airports in Florida, for example, have a high proportion of elderly passengers who might require longer times to traverse a given distance. People movers, moving sidewalks, and buses can improve transfer times in such airports.

Large hub airports typically require a longer time for transfer passengers than do small hub airports. For example, in the OAG, which lists standard minimum connection times for major airports in the United States, the average time required for interline transfers at large hub airports (approximately 45 minutes for domestic and 75 minutes for international connections) is nearly twice that for small hub airports.

Passenger movers

To speed passenger movement through the terminal and to lessen the inconvenience of walking long distances to board flights or to reach landside exits, some airports have turned to *passenger movers.* Several technologies are available, covering a broad spectrum of cost: buses, mobile lounges, moving sidewalks, and automated guideway systems. The choice of any of these involves a trade-off between their service characteristics and cost (capital and operating) against those of adding new gates or terminal wings. This trade-off is very sensitive to the rate of use, the specific vehicle chosen, and the cost of gate construction. Passenger movers tend to be more cost-effective than gates if the rate of use is high. Variation in traffic load is also important, and analysis indicates that passenger movers are best suited to serving those locations and intraterminal trips where there is a great fluctuation in demand.

Automated transit system station at McCarran International Airport, Las Vegas, NV. Clark County Department of Aviation.

Buses and mobile lounges add to airside surface traffic; they are also labor-intensive and therefore costly to operate. For these reasons, airports with finger piers or satellite terminals have sometimes opted for automated vehicles such as moving sidewalks or guideway transit systems. Moving sidewalks are not an entirely satisfactory option. They are costly to operate and maintain, and their speed must be slow to allow passengers time to step on and off safely; thus, they provide only a marginal decrease in passenger movement time, although they greatly reduce the effort of long passages through the terminal complex. Some experimentation with accelerating devices and transition techniques would permit greater line speeds and still afford comfortable and safe boarding and descent. If these experiments are successful, the utility of moving sidewalks will be greatly increased.

For longer distances or where the volume of traffic is large, automated guideway systems are sometimes practical. Several different types are available, varying principally in terms of propulsion, vehicle size, and complexity of the guideway network and control system. Reliability and train control system design were problems in the first systems installed at airports (Dallas-Fort Worth, for example), but the technology has improved rapidly and now appears to give good service at air-

Bus used in transporting passengers between loading gates and aircraft at Los Angeles International Airport. Los Angeles Department of Airports.

ports such as Atlanta and Orlando. Capital costs of vehicles and guideway construction remain high, and they are still difficult and expensive to maintain. The view of airport designers is that these systems are cost-effective only at a few very large airports, and there is reluctance to utilize this technology except as a last resort.

Ticketing

Airlines normally rent ticket counter space from the airport operator and manage this space on an exclusive-use basis. This leased area may include office space for administration and baggage handling. Airline personnel staff the ticket counters and operate according to procedures and standards set by the individual airline. The principal demand and operating factors influencing service level and capacity for the ticket counter and baggage check component are given in Table 10-5.

In general, each airline establishes its own service standards for this component on the basis of company policy and local competition. Airlines may operate counter positions to segregate passengers by class of travel (e.g., first class, frequent traveler) and by service required (e.g., checking baggage only, purchasing tickets). Baggage

Passenger movers such as the automated guideway system shown here at Tampa International Airport can shorten walking distances and speed passenger processing. Reynolds,Smith, and Hills.

handling facilities are at many airports the single largest airline component and may play a dominant role in facilities planning.

In some airports a single line might feed a bank of check-in positions. Service rates and preexisting lines determine the waiting time encountered by passengers in a peak period. Long lines do not necessarily indicate that the component has a capacity problem. The length of time required to go through the line and the amount of waiting room available for each person in the queue are generally the minimum criteria for judging service levels.

Passenger demand is determined primarily by scheduled flight departure times, types of aircraft, and load factors. Length of arrival time before a scheduled departure may be expected to vary by type of service offered and by size of airport. Some airports survey departing passengers to develop representative distributions of such arrival times. Surges of demand might occur within the peak period for the airport as a whole, particularly during arrivals of groups of passengers from airport buses or other high-occupancy ground transport vehicles. Average demand conditions over the course of a peak hour are generally an appropriate basis for making judgments about service and capacity. However, airline or ground access operations may create sharp variations in passenger demand, making it more appropriate at some airports to use shorter periods such as 15 to 30 minutes.

**Table 10-5 Demand and operating factors influencing service level
and capacity of ticket counter and baggage check**

Factor	Description
Number and type of position	Processing rates are function of position type (baggage check only, ticket purchase, frequent or first class traveler, etc.)
Airline procedures and staffing	Number of positions manned and processing times
Passenger characteristics	Number preticketed or with boarding pass, amount of luggage and distribution of arrival before scheduled departure influence demand loads, fraction of passengers by-passing check-in
Space and configuration	Available waiting area for lines approaching agent positions; banked or separate lines; conflict with circulation patterns
Flight type, schedule, and load	Basic determinant of number of people arriving at ticket area
Airline lease agreement and airport management practices	Counter use policy, as formalized in lease agreements, similar to gate issues and options

Increased use of advance ticketing and seat assignment has raised the fraction of passengers bypassing the ticket counter and baggage check component. At New York City's major airports, the fraction of passengers able to avoid stopping at the ticket counter has been observed to vary from almost none on international flights, for which passports must be checked, to more than 40 percent on airlines serving primarily business travelers.

Data from several U.S. large hub airports show that average processing or contact time per passenger at ticket counters varies widely. A sample of experience at several larger airports showed times in a range of 1.4 to 5.6 minutes. Typical processing time at express check-in counters in this sample is 50 to 70 percent of that for full-service counters. Processing times at any particular airport will depend on airline staff experience, flight market, and passenger characteristics, as well as on airline operating policies. Surveys are typically required to determine these times.

Technologies to speed ticket counter operations or to eliminate them altogether are being explored, both to reduce delays in the terminal and to cut airline personnel costs. *Computerized ticket systems* available today offer passengers advance reservations and sales, preassignment of seats, and automatic tagging of baggage. They will probably be used more widely by the major air carriers, some of whom might also offer them to small carriers under a service contract. A companion development is the *computerized aircraft manifest* that has been implemented by some airlines. These systems typically produce aircraft load sheets, passenger manifests, and automatic telex reservations. They greatly reduce the administrative work at the counter and expedite airline dispatch from the gate.

Ticket dispensing machines similar to those used for banking are now in limited use by some airlines at a few locations and for se-

Delta Air Lines ticket counter at Hartsfield International Airport.
Delta Air Lines Inc.

lected routes. Improvement of these machines so that they can handle a larger number of routes and fare structures could promote wider use, with corresponding reduction in the amount of activity that must be conducted at the ticket counter. This technology could also be extended to sale of tickets off the airport property. With the deregulation of travel agencies, the range of services provided by these firms has expanded, offering passengers an alternative to purchasing tickets at the airport. Travel agents now account for more than 75 percent of airline ticket sales in the United States. The entry of mass-marketing firms such as Sears and Ticketron, as well as home computers, into the air travel field could further decrease the need for ticketing at airport terminals, reducing airline personnel and equipment requirements, and alleviating congestion at terminal ticket counters.

Baggage handling

The handling of baggage, especially baggage claim at the end of a flight, is a common and—for passengers—particularly onerous form of delay in terminals. At most airports, baggage handling is the responsibility of the individual air carriers, but some airports operate a consolidated baggage service—either with airport personnel or on a contract basis—in the interest of speeding the process and reducing the cost. Reduction of the delays and passenger inconvenience associated with baggage handling has been approached in three ways: more efficient procedures for check-in and claim, automated handling and sorting, and elimination of some baggage handling by encouraging carry-on luggage.

One of the simplest and most widely applied methods to expedite baggage handling is *curbside check-in*. This separates baggage handling from other ticket counter and gate activities, thereby disencumbering those locations and allowing baggage to be consolidated and moved to aircraft more directly. Another method is replacement of the baggage claim carousel with loop conveyor belts that allow passengers greater access to their luggage without increasing the size of the claim area.

Sorting baggage, moving it to and from the apron, and aircraft loading and unloading are time-critical and labor-intensive operations. Technologies to improve this process include high-speed conveyors to transport baggage between the terminal and the flight line, often used in conjunction with pallets or containers that can be put on and taken off aircraft with labor-saving equipment. *Computerized bag-*

gage sorting equipment, capable of distributing bags with machine-readable tags, has been installed at some airports. These devices are not yet fully satisfactory because the encoding and reading of tags are time-consuming and somewhat unreliable.

To handle peak loads, automated systems must have a larger capacity because they are less flexible than manual systems. Redundancy is a must with an automated system, which increases the capital cost. As those automated systems improve and come into wider use, a further step is to install self-service systems that allow passengers to check and claim luggage either in the terminal, at the curbside, or at remote locations on or off the airport property. While such a development would be primarily a labor-saving measure by airlines and airport operators, it might also speed transit through the airport for many passengers.

The functional equivalent of automated, self-service baggage handling systems—and one that might be cheaper and more reliable—is expanded capacity within the aircraft for carry-on luggage. With the advent of stronger and lighter materials, aircraft designers have been able to reconfigure cabins to provide larger and more secure storage space on board. New aircraft universally contain such overhead storage bins, and many airlines have converted older aircraft to incorporate similar enclosed overhead storage. A further development might be provision of a common baggage space either within the cabin or in a special module that could be transferred to the cargo bay. Passengers entering and leaving the aircraft would pass through this space and handle their own baggage.

Passenger security screening

Passenger security screening occurs in concourse corridors at entrances to terminal gate areas or at the entry to gate lounges. Equipment configuration and staffing are the primary factors influencing capacity. Corridor width often controls screening capacity, determining the number of inspection channels that can be set up.

Each channel consists of metal-detecting device (*magnetometer*) through which a passenger walks and one or sometimes two x-ray devices for inspection of carry-on luggage. Inspectors may undertake additional screening at their discretion, including hand searching of carry-on items and close screening (using a hand-held magnetometer) of individual passengers.

Curbside baggage check-in at La Guardia Airport.
Port Authority of New York and New Jersey

Security is often supervised by the airport operator. Sometimes airlines, in cooperation with the airport operator, hire security personnel themselves and establish their own procedures to supplement or replace those of the airport operator. Heightened concern over possible terrorist threats has led a number of airlines, especially overseas carriers, to augment their security screening procedures.

Demand and operating factors influencing service level and capacity for passenger security screening are given in Table 10-6. Because of the steady flow of passengers served at most security screening areas and because the security screening is among the last of several possible barriers facing departing passengers, short-term capacity of this component is the primary concern—lines typically build and clear over short periods. Assessment of delays related to security screening is usually made with respect to a peak on 1-hour period, but attention should also be given to the shorter time over which service quality can decline.

The timing of passengers' arrival at the gate for flight departure determines the basic demand on security screening facilities. Patterns of this timing have been documented at specific airports. When such data are not available, arrival patterns can be estimated from passenger arrival times at the airport if allowance is made for the several parallel paths by which passengers reach the security screening area. In addition to passenger demand, other people accompanying passengers to the gate area—nontravelers—typically must pass through security screening as well.

Table 10-6 Demand and operating factors influencing service level and capacity of passenger security screening areas

Factor	Description
Number of channels, space, and personnel	Influences number of passengers processed per unit time (magnetometer and x-ray considered separately)
Type, equipment sensitivity, and airport/airline/agent policy and practice	Determines average service time per passenger and likelihood of close inspection
Passenger characteristics	Amount of hand luggage, mobility, and patterns of arrival influence average service time as well as number of passengers
Building layout and passenger circulation patterns	Interference among pedestrian flows can influence flow rates and create congestion
Flight schedule and load	Basic determinant of number and direction of people on concourse

Processing rates at the security screening area are affected by the number and size of pieces of hand luggage carried on. Holiday travelers, tourists, and business travelers seeking to avoid checking baggage might have a larger number of items to be inspected. High percentages of passengers in wheelchairs or children in strollers might also lead to slower processing.

To reduce the total number using the security screening area, many airports have posted signs discouraging nontravelers from entering the secure area. This restriction is enforced in some airports by requiring passengers to show their tickets or boarding passes before entering the security screening area. The sensitivity of magnetometers can be varied to pick up smaller amounts of metal on the passenger's person. Less sensitive settings will tend to decrease average service time by reducing the frequency of intensive inspections.

When passengers arrive at rates exceeding the service rate of the security screening area, lines form. The delays associated with waiting in this line are the principal basis for judging the service level of the passenger security screening area. In some situations, space for passengers to line up may be limited, and crowding might become another important element of service level. Data on passenger delays and line lengths for security screening is not generally available. However, practice at U.S. airports suggests that such delays are encountered only rarely. A delay of 5 minutes, for example, at a facility with service and demand characteristics producing an average service time of 0.50 minute per passenger would indicate an average queue length of 9 to 10 passengers. At typical peak-period passenger volumes, small differences between service and arrival rates can rapidly cause large lines to build. Persistence of such lines during a peak hour is often evidence of a capacity problem at the security screening area.

New technology for screening cargo and baggage is being investigated. The aim is both to speed the screening process and to increase the thoroughness and reliability of detection. The new systems under development make use of improved bomb and explosive sensing techniques such as vapor detection, bulk detection, and computerized tomography.

Customs and immigration

Passengers arriving on international flights must generally undergo customs and immigration formalities at the airport of their initial landing in the United States. *Federal Inspection Services (FIS)* conducts these formalities, which include passport inspection, inspection of baggage, and collection of duties on certain imported items, and sometimes inspection for agricultural materials, illegal drugs, or other restricted items.

In recent years, introduction of streamlined procedures for returning U.S. citizens, the "red channel, green channel" system for passing through customs, and computerized access to records at inspection stations have substantially speeded the flow of passengers at many airports. Flights from some Canadian and Caribbean airports are precleared at the originating airport, so arrival formalities are substantially reduced or eliminated. Nevertheless, the simultaneous arrival of several fully loaded widebody aircraft can bring a surge of demand that causes service levels to drop dramatically in the international arrivals area.

International passengers generally arrive in an area segregated from other parts of the airport. All passengers must leave the aircraft and proceed through customs and immigration at a flight's first arrival in the United States. There is little layover or transfer activity in international areas of U.S. airports. U.S. citizens currently proceed directly to baggage claim and then to customs, whereas foreign nationals must first clear immigration.

On arrival at one of the several inspection booths, foreign passengers present their passports and other documents and parallel lines form. In some busy airports, roving immigration officers examine documents of passengers in queues, helping to ensure that all documents are in order and thereby reducing the average time required for each passenger to clear immigration.

At most U.S. airports, U.S. citizens' immigration and customs inspections are combined. Following reentry to the United States, U.S. passengers retrieve their baggage and proceed to customs inspection. Conditions at the baggage claim might become a capacity problem when too many people are crowded into the baggage claim area and baggage arrives slowly.

On the basis of declarations made by the arriving passenger and the judgment of the customs inspector, passengers might be required to open their luggage for inspection and might have to pay duties on imported goods. Most passengers proceed directly through an inspection station and exit to the arrivals lobby. The time spent waiting for and undergoing immigration and customs inspections and the conditions of crowding in which the passenger waits determine the service level and capacity of the FIS facility.

Although some airlines have full inspection facilities within their unit terminal areas, these facilities are always under the management of FIS officers. Airlines work with the FIS to ensure that flight arrival schedules are known and that an adequate number of inspectors is available to handle arriving passenger loads. However, variations in airline arrival schedules, government operating standards, and budget constraints may sometimes cause staffing shortages or excessive demand loads. Consequent passenger delays may affect the passengers' opinions of airline and airport operating efficiencies.

The demand and operating factors influencing service level and capacity of customs and immigration are given in Table 10-7. Capacity is generally determined over the short run—typically a peak period of 1 to 2 hours, during which several flights may arrive.

Flight arrival schedules are a major determinant of demand at the FIS facilities. Traffic loads are thus frequently influenced by the location

Table 10-7 Demand and operating factors influencing service level and capacity of customs and immigration

Factor	Description
Number of channels, space, and personnel	Inspector channels, U.S. citizen pass-through positions in immigration, "red-green" channel use in customs
Inspector	Average processing time per passenger, efficiency rate of selection for close inspection policy
Passenger characteristics	Fraction U.S. citizens, flight origin, citizenship of foreign nationals, baggage loads
Space and configuration	Available line space, access to and configuration of baggage display devices, use of carts
Flight schedule load	Basic determinant of number of people arriving at FIS areas

of an airport and the consequent predominant points of origin of arriving flights. Airports on the East Coast of the United States often have daily peak load periods in mid-afternoon and late afternoon, when flights from Europe arrive. West Coast airports with significant numbers of Asian flights might have a mid-morning peak.

Flight origins may also influence the degree of attention that arriving passengers receive from FIS inspectors. Flights from some parts of the world may receive careful examination because of concern for drug smuggling or may have large numbers of passengers whose visas and other entry papers are carefully examined. Flights from some countries carry large baggage loads, which places an extra burden on customs inspectors.

The number, size, and load factor of arriving aircraft can be used to estimate passenger loads at customs and immigration facilities. Walking speeds and distances from arrival gates to the inspection areas determine the distribution of actual passenger arrivals.

Operating procedures and planning standards for customs and immigration facilities are specified by the FIS. However, growth in international travel has made it difficult to maintain planning standards at many airports.

Very little information on actual performance of FIS facilities has been assembled, and the average processing rate of 50 passengers per hour per agent suggested by FAA guidance material is cited in many publications. However, it has been observed at New York City's John F. Kennedy International that average inspection rates can increase when conditions are crowded and passenger characteristics permit FIS officers to maintain inspection standards.

Lines may grow very long at some airports. During peak periods at John F. Kennedy International, which is by far the most frequently used point of arrival in the United States, foreign nationals might sometimes have to wait 20 minutes or more to clear immigration at the International Arrivals Building. The Port Authority of New York and New Jersey is now planning major expansion of these facilities. The wait for immigration and customs inspections and the crowding to which passengers may be subjected during these waits are the bases for determining service levels and capacity. A peak period of 1 to 1½ hours is usually appropriate to observe the impact of multiple flight arrivals at most international airports.

Landside access

It is a truism that nearly every airplane trip begins and ends with an automobile ride, and there is no clearer manifestation of our dependence on the automobile than at the terminal curbside and on the access roads to the airport. While the figures vary among airports, it is generally estimated that more than 90 percent of all airline passenger trips to and from airports are by private automobile or taxi. At medium and small airports, the figure is probably close to 100 percent because these communities tend not to have well-developed public transit providing a practical alternative to the automobile.

A further indication of the symbiosis between the airplane and the automobile is the emergence and growth of the car rental industry. This business has its origin in the need for air travelers to have transportation to and from airports in cities away from home. While many car rental firms have since branched out into other markets, the bulk of their business is still rentals to airline passengers, and revenues from this activity are a major source of income for airport operators.

Not all trips to the airport are made by airline passengers or those who come to meet travelers or drop them off. For airport workers (accounting for perhaps one-third of access trips) and calls by delivery vans, service representatives, and others with business on the airport property (also about one-third of all access trips), the automobile likewise predominates. Some (especially airport workers) come at times when public transit is not available or when service is infrequent, and they have almost no alternative but to drive to the airport and park.

At many airports, automobile traffic is a principal source of landside congestion and delay. Many major metropolitan area airports are suffering from capacity constraints imposed by landside congestion or lack of adequate access.

Only a few landside improvements and airport access projects are eligible for federal aid from the Airport and Airway Trust Fund. The Federal Highway Administration (FHWA) and the Urban Mass Transportation Administration (UMTA) also provide funds for landside development, and the airport operator or local airport authority contributes an important share through retained earnings and revenue bonds. Funding of landside investments is a complex multijurisdictional arrangement with wide variation from airport to airport. The capital improvements sponsored by FAA are limited to on-airport roadways, guideways, and walkways. Off the airport property, projects to improve landside access may receive FHWA and UMTA grants (Fig. 10-1) or be supported by state and local funds.

In general, the solution to landside access problems does not appear to be new technology, but application of management techniques to make better use of the facilities available and construction of new facilities (based on existing technology) to add to landside capacity. In a larger sense, there is also a need to look at the question of airport access from the perspective of the regional transportation system and to find ways to integrate the airport more effectively into the urban area it serves. Subsequent book sections focus on approaches that can be taken or applied more widely to alleviate the problem of traffic flow on the airport property and to reduce the cost and inconvenience of access from the surrounding metropolitan area.

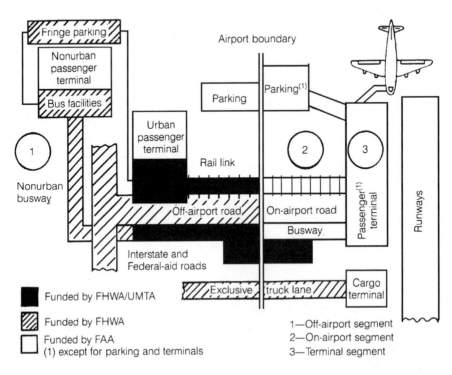

10-1 *Federal capital funding of airports and related facilities.*

Terminal curb front design

The terminal curb front provides temporary vehicle storage during passengers' transition between the terminal and the landside, and it is at the curbside that all passengers, except those using nearby parking or transit facilities, either enter or leave some form of ground transportation. A variety of pedestrians, private automobiles, taxis, buses, commercial delivery trucks, and hotel and rental car courtesy vans use the terminal curb area. Passengers might be carrying luggage to or from the terminal building, checking luggage at curbside facilities, and waiting for access to taxis or other vehicles. At some airports, passengers must cross frontage roads to reach parking areas from the terminal curb, slowing vehicular traffic circulation.

The principal demand and operating factors influencing service level and capacity for the terminal curb are summarized in Table 10-8. The primary determinant in the amount of curb frontage space required at a terminal is the length of time that vehicles stop for loading and unloading, referred to as the *dwell time*. For example, terminal designers estimate that reducing the average dwell time of those automobiles and taxis stopping at the terminal curb from 120 to 90 seconds can increase the capacity of a curb area by 15 to 20 percent.

Dwell time is influenced by whether drivers stop and leave their vehicles to accompany passengers into the terminal building or to meet or find an arriving passenger. Airports may seek to limit dwell times and overall congestion in the curb area through enforcement of regulations on access and by using signing and traffic management to separate user groups having substantially different demand characteristics. As an airport grows, parking and leaving vehicles along terminal curbs may be prohibited and efforts to channel automobile traffic directly to parking areas may be made. At large airports already practicing strict enforcement of traffic regulations, physical design changes often are the principal means for dealing with curb congestion. However, curb access is in general a major policy issue, requiring a balance among concerns of commercial operators and private automobile users, access service levels, and safety. The policy issue at many airports extends well beyond the technical questions of curb frontage design and vehicle demand characteristics.

Table 10-8 Demand and operating factors influencing service level and capacity of terminal curb

Factor	Description
Available frontage	Length of curb frontage modified by presence of obstructions and assigned uses (e.g., airport limousines only, taxi only), separation of departures and arrivals
Frontage roads and pedestrian paths	Number of traffic lanes feeding to and from frontage area; pedestrians crossing vehicle traffic lanes
Management policy	Stopping and dwell regulations, enforcement practices, commercial access control, public transport dispatching
Passenger characteristics and motor vehicle fleet mix	Passenger choice of ground transport mode, average occupancy of vehicles, dwell times at curb, passenger patterns of arrival before scheduled departure, baggage loads
Flight schedule	Basic determinant of number of people arriving and departing at given time in given area

Because private automobiles are the dominant ground access mode at most airports, they are the principal source of terminal curb frontage demand. Such demand can be reduced at some airports by increasing availability of convenient parking, which typically raises the proportion of motorists who enter or exit parking areas directly without stopping at the curb frontage, or by encouraging passengers to use off-airport check-in facilities if these are available.

Demand for curb frontage is also determined by flight schedules and particularly by the arrival pattern of originating passengers (how far in advance of the scheduled departure time they arrive at the airport) and the route through the terminal of terminating passengers (how long it takes them to travel from an arriving flight to the curb). Type of flight and trip purpose also influence terminal curb demand. For example, originating passengers on international flights are requested to arrive at the airport earlier than those aboard domestic flights. Terminating international passengers also are typically slower than domestic passengers to reach the curb frontage because of required customs and immigration procedures.

Passengers on business trips arrive at the airport closer to their departure time than those traveling for recreation or vacation. Deplaning business passengers, who might carry all their baggage aboard an aircraft and thus not need to stop at the baggage claim, reach the curb frontage sooner than those deplaning passengers who have checked bags. Transfer passengers at some airports use buses operating on frontage roads and thus also contribute to the demand on terminal curb facilities.

The curb frontage demand resulting from shuttle buses and courtesy vans might be related to the number of trips per hour they make to the terminal and not directly to number of passengers. The operators of these vehicles, seeking to ensure that all passengers are picked up promptly and reliably, may provide frequent service operated on specific headways and allow some vehicles to be underutilized in order to reduce waiting time for their patrons. Vehicle dwell time varies with type of vehicle, number in the vehicle, and baggage loads of passengers.

The most common forms of physical improvement are additional curb frontage, bypass lanes, multiple entry and exit points in the terminal building, remote park and ride facilities, and pedestrian overpasses or underpasses. These improvements are intended to increase the utilization of curb frontage by vehicular traffic or, in the case of park and ride, to reduce demand on the curb front by diverting passengers from private cars to high-volume vehicles. Walkways to segregate foot and vehicular traffic promote pedestrian safety and facilitate roadway traffic by eliminating conflicts between pedestrians and vehicles. Some terminals are designed initially or are retrofitted with two levels, an enplaning area on one level and deplaning area on the other level.

In some cases, procedural changes—either alone or in conjunction with low-cost physical modifications such as signing or lane dividers—are an effective alternative to expensive construction or remodeling of the curb front. For example, parking restrictions combined with strict enforcement will reduce curbside congestion and dwell time in discharging and boarding passengers. Short-term parking islands or reserved sections along the curb front, defined by roadway marking or simple dividers, could segregate vehicles picking up or discharging passengers from those that must handle baggage or enter the terminal for brief errands. Similarly, separation of private cars from taxis, buses, and limousines can diminish conflicts among these kinds of traffic and improve the flow to and from the curb front.

An effective approach at some airports has been provision of bus service from remote parking to the terminal and regulations to discourage bringing private automobiles to the terminal building. None of these measures is a substitute for adequate curbside capacity, but they can lead to more efficient use of the facilities available and perhaps compensate for deficiencies in terminal and curb front design.

Airport ground access

The roadways for access and circulation and public and private transit—both on and off the airport—make up the ground access system. When available, off-airport passenger check-in facilities or downtown terminals form part of this system. Typically only those off-airport elements of ground access that serve significant volumes of airport traffic are considered in planning and analysis. For example, a particular intersection far from the airport might be a constraint for one passenger but will have no material impact on airport operations. For many airports the access system extends only to the nearest interchange or intersection, whereas at those airports where most passengers arrive via a single primary route (such as the Sumner-Callahan tunnels in Boston or the expressway leading to Dulles International in Washington, D.C.) the access system may include many miles of a particular roadway or transit line.

Ground access is provided by an assortment of private and public transport modes. Except in those few cases where a rail transit system serves the airport, these ground access modes all use the metropolitan highway and street network and share the same roadways for circulation at the airport. For most U.S. airports, private automobiles and taxis are the principal access modes used.

Those accompanying or meeting passengers influence the demand on ground access systems. Such individuals overwhelmingly travel by private automobile, as do airport employees. Additional vehicle trips result from the delivery of cargo, priority packages, mail and terminal building and concession supplies, and the numerous service and maintenance requirements of an airport. The peak hours for employee and other highway travel not related to the airport and the conditions on the on-airport roadways most heavily used only by employees and airport operations differ from those for passenger traffic and are not addressed here.

The principal demand and operating factors influencing capacity and service conditions for ground access are summarized in Table 10-9. Although it is often necessary to view many of these factors on a metropolitan scale, the focus of capacity assessment is on the service provided between the terminal curb or parking area and the interchange linking the airport with the regional transportation system.

Access demand is primarily determined by the travel modes selected by passengers and visitors, the number of persons per vehicle, the circulation patterns of these vehicles, and how long before or after a flight a person arrives at or leaves the airport. Demand patterns of courtesy vehicles and scheduled limousines and buses might not be directly related to air passenger activity patterns. Access demand is

Shuttle bus service from various depots in and around the metropolitan area relieve auto traffic congestion at the airport.
Los Angeles Department of Airports.

Table 10-9 Demand and operating factors influencing service level and capacity of airport ground access

Factor	Description
Available modes and prices	Connections from various parts of the metropolitan area served, considering prices, comfort, and convenience, particularly with respect to baggage and required vehicle changes
Access times	Total, including wait for vehicles or access and travel from representative locations
Passenger characteristics	Fraction choosing each mode, vehicle occupancy, number of people accompanying passenger, other visitors, baggage loads, origination/destination share
Vehicle operator behavior	Fraction going directly to curb or to parking, weaving, curb dwell time, knowledge of traffic patterns
Flight schedule and load	Basic determinant of number of people using ground facilities
Facilities and background conditions	Highway and transit routes, interchanges; levels of traffic on facility for other than airport purposes; availability of remote check-in facilities

influenced by the extent of the public transportation system available, passenger trip purpose, the availability of parking, type of flight, and availability of alternative check-in areas. Cost of parking can have a particularly significant impact on access mode choice at large airports.

Ground access demand is generated by both originating and terminating passengers. At airports with multiple terminal buildings, the volume of connecting passenger transfers might influence the need for terminal-to-terminal shuttle bus service. At other airports, passenger transfers do not leave the terminal building and do not affect demand for either access or circulation. Circulation patterns are influenced by the location of the entrance and exit to parking and rental car areas, the availability and location of a recirculation road, the cost of short-term parking, and configuration of the terminals (single or multiple).

Driver familiarity with the roadway system and the complexity of the system significantly influence ground access operations. Complex road systems, such as those often found at large airports, require quick decision making by motorists unfamiliar with the airport and often involve frequent merging and weaving. Traffic control devices at grade intersections also influence system performance.

The management of taxi, limousine, and courtesy bus operations may also influence ground access operations. Control of taxi entry to the terminal area, issuance of taxi permits for airport service, and encouragement of limousine services are among the actions taken by management at some airports to improve ground access conditions. Control of cargo vehicles and employee access are also important at some airports.

Aside from expansion or improvement of the road network leading to the airport, most effort to facilitate airport ground access has focused on substitutes for the automobile. Bus or airline limousine service has proved workable in some cities, but patronage is generally low because of the infrequency of service or the inconvenience of getting between origin or destination and a centrally located bus terminal. Helicopter shuttle between the airport and city center has been tried, but it is expensive, unreliable because of weather, and objectionable to the community because of noise.

A solution that has been advocated by many planners is a rail rapid transit system, operated either exclusively to and from the airport or as part of a regional network. Cleveland, for example, built a rapid transit extension to Hopkins International Airport in 1968. Proposals to provide such service—either by construction of a new line to the airport or by linking an existing line to the airport by a feeder bus— have been advanced for several other cities.

In part, this interest has been stimulated by examples in foreign countries, which either have or are planning rail service to airports. Charles de Gaulle Airport in France has a rail station a little over a mile from the terminal with connection provided by shuttle bus. Amsterdam (Schiphol), Birmingham, Dusseldorf, Frankfurt, Gatwick, Heathrow, Orly, Vienna, and Zurich already have rail stations in or immediately adjacent to the airport terminal. Haneda Airport in

Japan has a monorail line from the center of Tokyo to the terminal, which brings passengers to within 300 feet of check-in counters. Toronto and Montreal (Dorval) in Canada have rail lines that are close by but not integral with the terminal (a connecting bus or taxi trip is needed to complete the link), and Montreal International (Mirabel) now has direct service from the airport to the downtown area with 13 intermediate stops.

Ridership statistics in the United States for existing transit linkages to major airports indicate an important, but distinctly limited, role for metropolitan rail systems. The most successful linkage is to Ronald Reagan Washington National Airport (DCA) via the modern and extensive Metrorail system. Transit has accounted for about 15 percent of trips to DCA and may reach 20 percent because the new terminal provides convenient access to transit. The next best performers are Atlanta's MARTA rail link to Hartsfield Airport, with a 9 percent market share, and Boston's MBTA rail link to Logan Airport, with a 7.5 percent market share. Transit links to Chicago O'Hare, New York JFK International, Philadelphia International, and Cleveland Hopkins airports all account for between 3 percent and 4 percent of airport access trips.

Experience to date suggests that public transportation (bus, rail, etc.) usually will not attract more than 30 percent of ground access trips to major airports. The same appears to be true in Europe where higher market shares are achieved only by linkages to extensive national rail systems that connect to cities beyond the metropolitan area served by the airport.

Unfortunately, rail transit is not a universal solution to the airport access problem. In most major U.S. cities, there is not a regional rail network to be tied into the airport, and without it there is little prospect that an exclusive line between downtown and the airport would be viable. Few passengers want to travel between the airport and the central business district, and even fewer want to go during rush hour. Rail transit, with its fixed routes and corridor structure, does not serve well in the U.S. setting, where there is wide dispersion of origins and destinations for airport passengers. The capital costs of such systems are likely to be high, and it is doubtful that operating expenses could be covered from the fare box, necessitating subsidy from the municipality or the airport.

Highway coverage is very good, with 70 percent to 90 percent of passengers within 45 minutes of the airport during peak travel periods. Transit coverage is poor, with less than 10 percent of travelers able to reach the Baltimore or Minneapolis airports in 45 minutes. Even in Boston, where the airport is linked to an extensive metropolitan rail system, only 25 percent of passengers can reach the airport within 45 minutes, and no more than 40 percent of passengers can reach the airport by transit, even if they allow 90 minutes for the trip. Because highway access is more convenient for most travelers, it accounts for most trips to airports.

There might be public resistance to building a system to serve airport users exclusively when other parts of the metropolitan area could profit perhaps more from rail rapid transit service. Finally, the service characteristics of rail transit do not lend themselves particularly well to airport trips. Passengers encumbered by baggage find rail transit inconvenient because there is no storage space on trains and narrow aisles might be difficult to negotiate with luggage in hand. If there are intermediate stops—as there almost certainly would be if the rail line attempts to serve more than a few who want to travel from city center to the airport—the trip is prolonged, and trains might be crowded with passengers riding for other purposes.

These arguments do not necessarily deny the validity of foreign experience, but they raise doubts about the viability of rail transit access to airports in this country—where we do not have the population densities, the existing urban rail network, and the tradition of public transit that are characteristic of Europe and Japan.

An alternative rail transit that accomplishes the same purpose but with greater flexibility and somewhat lower cost (Fig. 10-2) is the *remote airline terminal*, which is a facility for processing arriving and departing passengers at a site off the airport property and transferring them to the terminal by group transportation. The off-airport terminal might include facilities for ticketing, baggage handling, and parking. Connection with the airport might be provided by public transit, special airport bus, or helicopter shuttle. The technology to implement this concept exists, and it has been tried in several cities.

The popularity of the remote terminal concept has waned in recent years, largely because indirect costs tend to offset the benefits. Trip origins and destinations are becoming more and more scattered throughout the urban area, to the extent that trips to and from the city center now account for less than a quarter of airport patronage.

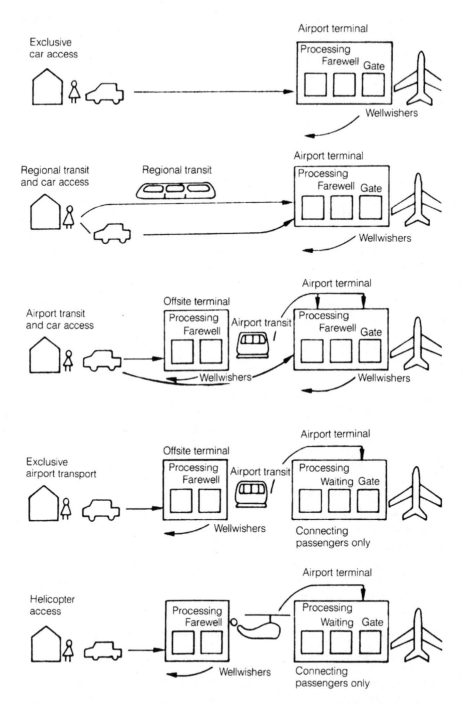

10-2 *Off-site passenger terminal concepts.*

On the other hand, the increasingly tighter restrictions on airport terminal and landside expansion might make this concept worth re-examining, particularly if a way can be found to build and operate a network of small dispersed facilities adapted to the urban-suburban pattern of business and residence in major metropolitan areas.

Parking areas

Parking areas consist of surface lots or multilevel garages used to store the vehicles of air passengers and visitors. Although parking and storage areas are also needed for employee vehicles, rental cars, taxis, and buses, these requirements have relatively little influence on the capacity or service level of the airport as viewed by a passenger. The focus of this section is therefore public parking.

For planning purposes, parking is divided into two or three general categories: short-term, long-term, and remote (which is usually long-term parking). *Short-term parking* is usually located close to terminal buildings and serves motorists dropping off or picking up travelers. These motorists usually remain at the airport for less than 3 hours. Some airports distinguish other periods of time as "short term." The most expensive parking is often found in the short-term lots.

Long-term parking serves passengers who leave their vehicles at the airport while they travel. With the low turnover rate and long duration of stay, long-term parking accounts for 70 to 80 percent of the occupied parking spaces at an airport, even though only 15 to 30 percent of all vehicles parked over the course of a year is represented.

Remote parking consists of long-term parking lots located away from the airport terminal buildings. Often buses or vans are available to transport passengers to the terminal. At some airports these parking facilities are called *shuttle lots* or, when used only during peak periods, *holiday lots.* Because parking rates at remote lots are less expensive than those for other airport parking facilities, these lots are often termed "reduced-rate" parking.

Entry to airport parking areas is usually controlled by automatic gates, and parking fees are collected by a cashier located in a booth at the exit. At some airports motorists leaving the parking facilities are delayed because there are insufficient cashiers. In addition to delays encountered entering and leaving parking areas, passenger service levels will also be affected by the distance to be walked between parked vehicles and the terminal and by the environment in which this walk occurs. At some airports weather-protected walkways improve passenger assessment of the service level. Other airports provide escalators, moving sidewalks, buses, people movers, or other mechanical assistance to reduce passenger walking distances and number of level changes.

The principal demand and operating factors influencing service level and capacity for parking areas are given in Table 10-10. Although the number of parking spaces provided is a snapshot measure of capacity, the total time required for access and egress influences the assessment of service level provided. Such factors as the allocation of parking between short- and long-term uses and parking prices influence service levels.

Demand at parking areas is characterized by accumulation of parked vehicles, which is measured by both length of time as well as number of spaces occupied. This accumulation is influenced by passenger arrival times at the airport and trip purposes. Business travelers have been found to be less sensitive to parking costs than those on pleasure trips and thus more likely to use more expensive, close-in, short-term parking. Passengers on vacation are more cost-sensitive but value their time less. They are more likely to seek reduced-rate, remote parking areas. Passengers who expect to be away for long trips have greater amounts of baggage and are more likely to be dropped off or greeted by motorists who use short-term parking.

Parking demand is in general very sensitive to the cost of parking. Effective parking capacity can be increased by altering parking fees to increase the cost difference between short-term and long-term parking and thus encourage price-sensitive motorists to divert to less expensive parking areas. General increases in parking fees may also encourage passengers to choose other means than driving their own automobiles for their trip to the airport.

Parking space needs are determined primarily by the amount of long-term parking because it generates the most space-hours. Because of their higher turnover rate, short-term spaces generate more entry and exit movements than do long-term spaces. Demand for automatic gates at the entry and cashier booths at the exit of the parking area is a function of the number of entries and exits, which,

Table 10-10 Demand and operating factors influencing service level and capacity of parking areas

Factor	Description
Access (enplaning)	
Available space	As a function of distance from terminal area, systems for reaching terminal, prices for parking, and availability of weather-protected waiting and walking areas
Access times	Total, including search for space, wait, and travel from remote locations
Passenger characteristics	Percentage of people driving, automobile occupancy, visitor ratios, length of stay
Pricing	Higher fees may suppress demand or divert some to lower-cost lots
Flight schedule	Basic determinant of number of people arriving at parking areas
Egress (deplaning)	
Access time	Total, including wait and travel to remote locations, with consideration for availability of weather-protected wait and walk areas
Exit position and employee efficiency	Number and direction to exits, service times to exit lots
Passenger characteristics	Fraction driving, automobile occupancy, length of stay
Flight schedule and load	Basic determinant of number of people arriving at parking areas

although not indicative of space needs or parking demand, may be significant for capacity estimation.

The number of parking spaces required to provide adequate service levels is normally greater than total parking demand. This is because at a large parking facility in which many areas cannot be seen simultaneously—for example, in a multilevel garage or extensive open lot—it is more difficult to find the last empty spaces. Thus a large parking facility may be considered full when 85 to 95 percent of the spaces are occupied, depending on its use by long- or short-term parking, size, and configuration.

The balance between long- and short-term parking is crucial to capacity estimation. As already noted, distribution of demand might be significantly influenced by parking fees. For example, when New York City's La Guardia was faced with a serious shortage of parking space, structured parking facilities were constructed, and all parking rates were raised significantly to substantially reduce long-term parking at the airport and make space available to satisfy short-term demand. Such a strategy generally required that adequate alternative transport services be available to meet the demand for airport ground access.

Besides determining the number of parking spaces available and the effective distance of spaces from terminal buildings, parking operators might be able to adjust the physical design of the parking lot entries and exits to reduce or avoid congestion and use informational signing to direct motorists to underutilized facilities. However, lengthening the pedestrian path between the parking lot and the terminal might reduce overall perceived service levels. Some airports are experimenting with "precashiering," in which passengers pay their parking fees before entering their vehicles, as a means to reduce delay and congestion at exit plazas.

Applications of technology to airport problems

In the search for solutions to capacity and delay problems, the value of new technology is typically measured by its ability to achieve one or more of the following:

1 Increased capacity.
2 Higher efficiency.
3 Greater safety.
4 Improved reliability.
5 Greater accuracy.
6 Lower cost.
7 Greater convenience.

The first two are direct benefits; they constitute relief of the problem of how to accommodate a higher level of demand. Safety is of prime importance, but it has little relationship to capacity and delay unless—as is often the case with procedures and rules—the requirement for safety precludes some measure for increasing capacity or throughput. If some new method of ensuring safety is found and it also allows a subsequent change in procedures or utilization of airport facilities, safety improvements might give rise to a secondary capacity-related benefit. Reliability, accuracy, cost, and convenience are operational benefits. They are worth seeking in and of themselves, but they have little direct relation to capacity except insofar as they are attributes that lead to adoption of new technology or hasten its implementation. (The description of airside and landside technologies presented in this chapter and chapter 9 touched on all of these prospective benefits.)

The emphasis has been on their potential to relieve capacity and delay problems, but other attributes have been cited where they appear relevant either to the future use of the technology or to the choice of one form of technology over another.

Key terms

passenger movers

computerized ticket systems

computerized aircraft manifest

curbside check-in

computerized baggage sorting equipment

Federal Inspection Services (FIS)

short-term parking

long-term parking

remote parking

Review questions

1 Briefly describe the demand and operating factors influencing service level and capacity in the following areas: terminal; passenger waiting area; transfer passengers; ticket counter and baggage check; passenger security screening; customs and immigration; terminal curb front; airport ground access; and parking areas.

2 Describe some of the passenger movement systems in the terminal designed to lessen the inconvenience of walking long distances.

- What are some problems associated with automated guide-way systems?

3 What are the major functions of the ticket counter? Describe several technologies designed to speed ticket counter operations. What is the major problem associated with ticket dispensing machines?

4 What is curbside check-in? What is the purpose of computerized baggage sorting equipment?

- What is being done to promote carry-on luggage?

5 How has passenger security screening affected service levels and capacity at major airports? What can be done to alleviate some problems associated with security screening?

- What is the "red channel, green channel" system for passing through customs?

6 If only a few landside improvements and airport access projects are eligible for federal aid from the Airport and Airway Trust Fund, how can this problem be addressed?

- The solution to landside access problems does not appear to be in new technology, but application of management techniques. Do you agree? Why?

- What are some of the common forms of physical improvement and management techniques used to expeditiously move traffic at the terminal curb front?

7 Define the ground access system. What are the factors affecting access demand?

- Discuss some of the pros and cons of rail transit between the airport and city center.

Suggested readings

Canadian Airport System Evaluation: Vancouver Airport. Report AK-14-06-031. Transport Canada, Ottawa, Ontario, 1981.

deNeufville, Richard. *Airport Systems Planning.* Cambridge, Massachusetts: The MIT Press, 1976.

Horonjeff, R., and F. X. McKelvey. *Planning and Design of Airports,* 4th ed. New York: McGraw-Hill, Inc., 1994.

Report of the Industry Task Force on Airport Capacity Improvement and Delay Reduction. Washington, DC: Airport Operators Council International, September 1982.

Airfield and Airspace Capacity/Delay Policy Analysis: FAA-APO-81-14. Washington, DC: Federal Aviation Administration, Office of Aviation Policy and Plans, December 1981.

Airport and Terminal-Area Operations of the Future. Washington, DC: Transportation Research Board, 1987.

Airport Landside Capacity. Washington, DC: Transportation Board, 1975.

Measuring Airport Landside Capacity. Washington, DC: Transportation Board, 1987.

Airport System Development. Washington, DC: U.S. Congress, Office of Technology Assessment, August 1984.

Airport Terminal and Landside Design and Operation. Washington, DC: Transportation Board, 1990.

Airport Landside Planning and Operations. Washington, DC: Transportation Board, 1992.

Intercity Passenger Rail, Washington, DC: U.S. general Accounting Office, March, 1997.

Part IV

The management process

11

Financial management

Outline

- Airport accounting
- Planning and budgeting
- Approaches to financial management at commercial airports
- Pricing of airport facilities and services
- Trends in airport financial management since deregulation

Objectives

When you have completed this chapter, you should be able to:

- Discuss the importance of accounting to airport financial management.
- Summarize the five major revenue sources under a typical airport's operating statement.
- Explain why it is so difficult to compare operating expenses between different airports.
- Discuss the importance of planning and budgeting in the financial management process.
- Distinguish between the residual-cost and compensatory approaches on airport-airline relationships.
- Define "majority-in-interest" and describe its implication for residual-cost airports.
- Describe the major sources of revenue for the airfield area, terminal area concessions, airline leased areas, and other leased areas.

- List and briefly describe the factors causing airport cost increases since deregulation.
- Discuss some of the effects of deregulation on airport financial management.

Airport accounting

Financial management of a major airport is comparable to that of a complex and highly diversified business enterprise. The airport provides a wide range of facilities and services for a diverse group of businesses and individuals. As a result, the impact of the airport's financial management not only affects the airport users, but also represents an important element in the growth and economic well-being of the community in which it is located.

Airport accounting involves the accumulation, communication, and interpretation of economic data relating to the financial position of an airport and the results of its operations for decision-making purposes. It differs from accounting procedures found in business firms because airports vary considerably in terms of goals, size, and operational characteristics. As such, it is very difficult to derive a unified accounting system that can be used by all airports. A system tailored to the needs of a large commercial airport might be impractical for a small GA airport or vice versa. Many airports have different definitions of what elements constitute operating and nonoperating revenues and expenses and sources of funds for airport development. Anyone attempting to compare the financial data of one airport to another, or against a group of similar airports, finds it extremely difficult to draw valid conclusions. Nevertheless, a good accounting system is needed for a number of reasons:

1 Financial statements are needed to inform governmental authorities and the local community regarding details of the airport's operations.
2 A good accounting system can assist airport management in allocating resources, reducing costs, and improving control.
3 Negotiating charges for use of airport facilities can be facilitated.
4 Financial statements can influence the decisions of voters and legislators.

One of the most important financial statements is the *operating statement*, which records an airport's revenues and expenses over a particular time period (quarterly and annually). Table 11-1 includes a sample of an operating statement for a fiscal period. The following discussion includes the major items appearing on an operating statement.

Operating revenues

Airport operating revenues can be divided into five major groupings: (1) airfield area; (2) terminal area concessions; (3) airline leased areas; (4) other leased areas; and (5) other operating revenue.

Airfield area The airfield area or airside of the airport produces revenues from sources that are directly related to the operation of aircraft:

1 Landing fees—scheduled and unscheduled airlines, itinerant aircraft, military or governmental aircraft.
2 Aircraft parking charges—paved and unpaved areas.
3 Fuel flowage fees—FBOs and other fuel suppliers.

Table 11-1 Sample airport operating statement for a fiscal period

Operating revenues		$740,000
Airfield area	$250,000	
Terminal area concessions	300,000	
Airline leased areas	110,000	
Other leased areas	70,000	
Other operating revenue	10,000	
Nonoperating revenues		20,000
Total operating revenues		$760,000
Operating expenses		$605,000
Airfield area	120,000	
Terminal area	260,000	
Hangars, cargo facilities, other facilities and grounds	75,000	
General and administrative expenses	150,000	
Nonoperating expenses		40,000
Total operating expenses		$645,000
Total operating income		$125,000
Depreciation		100,000
Net income		$ 25,000

Terminal area concessions The terminal area concessions include all of the nonairline users of the terminal area:

1 Food and beverage concessions (includes restaurants, snack bars, and lounges).
2 Travel services and facilities (includes checkrooms and lockers, flight insurance, restrooms, car rentals, and telephones).
3 Specialty stores and shops (includes boutiques, newsstands, banks, gift shops, clothing stores, duty-free shops, and so forth).
4 Personal services (includes beauty and barber shops, valet shops, and shoeshine stands).
5 Amusements (includes video arcades, movie and TV rooms, and observation decks).
6 Display advertising.
7 Outside terminal concessions (includes auto parking, ground transportation, hotels and motels).

Airline leased areas Airline leased areas include revenue derived from the air carriers for ground equipment rentals, cargo terminals, office rentals, ticket counters, hangars, operations, and maintenance facilities.

Other leased areas All of the remaining leased areas on the airport that produce revenue are brought together under other leased areas. Freight forwarders, fixed-base operators, governmental units, and businesses in the airport industrial area would be included under this category. All revenue derived from nonairline cargo terminals and ground equipment rentals to nonairline users would also be included.

Other operating revenue Other operating revenue includes revenues from the operation of distribution systems for public utilities, such as electricity and steam, and jobbing and contract work performed for tenants. Other miscellaneous service fees are also included under this category.

Nonoperating revenues

Nonoperating revenues include interest earned on investments in governmental securities, local taxes, subsidies or grants-in-aid, and selling or leasing of properties owned by the airport but not related to airport operations. The magnitude of nonoperating income can vary considerably between airports.

Operating expenses

Operating expenses, unlike revenues, can vary considerably between similar airports. The nature of airport expenses depends upon a number of factors including the airport's geographical location, organizational setup, and financial structure. Airports in the sunbelt do not experience the sizable snow removal and other cold-weather-related expenses that airports in colder climates must face. Some municipalities, counties, or local authorities absorb the costs of certain staff functions such as accounting, legal, planning, and public relations. Certain operating functions such as emergency service, policing, and traffic control might also be provided by local fire departments and local law enforcement agencies at some airports.

Operating expenses can be divided into four major groupings: (1) airfield area; (2) terminal area; (3) hangars, cargo, other buildings and grounds; and (4) general and administrative expenses.

Airfield area All maintenance and operating expenses associated with the airfield are included under this category:

1 Runways, taxiways, apron areas, aircraft parking areas, and airfield lighting systems maintenance.
2 Service on airport equipment such as cars and trucks.
3 Other expenses in this area such as maintenance on fire equipment and airport service roads.
4 Utilities (electricity) for the airfield.

Terminal area All maintenance and operating expenses associated with the terminal area:

1 Buildings and grounds—maintenance and custodial services.
2 Improvements to the land and landscaping.
3 Loading bridges and gates—maintenance and custodial services.
4 Concession improvements.
5 Observation facilities—maintenance and custodial services.
6 Passenger, employee, and tenant parking facilities.
7 Utilities (electricity, air conditioning and heating, and water).

8 Waste disposal (plumbing)—maintenance.

9 Equipment (air conditioning, heating, baggage handling)—maintenance.

Hangars, cargo facilities, other buildings, and grounds All maintenance and operating expenses associated with hangars, cargo facilities, other buildings, and grounds:

1 Buildings and grounds—maintenance and custodial services.

2 Improvements to the land and landscaping.

3 Employee parking—maintenance.

4 Access roadways—maintenance.

5 Utilities (electricity, air conditioning and heating, and water).

6 Waste disposal (plumbing)—maintenance.

General and administrative expenses All payroll expenses for the maintenance, operations, and administrative staff are included under this account. Other operating expenses for materials and supplies are included under general and administrative expenses.

Nonoperating expenses

Nonoperating expenses include the payment of interest on outstanding debt (bonds, notes, loans, and so forth), contributions to governmental bodies, and other miscellaneous expenses.

Depreciation

Some airports compute depreciation on the full value of facilities including federal and other aid, while other airports limit depreciation to only their share of the construction costs.

Planning and budgeting

Planning and budgeting are integral parts of any financial management process. Every airport must make short-term decisions about the allocation and scheduling of its limited resources over many competing uses; it must make long-term decisions about rates of expansion of capital improvements and funding sources. Both short-term and long-term decisions require planning. Planning is important because it

Water recycling as an effective way of reducing utility expenses.
Los Angeles Department of Airports.

1 Encourages coordinated thinking. No one department can act independently. A policy decision in a particular department affects the airport as a whole.

2 Helps develop standards for future performance. Without plans, the airport's measure of financial performance can be based only on historical standards. While past operating statements help to set these standards for the future, they should not necessarily serve as standards themselves.

3 Assists management in controlling the actions of subordinates. By planning, employees are provided a goal or standard to achieve.

4 Might help reveal potential problems for which remedial measures can be taken earlier.

5 Promotes smoother-running operations. For example, new equipment can be ordered in advance of its anticipated usage. With smooth, uninterrupted operations, the overall efficiency of the airport can be increased.

Once the airport has decided upon a plan of action for the future, these plans are incorporated into a written financial budget. *Budgets* are simply the planned dollar amounts needed to operate and maintain the airport during a definite period of time such as a year. Budgets are established for major capital expenditures such as runway resurfacing, taxiway construction, and new snow removal equipment as well as for operating expenses during the planning period.

In an airport maintenance department, there are labor expenses and a variety of other expenses for supplies, minor equipment purchasing and repair, and mechanical systems maintenance. The real expenses incurred during the year are a measure of the actual performance. The differences between actual expenses and the budgeted amount is called a *variance*. The variance measures the efficiency of the department.

Airports generally operate under one of three different forms of budget appropriation:

1 Lump-sum appropriation. A *lump-sum appropriation* is the simplest form of budget and generally only utilized by small GA airports. There are no specific restrictions as to how the money should be spent. Only the total expenditure for the period is stipulated. Obviously, this is the most flexible form of budget.

2 Appropriation by activity. Under this form of budget, appropriated expenses are planned according to major work area or activity with no further detailed breakdown. *Appropriation by activity* enables management to establish capital and operating expense budgets for particular areas such as airside facilities, terminal building area, and so forth. It also permits flexibility in responding to changing conditions.

3 Line-item budget. The *line-item budget* is the most detailed form of budgeting and is used quite extensively at the large commercial airports. Numerical codes are established for each operating and capital expense item. Budgets are established for each item and often adjusted to take into consideration changes in volume of activity. For example, as the number of passenger enplanements changes, budgets for the terminal building maintenance can be adjusted accordingly.

A very popular approach to budgeting today at many airports is the zero-base budget. The *zero-base budget* derives from the idea that each program or departmental budget should be prepared from the ground up, or base zero. This is in contrast to the normal budgeting practice, which builds on the base of a previous period. By calculating the budget from a zero-base, all costs are newly developed and reviewed entirely to determine their necessity. Various programs are reviewed and costed thoroughly and then ranked in degree of importance to the airport. Managers are presumably forced to look at a program in its entirety rather than as an expense add-on to an existing budget.

In drawing up a budget, the first step normally involves an estimate of revenues from all sources for the coming year. The next step is to establish budgets for the various areas of responsibility. When budgets are being investigated, predetermined, and integrated, the department managers who must live within the budgets are consulted about the amount of money available and help draw up budgets for their departments for the coming period. A manager who has some say about the budget and expenses is more inclined to make an added effort to keep down the actual expenses of the department.

Actual expenses are then checked against budgeted expenses frequently during the period that the budgets are in effect. Managers are supplied with figures of actual expenses so that they can compare them with budgeted expenses and investigate variances.

Approaches to financial management at commercial airports

At most commercial airports, the financial and operational relationship between the airport operator and the airlines is defined in legally binding agreements that specify how the risks and responsibilities of running the airport are to be shared. These contracts, commonly termed airport use agreements, establish the terms and conditions governing the airlines' use of the airport. *Airport use agreement* is used generically here to include both legal contracts for the airlines' use of airfield facilities and leases for use of terminal facilities. At many airports, both are combined in a single document. A few commercial airports do not negotiate airport use agreements with the airlines, but instead charge rates and fees set by local ordinance. The airport use agreements also specify the methods for calculating rates airlines must pay for use of airport facilities and services; and they identify the airlines' rights and privileges, sometimes including the right to approve or disapprove any major proposed airport capital development projects.

Although financial management practices differ greatly among commercial airports, the airport-airline relationship at major airports typically takes one of two very different forms, with important implications for airport pricing and investment:

1 The residual-cost approach, under which the airlines collectively assume significant financial risk by agreeing to pay any costs of running the airport that are not allocated to other users or covered by nonairline sources of revenue.

2 The compensatory approach, under which the airport operator assumes the major financial risk of running the airport and charges the airlines fees and rental rates set so as to recover the actual costs of the facilities and services that they use.

The residual-cost approach

A majority of the nation's large commercial airports have some form of *residual-cost approach* to financial management. Under this approach, the airlines collectively assume significant financial risk. They agree to keep the airport financially self-sustaining by making up any deficit—the residual cost—remaining after the costs identified for all airport users have been offset by nonairline sources of revenue (automobile parking and terminal concessions such as restaurants, newsstands, snack bars, and the like).

Although applications of the residual-cost approach vary widely, a simplified example can illustrate the basic approach (Table 11-2).

Most airports have a number of different cost centers. These include the airfield area, terminal area, and so forth as indicated earlier in this chapter. At a residual-cost airport, the total annual expenses, including administration, maintenance, operations, and debt service (including coverage) is calculated for each cost center, and offset by all nonairline revenues anticipated for that center. *Debt service coverage* is the requirement that the airport's revenue, net of operating and maintenance expenses, be equal to a specified percentage in excess of the annual debt service (principal and interest payments) for revenue bond issues. The coverage required is generally from 1.25 to 1.40 times debt service, thereby providing a substantial cushion that enhances the security of the bonds.

The residual between costs and revenues provides the basis for calculating the rates charged the airlines for their use of facilities within

Table 11-2 Comparison of residual-cost and compensatory methods of calculating airport fees

Requirement	Residual cost		Compensatory	
	Terminal	Airfield	Terminal	Airfield
Maintenance, operations, and administration	$ 40,000	$ 40,000	$ 40,000	$ 40,000
Debt service	40,000	20,000	40,000	20,000
Debt service coverage	10,000	5,000	10,000	5,000
Deposits to special funds	5,000	20,000	5,000	20,000
Other	5,000	15,000	5,000	15,000
Total requirement	$100,000	$100,000	$100,000	$100,000
Cost center from nonairline sources	−$50,000	−$50,000	NA	NA
Airline share (percent)	NA	NA	65	75
Residual cost	50,000	50,000	NA	NA
Activity level	6,500 square feet	100,000 pounds gross landing weight	6,500 square feet	100,000 pounds gross landing weight
Rental rate (per square foot)	$7.69	NA	$10.00	NA
Landing fee rate (per 1,000 pounds gross landing weight)	NA	$0.50	NA	$0.75

This is not a comparison of actual rate calculations but a simplified illustration. Rates are not necessarily higher under either approach but differ according to the volume of traffic, amount of debt, and other factors.

NA = Not applicable

Source: FAA

the cost center. Any surplus revenues would be credited to the airlines and any deficit charged to them in calculating airline landing fees or other rates for the following year.

The compensatory approach

Under a *compensatory approach*, the airport operator assumes the financial risk of airport operation, and airlines pay rates and charges equal to the costs of the facilities they use, as determined by cost accounting. In contrast to the situation at residual-cost airports, the airlines at a compensatory airport provide no guarantee that fees and rents will suffice to allow the airport to meet its annual operating and debt service requirements.

Although individual airports have adopted many versions of the compensatory approach, the simplified example set out in Table 11-2 illustrates the basics. First, for each cost center, a calculation would be made of the total annual expense of running the center, including administration, maintenance, operations, and debt service (with coverage). The airlines' shares of these costs would then be based on the extent of their actual use of facilities within each cost center. The airlines would not be charged for the costs of public space, such as terminal lobbies. Nor would they receive any credit for nonairline revenues, which offset expenses in the residual-cost approach but are disregarded under a compensatory approach in calculating rates and charges to the airlines.

Comparison of residual-cost and compensatory approaches

Residual-cost and compensatory approaches to financial management of major commercial airports have significantly different implications for pricing and investment practices. In particular, they help determine:

1 An airport's potential for accumulating net income for capital development.

2 The nature and extent of the airlines' role in making airport capital investment decisions, which can be formally defined in majority-in-interest clauses included in airport use agreements with the airlines.

3 The length of term of the use agreement between the airlines and the airport operator.

These differences, discussed below, can have an important bearing on an airport's performance in the municipal bond market.

Net income Although large and medium commercial airports generally must rely on the issuance of debt to finance major capital development projects, the availability of substantial revenues generated in excess of expenses can strengthen the performance of an airport in the municipal bond market. It can also provide an alternative to issuing debt for the financing of some portion of capital development. Residual-cost financing guarantees that an airport will always break even—thereby ensuring service without resort to supplemental local tax support—but it precludes the airport from generating earnings substantially in excess of costs.

By contrast, an airport using a compensatory approach lacks the built-in security afforded by the airlines' guarantee that the airport will break even every year. The public operator undertakes the risk that revenues generated by airport fees and charges might not be adequate to allow the airport to meet its annual operating costs and debt service obligations. On the other hand, because total revenues are not constrained to the amount needed to break even, and because surplus revenues are not used to reduce airline rates and charges, compensatory airports may earn and retain a substantial surplus, which can later be used for capital development. Since the pricing of airport concessions and consumer services need not be limited to the recovery of actual costs, the extent of such retained earnings generally depends on the magnitude of the airport's nonairline revenues. Market pricing of concessions and other nonairline sources of revenue is a feature of both residual-cost and compensatory airports.

Because the residual-cost approach is not designed to yield substantial revenues in excess of costs, residual-cost airports, as a group, tend to retain considerably smaller percentages of their gross revenues than do compensatory airports. A few residual-cost airports, however, have modified the approach to permit accumulation of sizable retained earnings for use in capital projects. For example, at Miami International certain airport-generated revenues are excluded from the revenue base used in calculating the residual-cost payable by the airlines; the revenues flow instead into a discretionary fund that can finance capital development projects.

Majority-in-interest In exchange for the guarantee of solvency, airlines that are signatory to a residual-cost use agreement often exercise a significant measure of control over airport investment decisions and related pricing policy. These powers are embodied in so-called majority-in-interest clauses, which are a much more common feature of airport use agreements at residual-cost airports than at airports using a compensatory approach.

Majority-in-interest clauses give the airlines that represent a majority of traffic at an airport the opportunity to review and approve or veto capital projects that would entail significant increases in the rates and fees they pay for the use of airport facilities. The combination of airlines that can exercise majority-in-interest powers varies. A typical formulation would give majority-in-interest powers to any combination of "more than 50 percent of the scheduled airlines that landed more than 50 percent of the aggregate revenue aircraft weight during the preceding fiscal year" (standard document wording).

This arrangement provides protection for the airlines that have assumed financial risk under a residual-cost agreement by guaranteeing payment of all airport costs not covered by nonairline sources of revenue. For instance, without some form of majority-in-interest clause, the airlines at a residual-cost airport could be obligating themselves to pay the costs of as-yet-undefined facilities that might be proposed in the 15th or 20th year of a 30-year use agreement. Under a compensatory approach, where the airport operator assumes the major financial risk of running the facility, the operator is generally freer to undertake capital development projects without consent of the airlines that account for a majority of the traffic. Even so, airport operators rarely embark on major projects without consulting the airlines that serve the airport. Potential investors in airport revenue bonds would be wary of a bond issue for a project lacking the airlines' approval.

Specific provisions of majority-in-interest clauses vary considerably. At some airports, the airlines that account for a majority of traffic can approve or disapprove all major capital development projects—any project costing more than $100,000. At other airports, projects can only be deferred for a certain period of time (generally six months to two years). Although most airports have at least a small discretionary fund for capital improvements that is not subject to majority-in-interest approval, the general effect of majority-in-interest provisions is to limit the ability of the public airport owner to proceed with any major project opposed by the airlines. Sometimes, a group of just two or three major carriers can exercise such control.

Term of use agreement Residual-cost airports typically have longer-term use agreements than compensatory airports. This is because residual-cost agreements historically have been drawn up to provide security for long-term airport revenue bond issues; and the term of the use agreement, with its airline guarantee of debt service, has generally coincided with the term of the revenue bonds. The vast majority of residual-cost airports have use agreements with terms of 20 or more years and 30 years or longer is not uncommon.

By contrast, probably only 50 percent of the compensatory airports have use agreements running for 20 years or more. Many of the compensatory airports have no contractual agreements whatever with the airlines. At these airports, rates and charges are established by local ordinance or resolution. This arrangement gives airport operators maximum flexibility to adjust their pricing and investment practices unilaterally, without the constraints imposed by a formal agreement negotiated with the airlines, but it lacks the security provided by contractual agreements.

Pricing of airport facilities and services

Major commercial airports are diversified enterprises that provide a wide range of facilities and services for which fees, rents, or other user charges are assessed. It was pointed out earlier in the chapter that most commercial airports, regardless of size, type, or locale, offer four major types of facilities and services: (1) airfield area; (2) terminal area concessions; (3) airline leased areas; and (4) other leased areas.

The facilities and services provided to users generate the revenues necessary to operate the airport and to support the financing of capital development. Smaller commercial airports and GA airports typically offer a much narrower range of facilities and services, for which only minimal fees and charges often are assessed. Revenue bases shrink as airports decrease in size, and many of the smallest do not generate sufficient revenue to cover their operating costs, much less capital investment. Among GA airports, those that lease land or facilities for industrial use generally have a better chance of covering their costs of operation than do those providing only aviation-related services and facilities.

The combination of public management and private enterprise uniquely characteristic of the financial operation of commercial airports is reflected in the divergent pricing of airport facilities and services. The private enterprise aspects of airport operation—the services and facilities furnished for nonaeronautical use—generally are priced on a market pricing basis. On the other hand, the pricing of facilities and services for airlines and other aeronautical users is on a cost-recovery basis, either recovery of the actual costs of the facilities and services provided (the compensatory approach) or recovery of the residual costs of airport operation not covered by nonairline sources of revenue. This mix of market pricing and cost-recovery pricing has important implications for airport financing, especially with regard to the structure and control of airport charges and the distribution of operating revenues.

The structure and control of fees, rents, and other charges for facilities and services are governed largely by a variety of long-term and short-term contracts, including airport use agreements with the airlines, leases, and concession and management contracts. For each of the four major groups of facilities and services outlined earlier in the chapter, the basic kinds of charges assessed at residual-cost and compensatory airports can be compared in terms of: (1) method of calculation; (2) term of agreement; and (3) frequency of adjustment.

Airfield area   The major fees assessed for use of airfield facilities are landing or flight fees for commercial airlines and GA aircraft. Some airports also levy other airfield fees, such as charges for the use of aircraft parking ramps or aprons. In lieu of landing fees, many smaller airports—especially GA airports—collect *fuel flowage fees,* which are levied per gallon of aviation gasoline and jet fuel sold at the airport.

At residual-cost airports, the landing fee for airlines is typically the item that balances the budget, making up the projected difference between all other anticipated revenues and the total annual costs of administration, operations and maintenance, and debt service (including coverage). Landing fees differ widely among residual-cost airports, depending on the extent of the revenues derived from airline terminal rentals and concessions such as restaurants, car rental companies, and automobile parking lots. If the nonairline revenues are high in a given year, the landing fee for the airlines might be quite low. In recent years, several airports—including Los Angeles and Honolulu International—have approached a "negative" landing fee. At some residual-cost airports, the landing fee is the budget-balancing item for the airfield cost center only. At such airports, the surplus or deficit in the terminal cost center has no influence on airline landing fees, and terminal rental rates for the airlines are set on a residual-cost or a compensatory basis.

The method of calculating landing fees at residual-cost airports is established in the airport use agreement and continues for the full term of the agreement. To reflect changes in operating costs or revenues, landing fees are typically adjusted at specified intervals ranging from six months to three years. At some airports, fees might be adjusted more often if revenues are significantly lower or higher than anticipated. Often, the nonsignatory airlines (those not party to the basic use agreement) pay higher landing fees than the signatory carriers. General aviation landing fees vary greatly from airport to airport, ranging from charges equal to those paid by the commercial airlines to none at all. Most landing fees are assessed on the basis of certificated gross landing weight. This practice of basing landing fees on aircraft weight tends to promote use of commercial airports by general aviation. Because most GA aircraft are relatively light (under 10,000 pounds), they pay very low landing fees at most commercial airports. The smallest GA aircraft often pay no fee. Residual-cost and compensatory airports alike have landing fees for GA aircraft that are generally so small as to be negligible, either as a source of revenue to the airport or as a deterrent to use of congested facilities.

At compensatory airports, airline landing fees are based on calculation of the average actual costs of airfield facilities used by the airlines. As in the case of residual-cost airports, each airline's share of these costs is based on its share of total projected airline gross landing weights (or, in a few cases, gross takeoff weight). In addition to fees determined by this weight-based measure, some airports assess a surcharge on GA aircraft during hours of peak demand. Presently, no major airports impose such peak-hour surcharges on commercial airlines to help ease congestion problems. Some airport managers and federal authorities feel that peak-hour surcharges could reduce congestion by giving airlines and other providers of air transportation services the opportunity to save money (and lower fares) by flying during uncongested periods. If peak-period demand continued to cause congestion, the increased revenue generated by the surcharges could help finance the expansion necessary to accommodate peak-hour traffic.

Landing fees at compensatory airports are established either in airport use agreements with the airlines or by local ordinance or resolution. The frequency of adjustment of the fees is comparable to that at residual-cost airports.

Terminal area concessions The structure of terminal concession and service contract fees is similar under both pricing approaches. Concession contracts typically provide the airport operator with a guaranteed annual minimum payment or a specified percentage of the concessionaire's gross revenues, whichever is greater. Restaurants, snack bars, gift shops, newsstands, duty-free shops, hotels, and rental car operations usually have contracts of this type. Terminal concession contracts are often bid competitively, and they range in term from month-to-month agreements to contracts of 10 to 15 years duration. (Hotel agreements generally have much longer terms, often running for 40 years or more.) Airport parking facilities might be operated as concessions; they might be run by the airport directly, or they might be managed by a contractor for either a flat fee or a percentage of revenues.

Terminal area concessions are changing rapidly. Airport food and retail products are moving out of the traditional terminal cafeterias and gift shops and into multistore food courts and retail lobbies that

The shops at Orlando International Airport offer a variety of helpful services and products with community-priced brand name and specialty items in a 28,000-square foot area in the main terminal that emulates a mall atmosphere. Greater Orlando Aviation Authority.

feature brand-name or specialty products priced competitively with off-airport stores.

Specialty stores also have become aware of the market that has emerged at airports, and many are intently working to capture a share of these customers. Meanwhile, traditional single-company airport concessionaires are realizing the need to adapt by either subcontracting with brand-name franchises or creating their own specialty shops.

These trends, sparked by changing air traveler demographics brought on by deregulation, have forced airports to reexamine the ways they manage their concessions and negotiate vendor contracts. More and more, these management decisions are based on individual airports' market demands. Airports are finding that they can offer high-quality goods at competitive prices in their terminals, mutually benefiting passengers, vendors, and the airport alike.

Airline leased areas   At both residual-cost and compensatory airports, airlines pay rent to the airport operator for the right to occupy various facilities (terminal space, hangars, cargo terminals, and land). Rental rates are established in the airport use agreements, in separate leases, or by local ordinance or resolution. Terminal space might be assigned on an exclusive-use basis (to a single airline), a preferential-use basis (if a certain level of activity is not maintained, the airline must share the space), or on a joint-use basis (space used in common by several airlines). Most major commercial airports use a combination of these methods. In addition, airports can charge the airlines a fee for use of any airport-controlled gate space and for the provision of federal inspection facilities required at airports serving international traffic. Some airports have long-term ground leases with individual airlines that allow the airlines to finance and construct their own passenger terminal facilities on land leased from the airport.

Among residual-cost airports, the method of calculating airline terminal rental rates varies considerably. If airline fees and charges are calculated on a residual-cost basis within each cost center, the method of calculating rental rates resembles that of the simplified example shown in Table 11-2. To arrive at the airline fee, total nonairline revenues generated within the terminal cost center are subtracted from the total costs of the center (administration, operations and maintenance, and debt service). Each airline's share is based on the square footage it occupies, with proration of jointly used space.

On the other hand, at residual-cost airports where receipts from airline landing fees alone are used to balance the airport budget, the terminal rental rates for the airlines can be set in various ways—on a compensatory basis (recovering the average actual costs of the facilities used), by an outside appraisal of the property value, or by negotiation with the airlines. In all cases, each airline's share of costs is based on its proportionate use of the facilities. Rental rates might be uniform for all types of space leased to the airlines, or they might differ according to the type of space provided—for example, they might be significantly higher for leases of ticket counters or office space than for rental of gate or baggage claim areas.

At residual-cost airports, the rental term for airline leased areas generally coincides with the term of the airport use agreement with the airlines. The frequency of adjustment of terminal rental rates ranges considerably—annually at many airports, but up to three to five years at others.

At compensatory airports, the method of calculating terminal rental rates for the airlines is based on recovery of the average actual costs of the space occupied. Each airline's share of the total costs is based on the square footage leased. Typically, rates differ according to the type of space and whether it is leased on an exclusive, preferential, or joint-use basis. The rental term for airline leased areas often coincides with that of the airport use agreement. (It is set by ordinance at airports that operate without agreements.) Rates are typically adjusted annually at compensatory airports.

Other leased areas A wide variety of arrangements are employed for other leased areas at an airport, which might include agricultural land, fixed-base operations, cargo terminals, and industrial parks. The methods of calculating rental rates and the frequency of adjustment differ according to the type of facility and the nature of use. What these disparate rentals have in common is that, like terminal concessions and services, they are generally priced on a market basis, and the airport managers have considerable flexibility in setting rates and charges in the context of market constraints and their own policy objectives.

Variation in the source of operating revenues

In general, revenue diversification enhances the financial stability of an airport. In addition, the specific mix of revenues might influence year-to-year financial performance. Some of the major sources of airport revenue (notably landing fees and terminal concessions) are affected by changes in the volume of air passenger traffic, while others (airline terminal rentals and ground leases) are essentially immune to fluctuations in air traffic.

The distribution of operating revenues differs widely according to factors such as passenger enplanements, the nature of the market served, and the specific objectives and features of the airport's approach to pricing and financial management. Airport size generally has a strong influence on the distribution of revenues. The larger commercial airports typically have a more diversified revenue base than smaller airports. For example, they tend to have a wider array of income-producing facilities and services in the passenger terminal complex. In general, terminal concessions can be expected to generate a greater percentage of total operating revenues as passenger enplanements increase. On average, concessions account for at least one-third of total operating revenues at large, medium, and small commercial airports, compared to about one-fifth at very small (nonhub) commercial airports and a smaller fraction still at GA airports.

Factors other than airport size also affect distribution of operating revenues. At commercial airports, for example, parking facilities generally provide the largest single source of nonairline revenues in the terminal area. Airports that have a high proportion of connecting traffic might, however, derive a smaller percentage of their operating income from parking revenues than do so-called "origin and destination" airports. Other factors that can affect parking revenues include availability of space for parking, the volume of air passenger traffic, the airport pricing policy, availability and cost of alternatives to driving to the airport (mass transit and taxicab service), and the presence of private competitors providing parking facilities at nearby locations off the airport property.

The approach to financial management, because it governs the pricing of facilities and services provided to airlines, significantly affects the distribution of operating revenues. Because so many other factors play an important role in determining revenue distribution, however, the mix of operating revenues at an airport cannot be predicted on the basis of whether the airport employs a residual-cost or compensatory approach. The mix of revenues varies widely among residual-cost airports. With airline landing fees characteristically picking up the difference between airport costs and other revenues at residual-cost airports, airfield area income differs markedly according to the extent of the airport's financial obligations, the magnitude of terminal concession income and other nonairline revenues, and the volume of air traffic.

Rise in airport costs

Despite significant growth in the number of passengers during the past two decades, airport charges per passenger more than doubled during this period. The greatest percentage of increase has been in the area of rent, which approximately equaled the amount of landing fees paid in the early 1980s but is now more than double the amount of landing fees. The reasons for this shift are obvious—relatively few new runways being constructed versus many expensive terminal expansions and upgrades.

At the same time that airport costs have been increasing, airline prices (yields) have continued to decline. Most forecasters predict that airfares will continue to decline and that the industry will remain fiercely competitive. Consequently, all aspects of the airlines' cost structure will remain under pressure. It is no surprise, therefore, that steadily increasing airport costs have been a source of contention between airlines and airports.

Airport cost increases have been driven primarily by the following factors:

1. Governmental mandates, including new security, environmental, Americans with Disabilities Act, and noise-related compliance costs.
2. Renewal and replacement of old facilities and equipment.
3. Airline requirements for support facilities.
4. Changing airline demand patterns that require additional hub facilities and leave excess facilities at some airports.

Apart from the average rate of growth of airport costs, there is also a significant disparity in cost growth by airport size. Larger airports have a greater need for infrastructure and, consequently, have experienced the greater cost increases. However, the significant increase in operating expenses at large airports is a concern, since it suggests that their expansion and modernization programs have not been accompanied by any increase in operating efficiency. Another explanation for the greater cost increases at large airports is the implementation of fee structures that are more favorable to these airports.

Airlines generally agree that infrastructure needs have driven a significant portion of airport cost increases. The debt service associated with major airport construction projects necessary to replace aging facilities inevitably increases total costs. However, most airlines are convinced that the U.S. system of airport rate regulation has itself made possible and, in some ways, encouraged the rapid growth of airport costs at medium and large airports.

This conclusion is based on the observation that most commercial airports in the United States are natural monopolies, which provide an essential service, and are therefore best thought of as public utilities. However, unlike other public utilities, whose rates have been regularly reviewed by public utility commissions, federal law has permitted airports to define their rate base broadly and to set rates to provide full recovery of all of their costs, without any meaningful scrutiny.

Airport operators are quick to point out that federal law generally requires them to reinvest any surpluses or overcollection in airport improvements and, therefore, the airlines ultimately receive the benefit of any airport income. Even assuming that airports fully complied with federal law on this subject, such forced reinvestment is clearly not a substitute for structural incentive designed to encourage airport operators to maximize efficiency in the first place.

With no legal impediments to discourage "cost-plus" behavior and few economic impediments to this behavior (because of airports' monopoly position), political forces act strongly to encourage exactly this behavior. Most communities would like to have a large modern airport terminal to serve as their "gateway," as well as the associated construction and airport jobs—especially when this can be accomplished without increasing taxes. Candid airport managers will admit that cutting costs will not advance their careers, but that building a new terminal may. In the airlines' view, the only significant competition among airports is best summarized as, "If your community has a new terminal, we need to build one, too."

The conflict between decreasing airfares and increasing airport costs has been compounded by the airlines' inability to deal with the airports' monopoly position.

Trends in airport financial management since deregulation

Federal deregulation of the airline industry has radically changed the market in which airlines—and airports—operate. Once subject to strict regulation of routes and fares, commercial air carriers are free to revise routes, adjust fares, and introduce or terminate service to particular airports as market conditions seem to warrant. This new freedom from federal intervention has had pronounced effects on the airline industry. It has spurred intense competition and even price wars among the airlines, led to reconfiguration of the route system, and encouraged the start-up of new carriers. For some of the established airlines, serious financial difficulties have ensued. Although deregulation has not caused radical changes in the financial management of airports, recent trends do reflect the uncertainties of a new, open market. Deregulation also appears to have accelerated certain shifts in management policy and practice that were underway before deregulation.

Since the early days of commercial air travel, would-be investors in airport revenue bonds have held long-term use agreements in high regard, considering them evidence of the airlines' commitment to serve an airport for long periods—spans usually coincident with the terms of bond issues. As the industry has matured, however, investors and analysts have increasingly recognized that an airport's financial stability—hence its capacity to generate a stream of revenue adequate to secure revenue bond issues—depends more on the underlying strength of the local air travel market than on long-term use agreements.

Deregulation has reinforced this shift, as the strength of the airlines' financial commitment to an airport is significantly diluted by their new flexibility to withdraw from a market virtually at will. Confidence has also been shaken by the financial problems now plaguing many airlines. Although changes in airport financial management occur very slowly (many standing use agreements I have run through the 1990s or later), three important trends in financial management are now emerging at major commercial airports:

1 Shorter-term contracts. Shorter terms for airport use agreements, nonairline leases, and concessionaires' contracts, and more frequent adjustment of rates and charges.

2 Modification of residual-cost approach. Modification of residual-cost rate making and majority-in-interest provisions, with

movement in the direction of more compensatory forms of financial management.

3 Maximization of revenues. Concerted effort by airport managers to maximize revenues by means of a variety of strategies intended to strengthen and diversify the revenue base of the airport.

Shorter-term contracts

Deregulation appears to have hastened a trend toward shorter-term airport use agreements that was already underway prior to 1978. Shorter-term contracts give airport operators greater flexibility to adjust pricing, investment policies, and space allocation to meet shifting needs in a deregulated environment. For example, several airports with long-term use agreements in force have given much shorter term agreements to air carriers that have begun serving the airport since 1978. Contracts for such recent entrants often run for five years or less, and they might take the form of yearly or even month-to-month operating agreements (similar to those used for air taxi and commuter operators). As existing long-term use agreements expire, many airport operators are negotiating shorter-term use agreements with all carriers serving the airport. In part, this reflects the fact that many postderegulation agreements have not involved major capital development programs requiring long-term bond financing. For example, while most older agreements provided carriers with "exclusive" rights to use their leased facilities, new agreements tend to restrict carrier rights to "preferential" or "common" use of their gates. Some new agreements also stipulate that carriers must either "use or lose" their gates and must agree to relocate to other gates when the airport requests.

Many airports are also shortening the terms of nonairline leases and contracts with concessionaires. Some are also moving to more frequent adjustment of rates and charges under existing agreements to meet the escalating costs of airport operation.

Modifications of residual-cost approach

In the past, the strength of airlines' collective guarantee to pay for any shortfall in airport revenue was an important factor permitting airports to raise money in the bond market. However, this factor has become significantly less important over time with respect to medium and large airports that have high levels of origination-and-destination traffic. The financial community has concluded: (1) that these airports will continue to have a certain base level of traffic, regardless of the carriers that enter or leave the market and (2) more importantly, that such airports will be able to raise their charges to a level sufficient to meet their needs in the absence of any airline guarantees or commitments.

As a result of this changing financial perception of medium and large origination-and-destination airports, these airports have tended to replace expiring residual agreements with other types of agreements or with no agreements at all. Newer agreements are more likely to be based on a compensatory rate-making approach, under which the airlines are required to pay all costs associated with the facilities they use (such as holdroom space and runways), but do not guarantee the overall costs of the airport. To the extent that parking, rental car, and concession revenues exceed the costs of the associated facilities, the additional revenues are retained by the airport for use at its discretion on airport projects. This approach has also weakened or eliminated majority-in-interest clauses.

In many cases, airports use a hybrid approach whereby a portion of the excess nonairline revenue generated is shared with the airlines—in the form of either a direct rebate or a rent reduction—while the remainder is retained by the airport. Both compensatory and hybrid agreements have enabled airports to accumulate large surpluses, which are increasingly attractive to cash-strapped municipalities. While current federal law requires airport revenues to be spent only for airport projects, several large airport systems are exempt from this requirement because they are grandfathered under federal legislation enacted in 1982. Those airport systems, which include the Port Authority of New York and New Jersey and the Massachusetts Port Authority, are permitted to use airport revenue to support other port facilities. Still other airports skirt the current legal requirement by making excess payments for indirect and direct costs to the local government and by enlarging the defined boundaries of the airport to include connecting roads and train systems.

Maximization of revenues

No matter how they approach financial management, many commercial airports are now seeking to increase and diversify their revenues by a variety of strategies. These include raising existing fees and rental rates, seeking more frequent adjustment of charges, using competitive bidding for concessionaires' contracts, increasing the airport's percentage of gross profits, exploiting new or untapped sources of revenue, expanding profitable concessions, increasing cargo operations, developing industrial parks and foreign trade zones (FTZs) on or around airport property, and leasing of unused airport property. These actions can provide additional immediate revenue as well as expanded future revenue streams that may improve the airport's ability to borrow funds. Expanded concessions may involve the addition of particular restaurants or stores, construction of concession areas outside of the main terminal to capitalize on connecting passenger traffic, or construction of in-airport facilities, such as the shopping mall at Greater Pittsburgh International Airport.

In addition to capitalizing on cargo opportunities, airports can actively market themselves to both large and small cargo carriers. Since cargo flights operate primarily during the evening and night hours, they do not directly conflict with passenger flight operations. Particularly if an airport has strong noise mitigation programs, or is centrally located geographically, it may be well positioned to encourage expanded cargo operations.

Moreover, by encouraging the development of industrial parks, or having airport land declared an FTZ, airports can develop revenues from otherwise unused property. Because noise constraints are not a major issue for industrial business and many companies value proximity to air service, airports can be excellent locations for industrial parks. Businesses located on airport land may be completely unrelated to aviation, but the rents they pay can bolster airport revenues. This revenue source is particularly significant since these nonairline revenues are not subject to fluctuations in passenger traffic in the same way that concessions, parking, and ground transportation revenues are. Similarly, the existence of an FTZ can spur tremendous economic development at and around an airport.

Perhaps the most significant new source of revenue since the passage of the Airway Safety and Capacity Expansion Act of 1990 has been the authorization to collect passenger facility charges (PFCs) (see chapter 7). Many airports have turned to this new revenue source. In general, this effort to diversify and expand revenue sources reflects the paramount importance of a guaranteed stream of income to assure an airport's financial success.

Key terms

airport accounting

operating statement

budgets

variance

lump-sum appropriation

appropriation by activity

line-item budget

zero-base budget

airport use agreement

residual-cost approach

debt service coverage

compensatory approach

majority-in-interest clauses

fuel flowage fees

Review questions

1 Define airport accounting. What is the purpose of a good accounting system?
   - Describe the five major areas under a typical airport's operating revenues. Why is it difficult to compare operating costs between airports?
   - Describe the major maintenance and operating expenses under the airfield area and terminal area.

2 List the primary reasons for planning and budgeting. What is a "variance?"
   - Describe the following forms of budget appropriation: (1) lump-sum appropriation; (2) appropriation by activity; and (3) line-item budget.
   - What is a "zero-base" budget?

3 Define *airport use agreement*. Compare the residual-cost approach with the compensatory approach to airport-airline relationships. What is debt-service coverage? What effect do the two major approaches to financial management have on net income, majority-in-interest, and term of use agreements?

4 What are the major sources of revenue for the following areas? (1) airfield; (2) terminal concessions; (3) airline leased areas; and (4) other leased areas.

- Discuss some of the factors that determine the variations in revenues between different airports.

5. What are the reasons for the significant rise in airport costs since deregulation? What is the basis for conflict between the airlines and airports concerning these cost increases?

6. Three important trends in financial management at major commercial airports since deregulation are shorter-term contracts, modification of the residual-cost approach, and maximization of revenues. Discuss these trends and give examples of each.

Suggested readings

Airport Financing—Comparing Funding Sources with Planned Development. Washington, DC: U.S. General Accounting Office, March 1998.

Airport Financing—Funding Sources for Airport Development. Washington, DC: U.S. General Accounting Office, March 1998.

"Analysis of U.S. Airport Costs Incurred by Airlines," American Association of Airport Executives and Airports Council International—North America, September 1993.

Campbell, George E. *Airport Management and Operations.* Baton Rouge, Louisiana: Claitor's Publishing Division, 1972.

Cook, Barbara. "A New Solution to an Old Problem—What to Do When the AIP Well Dries Up." *Airport Magazine.* November/December 1994.

Doganis, Rigas. *The Airport Business.* New York: Routledge, Chapman and Hall, Inc., 1992.

Eckrose, Roy A., and William H. Green. *How to Assure the Future of Your Airport.* Madison, Wisconsin: Eckrose/Green Associates, 1988.

Gesell, Laurence E. *The Administration of Public Airports,* 3rd ed. Chandler, Arizona: Coast-Aire Publications, 1992.

12

Organization and administration

Outline

- Airport ownership and operation
- The airport organization chart
- Airport management as a career
- The airport manager and public relations

Objectives

When you have completed this chapter, you should be able to:

- Describe the five types of public airport ownership and operation in the United States.
- Explain the purpose of an organization chart.
- Summarize the major responsibility and discuss the principal duties of the following positions: airport director, assistant director—finance and administration, assistant director—operations, and assistant director—maintenance.
- Identify at least 10 other positions found at a commercial airport.
- Discuss the educational and training requirements for an individual considering a career in airport management.
- Explain the importance of airport public relations.
- List the primary objectives of an airport public relations campaign.

Airport ownership and operation

Public airports in the United States are owned and operated under a variety of organizational and jurisdictional arrangements. Usually, ownership and operation coincide: commercial airports might be owned and operated by a city, county, or state, by the federal government, or by more than one jurisdiction (a city and a county). In some cases, a commercial airport is owned by one or more of these governmental entities but operated by a separate public body, such as an airport authority specifically created for the purpose of managing the airport. Regardless of ownership, legal responsibility for day-to-day operation and administration can be vested in any of five kinds of governmental or public entities: (1) a municipal or county government, (2) a multipurpose port authority, (3) an airport authority, (4) a state government, or (5) the federal government.

A typical *municipally operated airport* is city owned and run as a department of the city, with policy direction by the city council and, in some cases, by a separate airport commission or advisory board. County-run airports are similarly organized. Under this type of public operation, airport policy decisions are generally made in the broader context of city or countywide public investment needs, budgetary constraints, and development goals.

Some commercial airports in the United States are run by multipurpose port authorities. *Port authorities* are legally chartered institutions with the status of public corporations that operate a variety of publicly owned facilities, such as harbors, airports, toll roads, and bridges. In managing the properties under their jurisdiction, port authorities have extensive independence from the state and local governments. Their financial independence rests largely on the power to issue their own debt, in the form of revenue bonds, and on the breadth of their revenue bases, which might include fees and charges from marine terminals and airports as well as proceeds (bridge or tunnel tolls) from other port authority properties. In addition, some port authorities have the power to tax within the port district, although it is rarely exercised.

Another type of arrangement is the single-purpose *airport authority*. Similar in structure and in legal charter to port authorities, these single-purpose authorities also have considerable independence from the state or local governments, which often retain ownership of the airport or airports operated by the authority. Like multipurpose port authorities, airport authorities have the power to issue their own debt for financing capital development, and in a few cases, the power to tax. Compared to port authorities, however, they must rely on a much narrower base of revenues to run a financially self-sustaining enterprise.

Since the early 1950s, there has been a gradual transition from city- and county-controlled airports to the independent single or multi-purpose authorities. The predominant form is still municipally owned and operated, particularly the smaller commercial and GA airports; however, there are reasons for this transition:

1 Many airport market or service areas have outgrown the political jurisdiction whose responsibility the airport entails. In some cases there is considerable, actual or potential, tax liability to a rather limited area. In these cases the creation of an authority to "spread the potential or actual tax support" for the airport might be recommended. By spreading the tax base of support for the airport, more equitable treatment of the individual taxpayer can result and the taxpayers supporting the airport in most cases more nearly match the actual users of the facility.

2 Another advantage of authority control of an airport is that such an organization allows the board to concentrate and specialize on airport matters.

3 Aviation authorities can also provide efficiency of operation and economies of scale when several political jurisdictions, each with separate airport responsibilities, choose to combine these under one board. This has been done quite successfully in many areas of the country. Normally, the staff required by an airport authority will be quite small compared to the personnel requirements of a city or county government. This factor generally results in better coordination with the airport management team.

4 Authorities can also provide on-scene decision-makers, rates, and charges unclouded by off-airport costs, and with less political impact on the business of running the airport.

State-operated airports are typically managed by the state's department of transportation. Either general obligation or revenue bonding might be used to raise investment capital, and state taxes on aviation fuel might be applied to capital improvement projects.

Although several states run their own commercial airports, only a handful of large- and medium-size commercial airports are operated in this way, primarily in Alaska, Connecticut, Hawaii, Maryland, and Rhode Island. The federal government owns and operates the airport at Pomona (Atlantic City), New Jersey, which is part of the FAA Technical Center. The FAA manages this facility with capital development financed through congressional appropriations. The federal government also levies user taxes and disburses funds for the capital development of other airports through FAA's Airport Improvement Program discussed in Chapter 1.

Several small U.S. airports are managed by a private company generally operating under a fixed-fee contract with a local government. Examples include the airports at White Plains, New York, and Atlantic City, New Jersey. By contrast, many U.S. airports are managed by the local government, but contract out a significant number of airport functions to private contractors, including janitorial, security, maintenance, and concession management. Neither of these situations is particularly controversial, nor are the economics of these airports unusual.

The most controversial form of airport privatization consists of proposals to sell airports to private developers, who would then increase carrier fees sufficiently to assure an adequate return on their investment. To date, no such proposal has been implemented, primarily because of legal requirements relating to the payback of government grants, the possible loss of tax-exempt financing ability, and governance and liability concerns.

Airlines are always interested in proposals that lower their costs. However, the monopoly position of airport operators makes airlines wary of proposals that leave a private operator a free hand in airport pricing decisions. In addition, a number of airport "sale" proposals have not been driven by any desire to operate the airport more efficiently, but instead by the desire to raise money for the local government involved. Since this money must inevitably be paid back by airport users, the airlines have been particularly suspicious of these proposals. (See chapter 2 for a full discussion of the privatization issue.)

The airport organization chart

An *organization chart* shows the formal authority relationships between superiors and subordinates at various levels, as well as the formal channels of communication within the organization. It provides a framework within which the management functions can be carried out. The chart aids employees to perceive more clearly their position in the organization in relation to others and how and where managers and workers fit into the overall organizational structure.

The organization chart is a static model of the airport because it shows how the airport is organized at a given point in time. This is a major limitation of the chart, because airports operate in a dynamic environment and thus must continually adapt to changing conditions. Some old positions might no longer be required, or new positions might have to be created in order that new objectives can be reached; therefore, it is necessary that the chart be revised and updated periodically to reflect these changing conditions.

Airport management has changed so significantly over the past 25 years that it is difficult to say that any organization chart is typical or that the chart of one airport at any particular time is the one still in effect even a few months later; however, all airports do have certain common functional areas into which airport activities are divided. Understandably, the larger the airport, the greater the specialization of tasks and the greater the departmentalization. Figure 12-1 shows

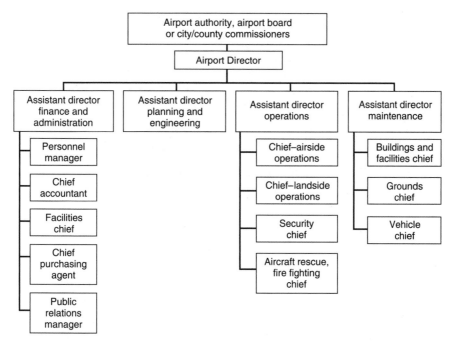

12-1 *Organizational chart for a commercial airport.*

the major functional areas and typical managerial job titles for a commercial airport.

Job descriptions

The following is a brief job description for each position shown in Fig. 12-1.

Airport director

The airport director is responsible for the overall day-to-day operation of the airport. He or she reports directly to the airport authority, the airport board or governmental commission charged with the development and administration of the airport. This individual directs, coordinates, and reviews through subordinate supervisors, all aircraft operations, building and field maintenance, construction plans, community relations, financial, and personnel matters at the airport. The airport director also:

1 Supervises and coordinates with airline, general aviation, and military tenants use of airport facilities.

2 Reviews airport tenant activities for compliance with terms of leases and other agreements.

3 Supervises enforcement of aircraft air and ground traffic and other applicable regulations.

4 Confers with airlines, tenants, the FAA, and others regarding airport regulations, facilities, and related matters.

5 Participates in planning for increased aircraft and passenger volume and facilities expansion.

6 Determines and recommends airport staffing requirements.

7 Compiles and submits for review an annual airport budget.

8 Coordinates airport activities with construction, maintenance, and other work done by departmental staff, tenants, public utilities, and contractors.

9 Promotes acceptance of airport-oriented activities in surrounding communities.

Assistant director—finance and administration The assistant director—finance and administration is charged with the responsibility for overall matters concerning finance, personnel, purchasing, facilities management, and office management. Specifically, this individual's duties include:

1 Fiscal planning and budget administration.

2 Ensuring accomplishment of basic finance functions such as accounts receivable and payable, auditing, and payroll.

3 Administering the purchasing function.

4 Administration and use of real property including negotiation of tenant leases and inventory control.

5 Personnel functions including compensation, employee relations, and training.

6 Ensuring adequate telephone and mail service.

7 Public relations.

Personnel manager The personnel manager is responsible for administering the airport personnel program. In such capacity, this individual's duties include:

1 Dealing with personnel problems involving position classification, compensation, recruitment, placement, transfers, layoffs, promotions, leaves of absence, supervisor-subordinate relationships, and working conditions.

2 Serving as equal rights and equal opportunity officer for the airport.

3 Handling Worker's Compensation cases.

4 Evaluating organization pattern, reviewing and recommending proposed departmental organization changes, and preparing position descriptions.

5 Conferring with employees and their supervisors on personnel problems.

6 Preparing personnel documents and maintaining personnel records.

7 Interviewing or supervising the interviewing of applicants for airport positions.

Chief accountant The chief accountant is responsible for financial planning, budgeting, accounting, payroll, and auditing. The principal duties include:

1 Coordinating, consolidating, and presentation of financial plans.

2 Administration of basic accounts such as general accounts, cost accounting, and accounts receivable and payable.

3 Administering budget; reviewing and analyzing actual performance at budget review sessions.

4 Supervising all receipts and disbursements.

5 Payroll administration.

6 Conducting periodic internal audit of all airport functions.

Facilities chief The facilities chief establishes criteria and procedures for the administration of all airport property. In this capacity, he or she is responsible for inventory control of all equipment and facilities. Principal duties and responsibilities of this individual include:

1 Identification and control of all property and equipment including periodic audits.

2 Evaluating and making recommendations concerning the most efficient use of airport real property utilization.

3 Soliciting tenants and concessionaires.

4 Developing policy and rate structure applicable to use of property by tenants and concessionaires.

5 Coordinating with purchasing and legal staff concerning tenant and concessionaire leases.

Chief purchasing agent The chief purchasing agent directs the procurement of materials and services to support the airport; he or she prepares, negotiates, interprets, and administers contracts with vendors. This individual's principal duties include:

1 Coordinating requirements for materials and services to be purchased.

2 Purchasing all materials and services.

3 Establishing bidding policies and procedures.

4 Working closely with facilities' chief and legal staff regarding contracts associated with purchasing equipment.

Manager of public relations The manager of public relations is the chief liaison officer between the airport and the surrounding community. In this capacity, he or she is responsible for all public relations activities including the development of advertising and publicity concerning the airport. This individual is also responsible for handling all noise and other environmental matters. Principal duties include:

1 Consulting with and advising airport management regarding public relations policies and practices.

2 Coordinating all publicity releases to the various media.

3 Supervising all airport guides and information booths.

4 Coordinating VIP visits to the airport.

5 Receiving and analyzing all public complaints regarding such things as noise and other environmental concerns.

6 Preparing answers to complaints and advising management as appropriate.

7 Sponsoring activities and special events to generate goodwill and public acceptance.

Assistant director—planning and engineering The assistant director—planning and engineering provides technical assistance to all airport organizations, and ensures the engineering integrity of construction, alteration, and installation programs. This individual also establishes industrial safety standards. Principal duties and responsibilities include:

1 Developing standards and specifications for construction, alteration, and installation programs; monitors such programs to ensure compliance therewith.

2 Reviewing all construction plans to determine technical integrity and conformance to aesthetic design standards.

3 Developing and publishing standards and procedures for industrial safety.

4 Participating in the negotiation of construction contracts.

Assistant director—operations The assistant director—operations is responsible for all airside and landside operations including security and crash, fire, and rescue operations. Principal duties include:

1 Directing the operations and security programs for the airport.

2 Coordinating and supervising security activities with field maintenance personnel, police and fire departments, federal agencies, and airport tenants.

3 Recommending and assisting in promulgating operational rules and procedures.

4 Supervising investigations of violations of airport regulations.

5 Preparing annual operations budget.

6 Directing monitoring of noise levels and coordinating noise level studies.

7 Participating in special programs relating to or affecting airport operations, such as studies of height limits around airport property and studies of noise control.

Chief—airside operations The chief—airside operations is responsible for all airfield operations. In this capacity, principal duties include:

1 Enforcing operating and security rules, regulations, and procedures concerning landing, taxiing, parking, servicing loading and unloading of aircraft, operation of vehicular traffic on the airfield, airline activities, and emergency situations.

2 Inspecting conditions of airfield lighting, runways, taxiways, and ramp areas.

3 Correcting hazardous conditions.

4 Coordinating airfield activities with maintenance and security personnel.

5 Assisting in all airfield emergency calls and disasters by notifying control tower to close runways, directing maintenance personnel, directing security officers in crowd control, and overseeing other safety considerations and activities necessary to resume normal airport operations.

Airside operations at Ronald Reagan Washington National Airport.
Federal Aviation Administration

6 Investigating and reporting on complaints and disrupted airport operations, including unscheduled plane arrivals, aircraft accidents, rule and procedure violations, airline activities, and other operations of the airport.

7 Assigning gate and parking spaces to all aircraft.

8 Coordinating special arrangements for arrivals and departures of important persons.

9 Completing all report forms pertaining to operations activities on assigned shifts.

10 Assisting in directing noise level studies with other departmental personnel.

Chief—landside operations The chief—landside operations is responsible for all landside operations. In this capacity, principal duties include:

1 Enforcing operating and security rules, regulations, and procedures concerning buildings, access roads, and parking facilities.

2 Exercising authority to halt hazardous or unauthorized activities by tenants, employees, or the public in violation of safety regulations and procedures.

3 Answering inquiries and explaining terminal use procedures and safety regulations to tenants.

4 Coordinating terminal building and other facility activities with maintenance and security personnel.

5 Coordinating all parking facility activities with tenants and transit companies.

6 Preparing personal injury and property damage reports and general incident reports.

7 Completing all report forms pertaining to operations activities on assigned shifts.

Security chief The security chief enforces interior security, traffic, and safety rules and regulations and participates in law enforcement activities at the airport. This individual also provides the public with information regarding locations and operations. Principal duties include:

1 Enforcing ordinances and regulations pertaining to parking, traffic control, safety, and property protection.

2 Patrolling facilities to prevent trespass and unauthorized or hazardous use.

3 Preventing public entry into dangerous or restricted areas.

4 Issuing citations and warnings for violations of specific provisions of airport rules and regulations.

5 Securing gates and locks and watching buildings and facilities for indications of fire, dangerous conditions, unauthorized entry, and vandalism.

6 Responding to emergencies and taking immediate action to control crowds, direct traffic, assist the injured, and turn in alarms.

7 Responding to calls for police service; participating in arrests; apprehending, or assisting members of the police department in apprehending, law violators.

8 Providing information to the public regarding locations and operations of the airport.

9 Assigning uniformed and armed personnel to patrol and stand watch, on a 24-hour basis, to protect and safeguard all persons and property on the airport.

Aircraft rescue, fire fighting chief The aircraft rescue, fire fighting chief develops procedures and implements accident, fire, and disaster plans. Principal duties include:

1 Conducting a training (continuing) program for all aircraft rescue, fire fighting personnel.

2 Developing and implementing all aircraft rescue and fire fighting programs.

3 Staffing and operating all aircraft rescue and fire fighting equipment on the airport.

4 Inspecting and testing all types of fixed fire prevention and extinguishing equipment on the airport.

5 Inspecting all facilities for fire and/or safety hazards.

Assistant director—maintenance The assistant director—maintenance is responsible for planning, coordinating, directing, and reviewing the maintenance of buildings, facilities, vehicles, and utilities. Principal duties include:

1 Developing, directing, and coordinating policies, programs, procedures, standards, and schedules for buildings, utilities, vehicle maintenance, and field facilities.

2 Coordinating work done by tenants and contractors.

International terminal building at San Francisco International Airport. San Francisco International Airport

3 Inspecting maintenance work for compliance with plans, specifications, and applicable laws.

4 Making recommendations as to adequacy, sufficiency, and condition of buildings, facilities, and vehicles.

5 Overseeing maintenance contracts.

Buildings and facilities chief The buildings and facilities chief is responsible for ensuring that buildings are adequately maintained with a minimum of cost. Types of maintenance required are primarily electrical, mechanical, plumbing, painting, carpentry, masonry, and cement work. Principal duties include:

1 Developing an approved maintenance schedule for all building maintenance requirements.

2 Assigning qualified personnel to perform maintenance.

3 Inspecting work for adequacy and compliance with requirements.

4 Developing special maintenance methods where necessary.

Grounds chief The grounds chief is responsible for ensuring that the grounds are maintained in good repair and that the landscape is adequately maintained. Principal duties include:

1 Developing approved schedules for maintaining all airport surface areas including paving, landscaping, and drainage systems.

2 Assigning qualified personnel to accomplish ground maintenance.

3 Inspecting work for adequacy and compliance with maintenance standards.

Vehicle chief The vehicle chief is responsible for the maintenance of all vehicles utilized by the airport. Vehicle maintenance includes tune-up, minor maintenance, washing and polishing, tires and batteries, lubrication, and fueling. Principal duties include:

1 Developing an approved vehicle maintenance schedule.

2 Coordinating schedule with users of airport vehicles.

3 Assigning qualified personnel to perform maintenance.

4 Inspecting all work to determine compliance with established maintenance standards.

5 Coordinating with purchasing to obtain vendor services as required.

6 Maintaining vehicle usage and maintenance records.

7 Coordinating with purchasing in developing a vehicle disposal and replacement program.

While the aforementioned positions represent a typical managerial structure at a commercial airport, there are numerous employees with a wide variety of job skills reporting to them. Some of the typical job titles found at major airports include the following:

- Accountant
- Administrative assistant
- Airport guide
- Airport noise abatement officer
- Painter
- Carpenter
- Plumber
- Air conditioning mechanic

- Software engineer
- Financial analyst
- Secretary
- Industrial engineer
- Public relations representative
- Buyer
- Auditor
- Student intern
- Contract analyst
- Personnel representative
- Facility planner
- Architect
- Drafter
- Custodian
- Electrician
- Elevator mechanic

- Equipment mechanic
- Equipment operator
- Operations assistant
- Heavy-duty equipment operator

- Cement finisher
- Auto mechanic
- Groundskeeper
- Sheet metal mechanic
- Welder
- Plasterer
- Tilesetter
- Construction inspector
- Civil engineer
- Security officer
- Firefighter
- Supervisor of operations
- Bus driver
- Maintenance foreman
- Tree surgeon
- Traffic painter and sign poster
- Truck operator
- Toolroom keeper
- Window cleaner
- Maintenance and construction laborer

Airport management as a career

There are many career paths within the field of airport management as evidenced by the wide variety of job descriptions under the previous section. Even the job of airport manager varies greatly. At one extreme is the manager of a large metropolitan airport, an appointee or civil service employee of the city government or airport authority, who heads a large staff of assistants and specialists through which he or she manages a highly complex organization. At the other extreme is the owner-manager of a small private field near a rural community. The latter might combine activities as airport manager with work in some other business.

Between these two extremes is the manager of a municipally owned or privately owned airport where there are a limited number of scheduled airline flights each day. Based at the airport are several FBOs and a number of aircraft owned by individuals and corporations. The typical manager of a medium-size airport deals with all segments of the aviation community including the airlines, general aviation, and federal and state agencies.

In the early days of aviation, an individual could become an airport manager if he or she was a pilot and had several years experience in some segment of the industry. Although the individual had to be able to manage the operation for the owner, his or her experience was likely to be in some area of flying rather than in business management.

Today an airport manager must be primarily a skilled and experienced executive with a broad background in all facets of aviation. It is no longer necessary that the manager be a pilot. Almost every airport manager's job situation is unique in some major respects because of the wide variety of size of airport and type of ownership and operation. There are also wide variations in government procedures in different communities. This sometimes causes the responsibilities, salaries, and authority of airport managers to be completely different from one city to the next. Even the job title varies. *Director of aviation, airport superintendent, executive director, airport director, general manager,* and other titles are often used instead of airport manager.

Duties of an airport manager

An airport manager is often part landlord and part business executive. As a landlord, the safe condition and operation of the airport is the manager's greatest responsibility. The maintenance of the airport buildings and land is also important. As a business executive, the manager is in charge of public relations; financial planning; profitable and efficient day-to-day operation; and coordination of airline, concession, and airport facilities to best serve the tenants and flying public.

The airport manager's primary duty is the safe and efficient operation of the airport and all its facilities regardless of its size. However, at least in the larger commercial airports, the manager does not have direct control over most flying activities. He or she must deal with all groups and individuals who use the airport facilities. These include (1) representatives of the airlines that schedule flights, maintain, and service their aircraft, and process passengers; (2) all segments of the general aviation community, including FBOs and individual and corporate owners and operators of aircraft; and (3) the government-employed staffs of the air traffic control facilities, customs, and so forth.

All of these groups can be regarded as tenants of the airport, carrying on their independent activities. Besides dealing with the companies and individuals directly concerned with flying, the manager is in contact with concessionaires who operate restaurants, shops, and parking facilities, and with the traveling public.

The size of the airport and the services it offers its tenants and the public play an important part in determining the airport manager's specific duties. Some of these duties were enumerated earlier in this chapter under job descriptions. A manager must formulate fiscal policy, secure new business, recommend and enforce field rules and regulations, make provisions for handling spectators and passengers, oversee construction projects, see that the airport is adequately policed, and airplane and automobile traffic is regulated.

The manager interprets the functions and activities of the airport to the city or other local government and to the public; he or she is a public relations expert as well as a business manager. This public relations function is extremely important and will be taken up at the end of this chapter in a separate section.

Not all of these duties are required of all managers of airports. Many airports are too small to have FAA-staffed control towers; others have no scheduled airline flights. In these airports the job is simpler, but the manager must usually do all of the work personally. In large airports, the manager has many assistants and supervises the work.

The job of airport manager is obviously not completed between 9 and 5. The hours are often irregular and most managers have some weekend and holiday work. They will often have to work at night. In emergency situations they will usually work additional hours. Difficult weather conditions, labor problems, personnel irregularities, and flight schedule changes are only some of the things that will affect job hours. Even when not actually working, most airport managers are on call.

Education and training

The major requirement for the job of airport manager is business and administrative ability; this means the ability to make decisions, to coordinate details, to direct the work of others, and to work smoothly with many kinds of people. Probably the best college program to follow is one that leads to a degree in aviation management. College courses in engineering; management; accounting; finance and economics; business and aviation law; and airline, general aviation, and airport management are good preparation for a career in airport management. Many schools that are members of the University Aviation Association (UAA) offer programs and courses that can be applied to the problems of managing an airport.

A number of the primary airports in the United States have one- or two-year internship programs that train college graduates for various aspects of airport management. Other individuals have started at a small GA airport where they become involved in all aspects of airport management—from maintenance and repair to attending city commission meetings. Some college graduates have taken jobs with aviation or airport consulting firms and after several years have moved into airport management. Many others have acquired experience in some other area of aviation before entering the field.

Because the position of airport manager is the top job in most airports, advancement generally comes by changing jobs—usually by working for a larger airport. In a large metropolitan airport, an individual usually works up from managing various departments to become an assistant manager or director and finally manager or director.

The important public service an airport provides along with its economic advantages to a community has caused city governments to recognize the need for professional management of airports. To meet the need, the American Association of Airport Executives (AAAE) initiated a program of accreditation for airport managers. A minimum of three years' work experience in airport management, an original paper on an airport problem, and the completion of a comprehensive examination are the major requirements of the accreditation program. The applicant must also be at least 21 years of age and of good moral character. Once an airport manager has completed these requirements the person may use the initials A.A.E. (Accredited Airport Executive) after his or her name and is eligible to vote at the business meetings of the American Association of Airport Executives. The airport managed by the person may be designated as an AAAE field.

Many career opportunities in airport management should become available in the years ahead because of expansion of facilities and attrition. As the number of new airports increases and the facilities of many existing airports expand, new managerial positions will be created. Many of these will not be top jobs, but the airport of the future will require assistant managers specializing in one part of the huge operation. Also, qualified people will be needed to replace those who retire.

Because the job of managing a medium-to-large commercial airport is a fascinating one that requires high qualifications, there will be tough competition for jobs; however, the motivated individual with a solid educational background and varied experience in the fields of aviation and management will find openings in a field of work that is and will remain comparatively small—but one that provides an interesting and challenging profession.

The airport manager and public relations

Unquestionably, one of the most important and challenging aspects of an airport manager's job is that of public relations. *Public relations* is the management function that attempts to create goodwill for

The landmark theme building at the Center of Los Angeles International Airport has 135-foot parabolic arches that accent an observation deck with a 360° view of the airport and surrounding area, a restaurant, offices, and employee cafteria. Los Angeles Department of Airports.

an organization and its products, services, or ideals with groups of people who can affect its present and future welfare. The most advanced type of public relations not only attempts to create goodwill for the organization as it exists, but also helps formulate policies, if needed, that of themselves result in a favorable reaction.

Aviation and airports have such great impact on our lives, and on the life of our nation, that it is difficult to find a person who has no knowledge or opinion of airports. Despite the tremendous growth in all segments of aviation over the past 25 years, and the resulting challenges, problems, and opportunities, aviation has not been exempted from the controversies that inevitably are part of any endeavor affecting or touching the lives of a large number of people. This controversy is the reason why every opinion, whether positive or negative, will be a strong one. The net result is that every airport has an image—either good or bad.

The great problems of airports are always related to the original and elemental images resulting from the collective opinions of the public. These images are really the balancing or compensating factors that correspond with the problems the public encounters with airports. These images are deposits representing the accumulated experience of jet noise, hours of struggle to reach the airport on clogged highways under construction, the frustration of trying to find a close-in parking place, the lines to obtain tickets, the time in waiting for luggage, and other inconveniences.

In this respect, some of the public will have an image of the airport as a very exciting place that makes major contributions to our society through commercial channels, and even more valuable contributions of a personal nature, by offering a means to efficient travel, and thus greater personal development and greater enjoyment of life.

Despite the hundreds of positive impacts of aviation, negative images do arise. Perhaps such negative images result from the fact that the industry has been so intent on the technological aspects of resolving problems that it has overlooked the less tangible components. The industry has the technology and resources to resolve many of the problems of the airport-airway system; however, the important link or catalyst in bringing together technology and community opinion is the airport public relations effort.

Both the airport and the community have a responsibility to work together to solve their mutual problems, attain desired goals, and ultimately achieve a better community. It takes continuing contributions—and sometimes sacrifices as well—to the general welfare on the part of individual citizens and the aviation industry to earn the opportunities and rewards of a good community for the public. This two-way relationship has its problems too. Many are spawned by misunderstanding that can arise and grow to disproportionate size, and in our context, result in a negative image for the airport and a loss of public confidence in the aviation industry. Ensuring that problems are met head-on, with full and explicit information made continuously available to the public to prevent misunderstanding, is the point at which airport public relations enters the picture.

Regardless of the size of an airport, there are several basic principles underlying the public relations process:

1 Every airport and every company and interest on the airport has public relations, whether or not it does anything about them.

2 Public goodwill is the greatest asset that can be enjoyed by any airport, and public opinion is the most powerful force. Public opinion that is informed and supplied with facts and fair interpretation might be sympathetic. Public opinion that is misinformed or uninformed will probably be hostile and damaging to an airport.

3 The basic ingredient of good relations for any airport is *integrity*. Without it, there can be no successful public relations.

4 Airport policies and programs that are not in the public interest have no chance of final success.

5 Airport public relations can never be some kind of program that is only used to respond to a negative situation. Good public relations has to be earned through continuing effort.

6 Airport public relations go far beyond press relations and publicity. It must interpret the airport interests to the public, and it should be a two-way flow with input and interpretation of public opinion to airport management and community leadership. It must use many means of reaching the various segments of the public interested in airport operations, and it must try to instill the public relations spirit into all facets of the airport's operation.

The airport and its public

Basically, every airport has four "publics" with which it deals, and despite the wide variance in size and scope of activities of airports, these publics are basically the same for all airports:

1 The external business public. These are the past, present, and future airport customers for all the services offered on an airport. It includes all segments of the business, government, educational, and general flying public.

2 The external general public. These are the local citizens and taxpayers, many of whom have never been to the airport but who vote on airport issues or who represent citizen groups with particular concerns.

3 The internal business public. These are the businesses and enterprises whose interests are tied directly to the airport—the airlines, FBOs, other members of the general aviation community, government officials, and other aviation and travel-oriented local businesses and trade organizations, and the employees of all of these enterprises.

4 The internal employee public. This group includes everyone who works for the airport and its parent organization.

These are the most important airport publics. These are the sources of vital information that management must have to know what and how it is doing, and they are the ones who must be informed and persuaded if any airport objective is to be achieved.

Public relations objectives

The primary objectives of an airport's public relations activities are as follows:

1 Establishing the airport in the minds of the external public as a facility that is dedicated to serving the public interest. Many airports work closely with the local chamber of commerce in developing a brochure or pamphlet citing various accomplishments and activities at the airport that would be of interest to the local business community and the community in general.

2 Communicating with the external public with the goal of establishing and building goodwill. The airport manager and other members of his or her staff often serve as guest speakers at various civic and social organizations. They also become active members of local or civic organizations in order to informally promote the airport and determine the pulse of the community. Public announcements of new developments at

Corporate aviation represents a significant amount of flight operations at commercial airports. Pascoe Building Systems

the airport are made through all media. This is a continuing part of the communications process.

3 Answering general and environmental complaints on an individual basis. It is important that the airport develop a good rapport with its neighbors and concerned citizen groups. Working closely with the airlines and other internal business publics, airport management attempts to work out such problems as noise by changing traffic patterns and adjusting hours of flight operation. Tours of the airport are given to various community groups in order for them to get a better understanding of operations. Civic-oriented activities are also conducted at the airport to improve relations with airport neighbors and address their concerns. Citizen participation in airport planning and public hearings is another means by which airport management is continually apprised of community feelings about airport related activities.

4 Establishing good working relationships with internal business publics whose interests are similar to those of airport management.

5 Promoting programs designed to enhance and improve employee morale.

Like any other facility that serves the total community, an airport requires total community understanding. A well-executed public relations program can make the community aware of the airport and its benefits and create an atmosphere of acceptance. Attitudes are not changed overnight, so the public relations effort must be a continuous campaign to build understanding and develop attitudes of acceptance.

Key terms

municipally operated airport

port authorities

airport authority

state-operated airports

organization chart

airport director

assistant director—finance and administration

personnel manager

chief accountant

facilities chief

chief purchasing agent

manager of public relations

assistant director—planning and engineering

assistant director—operations

chief—airside operations

chief—landside operations

security chief

aircraft rescue, fire fighting chief

assistant director—maintenance

building and facilities chief

grounds chief

vehicle chief

public relations

Review questions

1 Distinguish between a port authority and airport authority form of airport ownership and operation.

- Why have a number of formerly municipally owned airports transitioned into airport authorities over the past 30 years?

2 What is the purpose of an organization chart?

- Describe the principal responsibility of the four assistant directors.

- Describe some of the duties of the following positions: facility chief, community relations manager, chief—landside operations, and buildings and facilities chief.
- List 10 other positions found at a commercial airport.

3 Describe the principal duties of a typical airport manager at a medium-sized commercial airport.

- What educational and training requirements would best prepare an individual for such a position?
- What is the AAAE program of accreditation for airport managers?

4 Why is public relations such an important function of airport management? Describe some of the basic principles underlying the public relations process at an airport.

- What are the airport's "publics"?
- List and briefly describe the primary objectives of an airport's public relations activities.

Suggested readings

Ashford, Norman, H. P. Martin Stanton, and Clifton A. Moore. *Airport Operations*. London: Pitman Publishing Company, 1993.

Doganis, Rigas. *The Airport Business*. New York: Routledge, Chapman and Hall, Inc., 1992.

Odegard, John D., Donald I. Smith, and William Shea. *Airport Planning and Management*. Belmont, California: Wadsworth Publishing Co., 1984.

Eckrose, Roy A., and William H. Green. *How to Assure the Future of Your Airport*. Madison, Wisconsin: Eckrose/Green Associates, 1988.

Gesell, Laurence E. *The Administration of Public Airports*. San Luis Obispo, California: Coast Aire Publications, 1981.

Wiley, John R. *Airport Administration and Management*. Westport, Connecticut: Eno Foundation for Transportation, 1986.

13

Airport operations

Outline

- Pavement maintenance
- Snow removal
- Safety inspection program
- Bird hazards
- Aircraft rescue, fire fighting
- Security
- Ground support equipment

Objectives

When you have completed this chapter you should be able to:

- Describe some of the maintenance problems with asphalt and concrete runways.
- Distinguish between pavement maintenance and pavement rehabilitation.
- Distinquish between dynamic and viscous hydroplaning.
- Identify the three basic methods of removing rubber deposits and other contaminants from runways.
- Describe the major items included in a snow removal program.
- Describe how the three basic mechanical methods of snow removal are used.
- Identify four or five areas of concern under the following headings in an airport safety self-inspection program:

ramp/apron, runways, taxiways, fueling facilities, and buildings.

- Discuss several approaches to eliminating bird hazards.
- Describe the minimum ARFF requirements under FAR Part 139.
- List the basic requirements under FAR Part 107.
- Describe some of the major ground servicing equipment found at major airports.

Pavement maintenance

The airport surface is the beginning and end of every successful flight. The inspection, maintenance, and repair of the runways, taxiways, and apron areas ranks along with navigational aids and lighting in importance to airport management.

The first concrete runway was constructed in 1928 at the Ford Terminal in Dearborn, Michigan. During the next five years Cheyenne, Wyoming; Glendale, California; Louisville, Kentucky; and Cincinnati, Ohio were concrete-paved. By the middle of the 1930s, paving the airport surface became popular at civilian as well as military airports.

The technical advances during World War II brought a whole new concept to the aircraft industry, and required like attention to the takeoff and landing facility as well. No longer was the paved surface considered a luxury; there was load-bearing equipment to consider—large aircraft, heavily loaded, twisting, and grinding at the airport surface.

The criteria for airport paving were borrowed from the highway builders, who themselves had only 30 years in the business and were making new discoveries each day. It was soon apparent that a building experience in Miami carried little relevance for construction in Chicago—as the geology changes, so must the paving method.

Although early efforts at paving simply related the intended load, and some evaluation of the strength of subgrade material, to determine the thickness of pavement, by 1945 it was recognized that many other factors influenced pavement performance such as material quality, repetitions of load, climatic effects, distributions of load, mixed traffic, roughness, and maintenance. All of these factors were considered in pavement life.

Today, the average airport operator has inherited an airport surface constructed more than 30 years ago, and with it, arrivals and departures of aircraft that have grown in size, weight, and landing speed operating in all-weather conditions. New, heavier, multiwheel main-gear aircraft such as the B-777 and a growth version of the B-747 were not foreseen when current standards were developed. The increased aircraft weights and other design difficulties of new generation aircraft will tend to stimulate construction of heavier and more expensive pavements as part of the solution.

A new testing facility at the FAA's Atlantic City Technical Center is helping to pave the way into the future for airports. Opened in early 1999, the National Airport Pavement Test Machine, a joint project of the FAA and the Boeing Company, is capable of testing pavement loads of up to 75,000 pounds per aircraft wheel in simulated 18-wheel configurations, as well as a variety of other tasks. A working group comprising representatives from FAA, airports, airlines, aircraft manufacturers, and research scientists met for over a year to establish testing priorities for the facility.

The test machine is fully enclosed, with pavement test sections built by conventional construction equipment and techniques to replicate actual field construction. Testing is conducted year-round 24 hours a day and in a fully automated mode.

The pavement test section is about 900 feet by 60 feet, allowing for the simultaneous testing of nine different pavement cross sections. Simulated aircraft loading is applied with an electrically driven vehicle operated on railroad rails. Hydraulic actuators provide the desired wheel loads. Movable wheel modules allow the wheel groups to be moved up to 20 feet in any direction.

The machine also will be able to test for pavement loads that exceed the expected gross weight of the new generation of wide-body aircraft, which likely will be double-deckers weighing in at more than 1.2 million pounds.

Aircraft manufacturers are confident that today's pavement will be able to withstand the gross weights of tomorrow's larger aircraft. However, of more concern to many in the industry is not how much those planes will weigh, but how that weight will be distributed over the wheels. For example, the B-777 is not that big in terms of gross loads, but it is in terms of strut loads. In fact, it was the advent of the six-wheel-gear B-777 that really spurred the need for the facility. The test machine will be able to test pavement under a variety of wheel configurations of up to eight-wheel gears.

Data from in-pavement runway sensors at Denver International Airport is also being collected to measure the response of the aircraft to pavement and its effect on performance. Data from these instruments and from materials testing will be analyzed and used in FAA pavement research being conducted at their technical center.

Over the next five years, officials from government and industry will be working on the problem of developing new pavement design methods and standards. In addition to developing standard thickness criteria for new pavements, a universal design methodology is expected to address load transfer mechanisms at transverse and longitudinal joints, layered elastic design procedure, and finite-element and standard methodology for assessing the impact of large, heavy-footprint aircraft on existing and new pavements.

Runway Pavement

As soon as they are built, runways, like other airfield pavements, begin a gradual deterioration attributable to the effects of weathering and the action of aircraft traffic. Left unattended, such deterioration may affect the safe operation of aircraft takeoffs and landings. Proper runway construction and maintenance enhance the longevity of the pavement.

Runways can be constructed of flexible (asphalt) or rigid (concrete) materials. Concrete, a rigid pavement that can remain useful for 20 to 40 years, is typically found at large commercial service airports and at airports that formerly were military bases. Concrete runways can be laid out in square or rectangular slabs that may be divided by joints to allow for expansion and contraction as the weather changes. Asphalt, a flexible pavement that can deteriorate very quickly in cold climates and more slowly in mild ones, is the runway pavement at most small airports. With proper design, construction, and maintenance, an asphalt runway can last 15 to 20 years or more before needing rehabilitation.

Because of its nonrigid character, asphalt paving requires no visible joints or seams. Asphalt might be less expensive to install than concrete, but generally requires much more maintenance in the long run. Much depends on the preparation and grading, as well as vigilance and prompt attention to maintenance needs. Moisture is the primary enemy. If water does not drain off the surface and away from the pavement edging quickly, it will filter through to the subbase and weaken it to the point where the overlying courses sag and break open. Potholes appear as heavy rains wash away loose material.

After years of use, asphalt runways begin to lose their elasticity. Oxidation brings about physical changes in the asphalt material, which begins to lose its elastic qualities. Skin cracks will develop, allowing moisture to penetrate, unless the surface is resealed periodically. Patching of weakened areas as soon as weather conditions permit and renewal of the surface course can prolong the life of the runways considerably.

Concrete runways or taxiways are usually found at large airports with heavy air carrier traffic. Concrete has high load-bearing capacity in relation to thickness and high resistance to the destructive effects of weather. It also resists deterioration from oil or fuel spillage better than asphalt, and for this reason is generally used for parking ramps and around hangars at all types of airports. Jet fuel, incidentally, causes more harm than gasoline, because it evaporates more slowly.

Concrete, being a rigid material that expands and contracts with temperature change, is laid down in slabs separated by contraction and expansion joints. The joints are filled with flexible binder, which either compresses and extrudes or shrinks as the concrete contracts or expands. Over the winter, as the concrete contracts, the joints might separate enough to admit material that is essentially incompressible, such as sand or water when frozen.

When incompressible materials infiltrate the joints in concrete, tremendous pressures are generated during later expansion of the slabs, and the concrete might fracture in the joint area. This is known as *spalling*. The fractured edges permit rainfall to enter the subsurface with progressively destructive effect. Washing away of subbase can lead to empty spaces under the slabs, which in turn causes the slabs to rock and sometimes to break.

Incompressible material in the expansion joints can also cause the slabs to pop out—that is, to rise and slide over adjacent blocks. It can also cause slabs to buckle upward, cracking the surface and providing hundreds of avenues for water to enter the subbase. Considerable yardage of concrete surface can be destroyed in a relatively short time because an insignificant-appearing expansion joint has become filled with sand.

Even if the concrete slabs are misaligned only to a small degree they present a hazard. Landing gear, particularly nosewheels, can be damaged or sufficiently bent to prevent their retraction. Irregular surfaces can blow tires and wrench an airplane out of control. Periodic on-the-ground inspections can easily spot joint openings, surface cracks, and other problems before the runway becomes a hazard to aviation (Fig. 13-1). Most airport operations personnel are especially attentive to this precaution in the spring. The following are a few of the obvious indications of potential runway problems:

1 Ponding of water on or near runways and taxiways.
2 Buildup of soil or heavy turf at pavement edges, preventing water runoff.
3 Clogged or overgrown ditches.
4 Erosion of soil at runway edges.
5 Open or silted-in joints.
6 Surface cracking or crumbling.
7 Undulating or bumpy surfaces.

Pavement Management

A number of actions can be taken to repair the distresses that occur in concrete and asphalt pavements. The determining factor in selecting an action is the degree to which the pavement has deteriorated. Less deteriorated pavements generally require maintenance, while more extensively deteriorated pavements require rehabilitation. The FAA defines *pavement maintenance* as "any regular or recurring work necessary, on a continuing basis, to preserve existing airport facilities in good condition, any work involved in the care or cleaning of existing airport facilities, and incidental or minor repair work on existing airport facilities." A typical maintenance repair is crack sealing. The FAA defines *pavement rehabilitation* as the "development required to preserve, repair, or restore the financial integrity" of the pavement. One example of a rehabilitation project is a structural overlay (laying more asphalt on the runway surface). In the FAA's AIP Handbook, work items eligible for funds under airfield paving focus on construction and rehabilitation, including the reconstruction and repair of runways, taxiways, and aprons. Stand-alone crack sealing and other minor maintenance items are generally not eligible.

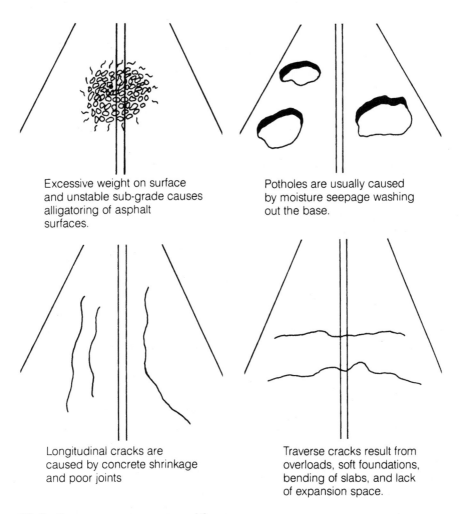

Excessive weight on surface and unstable sub-grade causes alligatoring of asphalt surfaces.

Potholes are usually caused by moisture seepage washing out the base.

Longitudinal cracks are caused by concrete shrinkage and poor joints

Traverse cracks result from overloads, soft foundations, bending of slabs, and lack of expansion space.

13-1. *Runway pavement problems.*

Though approaches to repairing pavements may differ, some experts note that appropriately timed maintenance and rehabilitation forestalls the need to replace the pavement entirely, a far more expensive step. Maintenance and repairs, such as crack sealing, can minimize pavement deterioration. Similarly, rehabilitation, such as structural overlay, can extend the time needed until the pavement must be replaced. On the other hand, not conducting such work at the proper time can shorten pavement life.

A *pavement management system* evaluates the present condition of a pavement and predicts its future condition through the use of a pavement condition index. By projecting the rate of deterioration, a life cycle cost analysis can be performed for various alternatives, and the optimal time of application of the best alternative is determined.

During the first 75 percent of a pavement's life, its performance is relatively stable. It is during the last 25 percent of its life that pavement begins to deteriorate rapidly. The trick for airports is to predict as precisely as possible when that 75 percent life cycle point will be reached for a particular piece of pavement so its maintenance and rehabilitation can be scheduled at the appropriate times.

The longer a pavement's life can be stretched until it must be rehabilitated, the lower its life cycle costs will be. According to the FAA's own estimates, the total costs for ignoring maintenance and periodically rehabilitating poor pavement can be up to four times as high as the cost for maintaining that same pavement in good condition.

An accurate and complete evaluation of the existing pavement system is one of the key factors contributing to the success of a maintenance project. Major strides are being made in this area with the development and application of nondestructive testing (NDT).

One of the most effective and valuable of the nondestructive techniques is *vibratory* (or *dynamic*) *testing*. This technique measures the strength of the composite pavement system by subjecting it to a vibratory load and measuring the amount the pavement responds or deflects under this known load. Of the many devices available to perform these tests, one of the most popular is the Road Rater. This device can perform a test in approximately 12 seconds and is very maneuverable.

Pavement evaluations in the past normally included large numbers of expensive and time-consuming destructive tests such as cores, borings, test pits, and so forth. Selected on a visual or random basis, the locations at which these tests were performed yielded results of varying degrees of success. Unfortunately, taking enough tests to provide reasonable assurance that the results were meaningful also meant high costs and expensive runway shutdown time.

Taking advantage of the economy and speed of vibratory testing, it is possible to saturate the pavement system with tests to determine a very minimum number of locations at which destructive tests can be performed for a complete and accurate evaluation of a pavement and its components. Additionally, the results frequently point out other factors contributing to pavement weakness such as drainage deficiencies.

Resurfacing an apron area. Phillips Fibers Corporation

Rigid (concrete) pavements may also be examined with this technique to evaluate the likelihood of voids, extent of pumping, load transfer qualities, and the degree to which cracked sections reseat themselves under traffic loadings. These considerations determine the amount and type of remedial or preventive maintenance appropriate to prepare the concrete pavement system so that it will perform adequately after it is overlayed.

As for the service roads, flexible pavement methodology is used to translate the vibratory test results directly into the thickness of asphalt overlay required to strengthen the pavement to serve present and projected traffic loads with a minimum of maintenance. Particularly weak areas requiring additional investigation for possible digout are also examined.

The testing of the airport surface will reveal maintenance needed to upgrade the pavement system to the specifications as outlined in the airport manager's long-range plan. Products and methods for pavement maintenance are changing rapidly. Environmental conditions require different applications of similar materials and methods of construction. Solutions to the problem of pavement maintenance take on specific characteristics as they apply to individual airport problems.

Maintenance in general substantially reduces the need for extensive repairs or replacement of deteriorating airport surfaces. The ultimate solution to pavement difficulties is to discover and repair them before they get expensive. Airport operations personnel normally make daily inspections of pavement surfaces, note emerging problems, and call for technical assistance. Periodically, an inspection with a civil engineer is made to check on the more subtle forms of pavement distress.

Runway surface friction

Runway pavement surface friction is threatened by normal wear, water, contaminants, and pavement abnormalities. Repeated traffic movements wear down the runway surface. Wet weather can create dynamic or viscous hydroplaning. *Dynamic hydroplaning* is a condition where landing gear tires ride up on a cushioning film of water on the runway surfaces. *Viscous hydroplaning* occurs when a thin film of oil, dirt, or rubber particles mixes with water and prevents tires from making sure contact with pavement. Contaminants, rubber deposits, and dust particles accumulate over a period of time and smooth the textured surface. The pavement itself might have depressed surface areas that are subject to ponding during periods of rainfall.

An aircraft makes contact with the runway. As the tires spin up to the speed of the aircraft, slippage occurs—heat is generated, a thin layer of rubber vulcanizes and bonds with the asphalt or concrete runway. With each successive landing, the layer of rubber builds and the antiskid character of the runway decreases. If it rains, it is possible that 100 percent of the braking ability will be lost.

The most effective and economical method of reducing hydroplaning is *runway grooving*. One-quarter-inch grooves spaced approximately one and one quarter inch apart are made (generally with diamond blades) in the runway surface. These safety grooves help provide better drainage on the runway surface, furnish escape routes for water under the tire footprint to prevent dynamic hydroplaning, and offer a means of escape for superheated steam in reverted rubber skids. Grooving also assists in draining surface areas that tend to pond, reducing the risks of spray ingestion, fluid drag on takeoff, and impacting spray damage.

Unfortunately, the grooves become filled with foreign matter and must be cleaned periodically. The FAA suggested schedule for friction surveys is shown in Table 13-1.

The removal of rubber deposits and other contaminants includes use of (1) high-pressure water; (2) chemical solvents; and (3) high-velocity impact techniques.

Table 13-1 FAA suggested schedule for friction surveys

Annual aircraft operations	Friction survey
Less than 12,000	When required
12,000–30,000	Once every two months
30,000–50,000	Once every month
50,000–100,000	Once every two weeks
100,000–200,000	Once every week
200,000 and above	Twice a week or more as required

Source: FAA

1 The *high-pressure water* method has been used very success-fully. The principle is based on high-pressure water jets aimed at the pavement surface to blast contaminants off the pavement surface. The technique is clean and removes deposits in a minimum of runway downtime. High-pressure water equipment operates between 5,000 and 8,000 psi and is capable of pressures exceeding 10,000 psi, and may be used when the temperature is 40°F and rising.

2 *Chemical solvents* have also been used successfully to remove contaminants from both portland cement and asphalt runways. Chemicals must meet Environmental Protection Agency (EPA) requirements. Acid-based chemicals are used on concrete runways and alkaline chemicals on asphalt.

3 The *high-velocity impact* method consists of throwing abrasive particles at high velocity at the runway surface. This technique blasts contaminants from the surface and can be adjusted to produce the desired surface texture. The abrasive material is propelled mechanically from the peripheral tips of radial blades in a high-speed, fanlike wheel. This reconditioning operation may be carried out during all temperature conditions and seasons except during rain, or in standing water, slush, snow or ice.

Snow removal

In the northern states, snow removal represents a significant portion of an airport's maintenance budget. How effective this expenditure will be depends on the ability of management to plan and execute an efficient snow removal program. Such a plan normally includes the following items:

1 A brief statement of the purpose of the plan.

2 A listing of the personnel and organizations (airport and other) responsible for the snow removal program. Many airports hire additional personnel during the winter months or utilize personnel from the streets and sanitation department on an emergency basis.

3 Standards and procedures to be followed. There are a number of excellent sources that airport management uses in preparation of this aspect of their snow removal program. They include the *Air Transportation Snow Removal Handbook* published by the ATA and FAA Advisory Circular 150/5200-30A *Airport Winter Safety and Operations*. The AAAE also sponsors an annual International Aviation Snow Symposium at which workshops are held covering all aspects of snow removal.

4 Training. Because the airport snow removal program requires special skills, a training program is normally an integral part of the plan. This includes classroom training in such areas as airport orientation, snow removal standards and procedures, use of various types of equipment, aircraft characteristics (capabilities and limitations), description of hazards and problem areas on the airport, communications, and safety procedures. On-site training includes a review of operational areas and hazards, test runs with equipment to accustom operators to area dimensions and maneuvering techniques, and communications practice while on the job.

5 Air traffic control, safety considerations, inspection standards, and notice to airmen (NOTAM) responsibility.

Timing

Knowing when to implement the snow removal program in order to maintain safe operations and avoid unnecessary repetition of certain activities is critical and generally learned through experience. Weather forecasts including the following information can be helpful in this regard:

1 Forecasted beginning of the snowfall.

2 Estimated duration, intensity, and accumulation.

3 The types of precipitation expected.

4 The wind direction during the snowfall and anticipated wind direction changes and associated velocities.

5 Temperature ranges during and after the snowfall.

6 Cloud coverage following the snowfall.

Snow removal is generally geared to the operational limitations of the most critical aircraft using the airport. Large jet aircraft have a takeoff limitation of ½ inch of heavy wet snow or slush, and 1 inch of snow of medium moisture content. This means that removal operations must get underway before such conditions occur, and must continue without interruption until the storm is over and snow removal has progressed to the point where aircraft operations may be carried on with safety.

Snow removal operations normally are started on the active "into the wind" runway, and progress to other inactive runways and taxiways. At the same time this work is proceeding, snow clearing from ramps, aircraft loading positions, service areas, and public facilities also takes place, as all of these areas are closely related in the overall operation of an airport facility.

Equipment and procedures

There are two basic methods of removing snow and ice: (1) mechanical and (2) chemical. Most removal is accomplished by mechanical means, since the chemical methods available for use in aviation are costly and not as effective as those available for highway use. Underground hot water and electrical heating systems are used in the ramp area at some large airports, but these are very expensive to construct and maintain.

The three mechanical methods of snow removal include plows, blowers or throwers, and brushes. These are illustrated in Fig. 13-2. Snowplows available for airport use do not differ significantly from those used on the highway. Blades are available in steel, steel with special carbide steel cutting edges, rubber, and polyure-thane. The traditional steel edge works most effectively on dry-packed snow, but is not as effective in slush removal and will not last as long as the rubber or polyurethane edges. The carbide steel edge gives longer life than the traditional steel edge, cuts packed snow more effectively, and can be more effective in the removal of ice that is not bound to the pavement surface.

The rubber blades have a longer life than the steel blades, make less noise and vibration (which contributes to the operator's comfort),

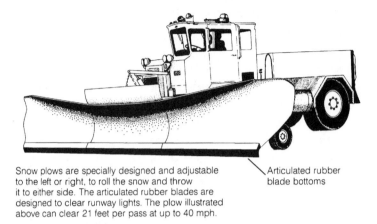

Snow plows are specially designed and adjustable
to the left or right, to roll the snow and throw
it to either side. The articulated rubber blades are
designed to clear runway lights. The plow illustrated
above can clear 21 feet per pass at up to 40 mph.

Articulated rubber
blade bottoms

A snow blower or thrower such as the one illustrated
above can clear windrows at speeds of 35 mph
and handle as much as 3,000 tons per hour.

A snow brush shown above can clear a heavy snowfall
in one operation. Angled up to 45 degrees, the 14 foot long brush scatters snow
up to 50 yards to either side. Variable speed control can be set to slow
speeds for sweeping surface dirt up to 550 rpm to clear heavy slush. By means
of an air deflector snow is thrown high to be carried away by the wind, or low to
avoid blowback.

13-2 *Snow removal equipment.*

and work well on slush, although not as well as steel on a dry or
packed snow. The rubber blades cost considerably more than the
steel blades, but generally last 5 to 10 times longer, depending on
how carefully they are maintained.

The snow blower or thrower is the primary mechanical device for
removal of hazardous snow accumulations such as windrows and

snow banks. Blowers are frequently used to clear taxiways, ramps, and parking areas prior to windrow removal on the runway.

Snow brushes are primarily used to clean up the residue left on the surface by the plow or the blower. They are also used to clear surfaces of a light snow and to remove sand spread on the runway to improve friction. The brush is the only unit of the three basic types of equipment that has year-round use on the airport. Runways and taxiways can be kept clean and free of debris with the brush, which prevents foreign object damage (FOD) to propellers or turbine engines. The brush will ordinarily have the slowest operating speed of the three types, and because of its relative ineffectiveness in removing any appreciable snow accumulation, will not be useful as the initial attack machine on most snowfalls. Its use, however, can eliminate the problems caused by freezing residue on the surfaces and the concern that aircraft operators have regarding turbine ingestion and propeller erosion caused by loose, dry sand on the runway.

Brushes are available with either steel or synthetic bristles. The steel bristle cuts better, but the nylon or polypropylene bristle is more effective on very wet snow or slush.

Snow removal equipment is expensive, but losses in revenue sustained by an airport closed by snow for several days would almost pay for the equipment needed to clear it.

Snow removal procedures Snow removal normally begins as soon as there are traces of precipitation on the runways and continues until the job is done. Snow is usually allowed to accumulate to 1 inch on ramp areas before airport personnel or contractors are called in to remove it. This accumulation is normally trucked to a snow dump in an outlying area of the airport.

Snow clearance operations on the runways are normally carried out by a chain of four or five vehicles working in an echelon formation. First the plows move down the runways at speeds up to 35 mph and move the snow to the pavement edges. This is normally followed by the snow blowers or throwers, which disperse the windrowed snow into the open areas beyond. The snow brushes are used for cleaning snow from semiflush-type fixtures such as in-runway lighting installations, and for the removal of slush and very light snow accumulation.

At O'Hare International, the world's busiest airport, clearing the longest runway (11,600 feet) of 2 to 3 inches of snow takes about two hours. Under the worst conditions it can take six hours or longer.

Ice accumulation Although snow is an important and serious problem in airport maintenance operations, ice is the most difficult problem to cope with and presents the greatest hazards to aircraft operations. Many airports attempt to control such conditions through the use of sand. Unfortunately, dry sand spread on runways and taxiways is quickly removed by aircraft engine blast, so a means of securing the sand to the ice is necessary. The most successful method uses conventional weed-burning equipment. The procedure is to apply sand to the icy surface by hydraulically powered and operated truck spreaders. These lay down a uniform layer of sand. This is immediately followed by the flame-thrower type burner units, which heat the sand particles and melt the ice sufficiently to produce a coarse, sandpaper-like surface upon refreezing. Very satisfactory results are obtained, which normally last until thawing temperatures cause the sand particles to sink into the ice and the process must be repeated. This method of ice control normally is used when the ice thickness is one-quarter inch or more. It has the additional advantage of dissipating some of the ice through evaporation and weakening the ice structure by a honeycombing effect that takes place when the open flame embeds the sand particles into the ice.

Snowplows move the snow to the pavement edges where snow blowers disperse the windrowed snow. Federal Aviation Administration

Safety inspection program

Clearly one of the most important concerns of airport management is safety. The Federal Aviation Act of 1958 and FAR Part 139 Certification and Operations of Air Carrier Airports were primarily established in the interest of promoting safety. To ensure that these regulations are continuously met—and, in fact, exceeded—airport management carries out an extensive airport safety inspection program. The frequency of inspection of each item will vary, but certain facilities and equipment must be inspected daily. Some of these items include runways, taxiways, and navigational aids. Other elements are normally ranked in order of importance to safety and the frequency of inspection is established. The FAA Airport *Certification Program Handbook* suggests the following general categories in which emphasis on elimination, improvement, or education should be placed:

1 Hazards created by weather conditions, such as snow, ice, and slush on or adjacent to runways, taxiways, and aprons.

2 Obstacles in primary and transition surfaces and in approach, takeoff, taxi, and apron areas.

3 Protection of the public.

4 Hazards created by erosion, or broken or damaged facilities in the approach, takeoff, taxi, and apron areas.

5 Hazards occurring on airports during construction activity, such as holes, ditches, obstacles, and so forth.

6 Bird hazards on or adjacent to the airport.

7 Inadequate maintenance personnel or equipment.

Additionally, FAA Advisory Circular 150/5200-18B *Airport Safety Self-Inspection* establishes a checklist primarily designed for operators of GA airports. This list includes some of the more important items that are often overlooked and result in damage to aircraft and injury to people. The following example taken from this source is not all-inclusive, but it does give an idea of the areas of major concern to an airport manager at a typical GA airport.

Ramp/apron—aircraft parking areas

1 Unsealed pavement cracks, weak or failing pavement, buildup of shoulders causing entrapment of water, poor drainage, and growth of vegetation.

2 Adequate parking and tiedown areas are provided and they are well clear of taxiways and are prominently marked.

3 Free of obstructions such as blocks, chocks, loose gravel, baggage carts, and so forth.

4 Deadlines are provided for spectator areas, passenger loading and unloading, cargo handling, and so forth.

5 Fuel trucks and other airport vehicles are parked in specified area away from aircraft.

6 No unauthorized vehicles permitted on ramp or apron.

7 "NO SMOKING" signs are prominently displayed in all areas where aircraft are being fueled.

8 Fire bottles are provided at apron and/or ramp and are in good working condition.

9 Directional signs are provided to direct aircraft.

10 Yellow centerlines are provided.

11 Flood lights, power outlets, and grounding rods in good condition.

Taxiways

1 Unsealed pavement cracks, weak or failing pavement, buildup or erosion of shoulders, poor drainage, and so forth.

2 Free of weeds or other obstructions.

3 Shoulders are firm, marked as necessary for easy reference, no washouts, and so forth.

4 Center (yellow) line is provided and is in good condition.

5 Hold line is provided and is clearly visible. No unauthorized vehicles and no livestock permitted on taxiways.

6 Necessary directional signs are provided and are so located as to be well clear of taxi areas.

7 Delineators and/or lights are provided and are in good order.

8 Is there a reminder sign at runup area? "USE YOUR CHECKLIST"

Runways

1 Runway lights and markers are clearly visible, are operated at correct brilliance, properly leveled and oriented, equipped with usable lamps of correct wattage, clear, clean lenses in runway lights, clean green lenses in threshold lights, unobstructed by vegetation.

2 Threshold properly marked and lighted.

3 Runway numbers in good condition (hard surface).

*4 End of runways flush with surrounding area (no lip).

*5 Overrun areas in good condition.

*6 Shoulders firm, no washouts, no holes or ditches and are clearly marked.

7 Clear line (white) in good condition.

8 Approach areas clear of obstructions. It should be noted whether views of ends of other runways are unobstructed by vegetation, trees, terrain or other obstructions, and whether unauthorized vehicles or livestock have access to the runways or airfield.

9 Procedures for removal of disabled aircraft from runways available at office.

(*Items 4, 5, and 6: Make a note of any unsealed pavement cracks, weak or failing pavement, poor drainage, birdbaths, buildup or erosion of shoulders, obstructing shoulders, and the like.)

Fueling facilities

1 Area is clearly defined and is located away from aircraft parking area.

2 Pumps are placarded as to octane and/or fuel grade.

3 Grounding means is provided for all refueling operations.

4 Fire bottles are provided and are in good condition.

5 Fuel hose and nozzle units are stored in clean area for protection from weather and contamination.

6 Filters are checked regularly and recorded.

7 Tanks are checked for water/contamination and recorded.

8 Locks are provided and used on fuel tank filler caps to avoid possibility of sabotage.

9 Fuel tank vents are checked.

10 Fueling area is kept clean, free of debris, and so forth.

11 Rags are stored in closed containers.

12 Oil is kept in storage bin or closet.

13 Oil cans are kept in drum or container.

14 "NO SMOKING" signs posted in area.

15 Stepladder is provided, properly stored, clean, and in good repair.

Buildings, hangars, shops

1 Clean and free of debris, junk, oil cans, used aircraft parts of no value, old batteries, tires, and so forth.

2 Fire protection with an adequate number of fire bottles in good operational condition and with dates of service record available. Fire and rescue equipment and first aid and emergency services. Smoke detectors and emergency lighting.

3 All tools, equipment, and so forth properly stored.

4 Paints, oils, dopes, and so forth kept in separate area, preferably fire proof.

5 "NO SMOKING" signs properly posted.

6 Restricted area signs posted.

7 Exit signs posted.

8 Buildings numbered—legible.

9 All rags and so forth in metal containers with lids.

10 Building provided with locks for security.

11 Area around buildings clean, free of weeds, junk, and so forth.

12 Signs properly posted to identify occupants of building.

Bird hazards

The FAA has reported a 107 percent increase in reported bird strikes since 1990, to more than 3,500 per year in 1998. It has been estimated that, between 1990 and 1998, wildlife aircraft strikes involving U.S. civil aircraft caused over $380 million per year in aircraft damage and over 461,000 hours per year of aircraft downtime.

A flock of birds sucked into a jet engine at takeoff can cause a dangerous stall, while a single large bird hitting an engine with the force of a bullet might smash a fan blade that can cost thousands of dollars to replace. Airport managers, as well as all other members of the aviation community, are aware of the hazards to flight that can be caused by birds. FAR Part 139 requires that airport operators must show that they have established instructions and procedures for the prevention or removal of factors on the airport that attract—or might attract—birds. Many airport managers call upon the expertise of an ornithologist to help analyze bird problems at their particular location. The ornithologist can provide useful data such as identification of species, estimates of the number of birds involved, habitat and diet, migrating characteristics, tendency to fly in flocks, and flight patterns. Most allowable control techniques are intended to cause birds roosting or feeding on the airport to go elsewhere and over-flights to use different routes away from the airport. There are a variety of control techniques available that can be used singly or in combination including:

1 Elimination of food sources through better planning and implementation of a regimen for vegetation management on the airport's property.

2 Elimination of habitat such as trees, ponds, building ledges, and other roosting areas. Proper water retention management, including better drainage and elimination of wetlands and low areas, is particularly important in discouraging bird populations.

3 Physical annoyance such as noisemakers, high-pressure water from fire hoses, and even papier-mâché owls to frighten birds.

4 Chemical treatment to cause dispersal and movement of flocks or death. Effective insect control would also be a part of chemical treatment.

5 Continual upgrading of scientific methods used in assessing the effectiveness of different bird control methods.

6 Better training and management of a team dedicated to bird hazard management.

7 Use of firearms or other mechanical means of killing.

The use of trained birds of prey, such as falcons and hawks, complements a number of other measures enacted in recent years in the fight against bird strikes. Several airports have turned to border collies as an effective way to chase birds.

Some of the listed techniques are not feasible. If large numbers are involved, the use of shotguns is generally ineffective. Chemical poisoning of nuisance birds is generally not allowed by the Environmental Protection Agency because of possible harmful side effects from the toxic agents and large concentrations of dead birds, both of which can pose significant public health hazards. Chemicals are available that, when mixed with food (usually grains), cause birds to exhibit erratic behavior and distress cries. These alarming reactions result in dispersal of flocks and the movement of individual birds to different locations. These chemicals are not for sale to the general public and may be applied only by personnel licensed by the EPA.

Jet, a two-year old border collie, has been specifically trained to chase birds from aircraft flight paths at Southwest Florida International Airport. Lee County Port Authority.

If this control procedure is used, the airport manager has to obtain the services of a pest control firm or use other and equipment available, people after proper training and licensing of personnel.

Evaluation of the various control techniques is the next step. Evaluation is relatively simple because it involves observations to determine if the presence of birds has been acceptably reduced. The airport manager cannot ignore possible bird hazards, even if a recent control program has been successful. Continuous monitoring is accomplished through the self-inspection program required by FAR Part 139.

The U.S. Air Force Safety Center has produced a historical model of bird migration using Geographic Information System (GIS) data for the 60 species responsible for most of the damage. The information has been incorporated into a Bird Avoidance Model that is used to give their pilots a "heads up" on where they may encounter large migrations of birds. In addition, the Air Force is contracting the development of a technique that will use Next-Generation Radar (NEXRAD) to detect near-real-time bird migrations and is cooperating with the Army to develop a technique that employs both infrared cameras and ground radar. The ground radar will first be programmed to identify certain movements in specific locations. When activity or movement occurs, an infrared camera connected to the radar will record a heat signature of the activity coordinates and display the image to a monitor mounted in the tower or operations office. This technique will be able to spot birds roosting on a runway in poor visibility or even a deer crossing the active surface at night.

Aircraft Rescue, Fire Fighting

Seventy-five percent of all aircraft accidents occur within half a mile from the airport. Aircraft fires are rare, but an airport is not permitted to operate without an efficient fire service. Aircraft rescue, fire fighting (ARFF) services will turn out on full emergency standby on the slightest indication that something is wrong with a landing aircraft—a deflated tire, a circuit breaker out in any important system, a warning light in the flight deck. ARFF units turn out on average once a day at a major airport and are always on standby in bad weather or fog. During an emergency, ARFF personnel provide general emergency help, carrying stretchers and aiding disabled people.

Aircraft rescue, fire fighting (ARFF) vehicles such as the ones shown here at Detroit Metropolitan Airport are ready to leave at a moment's notice.

Aircraft fires are unusual because of the speed with which they develop and the intense heat they generate. Thousands of gallons of fuel could be spilled, presenting a complicated rescue effort that could involve an area of more than 18,000 square feet. It is imperative for the first vehicle or vehicles reaching the crash scene to be capable of controlling 90 percent of the fire within the practical critical area surrounding the fuselage within a minute or less. Such action would prevent the fuselage skin from parting and would keep the temperature inside the fuselage from reaching an intolerable degree.

Vehicles required and response time

Table 13-2 shows the minimum ARFF vehicles and extinguishing agents required under FAR Part 139 for various categories of certificated air carrier airport.

The index system shown in Table 13-2 is based on an area that must be secured to effect evacuation or protection of aircraft occupants should an accident involving fire occur. The protected area is equal to the length of the aircraft times a 100-foot width, the latter consisting of 40 feet on each side of the fuselage plus a 20-foot allowance

Table 13-2 Minimum ARFF requirements under FAA part 139

Airport category	Type aircraft	Vehicle	Extinguishing agent
Index A	More than 90 feet	One lightweight	500 pounds. of dry chemical or 450 pounds. of dry chemical and 50 gallons of water for foam production.†
Index B	More than 90 feet but less than 126	One lightweight and one self-propelled fire extinguishing vehicle	Same dry chemical requirements as Index A and 1,500 gallons of water for foam production.
Index C	More than 126 feet but less than 160 feet	One lightweight and two additional self-propelled fire extinguishing vehicles	Same dry chemical requirements as Index A and 3,000 gallons of water for foam production.
Index D	More than 160 feet but less than 200 feet	Same as Index C	Same dry chemical requirements as Index A and 4,000 gallons. of water for foam pro duction.
Index E	More than 200 feet	Same as Index C	Same dry chemical re quirements as Index A and 6,000 gallons. of water for foam produc tion

† If the airport expects to serve Index B turbine aircraft, 500 gallons of water for foam production is required.

Source: FAA

for fuselage width. The indexing system was based on this critical area concept, expressed in aircraft length, to provide more equitable protection to all aircraft using the airport.

FAR Part 139 indicates that a lightweight vehicle—which it theorizes would be the first one on the scene of the crash—must be able to reach the midpoint of the farthest runway from its assigned post within 3 minutes from the time the alarm is sounded. The second vehicle must be able to fulfill the same requirements in four minutes, and any subsequent vehicle in 4 ½ minutes.

Until the 1960s, airport firefighting equipment consisted of little more than modified versions of the gear used by municipal fire services. Now, every major airport is equipped with rapid intervention vehicles (RIVs) able to reach the runways within 2 minutes of an alarm. Heavy-duty vehicles are designed to cross rough ground to reach a distant runway (by a circuitous route; they cannot drive across active runways) or the overshoot or undershoot areas where most fatalities occur.

RIVs are fast trucks that carry foam, water, medical and rescue equipment, and lights for use in fog and darkness. Their crews begin holding operations to contain the fire and clear escape routes. Heavy-duty foam tenders follow. They are large, but fast and maneuverable, and carry about 10 times more foam than the RIVs. Turret-mounted foam guns swivel to project the foam up to 300 feet. Figure 13-3 shows several typical vehicles used by ARFF units.

Extinguishing agents

Most airport ARFF facilities are based on the quick delivery of foam extinguishing agents to the scene of a crash. Foam is the general selection because of the two basic ingredients—foam concentrate and water—can be brought to the scene and applied to the fire, if any, in a matter of minutes.

Foam smothers the flames and cools the surrounding area to prevent further outbreak of fire. Water is only really effective as a coolant. Dry powder (either sodium or potassium bicarbonate base) is most effective on localized fires in wheels or tires, or in electrical apparatus. Foam does have some limitations as an extinguishing agent. It must be applied in large quantities in what the National Fire Protection Association describes as "a gentle manner so as to form an im-

*Heavy-duty foam tender.*Oshkosh Truck Corporation

pervious fire-resistance blanket" when dealing with large flammable (usually fuel and/or hydraulic fluids) liquid spills.

The foam blanket, once applied, can be broken by wind, or clear water streams, or turbulence, or even the "heat baking" generated by residual heat in metals or burned-over surfaces. Applying a good blanket of foam and keeping it intact is a primary objective of any ARFF training program.

Foam is produced by mixing water, air, and a concentrate with suitable agitation, and then spraying it either as a stream or as a fog, depending on the type of fire faced. When properly applied, it will flow over a burning liquid and form a long-lasting blanket that seals off combustion-supporting air and quickly smothers the flames of even volatile vapors. Properly mixed and applied, it will be tough in the sense that it resists rupture from wind or heat or outside flames. A good foam will even reseal itself in the event that the blanket is torn.

Training

Training is a key ingredient in the overall effectiveness of the ARFF team. There are two basic challenges to airport management in this regard. The first challenge can best be described as a requirement to initially train ARFF personnel and then to maintain a high state of readiness for extended periods of time during which they are seldom called upon to fully utilize the training they have received. Many airport ARFF personnel never become involved in a full-scale aircraft crash that would demand utilization of all training skills.

The light rescue unit illustrated on the left can carry 300 pounds of dry powder sodium bicarbonate in two units pressurized by carbon dioxide. Each discharge nozzle can eject powder at the rate of 3 pounds per second over a range of 39 feet.

The heavy-duty fire tender illustrated on the right can discharge over 10,000 gallons of water or foam a minute through its monitor and over 1,000 gallons through each of its two hand-lines, while moving forward or backward.

The tank holds 200 gallons of foam concentrate and is designed so that the base slopes down to a sump.

The four-person four door cab is made of double-skinned insulated aluminum.

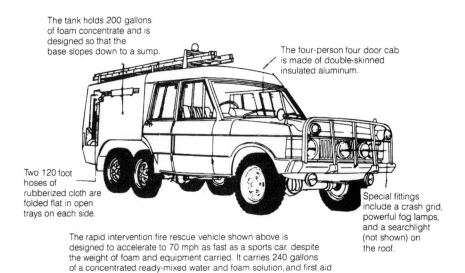

Two 120 foot hoses of rubberized cloth are folded flat in open trays on each side.

Special fittings include a crash grid, powerful fog lamps, and a searchlight (not shown) on the roof.

The rapid intervention fire rescue vehicle shown above is designed to accelerate to 70 mph as fast as a sports car, despite the weight of foam and equipment carried. It carries 240 gallons of a concentrated ready-mixed water and foam solution, and first aid and rescue equipment. It is used to contain the fire and keep aircraft escape routes open until the main fire fighting force arrives. This versatile chassis can be fitted with stretchers and other special equipment, for use as an ambulance.

3-3 *Typical ARFF vehicles.*

The second challenge is maintaining a suitable degree of interest and alertness within all members of the team. This aspect is primarily accomplished through an intensive in-service training program. Aircraft rescue, fire fighting personnel must develop a complete understanding and proficiency in the following areas:

1 All special hazards on the airport and surrounding area.

2 Airport water systems including the location of all fire hydrants.

3 Radio procedures.

4 Use of apparatus and equipment.

5 Aircraft types using the airport.

6 Hot drill fires.

7 Self-contained breathing equipment.

8 Emergency medical care.

9 Salvage and overhaul.

10 Building construction.

Security

FAR Part 107—Airport Security prescribes security rules for airport operators serving certificated air carriers. It became effective on March 18, 1972, and was largely in response to a wave of bomb threats and hijacking attempts in the early 1970s. Under this regulation, airport operators are required to prepare and submit to the FAA in writing a security program containing the following elements:

1 A listing of each "air operations area" (those used or intended to be used for landing, takeoff, or surface maneuvering of aircraft).

2 Identification of those areas with little or no protection against unauthorized access because of a lack of adequate fencing, gates, doors with locking means, or vehicular/pedestrian controls.

3 A plan for upgrading the security for air operations areas with a time schedule for each improvement project.

Further, under this part, the airport operator must implement a master security plan in the time frame approved by the FAA and also require persons and vehicles allowed in the air operations areas to be suitably identified. In effect, the guidelines for Part 107 are "if you find a door open, lock it; an unprotected area, fence it; an area in darkness, light it; and someone you don't know, find out who he is." Adherence to these rules keeps honest people out of restricted areas and makes it easier to spot those people with dishonest intentions.

FAA's interest in aviation security under Part 107 is limited to security "as it affects or could affect safety in flight." It does not extend to security in automobile parking lots or terminal areas distant from the landing area. However, compliance with these regulations unquestionably has beneficial fallout in other areas of the airport. Most airport operators include such areas in their master security program.

The airport security system consists of various parts. Table 13-3 demonstrates the various components of the airport security system and the functions carried out within each component.

Airport security starts at the perimeter fence, which normally has a 10-foot clear area on either side. Some airports use microwave fences in remote areas, which flash a warning of intruders to airport security personnel. Other remote facilities such as cargo terminals are often targets for thieves and pilferers. Security in this area has been strengthened considerably in recent years. Most cargo areas are well-lit and allow trucking firms only in certain designated areas. Armed security guards, closed-circuit TV with zoom lens cameras, videotape recording, and a twin-lock system for high-value articles (one key held by security personnel and the other by designated air-line personnel) are all part of the cargo area security program. At most major airports, bonded stores for duty-free goods and surveil-lance cages for valuable cargo reduce all but organized pilferage and theft during delivery or loading.

Terrorism is the worst threat, and airports and airlines at risk may have air cargo x-rayed, or have containerized cargo routinely de-compressed for 12 hours in remotely sited chambers to reduce the possibility of bombs exploding in aircraft cargo holds.

Airport operations Control Center at Fort Lauderdale-Hollywood International Airport. Broward County Aviation Department.

Table 13-3 The airport security system

Security component	Functions
Perimeter security	Posting, fencing, gates and other openings, light placement and protection
Cargo security	Security guards, lighting, closed-circuit TV, high-value property cages, pressure chambers, and fencing
Terminal security	Surveillance of jetway access, ramp doors, alarm systems, fire sensors and protection, screening personnel
Ramp security	Surveillance of jetway access, ramp doors, alarm systems, fire sensors and protection, screening personnel
Parked aircraft control	Screening airport and airline personnel, alarm systems for parked aircraft, aircraft security survey
Aircraft movement	Screening airport and airline personnel, alarm systems for parked aircraft, aircraft security survey
Passenger flow control	Flow holding, camera surveillance, prede parture screening
Baggage and cargo screening	X-ray inspection, carry-on luggage, screening, luggage surveillance from drop-off to loading, personnel screening
Predeparture gate screening	Screening passengers, body search, screening airport and airline personnel, x-ray inspection of carry-on luggage
Crew screening	Background checks, training, predeparture screening
Intelligence and communications	Telephone and radio communications, emergency power, bomb threat contingency plans, evacuation plans

Police officers on bicycles provide security and assistance to travelers.
Lee County Port Authority.

When smuggling was the major airport crime, the passenger was rarely subjected to the indignity of personal search. The scourge of hijackings by politically motivated terrorists has changed that. Mechanical aids are increasingly being used in the search process at most commercial airports (Fig. 13-4).

A combined check-in desk, electronic weighing unit with digital readout, and x-ray security is replacing the airline check-in desk at some major airports. One monitor can cover several desk points. A specially trained operator monitors the TV screen. If a suspicious object is detected, the doors leading to the main baggage conveyor system can be closed while the object is examined from all angles and from close up. If the contents are passed, the operator opens the doors to release the baggage.

Passenger carry-on luggage is handled in much the same manner in the area leading to gate positions. Luggage is placed on a small conveyor belt that moves it past cameras that take an automatic x-ray television picture of the contents. This picture is transmitted onto the screen, where an operator can immediately pick out any objects that look as if they might have an aggressive purpose. The owner of any luggage that arouses suspicion is then asked to open it. In the vast majority of cases, what showed up on the television screen as pos-

TV monitor has a zoom control to allow close-up inspection of any suspicious object. Full tilt control enables the operator to examine a suitcase from various angles. Metal shows up densely, other materials as shadows.

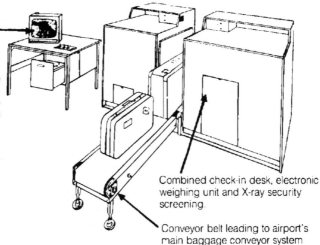

Combined check-in desk, electronic weighing unit and X-ray security screening.

Conveyor belt leading to airport's main baggage conveyor system

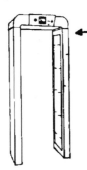

This metal-detection gateway has an electromagnetic field between doorframe-sized metal columns. Ferrous or nonferrous metal carried through by a passenger disturbs the magnetic field, the disturbance registers on a control panel, and an alarm sounds. Sensitivity can be reduced so as not to pick up the metal fastenings on clothes. The machine can be controlled by one person stationed away from the gateway and will not affect heart pacemakers, magnetic recording tape, or magnetically coded credit cards.

A portable explosives detector gives an audible alarm within 4 seconds of detecting explosive vapor. The probe, inserted into a handbag or suitcase, or passed over hands, clothing or containers, takes a sample of air. This is fed into the briefcase, which contains an electronic sensor unit, a rechargeable nickel-cadmium battery, and a bottle containing argon gas, to detect and register the contents. The detector can respond to explosive vapor concentrations of 1 part per several million parts of air, and can detect traces of explosives on any material hours after contact, but it will ignore vapors from lighter fluid and cleaning fluid.

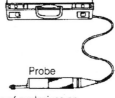

Probe

13-4 *Passenger security devices.*

sibly a weapon turns out to be an innocent household item such as an aerosol spray or a cigarette lighter.

More often than might be expected, lifelike toy pistols or knives being taken home as souvenirs are found by the process. Usually they are taken from the owner, given to the airline cabin staff for the journey, and returned to the owner at the end of the flight. Very infrequently a real weapon that just might have been intended for a hijacking attempt is found. A police investigation always follows such discoveries.

Meanwhile, the passengers themselves are passing through a magnetic gate that sounds an alarm when it detects metallic objects upon the person. As in the case of the baggage, most of the items picked up by the gateway prove to be innocuous—keys, lighters, cameras, and so forth—but an alert is immediately followed by a body search.

The security staff is also trained to recognize the "profile" of typical hijackers—facial appearance, the manner in which they are likely to comport himself during the security procedures, dress, and the baggage they are is likely to be carrying.

The funding of the security operations is divided among the FAA, the air carriers, and the airport operators. The FAA is responsible for paying the salaries and costs associated with its oversight of air carrier and airport security programs, including security inspections of screening operations at airports, and for aviation security research and development activities. Air carriers are responsible for paying for the security personnel and checkpoint screeners, screening equipment, such as x-ray machines and metal detectors, and the operation and maintenance costs of that equipment. Airport operators are responsible for paying for law enforcement officers, access control systems, and perimeter fences and lighting. Currently, airport operators can fund certain security functions, such as perimeter fencing, with funds from the FAA's Airport Improvement Program.

The Federal Aviation Reauthorization Act of 1996 mandated that the FAA: (1) study and report on the current security responsibilities at airports and the potential sources of funding for these activities, (2) certify screening companies, and (3) improve the training and testing of security screeners through the development of performance standards for security-screening services. While the FAA currently has training and testing requirements for screeners, it does not have a requirement that screening companies be certified.

Ground support equipment

A considerable amount of specialized ground handling equipment is used to service aircraft at a major airport. This equipment represents a major and ever-increasing investment for the airlines, airline contracting services, or airport operators. Its adequacy and reliability are also a primary factor in airline operating efficiency and on-time performance. A quick turnaround is essential to airline profitability but just as important to airport management in assigning gate positions to new arrivals in an expeditious manner.

Between landing and takeoff an aircraft must be unloaded, cleaned, refueled, loaded up with passengers, baggage, food, water, cargo, and duty-free goods in the case of international flights, all in the shortest possible time. Figure 13-5 shows a typical positioning of servicing and loading equipment for a B-747 with cargo side door on the main deck. The B-747 is designed so that 250 to 300 passengers and their baggage can be unloaded, and the plane refueled, serviced, and reloaded, within a normal turnaround time of 30 minutes. To do this, 16 or more vehicles might be assembled around the

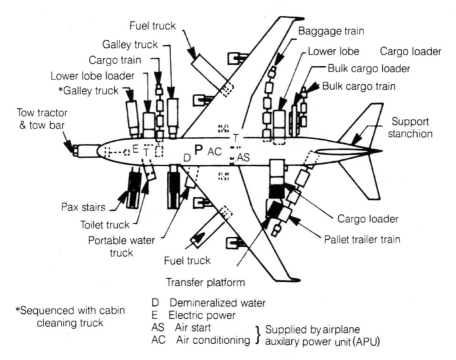

13-5 *Boeing 747 turnaround service.*

plane at once. Routine maintenance checks of the airframe, engines, tire pressure, lights, brakes, and other essentials take about 25 minutes. Minor problems reported by the crew are also corrected. Refueling at a rate of 20 gallons a second takes about 20 minutes. All other servicing goes on simultaneously. Figures 13-6 through 13-9 illustrate some of the major ground support equipment servicing aircraft on the apron area.

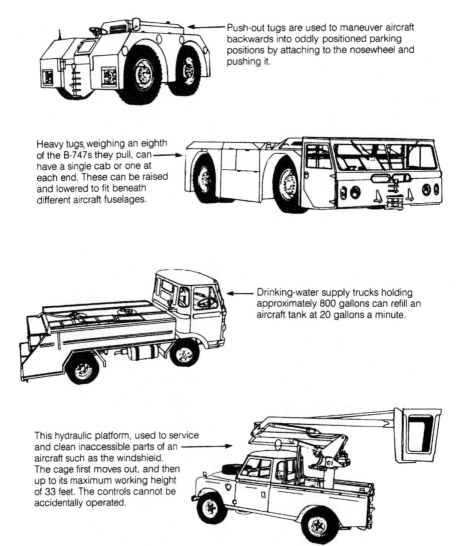

Push-out tugs are used to maneuver aircraft backwards into oddly positioned parking positions by attaching to the nosewheel and pushing it.

Heavy tugs, weighing an eighth of the B-747s they pull, can have a single cab or one at each end. These can be raised and lowered to fit beneath different aircraft fuselages.

Drinking-water supply trucks holding approximately 800 gallons can refill an aircraft tank at 20 gallons a minute.

This hydraulic platform, used to service and clean inaccessible parts of an aircraft such as the windshield. The cage first moves out, and then up to its maximum working height of 33 feet. The controls cannot be accidentally operated.

13-6 *Ground support equipment for aircraft movement and servicing.*

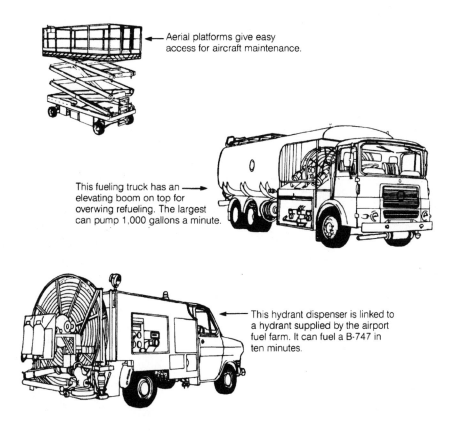

Aerial platforms give easy access for aircraft maintenance.

This fueling truck has an elevating boom on top for overwing refueling. The largest can pump 1,000 gallons a minute.

This hydrant dispenser is linked to a hydrant supplied by the airport fuel farm. It can fuel a B-747 in ten minutes.

Ground power units (GPUs) are used to start aircraft engines and give power to their electrical systems on the ground when the engines are not running. Though useful on busy aprons, they are not needed at airports that supply power from a central power source, or by aircraft with auxiliary power units (APUs). These are auxiliary engines that provide an alternative power supply independent of the main engines.

13-7 *More ground support equipment for aircraft movement and servicing.*

Forklift trucks with rapid lift and lower speeds may load small cargo units.

A double-deck loader used to load air cargo pallets, has two scissor-lift platforms. The lower rises to 9 feet and the upper deck, mounted on a 9-foot chassis, can extend up to the 18-foot deck height of a Boeing 747. This arrangement facilitates faster air cargo handling. While the top pallet is being unloaded, the next one is readied for collection on the deck below.

Transporters are very specialized pieces of equipment designed and used to carry containers and pallets 20 inches level over the ground and transfer them to or from other rollerized equipment such as dollies, fixed racks, or loaders.

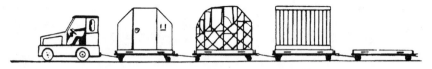

Pallet dollies are one of the most numerous pieces of equipment found on the apron area. The tractors come in various designs and can be used to tow baggage or cargo dollies.

13-8 *Ground support equipment for cargo loading.*

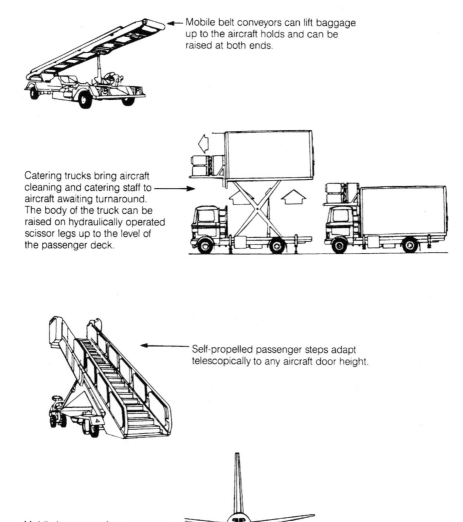

Mobile belt conveyors can lift baggage up to the aircraft holds and can be raised at both ends.

Catering trucks bring aircraft cleaning and catering staff to aircraft awaiting turnaround. The body of the truck can be raised on hydraulically operated scissor legs up to the level of the passenger deck.

Self-propelled passenger steps adapt telescopically to any aircraft door height.

Mobile lounges reduce congestion by conveying passengers to aircraft parked away from the terminals. Their extendable and lateral-moving gangways scissor-lift to enclose any aircraft door or terminal gate. They protect passengers from noise and weather. A mobile lounge can carry up to 150 passengers up to 20 mph.

13-9 *Ground support equipment for passenger and commissary servicing.*

Key terms

spalling

payment maintenance

payment rehabilitation

payment management system

vibratory (dynamic) testing

dynamic hydroplaning

viscous hydroplaning

runway grooving

airport safety self-inspection

FAR Part 107 Airport Security

Review questions

1 Why are new pavement design methods and standards being studied at the FAA's Technical center in Atlantic City?

   • Describe some of the tests being performed.

2 Asphalt runways might be less expensive to install than concrete, but generally require much more maintenance in the long run. Explain why.

   • What is the major problem with concrete runways? List some of the obvious indications of potential runway problems.

   • What is meant by vibratory (or dynamic) testing?

3 Distinguish between pavement maintenance and pavement rehabilitation.

   • What is a pavement management system?

4 Distinguish between dynamic and viscous hydroplaning. How does runway grooving help reduce hydroplaning?

   • Describe the three common methods of removing rubber deposits and other contaminants from runways.

5 Identify and briefly describe the major considerations in a snow removal program. Give two sources of additional information regarding snow removal.

   • Why is timing so important in an effective snow removal program?

- Describe how the three mechanical methods of snow removal are used together in clearing a runway.
- Describe one successful method of removing ice from the runway.

6 List and briefly describe four or five major concerns in a safety self-inspection for the following areas: ramp/apron area, taxiways, runways, fueling facilities, and building areas.

- Why would an airport manager want to consult with an ornithologist? List four or five bird control techniques.

7 What are the minimum requirements under FAR Part 139 for ARFF vehicles and extinguishing agents?

- What are RIVs?
- Why is foam the most prevalent extinguishing agent?
- What are some of the key elements in an ARFF training program?

8 What are the basic requirements under FAR Part 107?

- Describe some of the major security devices used at a typical commercial airport.
- Who is responsible for funding security operations?
- Describe some of the major ground support equipment used in moving and servicing aircraft; in loading cargo, baggage, and passengers.

Suggested readings

FAR Part 139   Certification and Operations of Air Carrier Airports
FAR Part 107   Airport Security

DOT/FAA advisory circulars

91-6A   Water, Slush, and Snow on the Runway
91-13C   Cold Weather Operation of Aircraft
91-53A   Noise Abatement Departure Profile
108-1   Air Carrier Security
109-1   Aviation Security—Acceptance and Handling Procedures
                   Indirect Air Carrier Security
150/5200-4   Foaming of Runways
150/5200-6A   Security of Aircraft at Airports

150/5200-8   Use of Chemical Controls to Repel Flocks of Birds at Airports

150/5200-12A   Fire Department Responsibility in Protecting Evidence at the Scene of an Aircraft Accident

150/5200-13   Removal of Disabled Aircraft

150/5200-18   Airport Safety Self-Inspection

150/5200-23   Airport Snow and Ice Control

150/5200-28A   Notices to Airmen (NOTAMS) for Airport Operators

150/5200-30A   Airport Winter Safety and Operations

150/5200-31   Airport Emergency Plan

150/5200-32   Announcement of Availibilty: Bud Strike Incident/Ingestion Report

150/5200-33   Hazardous Wildlife Attractants on or near Airports

150/5210-2A   Airport Emergency Medical Facilities and Services

150/5210-5B   Painting, Marking, and Lighting of Vehicles Used on an Airport

150/5210-6C   Aircraft Fire and Rescue Facilities and Extinguishing Agents

150/5210-7B   Aircraft Fire and Rescue Communications

150/5210-7C   Aircraft Rescue and Firefighting Communications

150/5210-9   Airport Fire Department Operating Procedures During Periods of Low Visibility

150/5210-10   Airport Fire and Rescue Equipment Building Guide

150/5210-12   Fire and Rescue Service for Certificated Airports

150/5210-13A   Water Rescue Plans, Facilities, and Equipment

150/5200-14   Airport Fire and Rescue Personnel Protective Clothing

150/5200-15   Airport Rescue and Firefighting Station Building Design

150/5210-17   Programs for Training of Aircraft Rescue and Firefighting Personnel

150/5210-18   Systems for Interactive Training of Airport Personnel

150/5210-2-   National Fire Protection Association (NFPA) Aircraft Familiarization Charts Manual

150/5220-4   Water Supply Systems for Aircraft Fire and Rescue Protection

150/5220-10   Guide Specification for Water/Foam Type Aircraft Fire and Rescue Trucks

150/5220-11   Airport Snowblower Specification Guide

150/5220-13B   Runway Surface Condition Sensor Specification Guide

150/5220-14   Airport Fire and Rescue Vehicle Specification Guide

150/5220-17A	Design Standards for an Aircraft Rescue and Fire-fighting Training Facility
150/5220-18	Building for Storage and Maintenance of Airport Snow and Ice Control Equipment and Materials
150/5220-19	Guide Specification for Small Agent Aircraft Rescue and Fire Fighting Vehicles
150/5220-20	Airport Snow and Ice Control Equipment
150/5230-3	Fire Prevention During Aircraft Fueling Operations
150/5230-4	Airport Fuel Storage, Handling, and Dispensing on Airports
150/5280-1	Airport Operations Manual
150/5300-11	Announcement of Availability Report No. FAA-AAS-80-1, National Runway Friction Measurement Program
150/5320-5B	Airport Dranaige
150/5320-6C	Airport Pavement Design and Evaluation
150/5320-12B	Measurement, Construction, and Maintenance of Skid Resistant Airport Pavement Surfaces
150/5320-14	Airport Landscaping for Noise Control Purposes
150/5320-15	Management of Airport Industrial Waste
150/5320-16	Airport Pavement Design for the Boeing 777
150/5335-5	Standardized Method of Reporting Airport Pavement Strength
150/5370-2C	Operational Safety on Airports During Construction
150/5370-6B	Construction Progress and Inspection Report—Airports Grant Program
150/5370-11	Use of Nondestructive Testing Devices in the Evaluation of Airport Pavements
150/5370-12	Quality Control of Construction of Airport Grant Projects
150/5370-13	Offpeak Construction of Airport Pavements Using Hot-Mix Asphalt
150/5370-14	Hot Mix Asphalt Paving Handbook
150/5380-5B	Debris Hazards at Civil Airports
150/5380-6	Guidelines and Procedures for Maintenance of Airport Pavements
150/5380-7	Pavement Management System

14

Airport relations with tenants and the public

Outline

- The airport as landlord
- Liability insurance
- Aircraft noise

Objectives

When you have completed this chapter you should be able to:

- Describe how airport-airline relations concerning use agreements have changed since deregulation.
- Describe a typical airport-concessionaire agreement.
- Discuss some of the liability exposures that an airport experiences.
- Summarize the coverages afforded under an airport premises liability policy.
- Highlight the FAA's role in noise abatement.
- Discuss some of the problems of noise as it relates to land use around the airport.
- Identify the noise abatement programs eligible for federal aid.
- Describe some of the restrictions imposed upon aircraft operators to control noise.

The airport as landlord

A major commercial airport is a huge public enterprise. Some are literally cities in their own right, with a great variety of facilities and services. While the administration of these facilities is generally the responsibility of a public entity, such as a department of city government or aviation authority, airports also have a private character. They must be operated in conjunction with airlines that provide air transportation service and with concessionaires, FBOs, and other firms doing business on airport property. This combination of public management and private enterprise creates a unique landlord-tenant relationship.

Airport-airline relations

From the airlines' perspective, each airport is a point in a route system for the loading and transfer of passengers and freight. In order to operate efficiently, air carriers need certain facilities at each airport. These requirements, however, are not static; they change with traffic demand, economic conditions, and the competitive climate. Before airline deregulation in 1978, response to changes of this sort was slow and mediated by the regulatory process. Carriers had to apply to the Civil Aeronautics Board (CAB) for permission to add or to drop routes or to change fares. CAB deliberations involved published notices, comments from opposing parties, and sometimes hearings. Deliberations could take months, even years, and all members of the airline-airport community were aware of a carrier's intention to make a change long before the CAB gave permission. Since the Airline Deregulation Act of 1978, air carriers can change their routes without permission and on very short notice. With these route changes, airline requirements at airports can change with equal rapidity.

In contrast to airlines, which operate over a route system connecting many cities, airport operators must focus on accommodating the interests of a number of users at a single location. Changes in the way individual airlines operate might put pressures on the airport's resources, requiring major capital expenditures or making obsolete a facility already constructed. Because airports accommodate many users and tenants other than the airlines, airport operators must be concerned with efficient use of landside facilities that are of little concern to the carriers, even though carriers' activities can severely affect (or be affected by) them.

Good airport-airlines relations are a critical component in the operation of a commercial airport. Los Angeles Department of Airports

Despite their different perspectives, air carriers and the airport management have a common interest in making the airport a stable and successful economic enterprise. Traditionally, airports and carriers have formalized their relationship through airport use agreements (discussed in chapter 11) that establish the conditions and methods for setting fees and charges associated with use of the airport by air carriers. Most agreements also include formulas for adjusting those fees from year to year. The terms of a use agreement can vary widely, from short-term monthly or yearly arrangements to long-term leases of 25 years or more. Within the context of these use agreements, carriers negotiate with the airport to get the specific airport resources they need for day-to-day operations. For example, under the basic use agreement, the carrier may conduct subsidiary negotiations for the lease of terminal space for offices, passenger lounges, ticket counters, and other necessities.

Long-term agreements between airports and major airlines have traditionally been the rule. One reason is the long-lived nature of the investments involved. A runway might have an economic life of a decade or more, a terminal even longer. When an airport undertakes such an improvement for the benefit of the airlines, the airport might want long-term leases to help ensure that carriers will continue to use the facility and help pay for it. At some airports the use agreements and leases might hold all signatory carriers jointly and severally responsible for payments; at others, airlines might be individually responsible for improvements made for their benefit.

In the past, the major airlines operated as virtual regulated monopolies with clearly defined markets and better credit risks than individual airports. In recent years, the perception of airlines as stable and the airports as risky has begun to change. Since deregulation, airlines are no longer under an obligation to serve a particular city, nor are they protected from competition by other carriers. They are free to compete, to change their routes, and to go out of business. On the other hand, certain airports have demonstrated that they are creditworthy and have strong travel markets. Regardless of what happens to an individual airline, these strong airports will continue to be served. In these locations, long-term agreements with individual carriers have become less important for airports seeking financing than the underlying economic strength of the community.

Because of the frequent route changes since deregulation, short-term use agreements and leases are becoming more common. Although the cost to the carrier of a short-term lease might be higher, it has the advantage of allowing greater flexibility for both the carrier and the airport. A carrier testing a new market might not be able or willing to enter a long-term agreement or to assume responsibility for capital improvements until it is sure that the market will be profitable. At the same time, an airport might not want to enter into a long-term agreement with a new carrier that has not yet established a reputation for reliability. At some airports, several different kinds of use agreements may be in effect simultaneously.

As with major airport planning decisions, negotiations related to the day-to-day needs of the carriers have traditionally been carried out between airport management and a negotiating committee made up of representatives of the scheduled airlines that are signatories to use agreements with the airport. In the past, negotiating committees have been an effective means of bringing the collective influence of the airlines to bear on airport management.

The nature of negotiations at some airports has changed radically since deregulation. Under regulation, the major carriers—though competitors—had reasonably similar interests and needs. They did not really compete on the basis of price, and the regulatory process guaranteed that no member of the community could surprise the others with sudden changes in operating strategy. The carriers' representatives were a small group of people who sat on the same side of the negotiating table at many different airports. Carriers generally worked with one another in an atmosphere of cooperation and presented a common position in negotiating with the management of an individual airport.

Since deregulation, however, the environment has been characterized by competition rather than cooperation. Carriers might radically alter their routes, service levels, or prices on very short notice. They are reluctant to share information about their plans for fear of giving an advantage to a competitor. These factors make group negotiations more difficult. Some airport proprietors have complained that in this competitive atmosphere, carriers no longer give adequate advance warning of changes that might directly affect the operation of the airport.

The days when most major airports are dominated by a few large airlines with long-term agreements might be passing away. One reason is the proliferation of air carriers since deregulation. The wide variation in aircraft size and performance, number of passengers, and markets served means that different classes of carriers require somewhat different facilities. Commuter carriers, with their smaller aircraft, usually do not need the same gate and apron facilities as major carriers. While there were commuters before deregulation, they are coming to constitute a larger portion of users at many airports. Other new entrants, including "no-frills" carriers, might also have different needs from those of conventional air carriers—for example, they might want more frequent gate access, but less baggage handling. These minority carriers might come to wield more power in negotiating with the airport for what they need and might challenge major carriers for a voice in investment decisions at an airport.

Airport-concessionaire relations

Services such as restaurants, bookstores, gift shops, parking facilities, car rental companies, and hotels are often operated under concession agreements or management contracts with the airport. These agreements vary greatly, but in the typical *concession agreement*, the airport extends to a firm the privilege of conducting business on airport property in exchange for payment of a minimum annual fee or a percentage of the revenues, whichever is greater. Some airports prefer to retain a larger share of revenues for themselves and employ

Hotel above the terminal building at Miami International Airport.
Metro-Dade Aviation Department

an alternative arrangement called a *management contract,* under which a firm is hired to operate a particular service on behalf of the airport. The gross revenues are collected by the airport management, which pays the firm for operating expenses plus either a flat management fee or a percentage of revenues.

Revenues from concessions are very important to an airport. At some, concessionaires and their customers yield more revenue to the airport than airline fees and leases, resulting—in effect—in cross-subsidy of air carriers by nonaviation service concessions.

Parking and automobile rentals are typically large and important concessions at airports. Despite growth in the use of buses and other high-occupancy vehicles, the continued importance of parking and car rental revenues is indicative of the relationship between the airport and the automobile.

At a number of airports, the airport operator's share of parking and car rental fees (after concession or management fees are paid) represents the largest revenue source from the terminal area—and in some cases, larger than revenue from air carrier landing fees. At many locations, the parking and car rental firms operating on the airport are complemented by (or are in competition with) similar services operating off the airport.

Another important type of concessionaire is the FBO, who provides services for airport users lacking facilities of their own, primarily general aviation. Typically, the FBO sells fuel and operates facilities for aircraft service, repair, and maintenance. The FBO might also handle the leasing of hangars and rental of short-term aircraft parking facilities. Agreements between airports and FBOs vary. In some cases, the FBO constructs and develops its own facilities on airport property; in other cases the FBO manages facilities belonging to the airport. FBOs also provide service to some commuter and start-up carriers, especially those that have just entered a particular market and have not yet established (or have chosen not to set up) their own ground operations. The presence of an FBO capable of servicing small transport aircraft can sometimes be instrumental in a new carrier's decision to serve a particular airport.

In addition to concessionaires, some airport authorities serve as landlord to other tenants such as industrial parks, freight forwarders, and warehouses, all of which can provide significant revenue. These firms might lease space from the airport operator, or they might build their own facilities on the airport property.

Airport–general aviation relations

The relationship between airport operators and general aviation is seldom governed by the complex of use agreements and leases that characterize relationships with air carriers or concessionaires. General

The aviation department for Broward Community College is located on North Perry Airport in Pembroke Pines, FL. Broward County Aviation Department

General aviation aircraft such as the Cessna Skywagon shown here are flown for business and pleasure purposes. Federal Aviation Administration

aviation (GA) is a diverse group. At any given airport, the GA aircraft will be owned and operated by a variety of individuals and organizations for a number of personal, business, or instructional purposes. Because of the variety of ownership and the diversity of aircraft type and use, long-term agreements between the airport and GA users are not customary. GA users often lease airport facilities, especially storage space such as hangars and tiedowns, but the relationship is usually that of landlord and tenant. There are instances where owners and operators of GA aircraft assume direct responsibility for capital development of an airport, but this is not common, even at airports where general aviation is a majority user.

It must be remembered that while GA activities make up about half of the aircraft operations at FAA-towered airports, the average utilization of each aircraft is much lower than that of commercial aircraft. There are approximately 190,000 GA aircraft, compared to approximately 7,000 air carrier aircraft. Most GA aircraft spend most of the time parked on the ground. Only a small number—usually those operated by large corporations—are used as intensively as commercial aircraft.

Thus, at the airport, the chief needs of GA are parking and storage space, along with facilities for fuel, maintenance, and repair. While an airliner might occupy a gate for an hour to load passengers and fuel, a GA user might need to park an aircraft for a day or a week while the passenger conducts business in town. At the user's home base, long-term storage facilities are needed, and the aircraft owner might own or lease a hangar or tiedown spot. In most parts of the country, the chief airport capacity problem for GA is a shortage of parking and storage space at popular airports. At some airports in the Southwest and in California, waiting lists for GA parking spaces are several years long.

Some airport operators deal directly with their general aviation customers. The airport management might operate a GA terminal, collect landing fees, and lease tiedowns or hangars to users. At some airports, condominium hangars are available for sale to individual users. A corporation with an aircraft fleet commonly owns hangar space at its base airport. Often, however, at least some of this responsibility is delegated to the FBO, who thus stands as a proxy for the airport operator in negotiating with the individual aircraft owners for use of airport facilities and collecting fees.

Liability insurance

Airports and their tenants have the same general type and degree of liability exposure as the operator of most public premises. People sustain injuries and damage their clothing when they fall over obstructions or trip over concealed obstacles, and their automobiles are damaged when struck by airport service vehicles on the airport premises. Claims from such accidents can be for large amounts, but claims stemming from aircraft accidents have even greater catastrophe potential. The occupants of aircraft might be killed or severely injured and expensive aircraft damaged or destroyed, not to mention injury to other persons or other types of property at or near an airport. Liability in such instances can stem from a defect in the surface of the runway, from the failure of airport management to mark obstructions properly, or failure to send out the necessary warnings and to close the airport when it is not in usable condition.

Airports and their tenants are liable for all such damage as is caused by their failure to exercise reasonable care. The principal areas in which litigation arises can be summarized under three main headings:

1 Aircraft Operations. Liability to tenants and the general public arising out of aircraft accidents, fueling, maintenance and servicing, and rescue efforts.

2 Premises Operations. Liability to tenants and the general public arising out of automobile and other vehicle accidents, elevators and escalators, police and security enforcement, tripping and

falling, contractual obligations, airport construction, work performed by independent contractors, and special events such as airshows.

3 Sale of Products. Liability to tenants and the general public arising out of maintenance and servicing, fueling, and food and beverage services.

Airport operators require that all tenants purchase their own insurance as appropriate for their particular circumstances and with certain minimum limits of liability. Generally, the airport operator is included as an additional insured under the tenant's insurance coverage; however, this does not relieve the airport operator from securing its own liability protection under a separate policy. The comprehensive coverage and limits of liability needed by most major airports far exceed what is required by the average tenant.

Airport liability coverage

The basic *airport premises liability policy* is designed to protect the airport operator for losses arising out of legal liability for all activities carried on at the airport. Coverage can be written for bodily injury and property damage. A number of exclusions apply to the basic policy, and consequently the insuring agreements must be amended to add certain exposures. By endorsement, the basic contract can be extended to pick up any contractual liability the airport might assume under various agreements with fuel suppliers, railroads, and so forth. Elevator liability and liability arising out of construction work performed by independent contractors might also be covered. The basic policy can also be extended to provide coverage for the airport that sponsors an airshow or some other special event.

For those airports engaged in the sale of products or services, the premises liability policy can provide coverage for the airport's products liability exposure. Aircraft accidents arising out of contaminated fuel originally stored in airport fuel storage tanks or even food poisoning from an airport restaurant would be examples. Aircraft damaged while in the care, custody, or control of the airport for storage or safekeeping can be covered by extending the premise's liability policy to provide hangarkeepers coverage.

The growth of aviation and airports during the past 30 years has increased the industry's exposure to liability claims. Airports invest thousands of dollars in purchasing adequate insurance coverage and limits of liability to protect their multimillion dollar assets. The courts have consistently held airport operators responsible for the safety of aircraft and the public as well as for the issuance of proper warning of hazards. In many cases, municipalities have not been immune, with courts determining that the operation of an airport is a proprietary or corporate function rather than a government responsibility.

Aircraft noise

Aviation noise is a fact of life at today's airports and a major—perhaps *the* major—constraint on airport expansion and development. Citizens living around airports have complained that aviation noise is annoying, disturbs sleep, interferes with conversation, and generally detracts from the enjoyable use of property. There is increasing evidence that high exposure to noise has adverse psychological and physiological effects. People repeatedly exposed to loud noises might exhibit high stress levels, nervous tension, and inability to concentrate.

Conflicts between airports and their neighbors have occurred since the early days of aviation, but airport noise became a more serious issue with the introduction of commercial jet aircraft in the 1960s. FAA estimates that the land area affected by aviation noise increased about sevenfold between 1960 and 1970. Even with this increase, the actual number of people affected by aviation noise is relatively small.

New aircraft are much quieter than earlier jets, and the noise levels at the busiest large airports have been reduced to the point that

An airline approaches Ronald Reagan Washington National Airport from the south. The Crystal City office and hotel complex in Arlington, Virginia, forms a backdrop. Federal Aviation Administration

community opposition has abated in some instances. Certain cities have been able to secure community agreement to proceed with airport expansion projects, including new runways. Expansion of terminal buildings, which implies an increase in air traffic, has also been accepted in other cities. On the other hand, noise levels threaten to increase as jet traffic is introduced at secondary airports in some metropolitan areas where the surrounding communities are pressing for curfews and other airport use restrictions.

Another trend that might intensify the noise issue is continuation of residential encroachment around airports. As more people come to live in noise impact areas, the opportunities for annoyance increase. Equally important, the public has become more sensitive to the issue, and it has become highly politicized. Airport neighbors have sued airports for mental anguish as well as the reduced property values related to noise exposure. Airport operators have begun to adopt noise abatement and mitigation measures so as to reduce their liability and protect themselves in legal proceedings. The noise issue has been instrumental in slowing or stopping several airport expansion programs.

Federal responsibilities

FAA's role is defined in a 1968 amendment to the Federal Aviation Act of 1958. The amendment charges the FAA administrator to "prescribe and amend such rules and regulations as he may find necessary to provide for the control and abatement of aircraft noise and the sonic boom."

The federal government pursues a program of aircraft noise control in cooperation with the aviation community. Much of the program is aimed at reducing noise at the source, through the use of quieter aircraft engines. The FAA adopted *Part 36 Certificated Airplane Noise Levels*, of the Federal Aviation Regulations in 1969, establishing noise certification standards for new design turbojet and transport category aircraft. In 1976, the Federal Aviation Regulations were amended, to provide U.S. operators until January 1, 1985, to quiet or retire the noisiest (Stage 1) aircraft. In 1977, the Federal Aviation Regulations were again amended, defining three "stage" levels to categorize aircraft noise emissions and requiring aircraft certificated after March 3, 1977, to meet the more demanding Stage 3 requirement.

The federal program to encourage the use of quieter aircraft has been effective. The retirement of early model four-engine aircraft provided tremendous benefits, lowering the residential population exposed to incompatibly high noise levels from an estimated 7 million people in 1975 to 1.7 million people in 1995. This improvement is remarkable because it took place during a period of substantial growth in air transportation, with enplanements more than doubling.

The reduction of aircraft noise at the source, by using quieter aircraft, is supplemented by an ambitious program to encourage compatible land uses in areas around airports. *Part 150 Airport Land-Use Compatibility Planning*, of the Federal Aviation Regulations, adopted in January 1985, establishes the system for measuring aviation noise in the community and provides information about the land uses that are normally compatible with various levels of noise exposure.

Part 150 encourages airport operators to develop *noise exposure maps* and *noise compatibility programs.* The noise exposure maps identify land use incompatibilities and are useful in discouraging any further incompatible development. Once the FAA determines that the noise exposure maps have been prepared in accordance with Part 150, the airport operator may submit a noise compatibility program, coordinated with affected parties, outlining measures to improve airport land use compatibility.

As of January 1993, 208 airports were participating in the Part 150 program, 155 had noise exposure maps in compliance with program requirements, and 135 had airport noise compatibility programs approved by FAA.

An FAA-approved Part 150 noise compatibility program clears the way for airports to obtain federal aid for noise abatement projects. A substantial amount of federal aid is available for preparing and implementing noise compatibility programs, with 10 percent of the annual Airport Improvement Program funds being reserved for this purpose. Large-scale projects have been undertaken in a number of major cities, including Atlanta, Baltimore, San Francisco, Seattle, and St. Louis, to relocate households or soundproof dwellings.

Further significant improvements are assured by the *Aircraft Noise and Capacity Act of 1990*, which requires the establishment of a national aviation noise policy, including a general prohibition against the operation of Stage 2 aircraft of more than 75,000 pounds after December 31, 1999. In addition to the phaseout of

Stage 2 aircraft, the act requires the establishment of a national program for reviewing airport noise and access restrictions. It is estimated that the phaseout of Stage 2 aircraft will reduce the population exposed to high noise levels to approximately 0.6 million people in the year 2000, a tremendous improvement over the situation in 1975 when 7 million people were affected. Further improvements after the year 2000 will depend largely upon advances in engine and aircraft design.

Measurement of noise

Several methods are used to measure aircraft noise and its effect on a community. The level of sound can be measured objectively, but noise—unwanted sound—is a very subjective matter, both because the human ear is more sensitive to some frequencies than others and because the degree of annoyance associated with a noise can be influenced by psychological factors such as the hearer's attitude or the type of activity in which she or he is engaged. Techniques have been developed to measure single events measured in units such as dBA (A-weighted sound level in decibels) or EPNdB (effective perceived noise decibels). These measure the level of noise in objective terms, giving extra weight to those sound frequencies that are most annoying to the human ear.

In some cases, annoyance is due not only to intensity of a single event, but to the cumulative effects of exposure to noise throughout the day. Methods to measure this effect objectively include aggregating single-event measures to give a cumulative noise profile by means of such techniques as the noise exposure forecast (NEF), the community noise equivalent level (CNEL), and the day-night average sound level (Ldn). FAA uses EPNdB to measure single-event aircraft noise as part of its aircraft certification process. FAA has established dBA as the single-event unit and the Ldn system as the standard measure of cumulative noise exposure to be used by airports in the preparation of noise abatement studies.

FAA has suggested, but not mandated, guidelines for determining land uses that are compatible with a given Ldn level. Ideally, residential uses should be located in areas below 65 Ldn. In the high noise impact areas (Ldn 80 to 85 or more), FAA suggests that parking, transportation facilities, mining and extraction, and similar activities are the most compatible.

Noise and land uses

The problem of aviation noise is intimately connected with the question of land use because one of the most effective insulators against annoying sound is distance. If possible, an airport should be surrounded by a noise buffer area of vacant or forested land, and the private property near the high noise impact area (under approach and departure paths and near aeronautical surfaces) should be used for activities that are less sensitive to noise: agriculture, highway interchanges, manufacturing, and other activities where a high level of ambient noise does not detract from performance. Unfortunately, many airports are surrounded by buildings devoted to incompatible activities: residences, schools, and auditoriums.

Zoning and land use planning are responsibilities of local governments. In many cases these governments have been unable or unwilling to provide mutual protection for airports and residential development. Land is a scarce resource in urban areas, and where there is great demand for housing and shopping centers, underutilized land around airports becomes extremely valuable. Even where local governments have enacted zoning ordinances to prevent encroachment, developers have been able to gain waivers. The tax revenues generated by the higher land uses might seem more important to city governments than the long-range need to protect the airport and the residential areas from one another. In some cases, local governments trying to enforce zoning rules have had them overturned when developers contested them in court.

At least part of the problem is ineffective intergovernmental cooperation. Few airports are located entirely within the borders of the municipality that owns and operates the facility. Surrounding municipalities might have conflicting practices, priorities, and philosophies of government, and each has separate zoning authority. For instance, St. Louis-Lambert Airport is surrounded by 29 municipalities, and Dallas-Fort Worth by 10. A municipality that owns an airport perceives advantages and disadvantages, and it must weigh the economic benefits of the airport against the problems of noise. A municipality that merely borders on an airport might see only disadvantages. Further, because the airport operator has sole liability for damage due to airport noise, some surrounding municipalities have felt little need to enforce zoning rules when complaints will not be directed to them but to the municipality that owns and operates the airport.

Even where sound intergovernmental agreements on zoning have been developed, time can erode them. When Dallas-Fort Worth airport was being planned and built, the surrounding municipalities developed agreements on zoning that were viewed as models of intergovernmental cooperation and coordination. Over the intervening years there have been changes in local government, in priorities, and in the local economy. There is now encroaching development such that Dallas-Fort Worth now has noise problems, despite its huge 17,600-acre size.

Local noise abatement programs

While aircraft are the source of noise at airports, aircraft operators are not liable for damage caused by noise. The courts have determined that the sole legal liability for aircraft noise rests with the airport operator. The federal government, by law and administrative action, has preempted control of aircraft in flight. Because the federal government is immune from suit (without its consent) and because the aircraft operate under federal regulation, litigants with complaints about aircraft noise have no recourse but to the airport operator. Courts have consistently held that the airport proprietor has the authority to control the location, orientation, and size of the airport and from that authority flows the liability for the consequences of its operation, including the responsibility to protect citizens from residual noise. Litigants have used various approaches in suing airports and have collected damages on the grounds of trespass, nuisance, and inverse condemnation.

Balancing their extensive exposure to liability claims, airport operators have some authority—albeit limited—to control the use of their airports in order to reduce noise. Basically, any restriction of operations at the airport must be nondiscriminatory. Further, no airport may impose a restriction that unduly burdens interstate commerce. The definition of "undue burden" is not precise, and restrictions at individual airports must be reviewed on a case-by-case basis. Restrictions must be meaningful and reasonable; a restriction adopted to reduce noise should actually have the effect of reducing noise. Finally, local restrictions must not interfere with safety or the federal prerogative to control aircraft in the navigable airspace.

Under FAR Part 150, airport operators can undertake noise compatibility studies to determine the extent and nature of the noise problem at a given airport. They can develop noise exposure maps indicating the contours within which noise exposure is greater than a permissible level. They can identify the noncompatible land uses within those contours and develop a plan for mitigating present problems and preventing future ones. Unfortunately, the airport operator's ability to prevent future problems is usually very limited. Unless the airport actually owns the land in question, the authority to make sure it is reserved for a compatible use is usually in the hands of a municipal zoning commission.

Many of these noise abatement programs allowed under current legislation are eligible for federal aid:

1 Takeoff and landing procedures to abate noise and preferential runway use to avoid noise-sensitive areas (which must be developed in cooperation with and approved by FAA).

2 Construction of sound barriers and soundproofing of buildings.

3 Acquisition of land and interests therein, such as easements, air rights, and development rights to ensure uses compatible with airport operation.

4 Complete or partial curfews.

5 Denial of airport use to aircraft types or classes not meeting federal noise standards.

6 Capacity limitations based on the relative noisiness of different types of aircraft.

7 Differential landing fees based on FAA-certificated noise levels or on time of arrival and departure.

FAA provides assistance to airport operators and air carriers in establishing or modifying flight paths to avoid noise-sensitive areas. In some cases, aircraft can be directed to use only certain runways, to stay above minimum altitudes, or to approach and depart over lakes, bays, rivers, or industrial areas rather than residential areas. Procedures might be developed to scatter the noise over several communities through some "equitable" rotation program. These noise abatement procedures might have a negative effect on airport capacity. They might require circuitous routing of aircraft or use of a runway configuration that is less than optimum with respect to capacity.

Restrictions on airport access or on the number of operations have an even more deleterious effect on airport capacity. One form of restriction is the night curfew, which effectively shuts down the airport during certain hours. Only a few airports have officially instituted curfews. One such is Washington National Airport, which has a curfew based on FAA-certificated noise standards. Aircraft with noise ratings more than 72 dBA on takeoff or 85 dBA on approach cannot use the airport between 10 P.M. and 7 A.M. This eliminates nearly all jet operations. Some other airports have reached informal agreements with carriers to refrain from operations after a certain hour, and some, like Cleveland, impose a curfew by not supplying jet fuel at night.

Air carriers are concerned about the spread of curfews as a noise abatement tool because they can play havoc with airline scheduling and reduce the capacity of the entire national airport system. Imposition of curfews at even two or three major airports on the East and West Coast could reduce the "scheduling window" for transcontinental flights to only four or five hours daily (Fig. 14-1) and would also affect flights within each region. Curfews are especially threatening to air cargo operators, whose business is typically conducted at night. Some see widespread imposition of curfews as a burden on interstate commerce, and hence unconstitutional.

Other types of airport access restrictions—excluding certain aircraft types, instituting special fees for noncomplying aircraft, or establish-

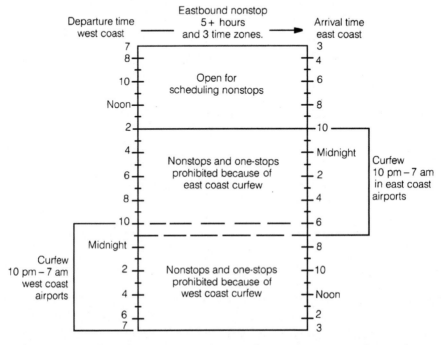

14-1 *Effects of curfews on scheduling transcontinental service.*
Federal Aviation Administration

ing hourly limits based on a "noise budget"—are subject to the legal tests of nondiscrimination and reasonableness. For example, the ban on jet aircraft instituted at Santa Monica Airport was struck down by the court in 1979 because many new technology jet aircraft that would have been banned by such a rule are quieter than the propeller-driven aircraft that would have been allowed to operate. A later ordinance by the city banning operations by aircraft with a single-event noise rating of 76 dBA was upheld. The court rejected the argument that enforcement of a local standard violates federal preemption. On the other hand, a federal court in 1983 struck down the curfew-quota system in effect at Westchester County Airport in New York. Under that system, an average of only six aircraft with noise ratings above 76 dBA were permitted to land between the hours of midnight and 6:30 A.M.

Both air carriers and airframe manufacturers have objected to the proliferation of local noise standards and noise-based quota systems. Boeing, for example, has pointed out that airlines are already in the process of replacing or reengining their noisier aircraft in response to FAA regulations. This replacement will require a large capital outlay on the part of carriers—capital that will have to be generated by continued operation of the aircraft they already have. If airports adopt local noise standards more stringent than FAA's, carriers will have to accelerate their fleet replacement programs in order to continue serving those markets. According to Boeing's estimates, such acceleration would be beyond the financial means of many airlines.

Federal funds are available to assist airport operators in soundproofing buildings or buying noise-impacted land. Usually, these are extremely expensive remedial measures, but a number of airports have been forced to undertake them. St. Louis Lambert Airport expects to spend about $50 million over the next 20 years under its Environs Plan. The airport has soundproofed some buildings and returned them to public use. In other cases, it has purchased land and resold it for more compatible use. In some cases, the land was "sterilized," that is, the buildings were torn down and the land left vacant as a noise buffer zone.

Key terms

concession agreement
management contract

airport premises liability policy

FAR Part 36 Certificated Airplane Noise Levels

FAR Part 150 Airport-Land Use Compatibility Planning

noise exposure maps

noise compatibility programs

Aircraft Noise and Capacity Act of 1990

Review questions

1 How have airport-airline relations concerning use agreements changed since deregulation?

- In the past, a joint airline negotiating committee would meet with airport management to discuss facility requirements and fees. Why is this practice changing?

2 What is a management contract? How does this arrangement differ from a typical concession agreement?

- Revenues from concessions are generally a minor portion of total revenue because of the incidental nature of their business on an airport. Do you agree? Why?

- What is the primary need of GA aircraft based at an airport?

3 What are some of the liability exposures a typical airport is subjected to in the course of conducting business?

- Litigation primarily arises from three areas. Give some examples under each area.

- Describe the coverages available under the airport premises liability policy.

4 Discuss the FAA's role in the control and abatement of aircraft noise. How is noise measured?

- What land use around the airport is compatible with aircraft operations?

- How have zoning and multigovernmental units around the airport exacerbated the problem of noise?

5 List the noise abatement programs eligible for federal aid. Explain some of the restrictions imposed on aircraft operations which are designed to reduce the problem of noise. Distinguish between noise exposure maps and noise compatibility programs. What is the primary purpose of the Aircraft Noise and Capacity Act of 1990?

Suggested readings

FAR Part 36 Certificated Airplane Noise Levels.

FAR Part 150 Airport-Land Use Compatibility Planning.

Aircraft Noise and Capacity Act of 1990.

Wells, Alexander T., and Bruce D. Chadbourne. *Introduction to Aviation Insurance and Risk Management.* Melbourne, Florida: Krieger Publishing Company, 1992.

DOT/FAA advisory circulars

91–53A   Noise Abatement Departure Profile.

91–66   Noise Abatement for Helicopters.

150/5020–1 Noise Control and Compatibility Planning for Airports.

Glossary

THIS GLOSSARY INCLUDES ALL KEY TERMS APPEARING AT THE ends of the chapters, as well as many other terms used in the text and others of significance in airport planning and management. The definitions are meant to be brief and straightforward, rather than technically precise and all-inclusive.

abandoned airport—An airport permanently closed to aircraft operations, which may be marked in accordance with current FAA standards for marking and lighting of deceptive, closed, and hazardous area on airports.

access/egress link—As used in the passenger handling system, the link that includes all of the ground transportation facilities, vehicles, and other modal transfer facilities required to move the passenger to and from the airport.

access/processing interface—As used in the passenger handling system, the link in which the passenger makes the transition from the vehicular mode of transportation to pedestrian movement into the passenger processing activities.

access taxiway—A taxiway that provides access to a particular location or area.

active based aircraft—Aircraft that have a current Airworthiness Certificate and are based at an airport.

actual runway length—The length of full-width usable runway from end to end of full-strength pavement where those runways are paved.

administrative building—A building or buildings accommodating airport administration activity and public facilities for itinerant and local flying, usually associated with general aviation fixed-based operations.

administrative management—A method of controlling airport access by setting quotas on passenger enplanements or on the number and type of aircraft operations that will be accommodated during a specific period.

advanced en route automation (AERA)—A traffic management system that will enable ATC personnel to detect and resolve problems concerning an aircraft's flight path on an approach to an airport. AERA will assist controllers in finding the open route closest to the preferred one if the latter is unavailable.

advisory circular (AC)—A series of external FAA publications consisting of all nonregulatory material of a policy, guidance, and informational nature.

aiming marker—A distinctive mark placed on the runway to serve as a point for judging and establishing a glide angle for landing aircraft. It is usually 1,000 feet from the landing threshold.

AIP Temporary Extension Act of 1994—Authorized the extension of AIP funding through 1994. Amended the percentage of AIP funds that must be set aside for reliever, commercial service, nonprimary, and system planning projects.

air carrier—A person who undertakes directly by lease, or other arrangement, to engage in air transportation. (FAR Part 1)

air carrier airport—An airport (or runway) designated by design and/or use for air carrier operations.

air carrier–certificated route—An air carrier holding a Certificate of Public Convenience and Necessity issued by the Civil Aeronautics Board to conduct scheduled services over specified routes and a limited amount of nonscheduled operations.

air carrier–commuter—An air taxi operator that (1) performs at least five round trips per week between two or more points and publishes flight schedules that specify the times, days of the week, and places between which such flights are performed; or (2) transports mail by air pursuant to a current contract with the U.S. Postal Service.

Air Commerce Act of 1926—Designed to promote the development of and stabilize commercial aviation. Included the first licensing of aircraft, pilots, and mechanics and established the first rules and regulations for operating aircraft in the airway system.

air marker—An alphanumeric or graphic symbol on ground or building surfaces designed to give guidance to pilots in flight.

air navigation facility (NAVAID)—Any facility used as, available for use as, or designed for use as an aid to air navigation, including landing areas, lights, any apparatus or equipment for disseminating weather information, for signaling, for radio direction-finding, or for radio or other electronic communication, and any other structure or mechanism having a similar purpose for guiding and controlling flight in the air or the landing or takeoff of aircraft.

Air Traffic Operations Management System (ATOMS)—FAA personnel record aircraft that are delayed 15 or more minutes by specific cause (weather, terminal volume, center volume, closed runways or taxiways, and NAS equipment interruptions).

aircraft—A device that is used or intended to be used for flight in the air. (FAR Part 1)

aircraft capacity—The rate of aircraft movements on the runway/taxiway system that results in a given level of delay.

aircraft mix—The types of categories of aircraft that are to be accommodated at the airport.

Aircraft Noise and Capacity Act of 1990—Establishes a national aviation noise policy, including a general prohibition against the operation of Stage 2 aircraft of more than 75,000 pounds after December 31, 1999.

aircraft operations—The airborne movement of aircraft in controlled or noncontrolled airport terminal areas and about given en route fixes or at other points where counts can be made. There are two types of operations—*local and itinerant*. Local operations are performed by aircraft that: (1) Operate in the local traffic pattern or within sight of the airport; (2) are known to be departing for, or arriving from, flight in local practice areas within a 20-mile radius of the airport; (3) Execute simulated instrument approaches or low passes at the airport. Itinerant operations are all aircraft operations other than local operations.

aircraft rescue, fire fighting chief—Develops procedures and implements aircraft rescue, firefighting, and disaster plans.

aircraft tiedowns—Positions on the ground surface that are available for securing aircraft.

Airline Deregulation Act of 1978—Marked the beginning of the end of economic regulation of the certificated air carriers by the CAB. The Act called for the gradual phaseout of the CAB with its termination on December 31, 1984. All remaining essential functions were transferred to DOT and other agencies.

Airline Operations Center Network (AOCNET)—A private intranet that provides an enhanced capability for the FAA and airline operations control centers to rapidly exchange and share a single integrated source of CDM-related aeronautical information concerning delays and constraints in the NAS.

airport—An area of land or water that is used or intended to be used for the landing and takeoff of aircraft, and includes its buildings and facilities, if any. (FAR Part 1)

airport access plans—Proposed routing of airport access to the central business district and to points of connection with existing or planned ground transportation arteries.

airport accounting—Involves the accumulation, communication, and interpretation of economic data relating to the financial position of an airport and the results of its operations for decision-making purposes.

Airport and Airway Development Act Amendments of 1976—Extended the 1970 Act for five years and included a number of amendments including the types of airport development projects eligible for ADAP funding, increased the federal share for ADAP and PGP grants, and initiated a number of studies concerning the National Airport System Plan (NASP).

Airport and Airway Development Act of 1970—A federal aid to airports program administered by the FAA for the ten-year period ending in 1980. Over $4.1 billion was invested in the airport system during this period.

Airport and Airway Improvement Act of 1982—Reestablished the operation of the Airport and Airway Trust Fund with a slightly revised schedule of user taxes.

Airport and Airway Revenue Act of 1970—Created an airport and airway trust fund to generate revenues for airport aid. Taxes included an 8 percent surcharge on domestic passenger fares, a $3 surcharge on international passenger tickets, a 7 cent surcharge on fuel, a 5 percent surcharge on airfreight waybills, and an annual registration fee of $25 on all civil aircraft.

Airport and Airway Safety and Capacity Expansion Act of 1987—Extended the Airport and Airway Improvement Act for five years. Also provided that 10 percent of funding be available for disadvantaged small businesses.

Airport and Airway Safety, Capacity, Noise Improvement, and Intermodal Transportation Act of 1992—Authorized the extension of AIP funding through 1993. Expanded eligibility under the Military Airport Program and State Block Grant Program.

airport authority—Similar to a port authority but with the single purpose of setting policy and management direction for airports within its jurisdiction.

airport beacon—A visual navigation aid displaying alternating white and green flashes to indicate a lighted airport or white flashes only for an unlighted airport.

airport configuration—The relative layout of component parts of an airport such as the runway-taxiway-terminal arrangement.

Airport Development Aid Program (ADAP)—A federal aid to airports program established under the Airport and Airway Development Act of 1970 for the development of airport facilities.

airport director—Sometimes referred to as airport manager or supervisor, the person responsible for the overall day-to-day operation of the airport.

airport elevation—The highest point of an airport's usable runways measured in feet from mean sea level.

airport geographical position—The designated geographical center of the airport (latitude and longitude) that is used as a reference point for the designation of airspace regulations.

airport identification beacon—Coded lighted beacon used to indicate the location of an airport where the airport beacon is more than 5,000 feet from the landing area.

airport imaginary surfaces—Imaginary surfaces established at an airport for obstruction determination purposes and consisting of primary, approach-departure, horizontal, vertical, conical, and transitional surfaces.

Airport Improvement Program (AIP)—A federal aid to airports program similar to ADAP covering the period from 1983 to 1987.

airport layout—The major portion of the airport layout plan drawing including existing and ultimate airport development and land uses drawn to scale.

airport layout plan—A plan for an airport showing boundaries and proposed additions to all areas owned or controlled by the sponsor for airport purposes, the location and nature of existing and proposed airport facilities and structures, and the location on the airport of existing and proposed nonaviation areas and improvements thereon.

airport layout plan drawing—Includes the airport layout, location map, vicinity map, basic data table, and wind information.

airport master plan—Presents the planner's conception of the ultimate development of a specific airport. It presents the research and logic from which the plan was evolved and displays the plan in a graphic and written report.

Airport Movement Area Safety System (AMASS)—Enhances the function of the ASDE-3 radar by providing automated alerts and warnings of potential runway incursions and other hazards.

Airport Noise and Capacity Act of 1990—Set a deadline date of December 31, 1999, for the elimination of Stage 2 aircraft in the contiguous United States, weighing more than 75,000 pounds.

airport of entry—See *international airport.*

airport premises liability policy—Designed to protect the airport operator for losses arising out of legal liability for all activities carried on at the airport.

airport requirements—First phase of the airport master plan that specifies new or expanded facilities that will be needed during the planning period. This involves cataloging existing facilities and forecasting future traffic demand. The planner compares the capacity of existing facilities with future demand, identifying where demand will exceed capacity and what new facilities will be necessary.

airport safety self-inspection—Provides a safety inspection checklist primarily designed for GA airports. (Advisory Circular 150/5200-18)

airport sponsor—A public agency or tax-supported organization, such as an airport authority, that is authorized to own and operate the airport, to obtain property interests, to obtain funds, and to be legally, financially, and otherwise able to meet all applicable requirements of current laws and regulations.

Airport Surface Detection Equipment (ASDE)—Radar equipment specifically designed to detect all principal features on the surface of an airport, including aircraft vehicular traffic, and to present the entire picture on a radar indicator console in the control tower.

Airport Surface Detection Equipment (ASDE-3)—A high-resolution ground-mapping radar that provides surveillance of taxiing aircraft and service vehicles at high-activity airports.

Airport Surveillance Radar (ASR)—Radar providing position of aircraft by azimuth and range data. It does not provide elevation data. It is designed for range coverage up to 60 nautical miles and is used by terminal area air traffic control.

airport system planning—Airport plans as part of a system that includes national, regional, state, and local transportation planning.

airport traffic area—Unless otherwise specifically designated in FAR Part 93, that airspace within a horizontal radius of 5 statute miles from the geographical center of any airport at which a control tower is operating, extending from the surface up to, but not including, an altitude of 3,000 feet above the elevation of the airport. (FAR Part 1)

airport traffic control service—Air traffic control service provided by an airport traffic control tower or aircraft operating on the movement area and in the vicinity of an airport.

airport traffic control tower (ATCT)—A central operations facility in the terminal air traffic control system, consisting of a tower cab structure, including an associated IFR room if radar equipped, using air/ground communications and/or radar, visual signaling and other devices, to provide safe and expeditious movement of terminal air traffic.

airport-to-airport distance—The great-circle distance, measured in statute miles, between airports as listed in the Civil Aeronautics Board's official airline route and mileage manual.

airport closed to the public—An airport not available to the public without permission from the owner.

airport open to the public—An airport open to the public without prior permission and without restrictions within the physical capacities of available facilities.

airport use agreement—Legal contracts for the air carriers' use of the airport and leases for use of terminal facilities.

air route—Navigable airspace between two points which is identifiable.

Air Route Surveillance Radar (ARSR)—A radar facility remotely connected to an air route traffic control center used to detect and display the azimuth and range of en route aircraft operating between terminal areas, enabling an ATC controller to provide air traffic service in the air route traffic control system.

Air Route Traffic Control Center (ARTCC)—A facility established to provide air traffic control service to aircraft operating on an IFR flight plan within controlled airspace and principally during the en route phase of flight.

airside facilities (aeronautical surfaces)—The airfield on which aircraft operations are carried out, including runways and taxiways.

airspace—Space in the air above the surface of the earth or a particular portion of such space, usually defined by the boundaries of an area on the surface projected upward.

airspace capacity—Includes the proximity of airports to one another, the relationship of runway alignments, and the nature of operations (IFR or VFR) in the area.

air taxi aircraft—Aircraft operated by the holder of an Air Taxi Operating Certificate, which authorizes the carriage of passengers, mail, or cargo for revenue in accordance with FAR Parts 135 and 121.

air taxi operator—An operator providing either scheduled or unscheduled air taxi service or mail service.

air traffic—Aircraft operating in the air or on an airport surface, exclusive of loading ramps and parking areas. (FAR Part 1)

air traffic clearance—An authorization by air traffic control, for the purpose of preventing collision between known aircraft, for an aircraft to proceed under specified traffic conditions within controlled airspace. (FAR Part 1)

air traffic control (ATC)—A service operated by appropriate authority to promote the safe, orderly, and expeditious flow of air traffic. (FAR Part 1)

Air Traffic Control Beacon Interrogator (ATCBI)—That part of the ATCRBS system located on the ground that interrogates the airborne transponder and receives the reply.

Air Traffic Control Radar Beacon System (ATCRBS)—A radar system in which the object to be detected is fitted with cooperative equipment in the form of a radio receiver/transmitter (transponder). Radio pulses transmitted from the searching transmitter/receiver (interrogator) site are received in the cooperative equipment and used to trigger a distinctive transmission from the transponder. This latter transmission rather than a reflected signal is then received back at the transmitter/ receiver site.

air transportation—Interstate, overseas, or foreign air transportation, or the transportation of mail by aircraft. (FAR Part 1)

airway—A path through the navigable airspace designated by appropriate authority within which air traffic service is provided.

Airways Modernization Act of 1957—Passed by Congress in response to several serious aircraft accidents and the coming of jet equipment, it was designed to provide for the development and modernization of the national system of navigation and traffic control facilities. Expiration was planned for June 30, 1960.

alphanumeric display—Use of letters of the alphabet and numerals to show altitude, beacon code, and other information about a target on a radar display.

alternate airport—An airport at which an aircraft may land if a landing at the intended airport becomes inadvisable. (FAR Part 1)

apportionment funds—Represent the largest funding category, making up approximately half of all AIP funding. For example, apportionment funds to primary airports are based on those airports' annual emplanements.

approach and clear zone layout—A graphic presentation to scale of the imaginary surfaces defined in FAR Part 77.

approach area—The defined area the dimensions of which are measured horizontally beyond the threshold over which the landing and takeoff operations are made.

approach clearance—Authorization issued by air traffic control to the pilot of an aircraft for an approach for landing under instrument flight rules.

approach control facility—A terminal air traffic control facility (TRACON, RAPCON, RATCF) providing approach control service.

approach control service—Air traffic control service provided by an approach control facility for arriving and departing VFR/IFR aircraft.

approach fix—The fix from or over which final approach (IFR) to an airport is executed.

approach gate—That point on the final approach course which is 1 mile from the approach fix on the side away from the airport or 5 miles from the landing threshold, whichever is farther from the landing threshold.

approach light beacon—An aeronautical beacon placed on the extended centerline of a runway at a fixed distance from the threshold.

approach light contact height—The height on the glide path of an instrument landing system from which a pilot making an approach can expect to see the high-intensity approach lights.

approach lighting system (ALS)—An airport lighting facility that provides visual guidance to landing aircraft by radiating light beams in a directional pattern by which the pilot aligns the aircraft with the extended centerline of the runway on the final approach and landing.

approach path—A specific flight course laid out in the vicinity of an airport and designed to bring aircraft in to safe landings; usually delineated by suitable navigational aids.

approach sequence—The order in which aircraft are positioned while awaiting approach clearance or while on approach.

approach slope ratio—The ratio of horizontal to vertical distance indicating the degree of inclination of the approach surface.

approach surface—An imaginary surface longitudinally centered on the extended centerline of the runway, beginning at the end of the primary surface and rising outward and upward to a specified height above the established airport elevation.

appropriation by activity—A form of budget where appropriate expenses are planned according to major work area or activity with no further detailed breakdown.

apron—A defined area, on a land airport, intended to accommodate aircraft for purposes of loading or unloading passengers or cargo, refueling, parking, or maintenance.

assistant director—finance and administration—Responsible for overall matters concerning finance, personnel, purchasing, facilities management and office management.

assistant director—maintenance—Responsible for planning, coordinating, directing, and reviewing the maintenance of buildings, facilities, vehicles, and utilities.

assistant director—operations—Responsible for all airside and landside operations including security and crash, fire, and rescue operations.

assistant director—planning and engineering—Provides technical assistance to all airport organizations, and ensures the engineering integrity of construction, alteration, and installation programs.

ATC data transfer and display equipment—Equipment for ATC facilities intended to provide a symbolic display of the data necessary for the control function by automatic means and providing for certain computation, storage, and recall of display data.

ATC System Command Center (ATCSCC)—A facility responsible for the operation of four distinct but integrated functions: Central Flow Control Function (CFCF), Central Altitude Reservations Function (CARF), Airport Reservation Position, and the Air Traffic Service Contingency Command Post (ATSCCP).

Automated Dependent Surveillance (ADS)—An onboard system that will replace verbal aircraft position reports, thereby enhancing surveillance coverage and accuracy in flight and on the airport surface.

Automated Radar Terminal Systems (ARTS)—Computer-aided radar display subsystems capable of associating alphanumeric data with radar returns. Systems of varying functional capability, determined by the type of automation equipment and software, are denoted by a number/letter suffix following the name abbreviation.

Automated Weather Observing System (AWOS)—Gathers weather data from unmanned sensors, automatically formulates weather reports, and distributes them to airport control towers.

Automatic Terminal Information Service (ATIS)—The continuous broadcast of recorded noncontrol information in selected high-activity terminal areas. Its purpose is to improve controller effectiveness and to relieve frequency congestion by automating the repetitive transmission of essential but routine information.

Aviation Safety and Capacity Expansion Act of 1990—This act authorized a passenger facility charge (PFC) program to provide funds to finance airport-related projects and a military airport program to finance the transition of selected military airfields to civil use.

Aviation Safety and Noise Abatement Act of 1979—Provides assistance to airport operators to prepare and carry out noise compatibility programs. Authorizes the FAA to help airport operators develop noise abatement programs and makes them eligible for grants under ADAP.

avigation easement—A grant of a property interest in land over which a right of unobstructed flight in the airspace is established.

balanced runway concept—A runway length design concept wherein length of prepared runway is such that the accelerate-stop distance is equal to the takeoff distance for the aircraft for which the runway is designed.

based aircraft—The total number of active general aviation aircraft that use or may be expected to use an airport as a home base.

basic data table—Shown on the airport layout plan drawing, it includes the airport elevation, runway identification and gradient, percent of wind coverage by principal runway, ILS runway when designated, normal or mean maximum daily temperature of the hottest month, pavement strength of each runway, and plan for obstruction removal, relocation of facilities.

basic runway length—Runway length resulting when actual length is corrected to mean sea level, standard atmospheric, and no gradient conditions.

basic transport airport (or runway)—An airport (or runway) that accommodates turbojet-powered aircraft up to 60,000 pounds gross weight.

basic utility (BU) airport—Accommodates most single-engine and many of the small twin-engine aircraft.

blast fence—A barrier that is used to divert or dissipate jet or propeller blast.

blast pad—A specially prepared surface placed adjacent to the ends of runways to eliminate the erosive effect of the high wind forces produced by airplanes at the beginning of their takeoff rolls.

bleed-off taxiway—A taxiway used as an exit from a runway to another runway, apron, or other aircraft operating area.

boundary markers—Markers indicating the boundary of the surface usable for landing and takeoff of aircraft.

break-even need—The annual revenue amount required to cover cost of capital investment and costs of administration, operation, and maintenance.

budgets—The planned dollar amounts needed to operate and maintain the airport during a definite period of time such as a year. There are capital budgets for major capital expenditures (such as runway resurfacing) and operating budgets to meet daily expenses.

building area—An area on an airport to be used, considered, or intended to be used, for airport buildings or other airport facilities or rights-of-way, together with all airport buildings and facilities located thereon.

building restriction line—A line shown on the airport layout plan beyond which airport buildings must not be positioned in order to limit their proximity to aircraft movement areas.

buildings and facilities chief—Responsible for assuring that buildings are adequately maintained with a minimum of cost.

Bureau of Air Commerce—Established in 1934 as a separately constituted bureau of the Department of Commerce to promote and regulate aeronautics. The bureau consisted of two divisions, the division of air navigation and the division of air regulation.

busy-hour operations—The total number of aircraft operations expected to occur at an airport at its busiest hour, computed by averaging two adjacent busiest hours of a typically high-activity day.

capacity—The ability of an airport to handle a given volume of traffic (demand). It is a limit that cannot be exceeded without incurring an operational penalty.

Category II operation—With respect to the operation of aircraft, means a straight-in ILS approach to the runway of an airport under a Category II ILS instrument approach procedure issued by the administrator or other appropriate authority. (FAR Part I)

causal models—Highly sophisticated mathematical models that are developed and tested using historical data. The model is built on a statistical relationship between the forecasted (dependent) variable and one or more explanatory (independent) variables.

Center Terminal Radar Approach Control Automation System (CTAS)—Will provide users with airspace capacity improvement, delay reductions, and fuel savings by introducing computer automation to assist controllers in efficiently descending, sequencing, and spacing arriving aircraft.

Central Flow Control Function (CFCF)—A function of the ATC Systems Command Center (ATCSCC) responsible for ensuring maximum efficient use of airspace by maintaining a dynamic hour-by-hour assessment of the ATC system conditions, including weather, staffing, outages, traffic demand, and system capacity. Using this real-time system status, the CFCF may initiate flow control actions including major rerouting of traffic on a system basis, approving or disapproving intercenter restrictions, or other actions deemed necessary to provide efficient flow of traffic and minimize delays.

centralized passenger processing—Facilities for ticketing, baggage check-in, security, customs, and immigration all done in one building and used for processing all passengers using the building.

certificated route air carrier—One of a class of air carriers holding Certificates of Public Convenience and Necessity issued by the Civil Aeronautics Board. These carriers are authorized to perform scheduled air transportation over specified routes and a limited amount of nonscheduled operations.

chief accountant—Responsible for financial planning, budgeting, accounting, payroll, and auditing.

chief—airside operations—Responsible for all airfield operations.

chief—landside operations—Responsible for all landside operations.

chief purchasing agent—Directs the procurement of materials and services to support the airport; prepares, negotiates, interprets, and administers contracts with vendors.

Civil Aeronautics Act of 1938—Created one administrative agency responsible for the regulation of aviation and air transportation. Under reorganization in 1940, two separate agencies were created: the *Civil Aeronautics Board*, primarily concerned with economic regulation of the air carriers; and the *Civil Aeronautics Administration*, responsible for the safe operation of the airway system.

Civil Aeronautics Administration (CAA)—Forerunner to the FAA, responsible for supervising the construction, maintenance, and operation of the airway system including enforcement of safety regulations.

Civil Aeronautics Board (CAB)—Responsible for the economic regulation of the certificated air carriers during the period from 1940 to 1985.

civil airport user categories—As used by airport planners, refers to the four major types of airports: certificated air carrier, commuter, general aviation, and military.

clear air turbulence (CAT)—Turbulence encountered in air where no clouds are present; more popularly applied to high-level turbulence associated with wind shear; often encountered in the vicinity of the jet stream.

clear zone—Areas constituting the innermost portions of the runway approach areas as defined in FAR Part 77.

closed airport—An airport temporarily closed to aircraft operations for maintenance, construction, or some other purpose while the operator is still in business.

closed field marking—Panels placed in the center of the segmented circle, or in the center of the field, in the form of a cross which will signify that the field is closed to all traffic.

closed runway marking—Panels placed on the ends of the runway and at regular intervals in the form of a cross, signifying that a runway is closed to all traffic.

Cockpit Information System (CIS)—Will process and display Flight Information Service (FIS) information and integrate it with navigation, surveillance, terrain, and other data available in the cockpit.

collaborative decision-making (CDM)—A joint FAA/industry initiative designed to improve traffic flow management through increased interaction and collaboration between airspace users and the FAA.

commercial service airports—Public-use commercial airports receiving scheduled passenger service and enplaning at least 2,500 passengers annually.

compensatory approach—A financial management approach under which the airport operator assumes the major financial risk of running the airport and charges the airlines fees and rental rates set so as to recover the actual costs of the facilities and services that they use.

computerized aircraft manifest—Produces aircraft load sheets, passenger manifests, and automatic telex reservations.

computerized baggage sorting equipment—A new technique to sort baggage through the use of machine-readable tags.

computerized ticket systems—Provide passengers advance reservation and sales, preassignment of seats, and automatic tagging of baggage.

concession agreement—An agreement between the airport and a concession regarding the conduct of business on airport property.

concourse—A passageway for passengers and public between the principal terminal building waiting area and the fingers and/or aircraft landing positions.

conical surface—A surface extending from the periphery of the horizontal surface outward and upward at a slope of 20 to 1 for the horizontal distances and to the elevations above the airport elevation as prescribed by FAR Part 77.

Consolidated Operations and Delay Analysis System (CODAS)—An improved aircraft delay reporting system. Using the FAA's Enhanced Traffic Management System and Aeronautical Radio Incorporated data it will calculate delay by phase of flight and will include weather data from National Oceanic and Atmospheric Administration.

Controller-to-Pilot Data Link Communications (CPDLC)—A data link service that will replace sets of controller/pilot voice messages with data messages displayed in the cockpit.

controlled airspace—Airspace designated as a continental control area, control area, control zone, terminal control area, or transition area, within which some or all aircraft may be subject to air traffic control. (FAR Part 1)

controlling obstruction—The highest obstruction relative to a prescribed plane within a specific area.

criteria for design and development—Specific performance measures used by airport planners in designing terminal building space requirements.

criteria for inclusion in the NPIAS—The principal criteria are: (1) that the airport has (or is forecast to have within five years) at least 10 based aircraft (or engines), (2) that it be at least a 30-minute drive from the nearest existing or proposed airport currently in the NPIAS, and (3) that there is an eligible sponsor willing to undertake ownership and development of the airport.

crosswind—A wind blowing across the line of flight of an aircraft.

crosswind component—A wind component that is at a right angle to the longitudinal axis of the runway or the flight path of the aircraft.

crosswind leg—A flight path at right angles to the landing runway off its upwind leg.

crosswind runway—A runway additional to the primary runway to provide for wind coverage not adequately provided by the primary runway.

curbside check-in—Designed to speed passenger movement by separating baggage handling from other ticket counter and gate activities and thereby disencumbering those locations, allowing baggage to be consolidated and moved to aircraft more directly.

daylight beacon operation—Operation of an airport rotating beacon during the hours of daylight means that the reported ground visibility in the control zone is less than 3 miles and/or the reported ceiling is less than 1,000 feet and that the ATC clearance is required for landing, takeoffs, and flight in the traffic pattern.

debt service coverage—The requirement that the airport's revenue, net of operating and maintenance expenses, be equal to a specified percentage in excess of the annual debt service (principal and interest payments) for revenue bond issues.

decentralized passenger processing—The passenger handling facilities are provided in smaller units and repeated in one or more buildings.

decibel (dB)—A unit of noise level representing a relative quantity. This reference value is a sound pressure of 20 micronewtons per square meter.

decision height (DH)—With respect to the operation of aircraft, means the height at which a decision must be made, during the ILS or PAR instrument approach, to either continue the approach or to execute a missed approach. (FAR Part 1)

defederalization—Refers to a proposal to withdraw assistance for major air carrier airports.

delay—The difference between the time an operation actually takes and the time that it would have taken under uncongested conditions without interference from other aircraft.

demand management—A method of controlling airport access by promoting more effective or economically efficient use of existing facilities. The two most prevalent methods are differential pricing and auctioning of landing rights.

Department of Transportation (DOT)—Established in 1966 to promote coordination of existing federal programs and to act as a focal point for future research and development efforts in transportation.

depreciable investment—The annual cost of capital invested in plant and equipment.

Development of Landing Areas for National Defense (DLAND)—A program approved by Congress in 1940 that appropriated $40 million to be spent by the CAA for 250 airports necessary for the national defense.

directional marker—An airway marker located on the ground used to give visual direction to an aircraft; consists of an arrow indicating true north and arrows indicating names and states of the nearest towns.

Discrete Address Beacon System (DABS)—A sophisticated air traffic control surveillance system capable of interrogating each airborne DABS transponder in an "all-call" mode or with a discrete address signal encoded for each specific aircraft operating in the system. The data acquired upon response from each transponder are then processed to provide range, azimuth, altitude, and identity of each aircraft in the system on an individual basis but in sequence on a programmed interro-schedule. Since aircraft are addressed individually in DABS, the surveillance system automatically provides a natural vehicle for a data link between ground and aircraft that can be used for ATC control purposes including the proposed intermittent positive control (IPC) concepts.

discretionary funds—grants that go to projects that address goals established by the Congress, such as enhancing capacity, safety, and security or mitigating noise at all types of airports.

displaced threshold—A threshold that is located at a point on the runway other than the beginning.

downwind leg—A flight path in the traffic pattern parallel to the landing runway in the direction opposite to landing. It extends to the intersection of the base leg.

dynamic hydroplaning—A condition where landing gear tires ride up on a cushioning film of water on the runway surfaces.

effective perceived noise level (EPNL)—Time-integrated perceived noise level calculated with adjustments for irregularities in the sound spectrum, such as that caused by discrete-frequency components (tone correction). The unit of effective perceived noise level is the decibel, with identifying prefix for clarification, EPNdB.

effective runway length—(a) Effective runway length for takeoff means the distance from the end of the runway at which the takeoff is started to the point at which the obstruction clearance plane associated with the other end of the runway intersects the runway centerline. (b) Effective runway length for landing means the distance from the point at which the obstruction clearance plane associated with the approach end of the runway intersects the centerline of the runway to the far end thereof. (FAR Part 121)

enplaned passengers—The total number of revenue passengers boarding aircraft, including originating, stopover, and transfer passengers, in scheduled and nonscheduled services.

enplaning air cargo—Includes the total tonnage of priority, nonpriority, and foreign mail, express, and freight (property other than baggage accompanying passengers) departing on aircraft at an airport, including origination, stopover, and transfer cargo.

en route air traffic control service—Air traffic control service provided aircraft on an IFR flight plan, generally by centers, when these aircraft are operating between departure and destination terminal areas.

en route flight advisory service (EFAS)—A specialized system providing near-real-time weather service to pilots in flight.

entrance taxiway—A taxiway that provides entrance for aircraft to the takeoff end of the runway.

essential air service—Guarantees air carrier service to selected small cities and provides subsidies (through 1988) if needed so as to prevent these cities from losing service.

executive aircraft operator—A corporation, company, or individual that operates owned or leased aircraft, flown by pilots whose primary duties involve pilotage of aircraft, as a means of transportation of personnel or cargo in the conduct of company business.

exit taxiway—A taxiway used as an exit from a runway to another runway, apron, or other aircraft operating area.

FAA high-density rule—Quotas imposed at selected airports based on estimated limits of the air traffic control (ATC) system and airport runway capacity.

Facilities and Equipment (F&E) Program—Provides funding for airports for the installsation of navigational aids and control towers, as necessary.

facilities chief—Establishes criteria and procedures for the administration of all airport property. Responsible for inventory control of all equipment and facilities.

fan noise—General term for the noise generated within the fan stage of a turbofan engine; includes both discrete frequencies and random noise.

FAR Part 77—Contains obstruction requirements at or near airports.

FAR Part 107, Airport Security—Prescribes security rules for airport operators serving certificated air carriers.

FAR Part 36, Certificated Airport Noise Levels—Establishes noise certification standards for new design turbojet and transport category aircraft.

FAR Part 150, Airport–Land Use Compatibility Planning—Designed to assist airport operators in determining the extent and nature of the noise problem at a given airport.

Federal Airport Act of 1946—A federal aid to airports program administered by the CAA (later the FAA) to give the United States a comprehensive system of airports. Over $1.2 billion in airport development aid funds were disbursed by the federal government during the Act's 24-year history.

Federal Aviation Act of 1958—Created the Federal Aviation Agency (FAA) with an administrator responsible to the President. The law retained the CAB as an independent agency and transferred the safety-rule-making powers to the FAA along with the functions of the CAA and the Airways Modernization Board.

Federal Aviation Administration (FAA)—Created by the act that established the Department of Transportation. Assumed all of the responsibilities of the former Federal Aviation Agency.

Federal Aviation Administration Authorization Act of 1994—Authorized the extension of AIP funding through 1996. Increased the number of airports eligible for Military Airport Program funding, universal access control, and explosives detection security.

Federal Aviation Agency (FAA)—Established in 1958 to regulate, promote, and develop air commerce in a safe manner. FAA was also given the responsibility of operating the airway system and consolidating all research and development of air navigation facilities.

Federal Aviation Reauthorization Act of 1996—Authorized the extension of AIP funding through 1998. Various changes were made to the formula computation of primary and cargo entitlements, state apportionment, and discretionary set-asides.

Federal Inspection Services (FIS)—Conducts customs and immigration services including passport inspection, inspection of baggage, and collection of duties on certain imported items, and sometimes inspection for agricultural materials, illegal drugs, or other restricted items.

federal letters of intent (LOI)—Issued by the FAA for projects that will significantly enhance systemwide airport capacity.

final approach areas—Areas of defined dimensions protected for aircraft executing instrument approaches.

final approach (IFR)—The flight path of an aircraft which is inbound to the airport on an approved final instrument approach course, beginning at the final approach fix or point and extending to the airport or the point where circling for landing or missed approach is executed.

final approach (VFR)—A flight path, in the traffic pattern, of a landing aircraft in the direction of landing along the extended runway centerline from the base leg to the runway.

final controller—That controller providing final approach guidance utilizing radar equipment.

Final Monitor Aid (FMA)—The FMA is a high-resolution color display that is equipped with the controller-alert hardware and software that is used in the PRM system.

financial plan—An economic evaluation of the entire master plan development including revenues and expenditures.

finger—A roofed structure, with or without sidewalls, extending from the main terminal building or its concourse to the aircraft loading positions.

flareout—That portion of a landing maneuver in which the rate of descent is reduced to lessen the impact of landing.

flexible pavement—A pavement structure consisting of a bituminous surface course, a base course, and in most cases, a subbase course.

flight advisory service—Advice and information provided by a facility to assist pilots in the safe conduct of flight and aircraft movement.

Flight Advisory Weather Service (FAWS)—Flight advisory and aviation forecast service provided by the National Weather Service.

Federal Information Service (FIS)—A ground-based data server and data links to provide a variety of nonoperational control information to the cockpit such as weather and traffic information, special-use airspace status, notices to airment, and obstruction updates.

flight interface—As used in the passenger handling system, the link between the passenger processing activities and the flight.

flight plan—Specified information relating to the intended flight of an aircraft that is filed orally or in writing with air traffic control. (FAR Part 1)

Flight Schedule Monitor (FSM)—A primary component of the collaborative decision-making (CDM) system which collects and displays arrival information, retrieves real-time demand and schedule information, and monitors ground delay performance.

Flight Service Station (FSS)—A central operations facility in the national flight advisory system utilizing data interchange facilities for the collection and dissemination of NOTAM, weather, and administrative data and providing preflight and inflight advisory service and other services to pilots via air/ground communication facilities.

flight time—The time from the moment the aircraft first moves under its own power for the purpose of flight until the moment it comes to rest at the next point of landing ("block-to-block" time). (FAR Part 1)

flow control—Restriction applied by ATC to the flow of air traffic to keep elements of the common system, such as airports or airways, from becoming saturated.

free flight—A concept for safe and efficient flight operating capability under instrument flight rules (IFR) in which the operators have the freedom to select their path and speed in real time.

fuel flowage fees—Fees levied by the airport operator per gallon of aviation gasoline and jet fuel sold at the airport.

gate arrival—A centralized terminal building layout that is aimed at reducing the walking distance by bringing the automobile as close as possible to the aircraft.

gate position—A designated space or position on an apron for an aircraft to remain parked while loading or unloading passengers and cargo.

general aviation—That portion of civil aviation that encompasses all facets of aviation except air carriers holding a certificate of convenience and necessity from the Civil Aeronautics Board, and large aircraft commercial operators.

general aviation airports—Those airports with fewer than 2,500 annual enplaned passengers and those used exclusively by private and business aircraft not providing common-carrier passenger service.

general aviation itinerant operations—Takeoffs and landings of civil aircraft (exclusive of air carrier) operating on other than local flights.

general concept evaluation—A set of general considerations that an airport planner uses to evaluate and select among alternative concepts in a preliminary fashion prior to any detailed design and development.

general obligation bonds—Bonds that are issued by states, municipalities, and other general-purpose governments and backed by the full faith, credit, and taxing power of the issuing government agency.

general utility (GU) airport—Accommodates all general aviation aircraft.

glideslope transmitter—An ILS navigation facility in the terminal area electronic navigation system, providing vertical guidance for aircraft during approach and landing by radiating a directional pattern of VHF radio waves modulated by two signals that, when received with equal intensity, are displayed by compatible airborne equipment as an "on-path" indication.

Global Positioning System (GPS)—A satellite-based navigation system that will enhance user-preferred routing, reduce separation standards, and increase access to airports under instrument meteorological conditions (IMC) through more precision approaches.

ground access capacity—Existing and planned highway and mass transit systems in the area of the airport.

ground controlled approach (GCA)—A radar landing system operated from the ground by air traffic control personnel transmitting instructions to the pilot by radio. Approach may be conducted with surveillance radar only or with both surveillance and precision approach radar.

grounds chief—Responsible for assuring that the grounds are maintained in good repair and that the landscape is adequately maintained.

guidance light facility (GDL)—A lighting facility in the terminal area navigation system located in the vicinity of an airport consisting of one or more high-intensity lights to guide a pilot into the takeoff or approach corridor, away from populated areas for safety and noise abatement.

handoff—Passing of control of an aircraft from one controller to another.

height and hazard zoning—Protects the airport and its approaches from obstructions to aviation while restricting certain elements of community growth.

heliport—An area of land, water, or structure used or intended to be used for the landing and takeoff of helicopters. (FAR Part 1)

high-intensity light—A runway or threshold light whose main beam provides a minimum intensity of 12,000 candlepower in white light through a vertical angle of 3° and a horizontal angle of 6°.

holding areas—Run-up areas located at or very near the ends of runways for pilots to make final checks and await final clearance for takeoff.

holding bay—An area where aircraft can be held, or bypassed, to facilitate efficient ground traffic movement.

horizontal surface—A specified portion of a horizontal plane located 150 feet above the established airport elevation which establishes the height above which an object is determined to be an obstruction to air navigation.

hub—A city or a standard metropolitan statistical area requiring aviation services and classified by each community's percentage of the total enplaned passengers in scheduled service of certain domestic certificated route air carriers.

hydroplaning—The condition in which moving aircraft tires are separated from a pavement surface by a water or liquid rubber film or by steam, resulting in a derogation of mechanical braking effectiveness.

IFR airport—An airport with an authorized instrument approach procedure.

IFR conditions—Weather conditions below the minimum for flight under visual flight rules. (FAR Part 1)

ILS Category I—An ILS that provides acceptable guidance information from the coverage limits of the ILS to the point at which the localizer course line intersects the glide path at a height of 100 feet above the horizontal plane containing the runway threshold. A Category I ILS supports landing minima as low as 200 feet HAT and 1,800 RVR.

ILS Category II—An ILS that provides acceptable guidance information from the coverage limits of the ILS to the point at which the localizer course line intersects the glide path at a height of 50 feet above the horizontal plane containing the runway threshold. A Category II ILS supports landing minima as low as 100 feet HAT and 1,200 RVR.

ILS Category III—An ILS that provides acceptable guidance information from the coverage limits of the ILS with no decision height specified above the horizontal plane containing the runway threshold. See *ILS-CAT III A, B, C operations.*

ILS-CAT III A operation—Operation, with no decision height limitation, to and along the surface of the runway with a runway visual range not less than 700 feet.

ILS-CAT III B operation—Operation, with no decision height limitation, to and along the surface of the runway without reliance on external visual reference; and, subsequently, taxiing with external visual reference with a runway visual range not less than 150 feet.

ILS-CAT III C operation—Operation, with no decision height limitation, to and along the surface of the runway and taxiways without reliance on external visual reference.

inactive airport—An airport where all flying activities have ceased yet has remained in an acceptable state of repair for civil use and is identifiable from the air as an airport.

Initial Conflict Probe (ICP)—Provides controllers with the ability to identify potential separation conflicts up to 20 minutes in advance, and to do this with greater precision and accuracy.

inner marker (IM)—An ILS navigational facility in the terminal area navigation system located between the middle marker and the end of the ILS runway, transmitting a 75 megahertz fan-shaped radiation pattern modulated at 3,000 hertz, keyed at six dots per second and received by compatible airborne equipment indicating to the pilot, both aurally and visually, that the aircraft is directly over the facility at an altitude of 100 feet on the final ILS approach, providing the pilot is on the glide path.

in-runway lighting—A lighting system consisting of flush or semiflush lights placed in the runway pavement in specified patterns.

instrument approach—An approach to an airport, with intent to land, by an aircraft flying in accordance with an IFR flight plan.

instrument approach runway—A runway served by electronic aid providing at least directional guidance adequate for a straight-in approach.

instrument flight rules (IFR)—FAR rules that govern the procedures for conducting instrument flight. (FAR Part 91)

instrument landing system (ILS)—A system that provides, in the aircraft, the lateral, longitudinal, and vertical guidance necessary for a landing.

instrument meteorological conditions (IMC)—Meteorological conditions expressed in terms of visibility and ceiling less than the minimum specified for visual meteorological conditions.

instrument runway—A runway equipped with electronic and visual navigation aids and for which a straight-in (precision or nonprecision) approach procedure has been approved.

integrated airport system planning—As defined in the Airport and Airway Improvement Act of 1982, "the initial as well as continuing development for planning purposes of information and guidance to determine the extent, type, nature, location, and timing of airport development needed in a specific area to establish a viable, balanced, and integrated system of public use airports."

Integrated Terminal Weather System (ITWS)—A fully automated weather-prediction system installed at ARTCCs that will give both air traffic personnel and pilots better information on near-term weather hazards in the airspace within 60 nm of an airport.

Intermodalism—To improve the speed, reliability, and cost-effectiveness of the country's overall transportation system by integrating transportation strategy to promote intermodal exchanges among highway, railway, waterway, and air transportation.

international airport—(1) An airport of entry that has been designated by the Secretary of Treasury or Commissioner of Customs as an international airport for customs service. (2) A landing rights airport at which specific permission to land must be obtained from customs authorities in advance of contemplated use. (3) Airports designated under the Convention of International Civil Aviation as an airport for use by international commercial air transport and/or international general aviation. (4) As pertaining to ICAO facilitation, any airport designated by the contracting state in whose territory it is situated as an airport of entry and departure for international air traffic, where the formalities incident to customs, immigration, public health, animal and plant quarantine and similar procedures are carried out.

intersecting runways—Two or more runways that cross or meet within their lengths.

itinerant operations—All aircraft arrivals and departures other than local operations.

jet noise—The noise generated externally to a jet engine in the turbulent jet exhaust.

Joint Automated Weather Observation System (JAWOS)—Automatically gathers local weather data and distributes it to other air traffic control facilities and to the National Weather Service.

joint-use airport—An airport owned by the military, a public body, or both, where an agreement exists for joint civil-military fixed-based aviation operations.

judgmental forecasts—Forecasts based on intuition and subjective evaluations by an individual who is closely acquainted with the factors related to the variable being forecast.

Kelly Act of 1925—Authorized the Postmaster General to enter into contracts with private persons or companies for the transportation of the mail by air.

landing area—Any locality, either on land or water, including airports, heliports, and STOLports, that is used or intended to be used for the landing and takeoff or surface maneuvering of aircraft, whether or not facilities are provided for the shelter, servicing, or repair of aircraft, or for receiving or discharging of passengers or cargo.

landing rights airport—See *international airport.*

landing roll—The distance from the point of touchdown to the point where the aircraft can be brought to a stop, or exit the runway.

landing strip—A term formerly used to designate (1) the graded area upon which the runway was symmetrically located and (2) the graded area suitable for the takeoff and landing of airplanes where a paved runway was not provided.

landing strip lighting—Lines or rows of lights located along the edges of the designated landing and takeoff path within the strip. See *landing strip.*

landside operations—Those parts of the airport designed to serve passengers including the terminal buildings, vehicular circular drive, and parking facilities.

land use plan—Shows on-airport land uses as developed by the airport sponsor under the master plan effort and off-airport land uses as developed by surrounding communities.

land use zoning—Zoning by cities, towns, or counties restricting the use of land to specific commercial or noncommercial activities.

large aircraft—Aircraft of more than 12,500 pounds maximum certificated takeoff weight. (FAR Part 1)

large hubs—Those airports that account for at least 1 percent of the total passenger enplanements.

Lead-in Light Facility (LDIN)—A facility in the terminal area navigation system providing special light guidance to aircraft in approach patterns or landing procedures. Facility configuration consists of any number of flashers so located as to visually guide an aircraft through an approach corridor, bypassing high-density residential, commercial, or obstruction areas.

lighted airport—An airport where runway and associated obstruction lighting is available from sunset to sunrise or during periods of reduced visibility or on request of the pilot.

linear or curvilinear terminal—A type of simple terminal layout that is repeated in a linear extension to provide additional apron frontage, more gates, and more room within the terminal for passenger processing.

line-item budget—The most detailed form of budget and used quite extensively at the large commercial airports. Budgets are established for each item and often adjusted to take into consideration changes in volume of activity.

Local Area Augmentation System (LAAS)—A differential GPS system that provides localized measurement correction signals to basic GPS signals to improve navigation accuracy, integrity, continuity, and availability.

localizer beacon—An ILS navigation facility in the terminal area electronic navigation system, providing horizontal guidance to the runway centerline for aircraft during approach and landing by radiating a directional pattern of VHF radio waves modulated by two signals that, when received with equal intensity, are displayed by compatible airborne equipment as an "on-course" indication, and when received in unequal intensity are displayed as an "off-course" indication.

local operations—As pertaining to air traffic operations, aircraft operating in the local traffic pattern or within sight of the tower; aircraft known to be departing for, or arriving from, flight in local practice areas located within a 20-mile radius of the control tower; aircraft executing simulated instrument approaches or low passes at the airport.

local traffic—Aircraft operating in the local traffic pattern or within sight of the tower, or aircraft known to be departing for or arriving from flight in local practice areas, or aircraft executing simulated instrument approaches at the airport.

local VFR flight plan—Specific information provided to air traffic service units, relative to the intended flight of an aircraft under visual flight rules within a specific local area.

location map—Shown on the airport layout plan drawing, it depicts the airport, cities, railroads, major highways, and roads within 20 to 50 miles of the airport.

long-term parking—Designed for travelers who leave their vehicles at the airport while they travel.

low-intensity light—A runway or threshold light from which the light distribution through 360° of azimuth and a selected 6° in the vertical is not less than 10 candlepower in white light.

Low-Level Wind Shear Alert System (LLWAS)—Provides the air traffic control tower with information on wind conditions near the runway. It consists of an array of anemometers that read wind velocity and direction around the airport and signal the sudden changes that indicate wind shear.

lump-sum appropriation—The simplest form of budget and generally only used at small GA airports. There are no specific restrictions as to how the money should be spent.

majority-in-interest clauses—Found in some airport use agreements that give the airlines accounting for a majority of traffic at an airport the opportunity to review and approve or veto capital projects that would entail significant increases in the rates and fees they pay for the use of airport facilities.

management contract—An agreement under which a firm is hired to operate a particular service on behalf of the airport.

manager of public relations—Responsible for all public relations activities including the development of advertising and publicity concerning the airport.

marking—On airports, a pattern of contrasting colors placed on the pavement, turf, or other usable surface by paint or other means to provide specific information to aircraft pilots, and sometimes to operators of ground vehicles, on the movement areas.

medium hubs—Those airports that account for between 0.25 and 1 percent of the total passenger enplanements.

metering—Regulating the arrival time of aircraft in the terminal area so as not to exceed a given acceptance rate.

Microwave Landing Systems (MLS)—An instrument approach and landing system operating in the microwave frequencies (5.0–5.25 GHz/15.4–15.7 GHz) that provides precision guidance in azimuth, elevation, and distance measurement.

middle marker (MM)—An ILS navigation facility in the terminal area navigation system located approximately 3,500 feet from the runway edge on the extended centerline, transmitting a 75-MHz fan-shaped radiation pattern, modulated at 1,300 Hz, keyed alternately dot and dash, and received by compatible airborne equipment, indicating to the pilot both aurally and visually, that he or she is passing over the facility.

Military Airport Program (MAP)—A program established as a funding set aside under the Airport Improvement Program (AIP) to provide money for airport master planning and capital development for military airfields transitioning to civilian airports.

mobile lounge or transporter—Used to transport passengers to and from the terminal building to aircraft parked on the apron.

mode S data link—An addition to the ATCRBS transponder that permits direct, automatic exchange of digitally encoded information between the ground controller and individual aircraft.

moving target detection—An electronic device that will permit radar scope presentation only from targets that are in motion. A partial remedy for ground clutter.

multiplier effect—Revenues generated by the airport are channeled throughout the community.

municipally operated airport—An airport owned by a city and run as a department of the city, with policy direction by the city council and, in some cases, by a separate airport commission or advisory board.

National Airport System Plan (NASP)—A plan specifying in terms of general location and type of development the projects considered by the administrator to be necessary to provide a system of public airports adequate to anticipate and meet the needs of civil aeronautics. Replaced by the NPIAS. See *criteria for inclusion in NPIAS*.

National Airspace Redesign (NAR)—A large-scale analysis of the national airspace structure that began by identifying problems in the congested airspace of New York and New Jersey. The goal is to ensure that the design and management of the national airspace system is prepared as the system evolves toward free flight.

National Environmental Policy Act of 1969—Requires the preparation of detailed environmental statements for all major federal airport development actions significantly affecting the quality of the environment.

NPIAS levels of need—The NPIAS relates the airport system improvements to three levels of need: Level I—maintain the airport system in its current condition, Level II—bring the system up to current design standards, and Level III—expand the system.

National Plan of Integrated Airport Systems (NPIAS)—The Airport and Airway Improvement Act of 1982 required the FAA to develop the NPIAS by September 1984. The legislation called for the identification of national airport system needs, including development costs in the short and long run.

National Route Program (NRP)—Gives airlines and pilots increased flexibility in choosing their routes. This flexibility allows airlines to plan and fly the most cost-effective routes and increases the efficiency of the aviation system.

national system of airports—The inventory of selected civil airports that are highly correlated with those aviation demands most consistent with the national interest.

National Transportation Safety Board (NTSB)—Created by the act that established the Department of Transportation to determine the cause of transportation accidents and review on appeal the suspension or revocation of any certificates or licenses issued by the Secretary of Transportation.

navaid—Any facility used in, available for use in, or designated for use in aid of air navigation, including lights; any apparatus or equipment for disseminating weather information, for signaling, for radio direction finding, or for radio or other electronic communication; and any other structure or mechanism having a similar purpose for guiding or controlling flight in the air or the landing or takeoff of aircraft.

navigable airspace—Airspace at and above the minimum flight altitudes prescribed in the FARs, including airspace needed for safe takeoff and landing. (FAR Part 1)

Next-Generation Air/Ground Communications (NEXCOM)—A digital radio system designed to alleviate the problems associated with the current analog-based communication system.

noise compatibility programs—Outlines measures to improve airport land use compatibility.

noise exposure maps—Identify noise contours and land use incompatibilities and are useful in evaluating noise impacts and discouraging incompatible development.

noise level—For airborne sound, the same as sound level, unless otherwise specified.

nondepreciable investment items—Those assets such as the cost of land acquisition that have a permanent value even if the airport site is converted to other uses.

nonhub primary airports—Those airports that enplane less than 0.05 percent of all commercial passenger enplanements but at least 10,000 annually.

noninstrument runway—A runway intended for the operation of aircraft using visual approach procedures. See *visual runway*.

nonprecision approach procedure—A standard instrument approach procedure in which no electronic glideslope is provided. (FAR Part 1)

nonprecision instrument runway—A runway having an existing instrument approach procedure utilizing air navigation facilities with only horizontal guidance for which a straight-in nonprecision instrument approach procedure has been approved.

nose-in, angled nose-in, angled nose-out, and parallel parking— Aircraft parking positions at various angles with respect to the terminal building. The nose-in parking position is the most frequently used at major airports.

notice to airmen (NOTAM)— A notice containing information (not known sufficiently in advance to publicize by other means) concerning the establishment, condition, or change in any component (facility, service, or procedure) of, or hazard in, the National Airspace System, the timely knowledge of which is essential to personnel concerned with flight operations.

objective of the airport master plan— To provide guidelines for future development of the airport which will satisfy aviation demand and be compatible with the environment, community development, other modes of transportation, and other airports.

obstruction light— A light, or one of a group of lights, usually red, mounted on a surface structure or natural terrain to warn pilots of the presence of a flight hazard; either an incandescent lamp with a red globe or a strobe light.

obstruction marking/lighting— Distinctive marking and lighting to provide a uniform means for indicating the presence of obstructions.

Office of Management and Budget Circular A-95— Prior to July 1982, required that designated regional agencies review airport projects before federal grants were given.

O'Hare Agreement— An agreement established in the 1950s between the City of Chicago and the airlines that established a precedent in revenue bond financing which pledged the airlines to meet any shortfall in income needed to pay off the principal and interest on the bonds.

open-V runways— Two intersecting runways whose extended centerlines intersect beyond their respective thresholds.

operating statement— Records an airport's revenues and expenses over a particular time period (quarterly and annually).

operational activity forecasts— Includes forecasts of operations by major user categories (air carrier, commuter, general aviation, and military).

organization chart— Shows the formal authority relationships between superiors and subordinates at various levels, as well as the formal channels of communication within the organization.

other commercial service airports— Commercial service airports enplaning 2,500 to 10,000 passengers annually.

outer fix— A fix in the destination terminal area, other than the approach fix, to which aircraft are normally cleared by an air route traffic control center or an approach control facility, and from which aircraft are cleared to the approach fix or final approach course.

outer marker (OM)—An ILS navigation facility in the terminal area navigation system located 4 to 7 miles from the runway edge on the extended centerline transmitting a 75-megahertz fan-shaped radiation pattern, modulated at 400 hertz, keyed at two dashes per second, and received by compatible airborne equipment indicating to the pilot, both aurally and visually, that the aircraft is passing over the facility and can begin its final approach.

overrun—To run off the end of the runway after touching down on the runway.

overrun area—In military aviation exclusively, that area beyond the end of the designated runway with a stabilized surface of the same width as the runway and centered on the extended runway centerline.

parallel runways—Two or more runways at the same airport whose centerlines are parallel.

parallel taxiways—Two taxiways that are parallel to one another that allow traffic to move simultaneously in different directions at busy airports.

parking apron—An apron intended to accommodate parked aircraft.

Part 150 of the Federal Aviation Regulations—Established a system for measuring aviation noise in the community and for providing information about land uses that are normally compatible with various levels of noise exposure.

passenger facility charges (PFCs)—The Airway Safety and Capacity Expansion Act of 1990 authorized the imposition of PFCs at commercial service airports. The airport operator may propose collecting $1, $2, or $3 per enplaned passenger, domestic or foreign, to fund approved airport capital projects.

passenger handling system—A series of links or processes that a passenger goes through in transferring from one mode of transportation to another.

passenger movers—Designed to speed passenger movement through the terminal. Includes buses, mobile lounges, moving sidewalks, and automated guideway systems.

passenger processing link—As used in the passenger handling system, the link that accomplishes the major processing activities required to prepare the passenger for using air transportation.

pavement grooving—The mechanical serration of a pavement surface to provide escape paths for water and slush, to promote improved aircraft mechanical braking effectiveness.

pavement maintenance—Any regular or recurring work necessary on a continuing basis to preserve existing airport facilities in good condition, any work involved in the care or cleaning of existing airport facilities, and any incidental or minor repair work on existing airport facilities.

pavement management system—Evaluates the present condition of a pavement and predicts its future condition through the use of a pavement condition index.

pavement rehabilitation—Work required to preserve, repair, or restore the physical integrity of the pavement—for example, a structural overlay (laying more asphalt on the runway surface).

pavement structure—The combination of runway base and subbase courses and surface course that transmits the traffic load to the subgrade.

pavement subgrade—The upper part of the soil, natural or constructed, that supports the loads transmitted by the runway pavement structure.

pavement surface course—The top course of a pavement, usually portland cement concrete or bituminous concrete, that supports the traffic load.

personnel manager—Responsible for administering the airport personnel program.

pier finger terminal—A type of terminal layout evolving in the 1950s when gate concourses (fingers) were added to simple terminal buildings.

Planning Grant Program (PGP)—A federal aid to airports program established under the Airport and Airway Development Act of 1970 for approved airport planning and development project costs.

port authorities—Legally chartered institutions with the status of public corporations that operate a variety of publicly owned facilities, such as harbors, airports, toll roads, and bridges.

practical capacity—The number of operations (takeoffs and landings) that can be accommodated with no more than a given amount of delay, usually expressed in terms of maximum acceptable average delay.

precision approach—A standard instrument approach using a precision approach procedure. See *precision approach procedure.*

precision approach procedure—A standard instrument approach procedure in which an electronic glideslope is provided, such as ILS and PAR. (FAR Part 1)

precision approach radar (PAR)—A radar facility in the terminal air traffic control system used to detect and display, with a high degree of accuracy, azimuth, range, and elevation of an aircraft on the final approach to a runway.

precision approach runway—See *precision instrument runway.*

precision instrument runway—A runway having an existing instrument approach procedure utilizing an instrument landing system (ILS) or a precision approach radar (PAR). It also means a runway for which a precision approach system is planned and is so indicated by an FAA approved airport layout plan; a military service approved military airport layout plan; any other FAA planning document, or military service military airport planning document. (FAR Part 77)

Precision Runway Monitor (PRM)—The PRM system consists of an improved monopulse antenna system that provides high azimuth and range accuracy and higher data rates than the current terminal ASR systems. It will improve the accuracy of monitoring simultaneous approaches to parallel runways.

primary airports—Public-use commercial airports enplaning at least 0.01 percent of all passengers enplaned annually at U.S. airports.

primary radar—See *search radar.*

primary surface—A rectangular surface longitudinally centered about a runway. Its width is a variable dimension and it usually extends 200 feet beyond each end of the runway. The elevation of any point on this surface coincides with the elevation of its nearest point on the runway centerline or extended runway centerline.

primary taxiway system—Taxiways that provide aircraft access from runways to aprons and the service areas.

privatization—Shifting of government functions and responsibilities, in whole or in part, to the private sector.

public airport—An airport for public use, publicly owned and under control of a public agency.

public relations—The management function that attempts to create goodwill for an organization and its products, services, or ideals, with groups of people who can affect its present and future welfare.

public-use airport—An airport open to the public without prior permission and without restrictions within the physical capacities of available facilities.

quadradar—Ground radar equipment named for its four presentations: (1) surveillance, (2) airport surface detection, (3) height finding, and (4) precision approach.

radar (radio detection and ranging)—A device that, by measuring the time interval between transmission and reception of radio pulses and correlating the angular orientation of the radiated antenna beam or beams in azimuth and/or elevation, provides information on range, azimuth, and/or elevation of objects in the path of the transmitted pulses.

Radar Approach Control (RAPCON)—A joint-use air traffic control facility, located at a U.S. Air Force Base, utilizing surveillance and precision approach radar equipment in conjunction with air/ground communication equipment, providing for the safe and expeditious movement of air traffic within the controlled airspace of that facility.

radar beacon system—A radar system in which the object to be detected is fitted with cooperative equipment in the form of a radio receiver/transmitter (transponder). Radio pulses transmitted from the searching transmitter/receiver (interrogator) site are received in the cooperative equipment and used to trigger a distinctive transmission from the transponder. This latter transmission, rather than a reflected signal, is then received back at the transmitter/receiver site.

ramp—A defined area, on a land airport, intended to accommodate aircraft for purposes of loading or unloading passengers or cargo, refueling, parking, or maintenance.

regional airport planning—Air transportation planning for the region as a whole including all airports in the region, both large and small.

reliever airports—A subset of general aviation airports that has the function of relieving congestion at primary commercial airports and providing more access for general aviation to the overall community.

relocated threshold—An area preceding the runway arrows unusable for takeoff or landing.

remote parking—Consists of long-term parking lots located away from the airport terminal buildings. Buses or vans are available to transport passengers to the terminal.

residual-cost approach—The airlines collectively assume significant financial risk by agreeing to pay any costs of running the airport that are not allocated to other users or covered by nonairline sources of revenue.

revenue bonds—Bonds that are payable solely from the revenues derived from the operation of a facility that was constructed or acquired with the proceeds of the bonds.

rigid pavement—A pavement structure consisting of portland cement concrete that may or may not include a subbase course.

RNAV—A generic term that refers to any instrument navigation performed outside of conventional routes defined by the ground-based navigational aids or by intersections formed by two navigational aids.

rotorcraft—A heavier-than-air aircraft that depends principally for its support in flight on the lift generated by one or more rotors. (FAR Part 1)

runway—A defined rectangular area on a land airport prepared for the landing and takeoff run of aircraft along its length.

runway alignment indicator light (RAIL)—This airport lighting facility in the terminal area consists of five or more sequenced flashing lights installed on the extended centerline of the runway. The maximum spacing between lights is 200 feet, extending out from 1,600 feet to 3,000 feet from the runway threshold. Even when collocated with ALS, RAIL will be identified as a separate facility.

runway bearing—The magnetic or true bearing of the runway centerline as measured from magnetic or true north.

runway capacity—The number of aircraft operations that can be accommodated by a runway without undue delay to aircraft. Undue delays are when delays to departures average 4 minutes during the normal peak 2-hour period of the day.

runway centerline lighting system—The runway centerline lighting system consists of single lights installed at uniform intervals along the runway centerline so as to provide a continuous lighting reference from threshold to threshold.

runway clear zone—An area at ground level whose perimeter conforms to the runway's innermost approach surface projected vertically. It begins at the end of the primary surface and it terminates directly below the point or points where the approach surface reaches a height of 50 feet above the elevation of the runway end.

runway configuration—Layout or design of a runway or runways, where operations on the particular runway or runways being used at a given time are mutually dependent. A large airport can have two or more runway configurations operating simultaneously.

Runway Configuration Management—A software program that has been under development at Chicago O'Hare since 1980 that will assist controllers in establishing the most efficient combination of arrival and departure runways for given conditions of weather and demand.

runway contamination—Deposition or presence of dirt, grease, rubber, or other materials on runway surfaces that adversely affect normal aircraft operation or that chemically attack the pavement surface.

runway direction number—A whole number to the nearest one-tenth of the magnetic bearing of the runway and measured in degrees clockwise from magnetic north.

runway end identification lights (REIL)—An airport lighting facility in the terminal area navigation system consisting of one flashing white high-intensity light installed at each approach end corner of a runway and directed toward the approach zone, which enables the pilot to identify the threshold of a usable runway.

runway environment—The runway threshold or approach lighting aids or other markings identifiable with the runway.

runway gradient (effective)—The average gradient consisting of the difference in elevation of the two ends of the runway divided by the runway length may be used provided that no intervening point on the runway profile lies more than 5 feet above or below a straight line joining the two ends of the runway. In excess of 5 feet, the runway profile will be segmented and aircraft data will be applied for each segment separately.

runway grooving—One-quarter-inch grooves spaced approximately $1\frac{1}{4}$ inch apart made in the runway surface designed to provide better drainage, and furnish escape routes for water under the tire footprint to prevent hydroplaning.

runway length—landing—The measured length from the threshold to the end of the runway.

runway length—physical—The actual measured length of the runway.

runway length—takeoff—The measured length from where the takeoff is designated to begin to the end of the runway.

runway lights—Lights having a prescribed angle of emission used to define the lateral limits of a runway. Runway light intensity may be controllable or preset. Lights are uniformly spaced at intervals of approximately 200 feet.

runway markings—(1) Basic marking—markings on runways used for operations under visual flight rules, consisting of centerline marking and runway direction numbers, and if required, letters. (2) Instrument marking—markings on runways served by nonvisual navigation aids and intended for landings under instrument weather conditions, consisting of basic marking plus threshold marking. (3) All-weather marking—markings on runways served by nonvisual precision approach aids and on runways having special operational requirements, consisting of instrument markings plus landing zone marking and side strips.

runway occupancy time (ROT)—The time from when an approaching aircraft crosses the threshold until it turns off the runway or from when a departing aircraft takes the active runway until it clears the departure end.

runway orientation—The magnetic bearing of the centerline of the runway.

runway safety area—Cleared, drained, graded, and usually turfed area abutting the edges of the usable runway and symmetrically located about the runway. It extends 200 feet beyond each runway end. The width varies according to the type of runway. (Formerly called "landing strip.")

runway strength—The assumed ability of a runway to support aircraft of a designated gross weight for each of single-wheel, dual-wheel, and dual-tandem-wheel gear types.

runway surface lighting—Also referred to as "in-runway lighting," consisting essentially of touchdown zone (narrow gauge) lights, runway centerline lights, and exit taxiway turnoff lights, installed in the pavement.

runway threshold marking—Markings so placed as to indicate the longitudinal limits of that portion of the runway usable for landing.

runway visibility—Visibility determined by a transmissometer associated with the instrument runways or by an observer stationed at the approach end of a runway.

runway visual range (RVR)—An instrumentally derived value that represents the horizontal distance a pilot can see down the runway from the approach end; it is based on the sighting of either high-intensity runway lights or on the visual contrast of other targets, whichever yields the greater visual range.

satellite terminals—A type of terminal layout in which all passenger processing is done in a single terminal that is connected by concourses to one or more satellite structures. The satellite generally has a common waiting room that serves a number of gate positions.

scheduled service—Transport service operated over routes based on published flight schedules, including extra sections and related non-revenue flights.

search radar—A radar system in which a minute portion of a radio pulse transmitted from a site is reflected off an object and then received back at that site.

secondary radar—See *radar beacon system.*

secondary runway—A runway that provides additional wind coverage or capacity to expedite traffic handling.

secondary taxiway system—Taxiways that provide aircraft access from runways to hangars and tiedown areas not commonly associated with itinerant and service areas.

security chief—Enforces interior security, traffic, and safety rules and regulations and participates in law enforcement activities at the airport.

segmented circle—A basic marking device used to aid pilots in locating airports, and that provides a central location for such indicators and signal devices as may be required.

self-liquidating general obligation bonds—Like general obligation bonds, these bonds are backed by the full faith, credit, and taxing power of the issuing government body; however, there is enough cash flow from the operation of the facility to cover the debt service and other costs of operation that the debt is not legally considered as part of the community's debt limitation.

semiflush light—A light mounted in pavement capable of rollover by aircraft.

sequencing—Specifying the exact order in which aircraft will take off or land.

Set-aside funds—Available to any eligible airport sponsor and allocated according to congressionally mandated requirements for a number of different set-aside subcategories such as minimum allocations to all 50 states, the District of Columbia, and insular areas on the basis of land area and population.

short takeoff and landing (STOL) aircraft—An aircraft that, at some weight within its approved range of STOL operating weight, is capable of operating from a STOL runway in compliance with the applicable STOL characteristics, airworthiness, operations, noise, and pollution standards.

short-term parking—Usually located close to terminal buildings for motorists picking up or dropping off travelers. These motorists generally remain at the airport less than 3 hours.

shoulder—As pertaining to airports, an area adjacent to the edge of a paved surface so prepared to provide a transition between the pavement and the adjacent surface for aircraft running off the pavement, for drainage, and sometimes for blast protection.

simple terminal—A type of gate arrival terminal layout that consists of a common waiting and ticketing area with several exits onto a small aircraft parking apron.

simultaneous offset instrument approaches—An attempt to increase airport capacity and reduce delay at airports with closely spaced parallel runways by allowing pilots to fly a straight-but-angled instrument (and possibly autopilot) approach until descending below the cloud cover.

single runway—An airport having one runway.

site selection—Second phase of the airport master plan that evaluates airspace, environmental factors, community growth, airport ground access, availability of utilities, land costs, and site development costs.

slot—A block of time allocated to an airport user to perform an aircraft operation (takeoff or landing).

small aircraft—Aircraft of 12,500 pounds or less maximum certificated takeoff weight. (FAR Part 1)

small hubs—Those airports that enplane 0.05 percent to 0.25 percent of the total passenger enplanements.

spacing—Establishing and maintaining the appropriate interval between successive aircraft, as dictated by considerations of safety, uniformity of traffic flow, and efficiencies of runway use.

spalling—Fractured edges in and around the joint area of concrete due to the tremendous pressures generated during expansion and contraction of the slabs.

special-use airspace—Airspace controlled by the Department of Defense.

Standard Terminal Automation Replacement System (STARS)—Will replace outdated air traffic control computers with twenty-first century systems at nine large consolidated TRACONs and approximately 173 FAA and 60 DOD terminal radar approach control sites across the country.

state aviation system plans (SASP)—Plan for the development of airports within a state.

State Block Grant Program—Under this program, selected states are given responsibility of AIP grants at other than primary airports. Each state is responsible for determining which locations will receive funds within the state.

state-operated airports—Airports generally managed by the state's department of transportation.

STOLport—An airport specifically designed for STOL aircraft, separate from conventional airport facilities.

straight-in approach (IFR)—An instrument approach wherein final approach is commenced without first having executed a procedure turn. (Not necessarily completed with a straight-in landing.)

straight-in approach (VFR)—Entry into the traffic pattern by interception of the extended runway centerline without executing any other portion of the traffic pattern.

stub taxiway—A short connecting taxiway to an airport facility that serves as the only connection with the remaining airport complex.

subdivision regulations—Provisions prohibiting residential construction in intense noise exposure areas.

Surface Movement Advisor (SMA)—A system developed by the FAA and NASA to promote the sharing of dynamic information among airlines, airport operators, and air traffic controllers in order to control the efficient flow of aircraft and vehicles on the airport surface.

taxiway—A defined path, usually paved, over which aircraft can taxi from one part of an airport to another.

taxiway centerline lighting—A system of flush or semiflush in-pavement lights indicating the taxiway centerline.

taxiway safety area—A cleared, drained, and graded area, symmetrically located about the extended taxiway centerline and adjacent to the end of the taxiway safety area.

taxiway turnoff lighting—Single lights installed in the pavement at uniform intervals to define the path of aircraft travel from the runway centerline to a point on the taxiway.

taxiway turnoff markings—Signs or lights along the runways, taxiways, and ramp surfaces of an airport used to assist a pilot in finding his or her way.

technological improvements—Refers to new devices and equipment as well as operational concepts and procedures designed to relieve congestion, increase capacity, or reduce delay.

terminal apron—An area provided for parking and positioning of aircraft in the vicinity of the terminal building for loading and unloading.

terminal area—The area used or intended to be used for such facilities as terminal and cargo buildings, gates, hangars, shops, and other service buildings; automobile parking, airport motels and restaurants, and garages and vehicle service—facilities used in connection with the airport; and entrance and service roads used by the public within the boundaries of the airport.

terminal area capacity—The ability of the terminal area to accept the passengers, cargo, and aircraft that the airfield accommodates.

terminal building—A building or buildings designed to accommodate the enplaning and deplaning activities of air carrier passengers.

terminal facilities—The airport facilities providing services for air carrier operations which serve as a center for the transfer of passengers and baggage between surface and air transportation.

terminal finger—An extension of the terminal building to provide direct access to a large number of airport terminal apron gate positions.

terminal instrument procedures (TERPS)—Procedures used for conducting independent instrument approaches to converging runways under instrument meteorological conditions.

tetrahedron—A device with four triangular sides that indicates wind direction and that may be used as a landing direction indicator.

T hangar—An aircraft hangar in which aircraft are parked alternately tail to tail, each in the T-shaped space left by the other row of aircraft or aircraft compartments.

3 D UPT Flight Trials Project—An attempt to quantify the savings associated with unrestricted flight.

threshold—The designated beginning of the runway that is available and suitable for the landing of airplanes.

threshold crossing height (TCH)—The height of the straightline extension of the visual or electronic glideslope above the runway threshold.

threshold lights—Lighting arranged symmetrically about the extended centerline of the runway identifying the runway threshold. They emit a fixed green light.

throughput capacity—The rate at which aircraft can be brought into or out of the airfield, without regard to any delay they might experience.

time-series analysis or trend extension—The oldest and in many cases the most widely used method of forecasting air transportation demand. It consists of interpreting the historical sequence of data and applying the interpretation to the immediate future. Historical data are plotted on a graph, and a trend line is drawn.

total operations—All arrivals and departures performed by military, general aviation, and air carrier aircraft.

touchdown—(1) The point at which an aircraft first makes contact with the landing surface. (2) In a precision radar approach, the point on the landing surface toward which the controller issues guidance instructions.

touchdown zone—The area of a runway near the approach end where airplanes normally alight.

touchdown zone lighting—This system in the runway touchdown zone area presents, in plain view, two rows of transverse light bars located symmetrically about the runway centerline. The basic system extends 3,000 feet along the runway.

tower—See *airport traffic control tower*.

Tower Automated Ground Surveillance System (TAGS)—Intended to be used in conjunction with airport surface detection equipment at major airports, it will provide, for transponder-equipped aircraft, a flight identification label alongside the position indicator on the ASDE display.

Traffic Management System (TMS)—A new software that will perform several important functions to increase the efficiency of airport and airspace utilization.

traffic pattern—The traffic flow that is prescribed for aircraft landing at, taxiing on, and taking off from an airport (FAR Part 1). The usual components of a traffic pattern are upwind leg, crosswind leg, downwind leg, base leg, and final approach.

transitional surface—A surface that extends outward and upward from the sides of the primary and approach surfaces normal to the runway centerline that identifies the height limitations on an object before it becomes an obstruction to air navigation.

transition area—Controlled airspace extending upward from 700 feet or more above the surface of the earth when designated in conjunction with an airport for which an instrument approach procedure has been prescribed; or from 1,200 feet or higher above the surface of the earth when designated in conjunction with airway route structures or segments. Unless otherwise limited, transition areas terminate at the base of the overlying controlled airspace.

turnaround—A taxiway adjacent to the runway ends that aircraft use to change direction, hold, or bypass other aircraft.

turning radius—The radius of the arc described by an aircraft in making a self-powered turn, usually given as a minimum.

turnoff taxiway—A taxiway specifically designed to provide aircraft with a means to expedite clearing a runway.

typical peak-hour passenger volume (design volume)—The peak hour of an average day in the peak month that is used as the hourly design volume for terminal space.

undershoot—To touch down short of the point of intended landing.

unicom—Frequencies authorized for aeronautical advisory services to private aircraft. Services available are advisory in nature, primarily concerning the airport services and airport utilization.

upwind leg—A flight path parallel to the landing runway in the direction of landing.

utility airport (or runway)—An airport (or runway) that accommodates small aircraft excluding turbojet powered aircraft.

variance—The differences between actual expenses and the budgeted amount.

vehicle chief—Responsible for the maintenance of all vehicles utilized by the airport.

vertical takeoff and landing (VTOL)—Aircraft that have the capability of vertical takeoff and landing. VTOL aircraft are not limited to helicopters.

VFR airport—An airport without an authorized or planned instrument approach procedure; also, a former airport design category indicating an airport serving small aircraft only and not designed to satisfy the requirements of instrument landing operations.

VFR tower—An airport traffic control tower that does not provide approach control service.

VHF omnidirectional range (VOR)—A radio transmitter facility in the navigation system radiating a VHF radio wave modulated by two signals, the relative phases of which are compared, resolved, and displayed by a compatible airborne receiver to give the pilot a direct indication of bearing relative to the facility.

vibratory (or dynamic) testing—A technique used to measure the strength of a composite pavement system by subjecting it to vibratory load and measuring the amount the pavement responds or deflects under this known load.

vicinity map—Shown on the airport layout plan drawing, it depicts the relationship of the airport to the city or cities, nearby airports, roads, railroads, and built-up areas.

viscous hydroplaning—Occurs when a thin film of oil, dirt, or rubber particles mixes with water and prevents tires from making sure contact with the pavement.

visual approach—An approach wherein an aircraft on an IFR flight plan, operating in VFR conditions under the control of a radar facility and having an air traffic control authorization, may deviate from the prescribed instrument approach procedure and proceed to the airport of destination, served by an operational control tower, by visual reference to the surface.

visual approach indicator (VASI)—An airport lighting facility in the terminal area navigation system used primarily under VFR conditions. It provides vertical visual guidance to aircraft during approach and landing by radiating a directional pattern of high intensity red and white focused light beams that indicate to the pilot that the aircraft is "on path" if the pilot sees red/white, "above path" if white/white, and "below path" if red/red.

visual flight rules (VFR)—Rules that govern the procedures for conducting flight under visual conditions. (FAR Part 91)

visual meteorological conditions (VMC)—Meteorological conditions expressed in terms of visibility and ceiling equal to or better than specified minima.

visual runway—A runway intended solely for the operation of aircraft using visual approach procedures, with no straight-in instrument approach procedure and no instrument designation indicated on an FAA-approved airport layout plan, a military service approved military airport layout plan, or by a planning document submitted to the FAA by competent authority. (FAR Part 77)

vortices—As pertaining to aircraft, circular patterns of air created by the movement of an airfoil through the atmosphere. As an airfoil moves through the atmosphere in sustained flight, an area of high pressure is created beneath it and an area of low pressure is created above it. The air flowing from the high-pressure area to the low-pressure area around and about the tips of the airfoil tends to roll up into two rapidly rotating vortices, cylindrical in shape. These vortices are the most predominant parts of aircraft wake turbulence and their rotational force is dependent upon the wing loading, gross weight, and speed of the generating aircraft.

wake vortex—A phenomenon resulting from the passage of an aircraft through the atmosphere. It is an aerodynamic disturbance that originates at the wingtips and trails in corkscrew fashion behind the aircraft. When used by ATC it includes vortices, thrust stream turbulence, jet wash, propeller wash, and rotor wash.

Weather and Radar Processor (WARP)—Will collect and process weather data from Low-Level Windshear Systems (LLWAS), Next-Generation Weather Radar (NEXRAD), Terminal Doppler Weather Radar (TDWR), and surveillance radar, and disseminate this data to controllers, traffic management specialists, pilots, and meteorologists.

Wide Area Augmentation System (WAAS)—An augmentation of GPS that includes integrity broadcasts, differential corrections, and additional ranging signals; its primary objective is to provide accuracy, integrity, availability, and continuity required to support all phases of flight.

wind cone—A free-rotating fabric truncated cone that, when subjected to air movement, indicates wind direction and wind force.

wind rose—A diagram for a given location showing relative frequency and velocity of wind from all compass directions.

wind shear—Variation of wind speed and wind direction with respect to a horizontal or vertical plane. Low-level shear in the terminal area is a factor in the safe and expeditious landing of aircraft.

wind tee—A T-shaped free-rotating device to indicate wind direction. Sometimes capable of being secured for use as a landing direction indicator.

zero-base budget—Derives from the idea that each program or departmental budget should be prepared from the ground up, or base zero. By calculating the budget from a zero base, all costs are newly developed and reviewed entirely to determine their necessity.

Zulu time (Z)—Time at the Prime Meridian in Greenwich, England.

Abbreviations

AAS	Airport Advisory Service
AC	advisory circular
ADAP	Airport Development Aid Program
ADC	Air Defense Command
ADF	automatic direction finder
ADS	Automated Dependent Surveillance
AERA	advanced en route automation
AID	airport information desk
AIM	Airman's Information Manual
AIP	Airport Improvement Program
AIREP	air report
AIRMET	airmen's meteorological information
ALNOT	alert notice
ALS	approach lighting system
AMASS	Airport Movement Area Safety System
AMIS	aircraft movement information service
AOCNET	Airline Operations Center Network
ARP	airport reference point
ARSR	Air Route Surveillance radar
ARTCC	Air Route Traffic Control Center
ARTS	Automated Radar Terminal System
ASDE	Airport Surface Detection Equipment
ASQP	airline service quality performance
ASR	Airport Surveillance Radar
ATC	air traffic control (FAR Part I)
ATCRBS	Air Traffic Control Radar Beacon System
ATCSCC	ATC Systems Command Center

ATCT	airport traffic control tower
ATIS	Automatic Terminal Information Service
ATOMS	Air traffic Operations Management System
CAA	Civil Aeronautics Administration
CAB	Civil Aeronautics Board
CAT	clear-air turbulence
CDM	Collaborative decision-making
CFCF	central flow control function
CIS	Cockpit Information System
CODAS	Consolidated Operations and Delay Analysis System
CPDLC	Controller-to-Pilot Data Link Communications
CTAS	Center Terminal Radar Approach Control Automation System
DABS	Discrete Address Beacon System
dB	decibel
DF	direction finder
DH	decision height
DME	distance measuring equipment
DOT	Department of Transportation
EFAS	en route flight advisory service
EPNL	effective perceived noise level
F&E	facilities and equipment program
FAA	Federal Aviation Administration
FAR	Federal Aviation Regulations
FAWS	Flight Advisory Weather Service
FIS	Federal Inspection Services
FMA	Final Monitor Aid
FSM	Flight Schedule Monitor
FSS	flight service station
GCA	ground-controlled approach
GDL	guidance light facility

GPS	Global Positioning System
GS	glideslope
HAT	height above touchdown
ICAO	International Civil Aviation Organization
ICP	Initial Conflict Probe
IFR	instrument flight rules (FAR Part 91)
ILS	instrument landing system
IM	inner marker
IMC	instrument meteorological conditions
ITWS	Integrated Terminal Weather System
JAWOS	Joint Automated Weather Observation System
LAAS	Local Area Augmentation System
LDIN	Lead-in Light Facility
LF	low frequency
LOC	ILS localizer
MAP	Military Airport Program
MDA	minimum descent altitude (FAR Part I)
MEA	minimum en route IFR altitude
MLS	Microwave Landing System
MM	middle marker
MOCA	minimum obstruction clearance altitude
MSL	mean sea level
NAFEC	National Aviation Facilities Experimental Center
NAR	National Airspace Review
NAS	National Airspace System
NASP	National Airport System Plan
NAVAID	air navigation facility
NEXCOM	Next generation Air/Ground Communications
NOTAM	notice to airmen
NPIAS	National Plan of Integrated Airport Systems

NRP	National Route Program
NTSB	National Transportation Safety Board
OM	outer marker
OMNI	(See VOR)
PANCAP	practical annual capacity
PAR	precision approach radar
PFC	passenger facility charge
PGP	Planning Grant Program
PHOCAP	practical hourly capacity
PIREP	pilot report
PNL	perceived noise level
PRM	Precision Runway Monitor
RAIL	runway alignment indicator light
RAPCON or RAPCO	Radar Approach Control
RATCF	radar air traffic control facility
REIL	runway end identification lights
RNAV	area navigation
ROT	runway occupancy time
RVR	runway visual range
SALS	short approach light system
SASP	state aviation system plans
SECRA	secondary radar
SFL	sequenced flashing lights
SIGMET	significant meteorological information
SMA	Surface Movement Advisor
SMSA	standard metropolitan statistical area
STARS	Standard Terminal Automation Replacement System
STOL	short takeoff and landing
TACAN	tactical air navigation
TCH	threshold crossing height

TERPS	terminal instrument procedures
TRACON	Terminal Radar Approach Control
UHF	ultrahigh frequency
VAS	Vortex Advisory System
VASI	visual approach slope indicator
VFR	visual flight rules (FAR Part 91)
VMC	visual meteorological conditions
VOR	very high frequency omnidirectional range
VTOL	vertical takeoff and landing
WAAS	Wide Area Augmentation System
WARP	Weather and Radar Processor
Z	Zulu time

Index

Note: **Boldface** numbers indicate illustrations.

About the Author

Alexander T. Wells, Ed.D., is a consultant and adjunct professor in the Aviation Business Administration Department at Embry Riddle Aeronautical University. The author of a number of leading aviation industry texts, he also wrote *Commercial Aviation Safety*, Second Edition, also from McGraw-Hill.